NO SPARK OF MALICE

NO SPARK OF MALICE

THE MURDER OF MARTIN BEGNAUD

WILLIAM ARCENEAUX

LOUISIANA STATE UNIVERSITY PRESS

Baton Rouge

08 07 06 05 04 03 02 01 00   5 4 3 2

Designer: Amanda McDonald Scallan
Typeface: Adobe Caslon Regular
Typesetter: Crane Composition, Inc.
Printer and binder: Thomson-Shore, Inc.

Library of Congress Cataloging-in-Publication Data:
Arceneaux, William.
    No spark of malice : the murder of Martin Begnaud / William
Arceneaux.
        p.   cm.
    Includes bibliographical references and index.
    ISBN 0-8071-2447-8 (alk. paper)
    1. Begnaud, Martin, d. 1896.   2. Murder—Louisiana—History.
3. Cajuns—History.   I. Title.
    HV6533.L8A73   1999
364.15'23'0976356—dc21   99-15677
                                                                    CIP

The paper in this book meets the guidelines for permanence and durability of the Committee on Production
Guidelines for Book Longevity of the Council on Library Resources. ∞

For NaNa

No spark of malice rests within us, and we hope that now we are about to face our God we will receive your pardon.

—*Ernest Blanc, April 2, 1897*

CONTENTS

ILLUSTRATIONS

Simeon Begnaud

Jean Begnaud and family

Georges Bosseront d'Anglade, consul general of France in New Orleans

Father Ernest Forge

Father Ashley Knapp

Drawings made by Ernest Blanc in prison

Title page of *The Life, Crime, and Confessions of Ernest and Alexis Blanc*

Death warrant for the Blancs, signed by Governor Murphy J. Foster

The Blanc brothers on the scaffold

Begnaud family plot

Suspected grave of Ernest and Alexis Blanc

Ground-penetrating radar readings of Begnaud family plot and suspected
   Blanc grave

Maps

NO SPARK OF MALICE

The Acadian Triangle; Lafayette and surrounding parishes

Courtesy Louisiana Department of Transportation and Development

Prologue

Early on a beautiful spring morning, J. T. Mulkern stepped out on to the front porch of the stationmaster's home at Scott Station, a small, isolated railroad settlement nestled on the prairie of southwest Louisiana. The village lay in the heart of Acadiana, that section of the state pioneered by the French Acadians, descendants of the original European colonists of the maritime provinces of Canada and the American state of Maine. The railroad boss descended the steps, walked the length of his spacious front lawn, crossed the road that ran directly in front of the house and then crossed the tracks of the Southern Pacific Railroad that ran parallel to the road. A few steps past the tracks, Mulkern reached his destination, Begnaud's General Store, where his friend and neighbor, Martin Begnaud, lived and worked. As he had done countless times before, the stationmaster entered the dry goods establishment, called out Martin's name and strolled into the merchant's living quarters in the rear of the store, probably anticipating the distinctive aroma and taste of a good cup of strong Louisiana coffee. But he would not drink any coffee with his friend that morning. In his statements to reporters and law enforcement officers later that day, Mulkern never mentioned the unmistakable smell of death that had permeated Begnaud's General Store, nor how the smell had grown stronger as he approached the rear of the structure. Perhaps the horror of his discovery overwhelmed his olfactory senses. In any event, the scene encountered by J. T. Mulkern on that day, at that time, in that place, would haunt him all the remaining days of his life. The date was April 23, 1896.

Book I

THE MURDER

1

Scott Station, Louisiana: April 1896

Mother Nature has been good to Louisiana: picturesque lakes and mighty rivers, fertile soil, rich mineral deposits, abundant fish and game, lush forests, and broad prairies. These natural endowments notwithstanding, the state is not an ideal place to live. Mother Nature did not bless Louisiana's climate. Its summers are hot, humid, and stifling. Winters are unpredictable, mild and pleasant one day and cold and wet the next. And it rains a great deal all year long. But there are two months of respite, when the weather is frequently excellent: April and October. October is characterized by dry, cool days and cooler nights accompanied by the first hints of fall colors in the foliage. April typically offers warm days and cool nights amid a profusion of singing birds and budding flowers. April 1896 was a prime example. When James Thomas Mulkern walked out of the stationmaster's home at Scott Station early on the morning of April 23, 1896, skies were clear and the temperature was a comfortable sixty-seven degrees.

Prior to the arrival of the railroad in the last decades of the nineteenth century, this area of southwest Louisiana was indistinguishable from the rest of the vast Attakapas Prairie, which stretches westward from the great basins of the Mississippi and Atchafalaya Rivers in south central Louisiana all the way to Texas. The environment was extremely rural, consisting of small and large farms and *vacheries* (as the

Acadians called their ranches). The farms produced some cotton, but their primary output was in potatoes, corn, poultry, and other commodities for domestic consumption. The ranchers raised horses and cattle. The coming of the iron horse would forever change the lives and landscape of the region, as it would for the rest of the nation. But merely a road of iron over which steam-powered and coal-burning engines rolled with passenger cars and boxcars in tow was insufficient to stimulate the local economy deeply or alter the native culture radically. Such transformations required the construction of distribution centers on selected sites: in railroad parlance, terminals, stations, or depots. The creation of such facilities meant that cash-producing crops and livestock could be shipped to distant markets, passengers could board and disembark, and mail could be sent and received. These depots planted the seeds of urbanization, and communities developed around them.

One of the budding settlements had begun in 1880 when the Louisiana Western Railroad selected a site about five miles west of the village of Vermilionville, in Lafayette Parish, for the purpose of establishing a fully operational railroad station. The station was named for G. P. Scott, the superintendent in charge of constructing the track through that area of the prairie. Mr. Scott and his crew moved on to other jobs on other tracks and were never heard from again. Nevertheless when the L.W.R.R. asked leading citizens of the area to select a name for the new station, they were unable to agree on any other. By 1881, the Louisiana Western had constructed a depot and a section house and had provided for a large comfortable home for the stationmaster and his family. With these three buildings serving as the nucleus of Scott Station, an unassuming village slowly emerged, its economic development enhanced by the 1883 purchase of the L.W.R.R. by the Southern Pacific Railroad Company. By 1896, there stood within a half-mile radius of the station a large hotel/boardinghouse, a blacksmith shed, two taverns, three large mercantile stores, a sugar mill (although it only made molasses), five steam-powered cotton gins, numerous warehouses, several homes, two schoolhouses (one for blacks and one for whites), and a small cemetery. Approximately two hundred people lived in and around the village, and it served a country population of perhaps five times that number. Except for a few African American families and a handful of railroad employees, nearly all the denizens of Scott Station and its environs were Acadians.

With a few interesting anomalies, life in Scott Station in 1896 was typical of life in late-nineteenth-century rural America. Horse- and mule-drawn wagons and buggies were the chief means of transportation; lone horseback or muleback riders were less common but not unknown. Shotguns and hunting rifles were commonplace and were normally openly visible, but handguns were rare. Roads were few and in terrible condition, muddy when wet and dusty when dry. Religion was an important part of life. It is possible that there were non-Catholics in Scott Station in 1896, but no one knew of any. The nearest church was St. John the Evangelist, about five miles away in the town of Lafayette (Vermilionville had changed its name to Lafayette in 1884), but missionary priests were frequent Sunday visitors and mass was celebrated in private homes or outdoors, weather permitting. Electricity, the automobile, and the radio would not arrive until well into the twentieth century, but the little village took pride in its one telephone and, particularly, in the fact that one of its homes had indoor plumbing. Aside from the two weekly newspapers published in Lafayette and an occasional New Orleans daily, the people's chief sources of information and entertainment were their neighbors. And there wasn't much excitement, because life was quotidian. Sensational events, such as one read about in the newspapers, seemed never to happen in hamlets like Scott Station.

A favorite gathering place in any rural community of the era was the general store. Around the woodburning stove in winter and on the porch in summer, farmers and villagers would gather to visit, exchange gossip, and play dominoes or checkers. In Scott Station it was dominoes. Two taverns provided a modest night life. French was the language of choice, but most people knew enough English to communicate on a rudimentary level. Conversation was easy and informal, and nearly everyone had a nickname. After the weather and crop conditions, politics was a favorite topic, especially this April 23. Just two days before, statewide elections had taken place. On the ballot were candidates for governor and other state officials, together with several interesting parish races. The competitions for governor and sheriff had been controversial and hotly contested, and interest ran high. The results of the local races were tabulated and known by the next day, but official results of the statewide contests would not reach Scott Station until the 23rd. There can be little doubt what was on Stationmaster Mulkern's mind when early on that beautiful April morning he walked the short distance to the general store owned by his confrere Martin Begnaud.

Martin Begnaud's store stood on the north side of the railroad track, a short fifty yards to the east of the stationmaster's house on the south side. The store faced south toward the tracks, its main entrance about thirty yards from the railroad bed. The front section of the building was filled with inventory for retail sale, while comfortable living quarters were located in the rear. The central feature of the living quarters was Begnaud's bed, a handsome black-walnut piece with a high, carved headboard. When Mulkern made his way into the room, it was on this bed that Begnaud lay motionless. Rope had been used to tie his feet together and bind his hands tightly behind his back, and his mouth was gagged with a large red rag. A big man, his entire body was wrapped in calico cloth like a mummy. A strip of the calico had been torn off and made into a blindfold. The body, the bed linen, and the floor were drenched in blood that had already begun to dry and cake. Numerous large splotches darker than the blood-soaked linen appeared like red roses in the calico. These were the places where the murder weapon had pierced the body. The papers reported that Begnaud had been stabbed more than fifty times around the neck in the shape of a necklace, that his throat had been cut from ear to ear, and that he had been robbed of over $7,000. The next morning's headline in the French-language daily *L'Abeille de la Nouvelle-Orléans* (the *New Orleans Bee*) proclaimed MARTIN BEGNAUD ASSASSINÉ.

2

Scott Station, Louisiana: April 1896

News of J. T. Mulkern's gruesome discovery spread like a wildfire across the parish, and the telegraph wires out of Scott Station were soon burning with word of the murder of Martin Begnaud. The sheriff's office in Lafayette was notified immediately, and it, in turn, promptly informed the coroner. But the story was too hot to be contained inside the parish, and telegraph operators up and down the Southern Pacific Railroad line took it upon themselves to spread the news. Before the end of the day, correspondents from most of the New Orleans newspapers were "on the ground" (as journalists, even in those days, described their presence at the scene of a story) in Scott Station. All the local papers were published weekly and delivered on Saturday, so it was too early for them to publish the story of the murder, but not so for the metropolitan press. The interest of the big-city editors was piqued for two reasons: their papers were the only daily publications in south Louisiana and the whole region was considered part of their circulation and advertising area, and the brutality of the crime made it an ideal scoop for the sensationalistic yellow journalism that characterized the competitive New Orleans press in the 1890s. The next morning, headlines read MURDER MOST FOUL (the *New Orleans Times-Democrat*), MURDERED IN COLD BLOOD (the *Daily Picayune*), and UN CRIME PRÈS DE LAFAYETTE (the *Bee*). The local people, however, needed no headlines to stir their interest. The entire parish was in shock and the victim's family in deep mourning.

Sheriff Isaac "Ike" Broussard was out of the office when word of the murder of Martin Begnaud reached the Lafayette Parish Courthouse. Although several deputies quickly set out in search of him, he did not arrive at the crime scene until about ten o'clock. The parish coroner, Dr. Alphonse Gladu, arrived about an hour earlier and began a preliminary investigation. Gladu had immigrated from Canada after the American Civil War and opened a medical practice in the parish, where his expertise as a physician and his fluency in French made him popular among the Acadians. His considerable interpersonal skills were tested as he endeavored to clear out the dozens of friends, neighbors, and family members from Begnaud's General Store, and he also needed medical personnel to assist him. Murders requiring an inquest or coroner's jury in Lafayette Parish were rare, but this homicide was extraordinary. Gladu sent for more physicians, informing them that a serious emergency existed and requesting their immediate presence at Scott Station. Three responded: Dr. Fred Mayer, who lived near Ile Navarre, a beautiful cluster of live oaks about two miles to the southeast of the village, likely arrived first, and he was soon joined by Drs. John D. and Anatole R. Trahan, father and son physicians from Lafayette. The elder Dr. Trahan had practiced in the parish for over thirty years and was loved and respected by all. His reputation was probably a factor in his son's victory—just two days before—over the incumbent coroner. The vote had been 1,164 for A. R. Trahan and 1,053 for Gladu.

Lafayette Parish would have a new coroner for the next four years, but for now, Gladu was still in charge. Since the body had apparently been dead several hours, there was no time to lose in getting the investigation under way. Gladu convened a coroner's jury composed of himself and his three colleagues, and they carefully removed the ropes binding the victim's hands and feet, the blindfold, and the gag. Next, they unrolled the tightly wrapped calico cloth from around the body and found that Begnaud was fully clothed in the same attire he had worn the previous day. A close examination revealed fifty-two stab wounds in the area of the neck and chest caused by a triangular instrument in the shape of a stiletto. The heart had been pierced and the

Doctors: Gladu, Mayer, Trahan & Trahan

coroner →

jugular vein severed. There were no signs of a struggle. The coroner's jury rendered a verdict based on the facts before it: Martin Begnaud had bled to death as a result of the wounds inflicted upon him. The newspaper accounts claiming the stab wounds to be in the shape of a necklace and the neck to have been slit from ear to ear were based on interviews with Scott Station residents who saw the body of the dead merchant before the coroner arrived; the physicians made no mention of those findings. When the coroner's jury had completed its work, Dr. Gladu turned the corpse over to the Begnaud family, who prepared the body for burial the following day.

J. T. Mulkern and Simeon Begnaud, the victim's brother, business partner, and next-door neighbor, were the first two people interviewed by Sheriff Broussard when he arrived at the murder scene. Upon finding the body, Mulkern had raced over to Begnaud's Tavern to inform Simeon of his older brother's fate, and together they returned to the store. Simeon immediately noticed that his brother's safe was ajar. Martin had used the large iron safe to store money, receipts, and other important papers for both the saloon and the store, as well as small amounts of cash for friends and neighbors for whom the merchant acted as a banker. Simeon Begnaud first estimated that more than $7,000 in cash, gold coins, and silver certificates had been stolen, but later in the day, after the discovery of $2,500 in cash in an inconspicuous drawer, the estimate was reduced to $5,000, although some newspapers continued to report the larger amount. Simeon, like his brother, occupied living quarters in the rear of his business, and he reported to the sheriff that he had neither seen nor heard anything suspicious the previous night. The only other piece of information that proved useful came from Hervillen Blanchard, a local farmer, who claimed to have walked by Begnaud's store the previous night about eleven. Blanchard reported that he had heard voices inside the store and that he had recognized one of them as belonging to Martin Begnaud. The conversation had sounded normal, and he had seen no one. Additional interviews with other friends and neighbors of the victim led Sheriff Broussard to conclude that this murder was not the work of only one person. The forty-five-year-old Begnaud had been a big, strong man in excellent health. The sheriff's theory was that he had somehow been overpowered by two or more persons, almost certainly by persons with whom he was acquainted, for there were no signs of forced entry.

By noon, hundreds of men from all over the parish had gathered around Begnaud's General Store. The *Daily Picayune* summed up their state of mind: "Woe unto the guilty wretches if they are caught. Swift justice will be meted out beyond all peradventure." If the perpetrator or perpetrators could be found, there was no reason to wait for the law. The mood of the crowd could not have gone unnoticed by the sheriff. By early afternoon, the bloodhounds he had sent for finally arrived, and he wasted no time organizing a posse. After sniffing and howling and wailing for quite some time, the dogs struck off to the east at a lively pace, following the railroad track. About a mile down the track, the pack paused, appearing confused, and then turned north, in the direction of Boudreaux Plantation. But they moved only a few yards in that direction before returning to the tracks and heading south, only to hesitate once again. After some indecision, the pack turned eastward again, but it soon became clear that they had lost the scent. The comings and goings of the dozens of people on the grounds and in and out of the store had seemingly rendered it impossible for the bloodhounds to find a solid trail. The sheriff disbanded the posse and returned to the courthouse, where he telegraphed the chief of the New Orleans police for help.

Specifically, Broussard requested that Chief Dexter Sidney Gaster dispatch a homicide detective to Lafayette Parish to assist in the investigation. Broussard, like the coroner, undoubtedly felt overwhelmed, and reasoned that a big-city police detective would have more experience in investigating a homicide like this one. But Chief Gaster refused to even respond to Broussard's telegram. When pressed by reporters in New Orleans, he said that "just at this time it would be an impossibility to comply with the sheriff's request." Instead, Gaster recommended the sheriff "secure a competent negro to work on the case." New Orleans, in the 1890s, was a hotbed of racial tension. Lynchings and race riots were commonplace, and citizens spoke openly of race war as a real possibility. The overwhelmingly white New Orleans police force was on the front line in the battle for white supremacy, and the issue of race was a pervasive and insidious influence in all areas of law enforcement in the Crescent City. It is thus not surprising that Chief Gaster assumed Martin Begnaud's murderer or murderers to be black and a "competent negro" to be sufficient for tracking them down. But the Acadians of Scott Station knew their African American neighbors well enough to know that none of them was likely to be the killer, and Gaster's advice was ignored.

It was clear to everyone why Martin Begnaud had been murdered: $5,000 was a small fortune in 1896. Robbery was a crime as old as man, a crime people could understand. What Begnaud's neighbors could not understand was the brutal nature of the homicide, and why it should have been visited upon the enterprising merchant from Scott Station. As one contemporary observed, "It is no exaggeration to say that this awful crime has cast a gloom over the whole parish. It is the sole topic of conversation on the streets and in the homes. The belief seems to be general that the crime was committed by residents of this section, though the people are loath to believe that such fiends as those who perpetrated this diabolical deed live within the borders of Lafayette parish, which is deservedly reputed to be one of the most peaceful and law-abiding in the State." Moreover, the victim was a member of one of the largest Acadian families in the region, which had been among the first to pioneer the Attakapas Prairie. Although Martin Begnaud was no saint, the fact that people trusted him with their money leaves no doubt that he was highly regarded. A bachelor who lived alone, he was known to have taken in an occasional boarder who might be temporarily down on his luck, and one unusual practice of his gives special insight into his generous and trusting nature. When business was slow on hot summer days, Begnaud would occasionally go fishing, leaving the store unattended and unlocked with a tablet set up so his customers could take what they needed and record their purchases using the honor system. Shortly after the murder, a reporter for the *Times-Democrat* interviewed the victim's neighbors and wrote the following evaluation: "Mr. Begnaud was . . . one of the most popular men in this parish, and was a gentleman of the highest integrity, and enjoyed the esteem of people of all classes. Every man, woman and child was his friend."

The next morning, Friday, April 24, at 9:45 A.M., the bells of St. John the Evangelist began their woeful peal announcing the funeral mass. By ten o'clock the church was filled to capacity, with hundreds more mourners outside. Father Ernest Forge, pastor of St. John's, officiated. Born in 1837, in Loire, France, Forge had immigrated to Louisiana at age nineteen and attended Catholic seminary in New Orleans. He then spent his life ministering to the Acadians of south Louisiana, usually in remote missions. He had been assigned to the Lafayette church in 1881 from Breaux Bridge, where he had founded St. Bernard Catholic School in addition to serving as pastor. Father Forge's homily focused on the nature of the crime, the character of the victim, the importance of faith, and the duties of good citizenship. Delivered in French and translated by the Lafayette newspaper, it began: "This large assemblage had [sic] congregated here, actuated by two sentiments; affection and regret for the victim of the most atrocious crime in the annals of this parish; second, a sentiment of protestation against so heinous a deed. Here lies before us the inanimate body of him you loved so well, stricken down in the prime of manhood by the foul blows of midnight assassins." The reporters present noted that at this point in the sermon the entire congregation was in tears. Father Forge himself was so overcome with emotion that he was forced to interrupt his sermon several times. As best he could, the priest concluded his talk with a stern warning: "Religion is the basis of society and all good government. Take away this basis and human affairs descend into a state of revolution and anarchy. The evil deeds of men often go unpunished in this world and we cannot believe that crimes such as this shall fail to receive terrible retribution at the hands of a just God. It is a foul blot on the fair reputation of the parish and every law abiding citizen could not help but feel a deep sense of shame that any citizen should be implicated. Should the villains be captured justice should be meted out by constituted authority and not by unlawful proceedings. If otherwise the people should rely upon the certain vengeance sure to be administered in the next world."

Martin Begnaud had been preceded in death by his father, Alexandre, who died in 1883, three sisters, a brother, and twenty-three nieces and nephews (nearly all of the latter died in infancy). He was survived by his mother, Eliza, seven sisters, two brothers and seventy nieces and nephews. One of his surviving nieces, Carmen Arceneaux, was his only godchild; she was the sixteen-year-old daughter of Martin's sister Alexandrine and her husband, Jacques Arceneaux. Begnaud was buried next to his father in the Begnaud family plot in the St. John the Evangelist cemetery.

Seventy-nine-year-old Eliza Begnaud was especially devastated. Martin had been her favorite, and the two had been exceptionally close. Of her four sons, Joseph had died in 1893, Jean had his own large family to look after, and Simeon was always occupied with business, but Martin had habitually taken time for his widowed mother. Without fail, he had spent every Sunday with her, and sometimes visited during the week. In less than two years, the bereaved mother would join her husband and her beloved son in death.

At the funeral, several people also noted with empathy the deep sorrow expressed by two young French immigrants, Ernest and Alexis Blanc. Orphans who were exceedingly well liked by the people of Scott Station, they were employed as farmhands at Boudreaux Plantation and had been frequent visitors at Begnaud's General Store, both as customers and as friends of the proprietor. No one shed more tears at Martin Begnaud's funeral than these two young men.

3

Carencro, Louisiana: April 1896

The finding of the coroner's jury that the murder weapon was a triangular instrument shaped like a stiletto gave the sheriff his first clue and first suspect, Gustave Ludovic Balin. Mr. Balin seems to have arrived in Lafayette Parish only a few months earlier, but he had been in the surrounding area for a year or two. He claimed to have moved to Louisiana from Florida. He had first appeared in Acadia Parish, posing as a "Dr. Davidson." When a Crowley woman under his care died amid mysterious circumstances, he disappeared before authorities could question him. Dr. Davidson next turned up in Vermilion Parish with a new patent medicine, a miracle elixir guaranteed to cure almost any ailment. Although the actual ingredients of the concoction are unknown, when the people of the town of Erath discovered the formula, Davidson/Balin again found it necessary to leave town quickly. In Lafayette Parish, he presented himself as an Italian, or sometimes a Spanish, portrait painter with special talent in oils and an exalted reputation in Europe, but when the quality of his portraits proved unacceptable, he was reduced to painting and plastering houses, work for which he did possess some talent. The *Picayune* described him as "about 40 years old, medium height, dark complexion, rather slight in build, lithe and active as a cat." During his "Italian" period, Balin had bragged to some companions that he possessed the finest weapon in the world for killing a man, a handcrafted Italian stiletto.

Having heard of Balin's prized possession from an informant, Sheriff Broussard got to work as soon as he returned from the funeral and launched an investigation into the newcomer's background. Casting a dragnet of telegraph messages to sheriffs' offices in neighboring parishes, Broussard learned of Balin's quack medical activities, his propensity for drinking and gambling, and his current residence: a remote cabin—which Balin called a studio—near Carencro, about five miles north of Lafayette and about ten miles from Scott Station. But there was no real evidence to go with the mounting suspicion until later in the afternoon when the sheriff discovered that upon his arrival in Lafayette Parish, Gustave Balin had lived with Martin Begnaud for about a week. Owing to the deceased merchant's practice of taking in boarders from time to time, this knowledge in itself would have been deemed insignificant by most of the citizens, but to the sheriff it meant that Balin knew the victim and almost certainly knew that Begnaud kept large sums of money in his safe. The evidence was circumstantial, but it was more than enough for Broussard, who was under intense pressure from the community and the press to capture the guilty parties and to do so quickly. The sheriff and his deputies headed for Carencro, where they began making inquiries regarding Balin and his activities on the night of April 22.

Balin's fate was sealed when Broussard learned that the painter was a friend of Hampton Benton Jr. and that the two had been seen together the night of April 22. Unfortunately for Balin, his friend and the sheriff were sworn personal and political enemies. The Benton clan hailed from South Carolina; Hampton Benton Sr., a Civil War veteran, had migrated to Louisiana with his family after the war and settled in Lafayette Parish. They were Methodist, poor, and Anglo. "Hamp" Benton Jr., born in 1863, the oldest child, was strong and aggressive at six feet three inches tall. Perhaps in response to cultural snubs by the French speakers around him, Hamp had developed a defiant personality. He displayed little or no respect for authority and would back down to no man. His father eventually returned to South Carolina, but Hamp remained in Louisiana, where he married an Acadian girl, Odéide Gilbert. They lived near Carencro and by 1896 had nine children. Benton listed his occupation as farming but seems to have spent most of his time gambling and drinking. His wife, in contrast, was a kind, gentle, long-suffering woman who showered her children with love and affection. Most of the time it was all she had to give them.

Benton did not enjoy a spotless public reputation. In 1894 he had brutally murdered a man named B. J. Pope in Opelousas, and spent six months in the St. Landry Parish jail. He was released after a grand jury returned a "no true bill" in response to his plea of self-defense. He was also a known "regulator"—a member of a group of lower-class imitators of the Ku Klux Klan active in the South in the late nineteenth century—and had previously been arrested by Sheriff Broussard for carrying a concealed weapon. In a parish with 6,884 African Americans out of a total population of 15,964, the regulators were never out of "work," and Broussard hated them, not because they attempted to harass and intimidate blacks to keep them from voting, but because they operated outside the law, his law. The sheriff hunted down and broke up gangs of regulators with an unchecked ruthlessness. In response, no one had worked harder for Broussard's defeat in the recent election than Hamp Benton. Unfortunately for Benton, Ike had been reelected.

Further inquiries in the village of Carencro on April 24 only served to reinforce a scenario that was taking shape in the sheriff's mind. Broussard learned that around sunset on April 22, Hamp Benton had walked into the livery stable in Carencro and made arrangements to rent a sulky and a set of harnesses for the evening. When asked by the owner if he needed a horse, Benton said no, one had already been engaged. Around the same time, Gustave Balin had approached a black citizen of Carencro about renting his horse for the evening for sixty cents. The man was agreeable but refused to rent the horse without knowing Balin's destination because he wanted his horse back the next morning. Balin refused to divulge that information and negotiations were terminated abruptly. About seven o'clock, Benton and Balin were seen at a Carencro saloon drinking together. About eight, the owner of the livery stable ran into Benton in Carencro, probably at the same saloon, and suggested that he pick up the sulky and harnesses before the livery closed. Hamp asked the owner to leave the equipment outside the stable, saying he would pick it up later. Around half past nine Benton and Balin were reportedly engaged "in a low, earnest conversation" under a shed in Carencro. They were not seen again that night. The following morning the livery operator found that the sulky and harnesses had been returned and, from their muddy condition, had been used overnight. He also noticed that one of his horses, still lathered with sweat and now lame, had also been used the previous night, without payment and without permission. He suspected that Benton was responsible, but when confronted, Benton denied any knowledge and claimed that he had not used either the horse or the equipment the previous night.

With this information in hand, Sheriff Broussard and a deputy located Hamp Benton in Carencro late in the afternoon of the 24th and questioned him regarding his whereabouts on the night of the 22nd. Benton replied that he had spent the night at home with his wife and family. His alibi would be easy to confirm because the sheriff knew Odéide Benton would tell the truth, but that could wait. Broussard's immediate fear was that Balin, a transient, would learn that he was under suspicion and leave the area—so Broussard and his deputy proceeded to the "studio" of the artist. They found him at home, and searched the cabin thoroughly. The search turned up no stiletto but did reveal substantial traces of blood. Balin was taken to the courthouse for questioning, during which he denied both owning a stiletto and having seen Hamp Benton the night of April 22. He claimed he had an alibi and someone who could confirm it, but that person, an elderly Irish houseguest named Kenly, could not back up Balin's story, since he had been drunk that entire evening and could remember nothing. Upon reflection, the old Irishman did have one memory of that night or, rather, the next morning: he remembered Benton and Balin carrying him into Balin's cabin at dawn on April 23. With an unsubstantiated alibi, fresh blood in his cabin, and apparently having lied about being with Benton on the night in question, Balin was arrested for the murder of Martin Begnaud and placed under twenty-four-hour guard to protect him from lynch mobs.

The *New Orleans Times-Democrat* headlined, A SUSPECTED ITALIAN ARRESTED. Italians ranked right behind blacks as favorite targets in the New Orleans press's unending crusade for white supremacy; during the 1890s, about a dozen Italian immigrants were lynched in the city. In response to his arrest, Balin vigorously asserted his innocence, announced that he was a Frenchman, and demanded to see a representative of his government. Sheriff Broussard was not impressed. Meanwhile, Mrs. Benton could not confirm her husband's alibi; she and her children had gone to her father's house the night of April 22, after Hamp had not been home for several nights. It was not the first time that her husband had disappeared without word, but she thought that maybe this time he had deserted them for good. In fact, Benton had probably been out night-riding with his gang of regulators, since it was election week. With a more complete picture of events now at his disposal, Sheriff Broussard was able to put some flesh on the bones of his theory. He surmised that the mastermind behind the crime was Balin, who knew Begnaud and knew that he kept substantial sums of cash in his safe. That would explain motive as well as the culprits' ability to gain admission at such a late hour of the evening. Balin also was connected to the murder weapon, the famous stiletto, while Benton could have provided the transportation and the muscle and acted as the actual assassin.

The next day the entire parish was buzzing with news of the overnight developments in the case. Hamp Benton had learned of his imminent arrest and, remembering his treatment at the hands of Broussard the last time he had been arrested, vowed that it would not happen again. Benton sent word by personal messenger to Ike Broussard that he would kill the sheriff if he tried to arrest him. Although that threat may have been liquor-induced, Sheriff Broussard knew he had to proceed with caution. Several people suggested forming a posse to apprehend Benton, but Broussard rejected the idea, recognizing the potential for violence if a large group of Martin Begnaud's friends and neighbors had the suspect in their grasp. In an effort to prevent the development of a situation over which he might lose control, Broussard and his chief deputy, Thomas Mouton, a man whom he trusted completely, established a stakeout of Benton's home. Mrs. Benton and her children remained at her father's house. Hamp, who was inside alone, would eventually have to emerge to get water from the well or to use the outhouse. With chamber pots available inside, the lawmen correctly guessed it would be the well that would draw him out. The two peace officers hid in the bushes on either side of the well, and when

Benton reached down to lower the bucket, Broussard and Mouton emerged with their pistols cocked and aimed at point-blank range. To resist meant death, and Hamp, though mean, was not stupid. He was handcuffed and escorted via back roads to Lafayette.

It was now dusk and the sheriff had received word that a lynch mob had gathered around the courthouse. For whatever reasons, they were not interested in Balin. The newcomer was not well known, and the rumor mill had apparently not yet had time to sort out his role in the murder. But virtually everyone knew of Hamp Benton, either personally or by reputation, and since he was thought to be the actual assassin, he was the one the mob wanted. When they learned that the officers had gone out to arrest him, they waited on the courthouse square. The sheriff thus had to get his prisoner out of town, and he had a plan. Taking the necessary precautions to avoid being detected, he and Mouton led Benton to the back door of the home of John Charles Buchanan, an executive with the Southern Pacific Railroad who lived with his family near the Lafayette station. The sheriff asked Buchanan if the three men could hide out in his home for a few hours until it was time for the eastbound midnight train for New Orleans to depart. If Buchanan agreed and lent his assistance, Broussard and the deputy would hustle their prisoner on board the train just as it was pulling away.

No one had to explain to the Buchanan household the tense situation that existed in Lafayette on Saturday night, April 25, 1896, and the fact that the sheriff's plan placed them in considerable danger. Nevertheless, Mr. Buchanan agreed to cooperate, and the plan was executed exactly as envisioned. (The Buchanan children would always remember that night as one of the most exciting experiences of their childhood.) Likewise, no one had to explain to Hamp Benton the perilous position he was in. He offered no resistance and cooperated with his captors. When the sun rose on the morning of April 26, Sheriff Broussard was 150 miles east of Lafayette. He safely deposited his prisoner in the Jefferson Parish jail in Gretna, just across the Mississippi River from New Orleans. His instructions for the care of the prisoner were that he be kept in solitary confinement and provided with bread and water twice a day. Under no conditions was the prisoner to receive any visitors or any other sustenance. The only person authorized to call upon him was

Isaac Broussard. Later that morning, the two officers returned to Lafayette by train and found that the situation had settled down. Unable to find Benton, the crowd had dispersed sometime after midnight. A few days later, the sheriff returned to Gretna and moved his prisoner across the river to the Orleans Parish Prison. In the face of intense examination, Benton maintained his innocence.

4

Lafayette, Louisiana: July 1896

For several months beginning in May 1896, Isaac Broussard was a frequent passenger on the trains traveling between Lafayette and New Orleans. The purpose of his many trips was to interrogate his prisoner, but Hamp Benton would not confess to the murder of Martin Begnaud. Under Broussard's supervision, and with the assistance of big-city jailers presumably well versed in such methods, Benton was severely beaten and tortured. His fingernails were pulled out, and the bottoms of his feet were burned repeatedly with cigars. His diet never varied from the bread and water he was given twice a day, making the maggots that were allowed to accumulate in his swill his only source of protein. Odéide Benton and other family members begged Broussard to allow them to send or bring food to the prisoner, but the sheriff refused. Frequent motions for bail by Benton's attorney, Joseph Albert Chargois, were taken under advisement by the presiding judge, Conrad Debaillon, but bail was never granted. As the months of his imprisonment slowly passed and his physical condition weakened, Benton continued to profess his innocence. All the while, Gustave Ludovic Balin faced strenuous interrogation in the Lafayette Parish prison.

Balin's protestations that he was a French national, his constant demands for a lawyer, and his insistence that he be allowed to communicate with French officials in the United States caused Broussard to approach his interrogation with caution. The sheriff asked Father Forge, who was originally from France, to pay his prisoner a visit for the purpose of determining whether Balin was telling the truth concerning his nationality. Based on that interview, the priest reached two conclusions: the accused was a man of low moral character and—unfortunately—he was a Frenchman. Balin's accent and his familiarity with French place-names and current events were, in Forge's opinion, conclusive proof of his origins. Balin underwent intense interrogation but was not beaten or tortured; his diet, however, was the same as Benton's. Balin eventually recanted his story that the two men had not been together the night of the murder, but he claimed that the only thing they did was get drunk, so drunk that he had no memory of the events of the night. By and large, Benton told the same story. Balin accounted for the blood in his cabin by explaining that it had come from chickens he had decapitated, plucked, and cooked. (This part of his story was probably true, for much later it was discovered that among his many talents, Balin was also a chicken thief.) And, yes, he and Benton had discussed renting a sulky that evening, but it was to visit a woman, not to kill or rob anyone. On the key questions of the weapon and his participation in the crime, the painter remained steadfast: he did not own a stiletto and he was innocent. Sheriff Broussard continued to believe that Benton and Balin were guilty, and would not allow anything or anyone to interfere with his handling of the case. He thus forbade Balin any contact with the outside world.

The atmosphere in Lafayette Parish remained relatively calm during May and June. Most people believed that the right men were in custody and that it was only a matter of time until they confessed to the murder and disclosed the location of the stolen lucre. But by July patience began to wear thin. Now Balin, conveniently housed in the local jail, was the target of the people's aggression, and toward the end of the month ugly rumors about a lynch mob reached Broussard's ears. The renewed interest in the case was not purely a matter of lost patience. The last week of July was the week set aside for the Lafayette Parish grand jury to hear evidence of all serious crimes that had occurred in the past year, and when the members of that jury had been announced the previous October, Martin Begnaud had been on the list. But for his untimely demise, Begnaud would have been a sitting member of the grand jury weighing the evidence of his own murder. The irony was not lost on the citizens.

The night before Minos T. Gordy from Abbeville, district attorney for Lafayette and Vermilion Parishes, was scheduled to begin presentations to the grand jury, Sheriff Broussard and Deputy Mouton clandestinely removed Balin from his jail cell and boarded a train heading west. They got off at Lake Charles, where Broussard had made arrangements with the local sheriff to house Balin under an assumed name in the Calcasieu Parish jail. The next morning, July 28, the grand jury began considering evidence in the Begnaud case, and on August 1, they returned a "true bill" of indictment against Hampton Benton Jr. and Gustave L. Balin for the murder and robbery of the merchant from Scott Station. The indictment meant that when the district court convened for its fall session in October, Benton and Balin would be placed on trial for the crimes listed in the charge.

In the Lake Charles jail, Balin continued to be held in solitary confinement and remained on a diet of bread and water, but the restriction prohibiting his correspondence with the outside world was lifted. With an indictment in hand, Broussard seems to have felt secure enough to allow Balin to write his letters. The sheriff may also have believed that Hamp Benton was close to breaking and that his confession would implicate Balin. Over the next six months, the new resident of the Calcasieu Parish prison would launch a flurry of correspondence with the French consul general in New Orleans, the French ambassador in Washington, D.C., and with his uncle in France, apparently his closest living relative and a man of some influence. All of his letters had the same themes: he was innocent; he owned no stiletto; and they lynched people in this part of the world. He was obviously very frightened. His chief complaints were that he was unable to wash, had no clean underwear, endured long periods of solitude, and was forced to eat only bread and water. He pleaded that a lawyer be provided to defend him.

In an effort to determine the facts, the consul general, Georges Bosseront d'Anglade, in conjunction with the French embassy in Washington, began an investigation into the records of Gustave Ludovic Balin. The officials were not thrilled with their findings. Balin was a French citizen, and he came from a good family of the Vienne province in west central France. His uncle and namesake, Ludovic O. Forestier, the relative Balin had enlisted in his cause, was a respected veterinarian in the city of Lusignan. Gustave was evidently the black sheep of the family. He was a deserter from the French army (a fact that, for good reason, the prisoner never shared with Louisiana authorities). While stationed in Marseilles many years earlier as a member of a regiment of Hussars, he had assaulted a French officer and, in order to avoid court-martial, had deserted. Balin was thus an escaped fugitive wanted for a serious crime in his home country. Over the years, he had lived as something of a vagabond in Portugal, Australia, and South America before coming to the United States. His uncle, who obviously knew Gustave well, urged the consul general to secure legal representation for his nephew, but with the following caveat: "If he is guilty he should be punished, but if he is innocent he should be released." D'Anglade knew of Balin's background as early as July 1896, but kept this knowledge to himself; no one at the time ever learned of Balin's past. In the end, the consul general's office retained legal counsel who, in turn, informed the state attorney general, District Attorney Gordy, and Broussard of their intentions to monitor the progress of the case. In addition, d'Anglade reluctantly agreed to provide Balin with a lawyer when his case came to trial, supposedly in October. But October came and went without a trial.

At this time, an unwritten political agreement existed between the two parishes that formed the 17th Judicial District, Lafayette and Vermilion: the district judge and the district attorney would not come from the same parish. This informal accord evolved as a way to divide the spoils of public office equitably between the two political subdivisions and to ensure that the citizens of both parishes would be involved in the administration of the justice system. Although sometimes elections did not turn out as planned, those of April 1896 had produced the desired result, with Debaillon of Lafayette Parish winning as district judge and Gordy of Vermilion Parish winning as district attorney. It was fortunate for Mr. Gordy that he lived in Abbeville, where he was somewhat sheltered from the incredible pressures in Lafayette Parish to bring Benton and Balin to justice. Given the fact that the two men arrested for the murder of Martin Begnaud had already been convicted in the court of public opinion, and given the public's outcry for retribution and its impatience with the legal process, Gordy knew that he could likely win a conviction if he went to trial. But he also knew that without a confession, he really did not have a case. All of the evidence was circumstantial. There were no witnesses who could place Benton and Balin at the scene of the crime, no murder weapon had been produced, and the money taken in the robbery had failed to surface. The Tulane University Law School graduate decided to postpone the trial in hopes that a confession from one of the suspects would be forthcoming. But Balin—now armed with the promise of a lawyer and the knowledge that the representatives of his country were in communication with his jailers—found new courage and his intransigence stiffened, dirty underwear notwithstanding. And Benton—by now only a shell of his former self—was unyielding, despite Broussard's assurances of an impending confession. By the end of October, some people had begun to wonder if maybe, just maybe, the sheriff had arrested the wrong men.

Whispers gave way to open speculation that the two men in jail were innocent, and that the guilty parties were still at large. Up until now, the Begnauds of Scott Station had been quite supportive of Sheriff Broussard and his handling of the case. They had anticipated a swift conclusion to this tragic chapter in their family history, but with the advent of the cold, wet days of November, they began to lose hope. These misgivings became public on November 21, when the local papers contained a paid advertisement—in both French and English—signed by Simeon Begnaud on behalf of the family, offering a $1,000 reward "to any person or persons who will detect the evidence, and cause the arrest and conviction of the murderers of my brother, Martin Begnaud." The notice announced that the reward would remain in force for two years. It was no idle promise; Simeon had deposited $1,000 in the First National Bank of Lafayette, and directly below the notice was a signed confirmation by "S. R. Parkerson, Cashier." This was a clear message to Isaac Broussard that the Begnaud family had lost confidence in him. Their frustration was generally shared by the local population.

In case Broussard needed further proof of the Begnauds' feelings, around the first of December the family let it be known that because the duly elected officers of the law had been unable to make progress leading to the arrest of those responsible for the crime, they had secured the services of an attorney who would aggressively pursue their interests in the case. Their choice of this attorney was as interesting as it was deliberate. William Campbell was the young mayor of Lafayette and a highly intelligent and capable lawyer. But on top of that, he was a graduate of the Tulane University School of Law, where he had been a classmate and friend of District Attorney Gordy. Campbell's representation gave the Begnaud family a direct pipeline into the D.A.'s office. Moreover, Campbell headed a strong faction of the Democratic Party in Lafayette Parish that was a rival of a faction headed by Isaac Broussard.

An intense professional, Campbell began his inquiry by reviewing every aspect of the case that had thus far been assembled by the authorities. Accepting the premise that the perpetrators were acquaintances of the victim, the young attorney interviewed each member of the Begnaud family in the hopes of finding anything or anyone that might shed some light on the mystery. In the months immediately following the murder, the family had spent many long evenings speculating as to what might have happened on that terrible night. Growing doubts as to the guilt of Benton and Balin caused them to expand their discussions and consider other possibilities. The family shared everything with William Campbell, and he found one scenario particularly intriguing, a scenario first suggested by Martin's sister Philomène, Mrs. Olivier Boudreaux.

Ernest and Alexis Blanc were orphaned teenaged brothers from France who had arrived, seeking work, at Mrs. Boudreaux's father-in-law's plantation in the spring of 1894. Colonel A. D. Boudreaux had given them employment and allowed them to live in a small cabin about a hundred yards behind the big house at Boudreaux Plantation. Ernest had given his age as seventeen and Alexis, sixteen. They had been good workers and were exceedingly well liked by everyone on the plantation except Vallena, an aging black servant and former slave, who had always distrusted them. The plantation was only one mile east of

Scott Station, along the railroad track. The young Frenchmen spent most of their spare time in the village, where they became popular regulars. Several nights a week and on Saturday afternoons, one could usually find them in one of the saloons or stores of Scott Station. The locals seemed never to tire of the brothers' tales of growing up in Paris and traveling in Europe and the United States; the stories provided vicarious thrills, for many of the audience would never journey beyond the borders of their state, and some would not even leave the parish. The Blancs were polite, well mannered, and educated. Ernest was particularly talented. He was artistic and could draw and sketch people, animals, and still lifes with uncanny accuracy. He was also ambidextrous and could write with both hands at the same time in extraordinarily fine penmanship. What was truly astounding was that he could write the same material simultaneously in two different languages: one hand wrote in French while the other wrote in English. Ernest and Alexis became close friends of Martin Begnaud and spent many evenings spinning yarns and playing dominoes in the living quarters of his store.

The Blanc brothers were treated like family by the Boudreauxs. When Alexis had become seriously ill, Philomène—tenderhearted like her big brother and touched by the fact that this very sick orphan boy had no one to look after him—persuaded her husband to take Alexis into their home so she could care for him. Olivier and Philomène lived on a nearby farm on land acquired from his father. Alexis lived with them for about two months, sharing a room with their son André, who was the same age. As Philomène nursed Alexis back to health, there developed a special bond between nurse and patient.

Philomène explained to Campbell that the Blanc brothers appeared to have been genuinely devastated by the death of her brother. Then, about a week after the funeral, they informed the family that they had received a letter from a former tutor, a friend of their late father, who had recently arrived in New Orleans from France and was living at 97 Toulouse Street. The tutor, they said, had a small amount of "traveling money" for them. Vague as to its source, the brothers suggested that the money could have come from the sale of a painting owned by their father. In any case, the tutor was in New Orleans waiting for them to pick up their little windfall. It was their intention to use that money to return to France, they said, for they harbored strong desires to see their old home in Paris again and visit the grave of their mother. The Boudreaux family was surprised by the news, since they had been led to believe that the Blanc brothers had left nothing—no family and no possessions—behind in the old country. Yet because they were so well educated, the story of the tutor made sense, and no one connected their departure with the murder. After all, two men had already been arrested. On April 30, Colonel Boudreaux loaded up his two farmhands and their few possessions in his wagon and drove them to the railroad station to catch the afternoon train for New Orleans. It was like losing two members of his own family.

Philomène Begnaud Boudreaux was the first member of the family to sense that there might be a link between the Blanc brothers and the murder of her brother. She first became aware of the possibility in a conversation with Vallena, the old black servant who had spent her entire life on Boudreaux Plantation. Vallena had been Olivier's nurse from the time he was born until he was old enough to care for himself, and she confided in his wife freely. About a month or two after the departure of the French brothers, Vallena expressed to Philomène how pleased she was that the Blanc brothers were no longer employed at the plantation. Because of her advanced age, Vallena's chores had been substantially reduced, but one of her responsibilities was to keep all the kitchen utensils sharpened, and she used a large grindstone located behind the big house for that purpose. On several occasions—too many, in Vallena's opinion—she had been unable to perform her honing duties because the grindstone was being used by the two young Frenchmen. They were secretive about their activities around the grindstone and would never let Vallena see what they were sharpening. What irked Vallena most was that their covert labors were causing gouges in her precious grindstone. Good riddance, Vallena declared. Philomène began to ask herself what they might have been sharpening, and why they were so secretive about it. Could it have been some kind of weapon? She probably tried not to entertain such a horrible thought, but as summer gave way to autumn, she could not help but reflect on the two years that the Blanc brothers had lived among her family. One observation haunted her thoughts: the subtle signs of discomfort she remembered noticing in Alexis whenever she had been near him in the days just after the murder. Despite the closeness that had developed between Philomène and Alexis during his illness, in those last days—especially when she came to bid him adieu—he seemed uneasy. Perhaps it was something only a mother, or a surrogate mother, could sense. But she knew it was real. And, finally, as if to confirm her suspicions, there was the inescapable fact of their unexpected and abrupt departure. Colonel Boudreaux scoffed at his daughter-in-law's suspicions, but William Campbell did not.

The trail of the brothers Blanc was cold. It was now mid-December and they had already been gone from Scott Station—and probably Louisiana—eight months. Campbell reported Philomène's musings to Sheriff Broussard and suggested that the address at 97 Toulouse Street in New Orleans be explored for any possible leads. Broussard, who by now was desperate for any new developments in the case, directed a thorough investigation of not only that address but the entire neighborhood, but discovered nothing. Inquiries around Lafayette Parish turned up a couple of interesting items, but nothing concrete. The postmasters in Scott Station and Lafayette could not recall the Blanc brothers receiving any letters from either New Orleans or France the previous April. Also, the brothers had made a dental appointment a day or two after the murder but failed to keep it. Considered something of a luxury in those days, the dental appointment could have meant that the Blancs had come into some money. And a few citizens who spoke to or saw them on their last day in Louisiana thought that the brothers had rapidly gained weight, explained by the imagined stuffed money bags around their midsections. The sheriff sent out hundreds of telegrams to law enforcement agencies all over the country asking for their cooperation in locating Ernest and Alexis Blanc, two brothers, ages nineteen and twenty, wanted for murder in Louisiana. The New Orleans *Daily Picayune* gave the following description of the wanted men: Ernest was "five feet, eight inches tall, weighing about 160 pounds, full face with a glow in his cheeks, sandy hair soft as silk, blue eyes, well-curved mouth, a trace of a mustache, sensitive nostrils and proven of quick temper"; Alexis, "an inch or two shorter than his brother, brown hair and eyes, no hair on his face, thin of body and gentle as a woman." The sheriff's dragnet of telegrams, like the investigation of the Toulouse Street address, turned up nothing. The year came to a close with Hamp Benton and Gustave Balin still in jail and the Blanc brothers, based on their declared destination, probably somewhere in Europe.

Book II

THE PEOPLE

5

At the time of the murder of Martin Begnaud in the last decade of the nineteenth century, the Acadians of Louisiana constituted a unique, easily identifiable ethnic minority group in the American South. Whereas the vast majority of white southerners were of Anglo-Saxon descent, English-speaking, and evangelical Protestant in religion as well as culture, the Acadians were of French heritage, Francophone, and Roman Catholic. This anomaly remains so today. But the forces of modernity are unstoppable, and the intervening century has witnessed striking changes in the lives of these people. In the last decade of the twentieth century, the French language is rarely heard on the streets of the villages, towns, and cities of Acadiana. While still the dominant population group throughout south Louisiana, Acadians are no longer isolated and can be found living and working around the world. But the most striking change of all is that Acadians are no longer called Acadians, but "Cajuns." The term is a twentieth-century creation, an Americanization of the French *Cadien*, the short form of *Acadien*. *Cajun* came into general usage in the years following World War II and has achieved national and even international recognition in the last quarter of the twentieth century, as the rest of the world embraced the Cajuns and their culture, famous for its joie de vivre, complete with piquant cuisine, exotic music, and contagious dancing.

This extraordinary culture, unlike the term *Cajun*, is not of recent vintage. It was inherited by the Cajuns from their Acadian forebears who could "let the good times roll" with the best of their modern cousins. The origin of this zest for life is complex and multifaceted, but one thing is certain: it belies a deep scar that exists on the collective Cajun soul. The original Acadians understood that life was precious and that what remained after a hard day's work and religious worship should be enjoyed to the fullest. Martin Begnaud and his fellow Acadians—unlike most modern Cajuns—still possessed a common memory of the incredible price that had been paid by their forefathers so that they could live life as they chose to live it. In the words of historian George Bancroft, "I do not know if the annals of the human race keep the record of sorrows so wantonly inflicted, so bitter and so lasting as fell upon the French inhabitants of Acadia."

Who, then, are the Acadians/Cajuns, these descendants of the first European settlers of Canada? How did they end up on the shores of the Gulf of Mexico, thousands of miles from the land of their ancestors? And what is this ominous shadow from the past that hovers even today?

I am an Acadian. My mother's name was Regina Begnaud. Her grandfather was Jean Begnaud, brother of Martin. From childhood I have been told the account of my great-great-uncle's death. This is my family, these are my people, and this is their story.

Le Havre, France: April 1604

Three years before the English founded Jamestown and sixteen years before the *Mayflower* landed at Plymouth Rock, an expedition sponsored by the Company of Acadia and composed of four ships set sail from the French seaport of Le Havre on the English Channel. The date was April 7, 1604. Duly licensed by King Henry IV, the group was headed for the land of *Acadie* to found and develop a colony of the same name. Since at least 1497, French fishermen had harvested the teeming waters of the Grand Banks off modern-day Newfoundland. According to one theory, cartographers and explorers named the region Acadia because its rugged coastline, thick forests, and pastoral river valleys reminded them—at least in the spring and summer—of Arcadia, the paradise described in Greek mythology. Acadia's boundaries were vague, but the territory first claimed by France in 1604 would eventually correspond to today's Canadian maritime provinces of New Brunswick, Nova Scotia, and Prince Edward Island, as well as portions of Quebec and of the U.S. state of Maine. The Atlantic Ocean and the Bay of Fundy washed the shores of Acadia, the latter serving as the primary highway into its heartland.

Pierre du Gast, sieur de Monts, headed the expedition that would provide the new French dynasty, the Bourbons, with its first permanent settlement in New France. The 120 colonists spent the month of June exploring the "Baye Française" and by early July had selected a location for a settlement on its western shore, a spot they christened Ile St. Croix (now Dorchet Island, Maine). The members of the expedition were a hodgepodge of adventure seekers from all walks of life—Louis Hébert, a pharmacist from Paris, was typical of these first Acadians in his lack of preparation or experience. Hébert and his fellow colonists soon discovered the brutality of Canadian winters. Nearly half perished in that first winter of 1604–1605, and when spring arrived the survivors abandoned the settlement and moved to a more sheltered river valley on the eastern shore of the Bay of Fundy. They called the new village Port Royal. It became the first capital of Acadia and would remain the colony's most important urban center for as long as Acadia remained French.

In the course of the next hundred years, corresponding roughly to the seventeenth century, there emerged from the French colony of Acadia a new people with a new culture; these were the Acadians.

In the early years, mere survival was a major accomplishment in the Canadian wilderness. But for the assistance of the Micmacs, the dominant tribe of American Indians in the region, the colony might not have endured. The Micmacs taught the French how to spear salmon in the spring and fall, and introduced them to the fine art of trapping; in return, the early Acadians introduced the Micmacs to their religion, their language, and—in many cases—their love. Unlike English pioneers to the New World who immigrated with their entire families, unaccompanied males formed the vanguard of French exploration of the continent, and they had no reservations about consorting with the natives. As one writer observed, "From the very first the Indians had been friendly with the French, and many a dusky maiden of the forest became a stout housewife in an Acadian home."

But perhaps the single most important thing that bonded the French and the American Indians, not just in Acadia but throughout North America, was their mutual respect for the forests. Fundamentally hunters and gatherers, the Indians relied on the flora and fauna of the continent's primeval forests as their lifeblood. The Acadians' very different means of sustenance, creating new farmland by constructing dikes to drain the fertile marshes that ringed the coastal lowlands, allowed most of the interior woodlands to remain undisturbed so that trapping and lumbering could continue. The role of the Micmacs in the development of Acadia and its people would remain significant throughout the seventeenth century.

With every passing decade, as more French immigrated—meager though their numbers were—and as a survival mentality gave way to subsistence agriculture and eventually to a certain degree of creature comfort, the distinct culture of the Acadians increasingly took shape. There were several reasons for the sparseness of French immigration to Acadia. In 1608, Samuel de Champlain founded Quebec on a majestic plateau appropriately named the Plains of Abraham. Overlooking the St. Lawrence River, the site was and is a magnificent natural promontory. Quebec would soon become the political, economic, and cultural capital of New France, and as such, the recipient of the majority of attention and resources directed to the North American colonies by the mother country. Acadia thus remained a frontier society, isolated, self-sufficient, and independent.

Agriculture, fishing, and trapping were the basis of the economy, and it was not unusual for a family to run "a good-sized herd of cattle, as well as twenty or so pigs and the same number of sheep." The religious affiliation was Roman Catholic, but the people were not intolerant. A few French immigrants to *Acadie* were seamen, but the great majority came from peasant stock. In feudal Europe, peasants had little or no chance of becoming landowners, a status reserved for the crown, the nobility, and the church. But a plebeian's impossible dream in France of owning his own farm could come true on the Canadian frontier. For this reason, land ownership was the highest aspiration of every Acadian. In the words of Carl A. Brasseaux, a historian who is himself an Acadian, "Land ownership was the key to the settlers' modest social and economic aspirations. Products of a precapitalistic environment, they sought neither prestige nor affluence through land acquisition, but rather economic independence and a comfortable existence patterned upon their former agrarian life-style." Land was available, and the Acadians claimed it, homesteaded it, worked hard to keep it, and prospered. Their existence was by no means idyllic, however, owing to the ever-present threat of invasion by their more powerful and more populous New England neighbors.

Acadia was France's most vulnerable colony in North America because it lay directly in the path of the major sea route between Europe and North America, a route plowed regularly by the British navy. Quebec, in contrast, enjoyed the advantage of a more interior location, and the cliffs of the Plains of Abraham were considered an ideally defensible position militarily. Also, for three months a year the waters of the St. Lawrence were frozen solid, and while no ships could depart, none could enter. The only other way to approach Quebec was overland, which meant a long, arduous, and dangerous journey from New York or Boston along routes occupied by France's Indian allies. Acadia, surrounded by water, could be easily invaded by sea from either the Atlantic Ocean or the Bay of Fundy, its European population was small compared with that of its New England neighbors, and its Indian population was likewise relatively small and friendly. New England farmers cast envious eyes on the fertile fields and orchards of Acadia, and New England fishermen disliked the competition from Acadian boats in what were some of the most prolific waters in the world. The fact that the Acadians were papists provided their Protestant neighbors an additional reason for hostility toward them.

In the seventeenth century, three military excursions against Acadia were launched from the English colonies, with varying degrees of success; a fourth invasion, in the first decade of the eighteenth century, would prove decisive. The first effort, in 1613, was led by an English privateer named Samuel Argall operating under a license from the London Company and its colony of Virginia. Argall conducted a slash-and-burn type of raid and succeeded in torching Port Royal. Besides constituting a nuisance, Argall's raids demonstrated Acadia's vulnerability to invasion from the sea. A more serious effort was made in 1654, when Robert

Sedgwick, a Massachusetts merchant, church member, and officer in the colonial militia, assumed command of a British fleet and sailed for Port Royal with an army of New England volunteers aboard. After a three-day siege, Sedgwick demanded and received the surrender of Port Royal in the name of Oliver Cromwell, the Puritan lord protector of England. While the protector's influence was apparent, the expedition was for the most part a military thrust from Massachusetts, rather than from the mother country.

For the next sixteen years, Acadia was an English colony. France was of no help during this time, being engaged in the war of the Fronde as several ambitious relatives of the little ten-year-old king, Louis XIV, lusted after the throne. Fortunately for the Acadians, Cromwell was too busy slaughtering Catholics in Ireland and fighting monarchists in England to devote much time to a small colony across the Atlantic. In exchange for keeping the occupying British garrison well supplied, the Acadians were allowed to govern themselves under a council headed by Guillaume Trahan. Comfortable with the arrangement, the British military commanders vetoed the urgings of Massachusetts leaders that the Acadians be removed and their lands turned over to Protestant New Englanders. The years of British occupation were generally tranquil, and Acadia was returned to France in 1667 by the Treaty of Breda.

For the next thirty-three years, Acadia enjoyed peace with her more powerful neighbors. But in 1690, with the outbreak of King William's War, a New England fleet of more than a thousand men commanded by Sir William Phips invaded Acadia and destroyed Port Royal. Many Acadians were incarcerated at Boston as prisoners of war. Phips, a native of Massachusetts who had earned a reputation as a soldier of fortune, was interested in Acadia for the sole purpose of looting Port Royal and parlaying his military success into a lucrative government post. The 1697 Treaty of Ryswick terminated hostilities between England and France, and at century's end Acadia was once more restored to French rule. It should be noted that there is no evidence that the Acadians planned or even entertained the idea of retaliation against their Protestant neighbors. They had no designs on New England; it contained nothing they needed or wanted.

During the course of the seventeenth century, in the vast interior of the continent far from Acadia, France made its bid for primacy in North America. French policy in New France was twofold. It was materialistic, with the search for a water route to the Orient and the attempt to develop a profitable economy, and it was altruistic, with the sincere desire to convert the American Indians to Catholicism. To experienced mariners and cartographers of the time, the Gulf of St. Lawrence and the St. Lawrence River appeared to be the most likely entrance to the "Northwest Passage," and both, thanks to Samuel de Champlain, were under French control. From 1608, the year he founded Quebec, until his death there in 1635, Champlain—whom Francis Parkman terms the "Father of New France"—held the St. Lawrence River Valley for France and never gave up searching for an all-water route across the continent. The Society of Jesus—*les jésuites*—and to a lesser extent, the Recollects, a Franciscan mendicant order, preached the gospel. The fabled independent French traders known as *coureurs des bois* and their licensed counterparts, *les voyageurs*, worked to stimulate the economy, the basis of which was fish, timber, and especially fur. The success of these groups was inextricably linked to Champlain's leadership, as he proved to be a master diplomat, owing to his genuine interest in the Indians' spiritual welfare, his ability to speak their language, and his willingness to enter their lodges, smoke the peace pipe, and make big medicine. Champlain had many reasons to build friendships with the native population, but their talk of great waters that lay to the west surely provided much incentive.

The Indians had not lied. Past the rapids at Montreal, the St. Lawrence River flowed into the first of five incredibly large lakes, each as large as a small European country, the collective area being almost twice the size of England. Before his death, Champlain himself explored Lakes Ontario and Huron, and the *voyageurs* who succeeded him charted Erie, Michigan, and Superior. All official expeditions were accompanied by Indian guides, interpreters, and dark-robed Jesuits, and wherever a trading post was built, a mission was constructed nearby. By midcentury an impressive chain of French outposts dotted the shores of the Great Lakes, and the inhabitants of these shores spoke of still another great body of water that lay to the west.

By 1672, a new governor of New France, the count de Frontenac, and his able intendant, Jean Talon, were ready to make the great push for the discovery of the westward passage. For several years now they had dispatched *voyageurs* westward with strict instructions for keeping diaries and charts. The findings confirmed what the Indians and *coureurs des bois* had been saying for years: to the west of the Great Lakes lay a "great water," the mythic Mitchisipi, as it was known in Indian lore, which emptied into the sea. The burning question was, did it flow west or south? The man chosen to find the answer was Louis Jolliet, a young but dependable merchant/trader with a gift for Indian languages. In the first week of October 1672, Jolliet and his party departed Quebec. Their destination was the Jesuit mission of Saint Ignace at the Straits of Mackinac, at the top of Lake Michigan, where they would winter and rendezvous with the spiritual leader of the expedition, Father Jacques Marquette. Father Marquette, an experienced missionary, knew the tribes of the Great Lakes region well and was admired and respected by all who knew him, red or white. The following May, Jolliet, Marquette, and five other Frenchmen departed Saint Ignace in two canoes for what would become one of North America's most important historic trips.

Over the centuries, the legendary journey of Jolliet and Marquette has been told and retold by numerous scholars in numerous texts, but for our purposes it is sufficient to recount that on June 15, 1673, they reached the Mississippi River via the Wisconsin Portage, and headed downriver until they reached the mouth of the Arkansas River on July 15. There, the chiefs of the Arkansas Indians warned them of hostile tribes farther south. Jolliet and Marquette decided to take this advice seriously; two days later they turned their canoes around and prepared to face the powerful Mississippi current. But they had come far enough to announce to the world that the great water did not flow west, but south, and that it did not empty into the Pacific Ocean, but into the Gulf of Mexico. *Les voyageurs* returned via the Illinois River and the Chicago Portage.

Father Marquette did not return to Quebec with the other members of the expedition, choosing instead to remain in the Illinois country tending to the spiritual needs of his native flock. Primitive living conditions and brutal winters exacted their toll: Jacques Marquette was thirty-eight years old when he died on May 18, 1675, among his beloved Indians on the shores of Lake Michigan.

After wintering at the Jesuit mission of Sault Sainte Marie, Jolliet reached Quebec in July 1674. By August, accounts of the discoveries of Jolliet and Marquette had been published and word of their impressive accomplishments spread rapidly throughout Europe. Several major findings were revealed. The Mitchisipi was not the missing link in the search for the Northwest Passage, and the search would go on. The size and resources of the heartland of the North American continent were far greater than previously imagined. This was especially true of the upper Mississippi River Valley, where herds of bison were said to roam in numbers so large that they could not be counted. In Quebec, the Illinois country was already being referred to as the "El Dorado" of furs, and it was as yet unclaimed—a fact not lost on the governor of New France.

Count de Frontenac's choice to follow up the discoveries of Jolliet and Marquette was Robert Cavelier, sieur de La Salle. Frontenac and La Salle's objectives were to claim for France the entire Mississippi River Valley, to build trading connections in the Illinois country, and to establish a colony at the mouth of the great river. Frontenac had dreams of becoming very rich, and La Salle, who perceived himself as a man of destiny, envisioned a French colonial empire that would stretch from the Gulf of St. Lawrence to the Gulf of Mexico. In the spring of 1682, after spending a number of years building forts in the Illinois country to solidify French influence in the region, La Salle's expedition rode the swift downstream current of the Mississippi to a point near its mouth where it opens into three broad channels; La Salle followed one, and Henri de Tonty, his aide-de-camp, and Jacques d'Autray, one of his most capable young officers, followed the other two. Each found the open, salt waters of the Gulf of Mexico a few miles distant. On April 9, the entire party assembled for a formal ceremony in which La Salle read a proclamation claiming all the lands drained by the Mississippi River for Louis XIV, King of France and Navarre. He named it the "Land of Louis," in French, *la Louisiane.* Jacques de la Metairie, a royal notary who accompanied the expedition for this specific purpose, placed his seal on the document to make the proclamation official.

Upon his return to France, La Salle was given a hero's welcome. King Louis endorsed his plan to build a colony at the mouth of the Mississippi, and investors were eager to put up large sums in exchange for a piece of *la Louisiane*. On July 24, 1684, La Salle set sail once again, from La Rochelle, with an expedition whose mission was to establish a colony at a suitable location near the mouth of the river. This voyage was a calamity. The would-be colonists crossed the Atlantic, sailed around Florida, and entered the Gulf of Mexico, but the mouth of the Mississippi eluded them. After eight months, in March 1685, they landed at modern-day Matagorda Bay in Spanish Texas, about four hundred miles west of the mouth of the Mississippi. There were no signs of La Salle's previous visit, no familiar, friendly Indians, and no Tonty and d'Autray, who were expected to rendezvous with them and bring reinforcements and supplies. The captain of the *Joly*, the one ship not wrecked or captured by the Spanish navy, sailed back to France, and the members of the now stranded expedition built a fort. After two years of isolation, hostile natives, rattlesnakes, and low morale, La Salle concluded that something had gone dreadfully wrong. On January 7, 1687, he headed north with a small detachment in search of his countrymen and the great river. He never found them. Some of the group mutinied, and on March 19, near the Trinity River, La Salle was shot from ambush by the surgeon of the expedition. Estimates vary, but of the 280 men, women, and children who accompanied La Salle to the New World, there were fewer than a dozen survivors.

An immediate follow-up to the failed expedition was precluded by the outbreak of war between England and France, the fourth major military contest between the two nations in the seventeenth century. The end of King William's War in 1697 and a new champion at court for the cause of Louisiana were instrumental in reviving La Salle's dream. Louis XIV's minister of the navy, Count Pontchartrain, recognized the strategic and economic advantages of a viable colony in Louisiana and urged the king to permit a second attempt at settlement. Louis consented, and a North American was chosen to lead the effort. Canadian-born Pierre Le Moyne, sieur d'Iberville, a navy captain who had distinguished himself at sea, was appointed governor-general of Louisiana with instructions to explore the area, build a fort, and search for pearls, mulberry trees (for France's growing silk industry), and mineable ores and minerals. Iberville and his squadron set sail from Brest on October 24, 1698, and reached the northern shores of the Gulf of Mexico on January 24, 1699. The site Iberville chose for his fort, Fort Maurepas, was near a village of friendly Indians called the Biloxi, the extant site of Biloxi, Mississippi. Construction was completed on March 2, 1699, Mardi Gras Day, and the fleur-de-lis fluttered once again in the lower Mississippi Valley.

As the seventeenth century closed, France held an enviable position on the North American continent. She laid claim to its heartland, from the Great Lakes to the Gulf of Mexico, and she controlled the entrance to the two great rivers that allowed access into the continent's interior, the St. Lawrence and the Mississippi. Frenchmen had built a line of forts along the banks of the rivers and the Great Lakes, and although these outposts were separated by vast distances and thinly manned, they were enough to establish King Louis's claim and authority. Louisiana would soon be divided into two colonies: Upper Louisiana (the Illinois country) and Lower Louisiana; they joined Acadia, Hudson Bay, Newfoundland, and Quebec in Canada to constitute New France at the dawn of the eighteenth century. But power, politics, and people were shifting in both Europe and North America, and the Acadians would be the first to feel the consequences.

6

Annapolis Royal, Nova Scotia: December 1713

In 1700, Charles II of Spain, the last of the Spanish Hapsburgs, died childless and bequeathed his kingdom and its vast colonial empire to his sister's son Philip, the duke of Anjou. Philip's claim was certainly defensible, but there was one major problem: the duke of Anjou was a Bourbon, the grandson of Louis XIV. King Louis knew that the rest of Europe would never acquiesce in the concentration of such power in the hands of one dynasty, and that if his family's claim was pursued, it would mean war. But he was determined that his grandson would become Philip V, king of Spain and the Indies. In consequence, all the rest of Europe declared war on France and Spain.

It was during this conflict—the War of the Spanish Succession, or Queen Anne's War, as it was known in the Thirteen Colonies—that the fourth and final invasion of Acadia by the English and her colonists took place. When peace was finally declared in 1713 by the Treaty of Utrecht, Louis XIV had achieved his goal, but at a very high price. Philip was recognized as the rightful king of Spain and the Indies, but the rest of Spain's possessions in Europe were lost to her forever: the Netherlands, Naples, Sardinia, and Milan were ceded to Austria, Sicily to Savoy, and Gibraltar and Minorca to England. In North America, France was forced to surrender Hudson Bay, Newfoundland, and the Acadian peninsula to Great Britain. With its large and industrious population and its strategic location, Acadia was the prize. The new owners of this portion of the colony soon renamed it Nova Scotia. The Acadians living on the peninsula thus became British subjects in 1713, but their souls remained French. With the threat of periodic invasions from New England removed, the Acadians retained their culture and their property and thrived economically. It was during these years that they came to think and speak of themselves as a nation, the "Neutral French." N. E. S. Griffiths, probably the foremost authority of the pre-dispersal period of Acadian history, terms this period the "Golden Age" of the Acadians.

In addition to officially transferring the Acadian peninsula to England, the Treaty of Utrecht contained clauses that set forth, in general language, the rights and responsibilities of the Acadians as British subjects. They were given one year to move wherever they chose, and they were permitted to take all their possessions with them. If they chose to remain, they were guaranteed the right to practice their religion. Later in the year, Louis XIV emptied France's prisons of all Protestants jailed because of their religious beliefs. Queen Anne was so moved that she felt compelled to reciprocate, and she wrote her new governor in Nova Scotia "to continue our subjects, to retain and enjoy their said lands and tenements without molestation, as fully and freely as our other subjects do or to sell the same, if they shall rather choose to remove elsewhere." (The queen may also have reserved a special place in her heart for the little colony since its capital, Port Royal, had been renamed Annapolis Royal in her honor.)

Armed with these royal guarantees, few Acadians availed themselves of the option of leaving Nova Scotia within one year. They had good reason to remain. At least five generations of their people had worked and struggled and persevered against the elements, the wilderness, and the sea to own their own land, and by now, many were prosperous. The Acadian farms were located in the most fertile valleys and meadows, and their herds, flocks, and orchards represented dowries for daughters and a start in life for sons. Besides, this was not the first time English rule had been imposed on Acadia. On previous occasions, once the fighting had subsided, accommodations had been reached and life had not been unbearable. The Acadians also believed—and if the past is prologue, they had every good reason to do so—that British rule was only temporary; the French would be back. In fact, France remained a dominant force in the region. France still held the western shore of the Bay of Fundy (present-day New Brunswick), most of the Chignecto Isthmus connecting the Nova Scotia peninsula to the mainland, and Ile St. Jean (Prince Edward Island) and Ile Royale (Cape Breton Island). There was considerable migration on the part of the Acadians to French-held territory, but it was usually the result of economics and not politics.

The Acadians were the dominant society in Nova Scotia until 1755, and remained self-generating and self-sustaining. On their farms they grew beets, carrots, chives, onions, parsley, shallots, turnips, apples, cherries, pears, plums, cabbage, peas, rye, and wheat, and raised cattle, chickens, pigs, and sheep. Milk was the common drink, but wine and cider and rum were available. Fish and game were abundant. Visitors—both French and English—commented on the excellence and diversity of the cuisine and the hospitality of the hearth. It was generally accepted that an Acadian fisherman provided stiff competition for his New England counterpart, and Acadian seamen were noted for their huge catches of the precious cod. Coal mines, owned and operated by Acadians, were increasingly important in the region. But the great prize was the farmland, unmatched in its fertility, particularly when compared with the rocky soil of New England.

Acadia seemed favored in other ways as well. Epidemics of smallpox, typhoid, scarlet fever, and other dreaded plagues of the time were unknown there. The wholesome lifestyle produced healthier mothers and children, making for low infant mortality. In 1713 the Acadian population of Nova Scotia was estimated to be about 2,500; by 1755 it had reached an estimated 18,000, and this did not include several thousand more living on the western and northern shores of the Bay of Fundy and the outer islands. The presence of such a large and prosperous French-speaking Catholic population just across the sea from Boston would become a major propaganda tool of the faction of New Englanders eager for the elimination of the Acadians.

The loss of the Acadian peninsula, Hudson Bay, and Newfoundland forced France to acknowledge the vulnerability of her remaining colonies on the continent, Canada and Louisiana. The result was the construction of Louisbourg and New Orleans. To protect and secure Canada, her most prosperous and populous colony in North America, France built a massive fortress and naval base on the northern coast of Ile Royale at the entrance to the Gulf of St. Lawrence. Based on plans drawn by the great military engineer Vauban, Louisbourg was deemed impregnable and its large, permanent fleet of warships capable of checking any attempt to take Quebec. To solidify her position on the Gulf of Mexico and to prevent an invasion of the North American heartland via the Mississippi, France constructed and garrisoned a new settlement actually on the river, near its mouth. *La Nouvelle Orléans* was named for the current regent of France, the notorious duke of Orléans. Established in 1718, it shortly became the capital of *la Louisiane.*

The founder of Louisiana, Iberville, was a casualty of the War of the Spanish Succession: recalled to active duty, he died, probably of yellow fever, in the captain's quarters of his ship in July 1706. His younger brother, Jean Baptiste Le Moyne, sieur de Bienville, succeeded him as governor of the territory. Bienville devoted his entire career, forty-four years, to making Louisiana grow and prosper. It was not an easy task, but his dedication earned him the respect of historians and the title "Father of Louisiana." The opportunity for quick profits from furs was not an option as it was in beaver-teeming Canada. Furthermore, Louisiana's Indian population was small; some were hostile and some were friendly, but a thriving trade with the aboriginal population held few opportunities. And while Canada had brutal winters, Louisiana had brutal summers, during which the French pioneers encountered malaria, yellow fever, and dysentery, among other diseases. At one point, in an attempt to encourage immigration, the French government offered to release convicts if they would volunteer to immigrate to Louisiana, but found that most preferred prison in France to freedom in a colony that they regarded as a deathtrap. As midcentury passed, Louisiana still relied on downriver grain shipments from the Illinois country and imports from France to survive, although with each passing year her economic situation improved. Underpopulation was a problem, as it was in all of New France. By 1766, the entire population of Louisiana was only about ten thousand, most in and around New

Orleans but with active posts or forts at Biloxi and Mobile on the Gulf Coast, Natchez on the Mississippi River, Natchitoches on the Red River, and the small, remote Attakapas Post on Bayou Teche about 150 miles west of the capital.

New Orleans was virtually the only economic bright spot in the colony. It was the population center and eventually became a thriving and robust seaport. And it did its best to earn the reputation bestowed upon it by its namesake, the famous duke, who was described by one French historian as "witty, charming, clever, scandalous, unaccountable and a man who drank to excess." In the process of developing its identity, New Orleans also gave France what it needed: a formidable and permanent presence on the Gulf of Mexico at the mouth of the Mississippi River.

France was fortunate that her position in the lower Mississippi Valley was never contested militarily by another European power; it would have been difficult to defend such a large area with so few Frenchmen. But with the exception of a few Indian uprisings, Louisiana enjoyed peace during the French colonial period. Things were not as favorable for Canada. The continent, as big as it is, was not big enough for both France and Britain. War was inevitable. The proximity of the Acadian homeland to the centers of French power in North America, Quebec and Louisbourg, was of genuine concern to Britain's colonial administrators, for whom the issue was how to neutralize the role of the Acadians in any future conflict. Their solution was to require the Acadians of Nova Scotia to take an unconditional oath of allegiance to the king of England. This policy was incongruous on its face, for these Acadians had become British subjects by terms of the Treaty of Utrecht, and the conditions of their citizenship were established by Queen Anne's declaration. But under intense political pressure from New England, the Board of Trade in London and the governors of Nova Scotia pursued the issue of the oath off and on and with more or less vigor until 1755.

The Acadians, demonstrating a stubbornness that would prove to be at once their greatest strength and their greatest weakness, refused to take the unconditional oath. As a counteroffer, they proposed to take a conditional oath that contained provisions ensuring their religious freedom, property rights, recognition as a distinct community, and neutrality in any war between England and France. It was the latter provision, of course, that disturbed the British; they insisted that the Acadians stand with England. The Acadians refused; they could not bring themselves to bear arms against France. Some have called it loyalty, others obduracy; some have called it fierce independence, others stubbornness; some have called it courage, others intransigence; but by any description, the Acadians paid a high price for their refusal.

English demands and Acadian counterproposals continued until 1730, when an exasperated governor Richard Philipps—probably with his career on the line—ended the stalemate by misrepresenting the situation to both sides. He assured the Acadian delegates from the various settlements that England had accepted their proposals. Accepting his word, they signed the unconditional oath. Back in London, Philipps presented the rolls of signatures to the Board of Trade and proclaimed that the Acadians had abandoned their demands for neutrality. As Carl Brasseaux has put it, the governor "managed simultaneously to please and deceive all parties." These "Conventions of 1730," though mendaciously obtained, would provide the framework for the relationship between the Acadians and their British rulers for almost twenty years. Philipps's innovative diplomacy was later discovered, but neither side wished to reopen the issue. It was understood by all parties that the Acadians stood firm on the issue of neutrality.

The first real test of Acadian neutrality came during the War of the Austrian Succession (1740–1748), or King George's War, as it was known in America. French raids from Louisbourg and Quebec on English positions in Nova Scotia were conducted without Acadian assistance. Likewise, when a French priest, the abbé Jean Louis LeLoutre, who was considered something of a messianic figure by the Micmacs, led his Native American followers in raids against Annapolis Royal and other British installations in Nova Scotia, the Acadians refused to become involved. LeLoutre was a zealot who fervently believed the Acadians were in danger of losing their souls to the devil because they lived under English rule. He preached that they should give up their earthly possessions and remove themselves to French-held territory, where they might live in poverty in this life but gain everlasting salvation in the next. Typically, the Acadians were not impressed.

Frustrated, LeLoutre ordered his Micmacs to burn several Acadian settlements around Beaubassin along the Missagouash River, the boundary between English Nova Scotia and French territory on the Isthmus of Chignecto. As a result of LeLoutre's fanaticism, a few hundred Acadians were forced to cross the boundary into French territory in search of food and shelter, thus compromising the pledge of neutrality. But the Acadians were determined to honor their commitment. They took their identity as Neutral French seriously; they were French and they were neutral. While a few young Acadians undeniably fought alongside French troops during this period, and a few even joined forces with LeLoutre, the official policy of the Acadian leaders and the conduct of the overwhelming majority of the Acadian people was neutrality.

Knowledge of the role played by English military officer Paul Mascarene provides a key to understanding the Acadians' conduct during this period. During most of Richard Philipps's long tenure as governor of Nova Scotia (1717–1749), Philipps served as an absentee administrator. In 1731 he left Annapolis Royal never to return. Officially, he governed from London, but the real chief executive of the colony was Major Mascarene, who began as commander of the garrison at Annapolis Royal, then served as president of the Council of Nova Scotia, and finally, from 1740 to 1749, as lieutenant governor. Mascarene was a Huguenot, bilingual, and by nature a consensus builder, traits that made him popular among the Acadians. He understood and sympathized with the difficulty of the Acadians' position; they, in turn, reciprocated with their loyalty and cooperation. Mascarene's enlightened policies helped the Acadians succeed in maintaining their neutrality in the face of the challenges posed by King George's War.

With the advent of peace in 1748, life appeared to return to normalcy for the Acadians, but across the Bay of Fundy, anger, frustration, and disbelief reigned. In June 1745, Louisbourg, the "Gibraltar of New France," had been besieged by a force of four thousand New England militia and had surrendered after a six-week siege. Nevertheless, by the Treaty of Aix-la-Chapelle that ended the war, England returned Louisbourg to France. It was common knowledge in America that Europe and European concerns took precedence over colonial interests,

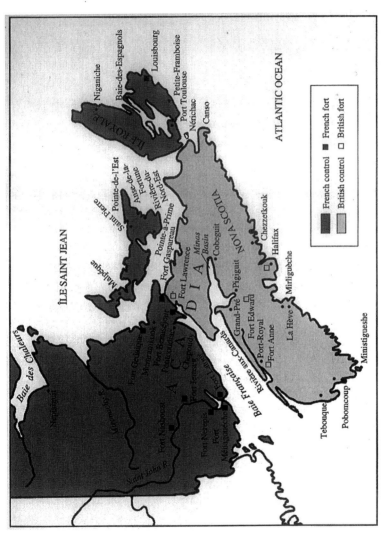

Acadia / Nova Scotia, 1750

Courtesy Center for Canadian Studies, Mount Allison University, Sackville, N.B.

but this dastardly act of betrayal at the hands of European diplomats sent an unmistakable message that reverberated throughout the thirteen English colonies: Americans were capable of defending themselves without the military assistance and diplomatic meddling of the mother country. In less than thirty years, those very colonies would be at war with Great Britain, but first they had to rid themselves of a common enemy: the French.

Because it was inevitable that there would be another war between England and France for primacy in North America, King George and his ministers in London made several strategic foreign policy decisions that forever altered the history of Nova Scotia and the Acadians. A key element of English preparedness was the establishment of a strong military presence in Nova Scotia. The plan had three components: the construction of a fortress on the Nova Scotia peninsula to rival Louisbourg, the large-scale immigration of Protestant settlers to counter the economic domination of the colony by the Acadians, and the establishment of strong military installations among the larger Acadian settlements. No expense was to be spared. In 1749 Colonel Edward Cornwallis was appointed governor with orders to implement these policies.

On the site of a small Acadian settlement on Chebuctou Bay, on Nova Scotia's Atlantic coast, Cornwallis began construction of the great naval fortress of Halifax. It was intended to serve as a barrier between Louisbourg and New England and to keep the sea lanes open between England and her colonies in the event of war. The British also hoped the construction of Halifax would help mollify public opinion in the colonies, where feelings were still smarting from the return of Louisbourg to France. The Annapolis Royal garrison was also reinforced, and two new forts were built in major Acadian population centers: Fort Edward in the Mines District, with a road connecting it to Halifax, and Fort Lawrence on the Chignecto Isthmus near Beaubassin. (Major Charles Lawrence, the officer in charge of building the latter fort, named it for himself.) Finally, Cornwallis began the process of recruiting two thousand German and Irish Protestants to settle a site south of Halifax that eventually became Lunenburg.

In the midst of all of these tasks, in 1750, Governor Cornwallis called a meeting of all Acadian leaders from each section of the colony. He demanded that every Acadian take the unconditional oath of allegiance to the king of England. Those who refused would be given their passports and must leave the country. The Acadians refused to take the oath. They countered Cornwallis's demands by citing the Conventions of 1730 and their official status as French Neutrals.

For a minority of Nova Scotia's Acadians, somewhere between two and four thousand, these new manifestations of British suzerainty in their homeland were unacceptable. They chose to migrate to contiguous or nearby colonies still under French rule. Their departure was orderly and peaceful. They were able to dispose of their possessions as best they could, and with the assistance of family and friends, with their oxen-drawn wagons filled to capacity, and in some cases with their flocks in tow, they left to join their countrymen living in the numerous Acadian settlements across the Missagouash River in French-held territory. These Acadian émigrés settled on Ile St. Jean, Ile Royale, and in eastern Quebec.

One family central to the present narrative was among those who chose to leave. Paul Doiron, a forty-year-old farmer, obtained passports for himself and his wife, Marguerite Michel, and, accompanied by their eight children, they left Nova Scotia. The Doirons' destination was Ile St. Jean.

The approximately 80 percent of the Acadian population who remained in Nova Scotia stood firm. For his part, Cornwallis did not press the issue of the unconditional oath. Even in 1751, when France built two new forts near the northern boundary of Nova Scotia, Cornwallis seemed to acknowledge the stance of the Neutral French. Fort Beausejour was constructed on the French side of the Missagouash River at the northern tip of the Bay of Fundy, almost in sight of Fort Lawrence. The smaller Fort Gaspereau, on the north shore of the Chignecto Isthmus, was built for the purpose of protecting the portage route to Ile St. Jean. On August 3, 1752, Cornwallis was recalled. The issue of the oath remained unsettled.

Colonel Peregrine Thomas Hopson succeeded Cornwallis as governor of Nova Scotia. From the standpoint of the Acadians, a wiser choice could not have been made. He was a man of honor and sensitivity, moderation and personal charm, with an inquiring mind that he used to make independent judgments. Governor Hopson's political independence and sense of fairness did not endear him to the merchants of Boston and their agents who had set up shop in Halifax in large numbers. He sided with the Acadians on the thorny issue of the oath of allegiance and even persuaded the Board of Trade in London to drop the matter. "Always," a principal historian of these events says of Hopson, "he emphasized the necessity of treating the Acadians as British subjects, dealing with them fairly in money matters, and redressing their wrongs." Hopson's relations with his French counterparts in Quebec and Louisbourg were excellent, and he even negotiated a peace treaty with the Micmacs.

If the news from Acadia was good, Acadian émigrés elsewhere in New France were also doing well, Paul Doiron among them. Doiron had settled in the community of Rivière du Nord-Est on Ile St. Jean, where he had become a wheat farmer on land acquired from a M. de Bonaventure. The Census of 1752 also lists Doiron as owning "live stock consisting of four bulls, three cows, two heifers, two sows, two pigs and twenty-five fowls or chickens." The best news, however, was the birth of the Doirons' first child in their new country, a little girl, Hélenne, eight months old when the census taker visited the family. Hélenne joined her eight older siblings, a traditionally large Acadian family: Roze, age 2, Joseph, 4, Auzitte, 6, Jean Baptiste, 8, Blanche, 10, Pierre Paul, 12, Anne Appoline, 15, and Margueritte Joseph, 17. For the Doirons and many others like them, the prospects for peace in the region and prosperity at home must have seemed bright. Then destiny intervened. In October 1753, after only fourteen months in office, Governor Hopson was forced to return to England owing to a serious eye problem. Charles Lawrence, by now a lieutenant colonel and also lieutenant governor, was left in charge of Nova Scotia. His ascension to power was a fateful event in the history of the Acadian people.

7

Halifax, Nova Scotia: July 1755

The history of every nation or culture is, to some degree, unique. But it is rare that a single year can so precisely cut through time that it literally rips apart the physical domicile of a people. For the Neutral French, the Acadians, that watershed year was 1755. From 1604 to 1755, the only place in the world where one could find an Acadian was in Acadia. True, in the first half of the eighteenth century, new names like the "Bay of Fundy" and "Nova Scotia" replaced *Baye Française* and *Acadie* on English maps, but the Acadian people remained. The Acadian diaspora began in 1755, the beginning of a thirty-year period during which Acadians could be found scattered throughout the Atlantic littoral: on the islands of St. Pierre and Miquelon in the North Atlantic and the Falkland Islands in the far South Atlantic, on the island of Corsica in the Mediterranean Sea and that of St. Domingue in the Caribbean, from French Guiana in the South American tropics to the Channel Islands of the North Sea, in the coastal regions of England and France, and, in North America, Canada, the thirteen English colonies (soon to become the United States), and the colony of Louisiana.

The essential historical facts are undisputed. On July 4, 1754, the French and Indian War began in North America when an army of Virginia militiamen under the command of Colonel George Washington was defeated at Fort Necessity in the Ohio River Valley. The following year, General Edward Braddock arrived to take charge of all British military operations in America. At a council of war at Alexandria, Virginia, in April 1755, Braddock approved a plan submitted by Governor William Shirley of Massachusetts and Lieutenant Governor Charles Lawrence of Nova Scotia to attack the French positions at Forts Beausejour and Gaspereau with militia from New England transported and supported by two large English fleets commanded by Admirals Boscawen and Mostyn. The governors believed the conquest of these two forts necessary to ensure the safety of New England. In June, both were rather easily overwhelmed and surrendered. The following month, however, brought news of the stunning defeat and death of General Braddock at the Battle of the Wilderness. As a result, fear and hatred of the French reached new levels of intensity throughout the English colonies.

In August 1755, Lawrence issued orders for the expulsion of the Acadians from Nova Scotia and from anywhere else they might be captured. His orders were specific: disarm the Acadians, burn their homes, churches, boats, crops, and fields, slaughter or scatter their flocks, and destroy the extensive network of dikes that held back the surging saltwater tides of the Bay of Fundy, allowing floodwaters to inundate the farmland and pollute the soil. The men were to be separated from the women and kept under heavy guard in holding pens until transport ships arrived; then men, women, and children were to be loaded on board and distributed among the Thirteen Colonies, from Massachusetts to Georgia. *Le Grand Dérangement*, the Great Disruption, had begun. It is entirely appropriate that the twentieth century, a century perhaps unequaled in its record of man's inhumanity to man, would coin a new term for this unique form of terror: ethnic cleansing.

Greed was the primary motivation of the English in their attempt to eradicate the Acadian people. It was no secret that the great merchants, land brokers, and fishing fleet owners of Massachusetts had long wanted to bring the economy of Acadia under their influence. They had enthusiastically encouraged and financially underwritten the previous invasions of Acadia launched from New England; only the Eurocentric character of French and English foreign policy had foiled their plans for making Acadia an appendage of Massachusetts. (Similarly, it is improbable that these ambitious New England expansionists could have achieved their goal of eliminating Acadian influence from Nova Scotia in the middle of the eighteenth century had it not been for the tense geopolitical situation that existed elsewhere in North America.)

Charles Lawrence was ultimately responsible for the expulsion of the Acadians from their homeland, but he did not act in a vacuum. He had coconspirators. We know from the record that Lawrence was a bachelor and a career military officer; that he had served in Nova Scotia for many years under Philipps, Mascarene, Cornwallis, and Hopson and thus knew the Acadians intimately; and that he was venal, egocentric, and intensely disdainful of the Acadians. Certainly the Acadians had their faults, but the last forty years had proved that mutual respect and cooperation between rulers and ruled was possible and, with the right leadership, could produce desirable results for all concerned. The administrations of Mascarene and Hopkins are good examples. It is probable that Lawrence was miserable under those regimes and found the thought of Acadians and Englishmen living in harmony to be anathema. And political comity was certainly not in the plans of his friends and associates in Boston and Halifax, merchants and fleet owners who viewed the Acadians as impediments to their commercial designs on Nova Scotia. Without consulting Governor Shirley of Massachusetts, who had succeeded Braddock as commander in chief, and without consulting the Board of Trade in London, Lawrence issued the orders for expulsion in August 1755.

He would never have such an opportunity again. To supplement his already formidable force of British regulars in the colony, Lawrence had at his disposal an army of over two thousand New England militiamen fresh from victory at Fort Beausejour already in Nova Scotia. Governor Shirley was temporarily missing in action, allowing Lawrence to act independently. The two large British fleets were idle and available for duty. War hysteria and anti-French sentiment were at fever pitch. With the well-documented refusal of the Acadians to take the unconditional oath of allegiance as his rationale, Lawrence hoped to present his superiors with a fait accompli. By November 1755, a large segment of Nova Scotia's Acadian population had been deported, but Lawrence would spend the remaining five years of his life (he died in 1760) hunting down and deporting Acadians from his part of the world. Lawrence's goal was to wipe out the Neutral French by distributing them among the larger English Protestant populations of the Thirteen Colonies. Those who survived the horrors of deportation would exist individually but not collectively. He desired the eradication of Acadian culture and, in time, its memory. As a reward for his initiative, Lawrence was promoted to full colonel in 1756 and named governor of Nova Scotia.

John Bartlet Brebner's chronicle of this most tragic chapter in North American history is unsurpassed. He identifies and charges by name the New Englanders who were Charles Lawrence's civilian co-conspirators: Benjamin Green, John Collier, William Cotterell, John Rous, Jonathan Belcher, and Charles Morris. Each of these men had committed his financial fortune to the success of a new Nova Scotia, a Nova Scotia free of Acadians and governed by Colonel Lawrence. It would be speculation to suggest that Lawrence was a secret business partner of this group, and still further speculation to suggest that Lawrence was the financial beneficiary of these admiring and grateful businessmen, but it seems highly probable that he was both.

Leaving *Acadie* was never an option for most Acadians; this was their home. By 1755, however, some Acadians had come to believe that forced exile might become a reality. But they assumed, logically, that such an undertaking would resemble the voluntary departures of 1750; it would be peaceful, orderly, and with a nearby destination: French Canada. Lawrence and his backers, however, never considered this humane approach to expulsion, for it would mean that after the war—when emotions had cooled—the Acadians would be free to return, reclaim their lands, and seek restitution for the unlawful expropriation of their property. After all, they were British subjects. For Lawrence's plans to succeed fully, the Acadians must be dispatched to faraway lands. It was for this same reason that he ordered the burning of Acadian homes, barns, crops, and churches and the flooding of their fields with seawater. He wanted the Acadians to see with their own eyes that there was nothing left for them in Nova Scotia.

It is unlikely that the Acadians could have avoided their tragic destiny even if they had agreed to take the unconditional oath of allegiance in 1755, 1754, or earlier. Their fate was sealed when Charles Lawrence assumed control of the colonial government. In August of 1754, the Council of Nova Scotia at Halifax, presided over by Lieutenant Governor Lawrence, received a petition from twenty-five Acadian émigrés from Louisbourg who wished to return home. They were granted permission to enter the colony on condition that they take the unqualified oath; they took the oath and were admitted. In October of the same year, a group of six families (twenty-eight persons) filed a similar petition, took the oath, and were readmitted. When the mass deportations began, however, Lawrence made no distinction between those who had taken the oath and those who had not. He imprisoned and expelled every Acadian man, woman, and child he and his soldiers could capture, including those émigrés who had returned in 1754 and had taken the unconditional oath. The issue of the unconditional oath, in Lawrence's hands, was reduced to a legal pretext.

It is impossible to capture in words the agony, the pain, the suffering, and the humiliation of the Acadian people during the years of expulsion, exile, homelessness, and wandering. Nonetheless, a few have tried. The most famous account is Henry Wadsworth Longfellow's epic poem *Evangeline: A Tale of Acadie,* published in 1847. Long regarded as one of the classics of American literature, the tragic life of Longfellow's Acadian heroine was required reading for most nineteenth-century American schoolchildren. Longfellow, however, made no claim to historical accuracy, freely exercising poetic license. Although *Evangeline* is an outstanding work of literature, the tale of *le Grand Dérangement* presented therein is a romanticized and sanitized version of the truth. The unvarnished raw facts speak for themselves. Hundreds of Acadians died of smallpox, dysentery, scurvy, and malnutrition on overcrowded, underrationed British ships. The Acadians had no natural resistance to these diseases, which were unknown in their homeland. Especially devastating was the variola virus, or smallpox. Unsanitary conditions on the ships reached epidemic levels when officials of a number of the English colonies refused to admit the Acadians. In some cases, the exiles were forced to live in squalid conditions on ships that remained anchored in harbors for months at a time while the ship's officers and colonial officials argued over the disposition of their human cargo. Hundreds died when put ashore, too weak to survive. Many more died of simple exposure. In some of the English colonies, orphan and some nonorphan children of the exiles were forcibly removed from their parents or guardians and placed in Protestant, English-speaking homes. There were some examples of charity extended to them, but not many. In some cases, beggary was necessary for survival. A group of 1,500 Acadians was unloaded in Virginia, but the colonial governor ordered them back on board. They were ferried across the Atlantic and placed in English prisons, where they remained for the next eight years. They were released when the war ended in 1763; of the original number, 866 were still alive.

With the fall of Louisbourg in 1758, Lawrence and his commanders moved to expel the entire Acadian population of the newly named Cape Breton and Prince Edward Islands, somewhere between three and four thousand people. (In that number was the Paul Doiron family, which now included ten children.) But Lawrence had nowhere to send them. The distribution of the Acadians from the outer islands to the Thirteen Colonies was no longer an option. The colonial governors were not pleased with having Nova Scotia's problems dropped on their doorsteps and had informed Lawrence that no more Acadians would be admitted into their domains. England's seaport jails, already filled to capacity with Acadians, were likewise not an option. Therefore, Lawrence ordered that the new exiles be transported directly to Europe and simply dumped at isolated, unguarded locations on the coast of France. Two of the British ships involved in this effort, the *Violet* and the *Duke William*, unseaworthy and badly overcrowded with 650 Acadians aboard, sank in the icy waters of the North Atlantic. There were 27 survivors. Of the approximately 3,000 remaining Acadians from Cape Breton and Prince Edward Islands herded aboard British transports destined for France, about 1,300 did not survive the transatlantic voyage; smallpox and dysentery were the official causes of those deaths. The survivors, including what was left of the Paul Doiron family, were put ashore near the French port of Cherbourg. Once the exiles were landed, the captain of the ship set sail without unloading the chests containing all their worldly possessions. Of the Doiron family, the father, the mother, and four children died in transit or shortly after arrival. Jean Baptiste, fourteen, was now the head of the family; little Hélenne was not among the survivors. Such was the fate of a once proud and independent people.

With the fall of Quebec in 1759, Governor Lawrence could move against the Acadians throughout the region with impunity, and he and his partners could begin to market the displaced people's coveted land. Lawrence and his backers lost no time promoting their new real estate development: by the end of 1763, roughly five thousand New Englanders had settled in Nova Scotia. They had pushed into vacated Acadian lands in the Minas Basin, Cobequid Bay, and Annapolis Royal areas, as well as the Isthmus of Chignecto. In all of England, only one voice was heard in protest, that of Edmund Burke: "We did, in my opinion, most inhumanely, and upon pretenses that, in the eye of an honest man, are not worth a farthing, root out this poor, innocent, deserving people, whom our utter inability to govern, or to reconcile, gave us no sort of right to extirpate."

From 1756, when all the proper declarations were signed, until 1763, when the Treaty of Paris ended hostilities, war raged around the globe. The Seven Years' War has been characterized as equaling the French Revolution in immensity and significance. It was a crushing defeat for the Bourbon dynasty and for their kingdoms, France and Spain. France was forced to cede to Great Britain all of Canada and all of Louisiana east of the Mississippi except the "Isle of Orleans," the little strip of land between the Mississippi River and Lake Ponchartrain on which Bienville had built New Orleans. France also ceded to England several of her rich sugar-producing islands in the Caribbean: Grenada, St. Vincent, Dominica, and Tobago. England agreed to return the conquered Cuba and the Philippines to Spain, but only in return for Florida. This was an important acquisition for Great Britain, for it would place the entire Atlantic coast of North America in her possession and remove an old adversary from her southern flank. And finally, by a secret treaty signed at Fontainebleau, Louis XV made France's exit from North America complete; he gave to his cousin, the king of

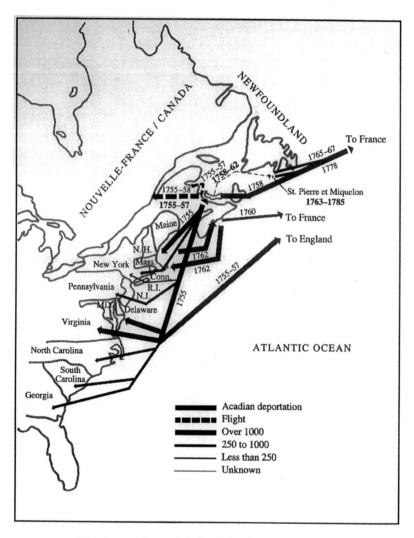

The deportation and flight of Acadians, 1755–1785

Courtesy Center for Canadian Studies, Mount Allison University, Sackville, N.B.

Spain, what was left of Louisiana—all the land west of the Mississippi River and the city of New Orleans—as compensation for the loss of Florida. *La Louisiane* became *la Luisiana*. New France was no more.

Another Acadian family central to this narrative was also on board the English ship whose passengers were so unceremoniously dumped on the French coast near Cherbourg. René Bernard and his wife, the former Marguerite Hébert, and their three daughters, Marie Madeleine, Anne Marie, and Marie Blanche, were natives of Beaubassin, Acadia, the part of the Chignecto Isthmus that remained under French control after 1713. With news of the fall of Fort Beausejour in June 1755, followed a few months later by word of the expulsions taking place in Nova Scotia, the Bernards escaped across Baie Verte to Ile St. Jean. That flight to safety won them three years of freedom. But in 1758, with the fall of Louisbourg, they were unable to escape Lawrence's net and were placed on the same overcrowded, smallpox-infested ship that carried the Doirons. If these two families had not been acquainted before, they certainly came to know one another as a result of their common destiny. Unlike the Doirons, the entire Bernard family survived the voyage. It is possible that René Bernard, who was about the same age as the late Paul Doiron, became a surrogate father to the orphaned Doiron children. In any event, both families made their way to the French seaport of Le Havre, where they lived for many years. Even though the Bernards had survived the difficult journey from North America, they found life in the waterfront slums of Le Havre hard, and every member of that family, save Marie Blanche, died in France in exile. What was left of these two families was united on January 7, 1766, when Blanche Bernard wed Jean Baptiste Doiron in the church of Notre Dame in Le Havre, France.

At the war's end in 1763, except for several hundred families who had managed to elude capture by hiding out in the upper reaches of the St. John and Miramichy River valleys or who had been given shelter by the Micmacs in the Nova Scotia interior and on the outer islands, the largest concentrations of Acadians could be found in three places: in North America, scattered among the thirteen English colonies and in a Halifax prison; in four British seaport detention centers, Bristol, Falmouth, Liverpool, and Southampton; and in several seaport cities on the English Channel and Atlantic coasts of France: Le Havre, Boulogne, St. Malo, and Rochefort. Canada, the desired destination of most of the Acadians who survived the *Grand Dérangement*, was no longer an alternative, because it now belonged to England.

The group that had been incarcerated at Halifax went on to play a special role in the Acadian diaspora. Led by Joseph and Alexandre Broussard, Simon Martin, and Jean and Michel Bourque, this group of Acadians had waged an effective guerilla campaign against the British from 1755 to 1759. But the fall of Quebec in 1759 caused them to recognize the hopelessness of their situation, and they surrendered and were imprisoned at Halifax for the duration of the war. Under the leadership of Joseph, *dit* Beausoleil, Broussard, some members of this Halifax group decided after the war to seek a new life in the Illinois country, the legendary El Dorado of Furs. They would pool their limited funds and charter a ship to the French West Indies, then on to Louisiana and up the Mississippi River to their ultimate destination. Broussard and 193 followers sailed from Halifax in November 1764 and arrived in New Orleans in February 1765. Louisiana was now a Spanish possession, but it would be another year before those authorities would arrive to take control. In the meantime, sympathetic and persuasive French officials were in charge of the colony's affairs. They offered to provide the exiles with foodstuffs, tools, muskets, building materials, and—most important—large land grants if the Acadians agreed to halt their journey and settle in Louisiana. Broussard and his followers decided to accept the offer.

This first group of Louisiana Acadians were given the opportunity to settle an area 150 miles west of New Orleans, on Bayou Teche, near the Attakapas outpost. On April 8, 1765, Beausoleil Broussard, commissioned captain in the militia and commandant of the Acadians, led his people to the "New Acadia." Soon after their arrival, on the site of a small chapel, they set about to build a church, which they named for the patron saint of France, St. Martin de Tours. The village that emerged came to be called St. Martinville. (Sadly, Broussard did not live to see his people multiply and prosper. He died on November 25, 1765.)

Through a communications network utilized by the exiles, other Acadians learned that many of their relatives and friends had become landowners in Louisiana, where people spoke French and practiced Catholicism. From New York to Charleston and most ports in between, Acadians sought passage to New Orleans. Many of these new arrivals acquired land grants along the banks of the Mississippi River north of New Orleans and in the Opelousas country. By 1770, when the first wave of Acadian immigration to Louisiana ended, about 1,500 exiles had resettled in the Spanish colony.

Those Acadians who came to Louisiana found the precious land they were seeking, although not without major adjustments and accommodations. Life in subtropical Louisiana was far different than in frigid Canada. Accordingly, the Acadians made numerous concessions to their new environment: wheat gave way to corn, moose to deer, codfish to catfish, lobster to crawfish, wool to cotton, beaver to muskrats, apples to figs, spruce to cypress, and sugar maple to sugarcane. But they were pioneers once again; they had each other; and, for the first time in their national history, they were governed by a friendly and supportive regime that needed them as much or more than the Acadians needed it.

Book III

THE RETURN

8

Scott Station, Louisiana: January 1897

In the late nineteenth century, the Acadians of south Louisiana still celebrated the Christmas season as their ancestors had done for centuries. Christmas Day was a religious holiday, a holy day of obligation on the calendar of the Roman Catholic Church. Everyone went to mass and no one was expected to work. It was a day for prayer, meditation, and thanksgiving; there were no feasts, no exchanges of presents, and no celebrating. But New Year's Day was quite different; it was a time to make merry. On New Year's Eve, every Acadian home with children or grandchildren could expect a visit from "Papa Noël," and the youngsters' anticipation and excitement were contagious. When they awoke on the first day of the new year, the empty stockings and baskets they had left around the fireplace the night before were filled with modest gifts from Papa Noël. Fresh fruit, a rarity at this time of the year, was always a favorite. If the family could afford it, a new pair of boots was left for a boy or a new bonnet for a girl, and maybe a shotgun for the young man of the house. Smaller children usually received homemade toys like carved farm animals, whistles, or toy locomotives.

If this was a typical New Year's Day, and there is no reason to believe it was not, Friday, January 1, 1897, was joyous on Boudreaux Plantation. Colonel A. D. Boudreaux, now in his seventy-eighth year and a widower for the past three, hosted his four sons and four daughters and their families for a day of feasting, dancing, drinking, and merriment. His daughters and daughters-in-law undoubtedly brought with them huge quantities of food, since the day's activities usually lasted past suppertime. Perhaps during the course of the day, when she had some time to herself, Philomène Boudreaux thought of her late brother Martin. And perhaps someone spoke of Ernest and Alexis Blanc. They had celebrated the last two New Year's Days with the Boudreaux family, but now they were presumably gone forever.

The first day of the new year had been mild, in the mid-sixties, but by nightfall it had begun to rain. The relative humidity recorded for Saturday, January 2, was 100 percent; it would be a windy, rainy day. A front was passing through, bringing winter weather behind it; by Monday, temperatures would drop into the mid-thirties.

At 11:16 P.M. Friday, the westbound Southern Pacific passenger train made its regularly scheduled stop at Scott Station. Two men got off the train. The station was deserted; if anyone witnessed their arrival, it was never reported. The two men watched the long liner pass in the night as it continued its westward trek. Then, probably with coat collars pulled up against the rain, shoulders hunched against the cold, and hands in their pockets, they began to walk along the railroad track toward the east, the direction from which they had come. The men passed Begnaud's General Store on their left. Perhaps they glanced at the building. After about a mile, they reached their destination. They climbed the steps of the big house at Boudreaux Plantation and knocked on the door. It was now just about midnight, and it probably took many knocks to awaken the old colonel. When he finally opened his front door, Ernest and Alexis Blanc were standing before him.

Colonel Boudreaux was very happy to see his two young friends. He found them unchanged, but travel-weary and wet and unkempt from walking in such foul weather. The three men talked into the early morning hours. The colonel was eager to hear of the Blancs' travels over the last nine months, and he almost certainly offered them leftovers from the New Year's Day feast. Given their condition, the brothers were probably ravenous. They spent the night in the big house and very likely slept most of the next day. Amid the nasty weather, and with many people nursing hangovers from the previous day's festivities, few were stirring about. Late in the afternoon, during a break in the weather, the two young Frenchmen decided to visit the nearby home of Olivier Boudreaux. Alexis was eager to see his old friend André.

Upon seeing the two men coming toward her home from a distance, Philomène Boudreaux was stunned and frightened. She was now certain that these two men were her brother's assassins, and she was alone in the house. Fearing for her own life, she quickly bolted the doors and pretended no one was at home. She did not respond to repeated knocks at the door. After a while, she heard the Blancs walking away. Only when Philomène thought it was safe did she peek through a window and see Ernest and Alexis headed in the direction of her father-in-law's house. Around dusk, when Olivier and the children returned home, Philomène related to her husband the incredible story: the Blanc brothers had returned and were apparently at Boudreaux Plantation. Together, Olivier and Philomène reached agreement on what must be done. They would not report their discovery to the sheriff, in whom they had lost confidence; instead, they would notify William Campbell immediately. Sundown comes early in January in Louisiana, and the rain was falling once again, but Olivier Boudreaux saddled up his horse and rode the four miles into Lafayette to the home of the attorney engaged by the Begnaud family.

From the information given him by Olivier, Campbell was reasonably sure no one but the Boudreaux family knew that the Blancs had returned to Scott Station. That knowledge, the terrible weather conditions, and the fact that it was already late on Saturday night gave him a little time to think and to plan. He sent Olivier home with instructions to say nothing to anyone. Campbell would notify the sheriff in the morning.

William Campbell was not a pious man, but he was deeply religious in the cerebral sense of the word. He regarded himself, and was regarded by others, as a student of the Bible. At one point he left the Catholic Church for a brief intellectual affair with Freemasonry. That experience sparked a lifetime avocation of comparing and contrasting the Catholic Bible—the Douay translation—and the Protestant King James Version. Given Campbell's legal training, it is not surprising that the Book of Daniel was one of his particular favorites, filled as it is with stories of Daniel applying his great wisdom to the solution of complex legal and moral dilemmas. In the Catholic Bible, Daniel 13:51 marks the beginning of the story of Susanna, a passage that does not appear in Protestant versions. Susanna, a beautiful young woman, was the married daughter of pious parents. Two men, judges and elders of the people, accused her of adultery, a crime punishable by death. They claimed to have witnessed her having sex with a young man, a stranger unknown to them, in a beautiful garden beneath the shade of a tree. In reality, both men had lusted after Susanna and both had been spurned. After they learned, by chance, of their mutual interest and rejection, the two plotted together to falsely accuse her. The virtuous Susanna maintained her innocence, but her case was hopeless in the face of such powerful witnesses. She was condemned to death. As she was being led to her execution, God heard her prayers and stirred the holy spirit in Daniel, who halted the proceedings. The prophet ordered everyone to return to court, then directed that Susanna's accusers be separated so he could question them individually. When pressed to explain the details of the assignation, the elders gave conflicting accounts, thus providing Daniel with irrefutable proof of their duplicity. Susanna was set free and her accusers were put to death in her place. William Campbell may have slept well that rainy Saturday night of January 2, 1897, or he may have lain awake thinking of the story of the virtuous Susanna. In any event, by the next morning, he had a plan.

Campbell's first obligation was to his clients, the Begnauds. Early Sunday morning, Simeon Begnaud was notified by messenger to meet his lawyer at Boudreaux Plantation. The message offered no explanation. Meanwhile, Campbell went to the home of Sheriff Isaac Broussard and outlined his plan for the arrest, incarceration, and interrogation of Ernest and Alexis Blanc. Although he would never have admitted it, Broussard probably knew that the two men currently being held for the murder of Martin Begnaud were innocent of that crime. Perhaps they were guilty of other crimes, but not that one. Frustrated by the lack of progress in the case and its negative impact on his reputation as a lawman, the sheriff leapt at this opportunity to redeem himself and agreed to follow Campbell's strategy. Campbell, Sheriff Broussard, and chief deputy Thomas Mouton, who boarded with the sheriff's family, arrived at Boudreaux Plantation about midmorning. Simeon Begnaud had already arrived and was waiting in the parlor with Olivier Boudreaux, the old colonel, and the Blanc brothers. The sheriff and his deputy went directly to the two young Frenchmen and arrested them for the murder of Martin Begnaud. Colonel Boudreaux was bewildered. The prisoners were handcuffed and escorted out of the house and into a prison wagon by the two lawmen and Campbell.

It seems safe to assume that before leaving, Campbell asked the witnesses to the arrest to keep the knowledge confidential, at least for a while. In Lafayette, Ernest Blanc was placed in the parish jail and Alexis in the corporate, or city, jail. Complete segregation was nearly impossible in these small jails, but Deputy Mouton was directed to keep the prisoners as isolated as possible. Campbell wanted the suspects to be alone with their thoughts, each wondering what the other might be saying to the authorities. The prisoners spent the rest of the day and night alone in their cells. Campbell knew that as soon as the general population learned of the arrest of the Blancs, citizens in the form of a lynch mob would demand justice, but he needed time to interrogate the brothers. The inclement weather and the fact that it was a Sunday and the end of the biggest holiday weekend of the year fit well with his plans. Most people remained indoors.

Early on Monday morning, January 4, the rain had stopped, the front had passed, and the temperature was a chilly thirty-eight degrees when Sheriff Broussard, Campbell, and Simeon Begnaud entered the jail cell of Alexis Blanc. At nineteen, Alexis was smaller than his older brother. He was soft-spoken and introverted, a follower, not a leader. Campbell thought he would be the easier to break. That supposition proved wrong. Under tough questioning, Alexis denied any role in the murder. As to his whereabouts the last nine months, he claimed that after New Orleans, he and his brother had journeyed to St. Louis, where they had worked in a hotel. Next they had visited Mexico and other places out west. From there, they had "tramped" back to New Orleans. When asked how much money had been in his possession when he left the parish nine months earlier, Alexis reported fifty dollars. "Lies," Campbell shot back. Then the lawyer set his trap. Quickly, Campbell told Alexis that he, the sheriff, and the Begnaud family knew what he and his brother had done. Campbell claimed that the authorities in Lafayette Parish had received regular weekly reports on the travels and the activities of the Blanc brothers, and that they had thus never really escaped but had been under constant surveillance. He said that the only remaining questions concerned the money: how much was stolen, how much was left, and where it was hidden? In exchange for the truth, Campbell offered Alexis and his brother protection: there would most certainly be a lynch mob, but there was still time for the sheriff to move the brothers to safety.

Campbell was bluffing about the surveillance, but the part about the lynch mob was no idle threat. Alexis remained quiet for a very long time, thinking; he appeared agitated, as if he was on the verge of speaking, perhaps confessing. Then he seemed to regain his composure and asked, "Have you seen my brother?" Surprised by the question, Campbell answered truthfully. They had not. The questioning continued, but Alexis would not utter another word. At 10:30 A.M. the interrogators left the jail cell.

Alexis's surprise question and Campbell's own equally surprising truthful answer apparently planted the kernel of an idea in the lawyer's mind. He would use a slightly different approach in the questioning of Ernest Blanc. After conferring briefly, the three men walked next door to the parish jail and, with the assistance of deputies, removed Ernest Blanc from his cell and marched him across the street to the courthouse and into the main courtroom. This was done for effect, to impress upon the prisoner the official nature of what was about to take place. Campbell spoke first: "We have just finished questioning your brother and he has confessed to everything." The only issue left unresolved, he stated, was how the money had been spent and how much was left. Ernest and Alexis had now been separated for twenty-four hours. Ernest knew that his little brother was weak, and he could only imagine what tortures Alexis had been put through. It was not difficult for him to believe Campbell's prevarication. "He promised me he never would," Ernest replied. He then broke down and confessed to the murder and gave a detailed account of the robbery and their travels over the last nine months. (They had actually journeyed to Paris before returning to the United States.)

When the interview with Ernest was finished, the sheriff began making the necessary arrangements with the Southern Pacific to transport his prisoners to safety. Campbell and Begnaud returned to the city jail and told Alexis what they had learned from his brother. As the Lafayette daily newspaper detailed in a 1955 feature, "When Alexis was told of his brother's confession, he also confessed, saying that he did not care to live longer, that trouble and sorrow had been his only portion since he had taken Begnaud's money." The younger Blanc confirmed that they had visited Paris after leaving Louisiana. Biblically inspired or not, William Campbell's plan had worked. The sheriff and deputy were on board the afternoon train for New Orleans with the two prisoners.

When Ike Broussard and Thomas Mouton returned to Lafayette the following day, the sheriff assigned the deputy responsibility for the excavations needed to find the murder weapon and a box belonging to Martin Begnaud that the brothers had used to carry the stolen money from the store. According to the Blancs, both items had been buried the night of the crime behind the little cabin on the plantation that had been their home for two years. As a courtesy and also to provide verification, Simeon Begnaud was invited to witness the dig. Valery Boudreaux, a son of the colonel who happened to be visiting his father that day, was also present.

The Blancs revealed that they had been very careful to replace the sod exactly as it had appeared before so that no one could tell the earth had been disturbed. The murder weapon, as described by Ernest, was a foot-long, three-sided pointed file, used to sharpen agricultural tools. Each angle of the file had been sharpened to almost razor quality, and the instrument of death had been fitted with a wooden handle. The file and the box were unearthed exactly where the Blancs said they would be found. Simeon identified the box as one that had belonged to his late brother. It was empty.

9

New Orleans: January 1897

Sheriff Ike Broussard placed few restrictions on visitors to the cell of Ernest and Alexis Blanc in Orleans Parish Prison, and the two young Frenchmen became the hottest topic of conversation on the streets of the Crescent City. Huge multicolumn and multiline articles appeared in all the city's newspapers, recounting the horrific nature of the murder, the exceptional character of Martin Begnaud, and the lives of the two brothers leading up to and following the crime. The Blancs gave countless interviews from their jail cell to aggressive reporters hungry for any information on the subject. Ernest did most of the talking and seemed to relish every opportunity to tell his story.

The Blanc brothers' lives as farmhands and sharecroppers on Boudreaux Plantation had been boring and financially unrewarding. All they had to look forward to was a life of hard work and marginal poverty. They thought they had found a way out when, sometime early in 1896, friend and neighbor Charles Breaux gave them a book on the life of the famous outlaw of the American West, Jesse James. James had been killed for reward money in 1882, but pulp novels about his exploits as a train and bank robber were popular through the end of the century. During times of severe economic depression in a rural America desperate for heroes, the James gang's exploits were more and more romanticized and exaggerated with each passing year. Jesse, his brother Frank, and the rest of the gang were fictionalized as modern-day Robin Hoods, leading adventurous lives and robbing rich, corrupt bankers and railroad magnates to give to the poor. The Blanc brothers had found their calling. They would emulate the lives of two other brothers, Jesse and Frank James.

Around the same time, Moss Brothers General Store in Lafayette advertised in the local papers the sale of Smith and Wesson revolvers—essential items for future outlaws. Exhausting their savings, Ernest and Alexis each purchased a pistol and bullets. With no money left to buy a suitable knife, they began to fashion a homemade version on the plantation whetstone from a large file that appeared to have been discarded by Colonel Boudreaux. By the end of March, all preparations had been completed, and they began to plan their first robbery. As they cast about for potential victims, Martin Begnaud was an obvious choice. They knew him well and knew his habits. He lived alone and kept large sums of money in his store. They selected the night of Monday, April 20, 1896, for the holdup. They would hide out in the ditch and high weeds between Begnaud's store and the railroad track and, at the appropriate time, make their move.

As outsiders unversed in Louisiana politics, the Blancs were probably unaware that Monday, April 20, was not a good choice. It was election eve, the day before one of the most hotly contested statewide elections of the century. There were too many people and too much activity in Scott Station for them to pull off their planned robbery without being detected. They returned the next night, April 21, but faced the same problem. It was election day; the polls had closed at Guidry's Dance Hall and everyone was clustering about, talking politics. But the night of April 22 was much more tranquil in the little village. From their hiding place in the tall weeds, the Blancs could see clearly inside Begnaud's Tavern next door. They could see men talking, drinking, and playing dominoes, and they could easily discern the big frame of Martin Begnaud in animated conversation. Around 11 P.M. the customers left and Martin spoke quietly with his brother, Simeon, on the front porch of the saloon. He then bid Simeon *bon soir,* returned to his store, and locked the door behind him. The Blancs had planned to accompany Begnaud into his store, but the merchant's long strides covered the short distance faster than they had anticipated. They quickly knocked. "Who's there?" asked Begnaud. The brothers identified themselves. The merchant replied through the door that it was late and that he was closed for the night. They were out of tobacco, Ernest said, and needed a smoke. Begnaud opened the door, smiled, invited them in, and went behind the counter to get the tobacco.

Each brother carried a loaded revolver in the waistband of his trousers, and Ernest was also armed with the file; their coats served to conceal the weapons. They had planned to pull out their revolvers as soon as Begnaud's back was turned, but they lost their nerve. The merchant handed them the tobacco and said he was tired and wanted to retire for the evening. Grasping for a reason not to be ushered out and remembering that he and his brother had skipped supper, Ernest blurted, "We are hungry, can you let us have a box of sardines?"

Begnaud replied that they could have all the sardines they wanted. As the merchant was wrapping the can, Alexis reached for a mousetrap and began talking to Begnaud about how it functioned. When he finished with the sardines, Begnaud walked over to Alexis, took the mousetrap from him, and began to demonstrate how it worked. While the shopkeeper was thus distracted, the brothers looked at each other, nodded, and drew their pistols. They demanded that Begnaud open the safe.

At first Begnaud thought they were joking, but they made it clear that they intended to take either his money or his life. He asked why they were doing this and said he would be happy to give them the money, but to no avail. Nervously, the merchant did as ordered. Once the safe was open, Alexis held the gun on Begnaud while Ernest tied his hands behind him with rope from the store's inventory. A red bandanna, also from the store, was tied around his mouth as a gag. "Then," the brothers were later quoted as saying, "we wrapped him up with calico just to make sure." They also blindfolded the shopkeeper with a strip torn from the bolt of calico. They made Martin lie down on his bed and tied his feet together with more rope. Ernest Blanc later observed that in that position, wrapped up as he was, Martin Begnaud "looked like a well-strung sausage." Then Ernest told the New Orleans reporters, "I own all; I tell you all. It was I who murdered the old man;

I who plunged the dagger again and again into his writhing form as he lay shuddering upon the bed, gasping and groaning and shrieking beneath the red handkerchief. Ah! how many times have I seen him since then! Oh God! at nights on lonely roads, in the sky, on fences, in bed, at all times."

When Ernest Blanc ended his murderous rapture fifty-two plunges later, he and Alexis emptied the contents of the safe into sacks and put the sacks in a box. Their night's work netted them $1,100 in gold coins, $1,300 in silver, and $700 in greenbacks, a total of $3,100. (They made $25 a month at Boudreaux Plantation.) The sacks were later fashioned into money belts that could be worn around the waist, enabling them to carry the very large and very heavy assortment of money on their bodies. They heard the hounds the afternoon of April 23, and as the baying grew louder and nearer, they were sure they had been caught. They could not believe their good fortune when the dogs turned away from the plantation. Their luck continued with the arrests of Benton and Balin. They knew then that it was safe to leave Scott Station.

"After having suffered for seven hours with these belts full of gold and silver, chewing at our bodies," the first thing Ernest and Alexis did when they arrived at New Orleans the night of April 30, 1896, was to "buy suitcases and take a hotel room to unload our burden." The next morning, fresh and rested, they took the train to Atlanta and from there to New York. They spent several days in New York, where they booked passage on a transatlantic steamer for Europe. After a six-day voyage, they arrived at Southampton, England, and the next day crossed the Channel to Le Havre, France. "We stayed a few days there, dressing ourselves in new clothes and tasting good wine and good French cuisine. It was thus, dressed like princes and with pockets full of gold, we made our triumphant entry into Paris, where we lived for a month and a half like millionaires, riding horseback, visiting all the theaters, and constantly tasting good wine and beautiful women. Soon weary of the life of debauchery, the love for travel once again got the best of us."

The brothers traveled across Belgium and England and then decided to return to the United States. They reached New York on July 12, and from there traveled cross-country by rail to San Francisco. The

Times-Democrat reported, "In the California metropolis they found their money was nearly exhausted, and they separated. Alexis, the younger, went to St. Louis, and Ernest, the elder, went to New York. But being separated they found was worse than being together, and they rejoined each other in St. Louis." They were now broke and essentially became tramps, riding the rails. From St. Louis, they rode the boxcars to El Paso, Texas, and spent some time in Mexico. Then they returned to Louisiana, to New Orleans. There, they said, they learned that Benton and Balin were still being held and awaiting trial, leading them to believe it was safe for them to return to Scott Station. In subsequent newspaper interviews, the brothers Blanc vociferously denied having their sights set on another victim, but this assertion was challenged by the *Times-Democrat,* which claimed that in a prison interview the Blancs identified their next target, another Scott Station merchant named Alcide Judice.

Aside from newspaper reporters, one of the first visitors to call on Ernest and Alexis in Orleans Parish Prison during that first week of January 1897 was J. A. Chargois, the attorney from Lafayette who had been retained to defend Hamp Benton. The two young Frenchmen freely admitted their guilt to Chargois, affirming that his client was being held for a crime that they had committed. Alexis was openly remorseful; Ernest was not. After his visit, Chargois held an impromptu news conference on the steps of the prison and declared that he had always known that his client was innocent. The entire case against Benton, he claimed, had been based on circumstantial evidence.

Two other men, not from the media and not even citizens of the United States, also made their way to Orleans Parish Prison that week. They, too, had a special interest in the case. The Blanc brothers must have been both surprised and honored by the jailhouse visit from two distinguished fellow countrymen: Georges Bosseront d'Anglade, the consul general of France in New Orleans, and his deputy, Henri Dessommes. They had come for two reasons. They were interested in the connection between these young men and Gustave Balin—the other Frenchman being held for the same crime—and, of course, they were interested in the general welfare of the two boys. The diplomats departed the prison with mixed feelings. They contacted their attorney with the news that Balin, a French army deserter, was innocent and must be released from prison. On the other hand, two French nationals, young, handsome, articulate, educated, and talented, must be punished.

On January 8, 1897, Sheriff Broussard boarded the westbound train to Lake Charles, picked up Gustave Balin, and returned with him that same day. Balin was placed in a cell in the Lafayette Parish prison. On January 9, Broussard boarded the eastbound train to New Orleans; he picked up Hamp Benton and returned with him the next day, placing him in the same jail as Balin. On January 12, Minos T. Gordy, the district attorney, dismissed all charges against Benton and Balin and set them free. Both men enjoyed a kind of celebrity status in the area. Balin became a designer and builder of Mardi Gras floats, but Benton was a broken man. In the words of his son, "he was never the same."

Later that same week, William Campbell, Simeon Begnaud, Sheriff Broussard, and Chief Deputy Mouton rode the train to New Orleans for the purpose of conducting follow-up interviews with the Blanc brothers. This was to be an official interrogation by the new special assistant district attorney, Campbell, assigned by his former classmate M. T. Gordy to be the lead prosecutor in the very high profile case. (Campbell was no longer acting as attorney for the Begnaud family.) The four men had all read with great fascination the voluminous accounts of the events of April 22, 1896, as described in the New Orleans papers. The newspaper confessions of Ernest and Alexis Blanc contained far more detailed information than the original admissions of guilt proffered by the brothers in Lafayette on the morning of January 4. In Orleans Parish Prison, the Blancs freely confessed again and reiterated to their Lafayette visitors all of the intimate details that they had previously divulged to the New Orleans reporters. Now, armed with a detailed, but unsigned, confession (by all indications, the Blancs were never asked to sign their statement), Campbell was eager to return home. The young attorney wanted to be with his wife, Ellen, pregnant and in the last days of her confinement. He returned to Lafayette in time to witness the birth of a son, Milton Campbell, born on January 17, 1897.

10

Lafayette, Louisiana: February 1897

The criminal term of the Seventeenth Judicial District Court of Louisiana, in and for the Parish of Lafayette, opened on Monday, February 8, 1897, the Honorable Conrad Debaillon presiding. Ed Voorhies, the veteran clerk of court for the parish, began his preparations well in advance of that scheduled date. He knew this term would be the most important of his career and perhaps the most historic in the legal annals of the parish. When Ernest and Alexis Blanc were brought before the bar of justice, all eyes in the state and many outside it would be focused on the town on Bayou Vermilion that served as the parish seat of government. Voorhies and the judge were undoubtedly determined that nothing go wrong. At 10 A.M., court was officially declared open and in session; Voorhies's handwritten record of the proceedings indicates that all four elected officers of the court were declared present: the judge, the clerk, District Attorney Gordy and Sheriff Broussard.

Exactly one month earlier, on January 8, 1897, Judge Debaillon had served Broussard with the *venire facias,* a judicial writ directed to the sheriff of a parish in which a case is to be tried commanding him that he "cause to come" before the court, on a certain day, a certain number of good, lawful, and qualified men of the parish for the purpose of impaneling a jury. In every Louisiana parish, a jury commission composed of four leading citizens appointed by the court and chaired by the clerk of court was responsible for gathering together the names of individuals for the purpose of forming jury pools for both the grand jury and the petit, i.e., trial, jury. For the grand jury pool, the jury commission was required to select the names of fifty "discreet" citizens. The four members of the Lafayette Parish Jury Commission for 1897 were Gustave Lacoste, Joachim Revillon, Albert Craig, and Alcide Judice. Once the sheriff received from them the names of the grand jury pool, his office notified each person on the list of the date and time he was to report in order to perform his civic duty. Every member chosen for the grand jury pool, except one man who no longer lived in the parish, was present in Seventeenth Judicial District Court on that cold morning of February 8.

The first order of substantive business was the presentation to the court of the list of possible jurors chosen. After reviewing the names and hearing from the sheriff and the clerk, Judge Debaillon excused four individuals from service, one for illness, two—a postmaster and a teacher—for special circumstances, and one because he was too old (over sixty). In open court, the judge selected J. Edmond Mouton to serve as foreman and then directed Broussard to draw fifteen names from a box to determine the remainder of the grand jury for the winter term. Judge Debaillon then administered the following oath:

> I [name] do solemnly swear that I will faithfully and diligently inquire and true presentment make of all such matters and things as may be given me in charge; the Counsel of the State, of my fellows and my own, I will keep secret; I will present no one from envy, hatred or malice, nor leave anyone unpresented for fear, favor, affection, reward or the hope thereof; but that I will present all things truly as they come to my knowledge, according to the best of my understanding, so help me God.

"The Judge then delivered his charge and instructions to the Grand Jury," an eyewitness to the proceedings reported, "and they then retired to their room of deliberations in charge of the Sheriff." Under normal conditions, the charge and instructions of the judge to the grand jury would have been perfunctory, but the publicity and interest in this session of his court, and the fact that his courtroom was full of reporters, gave Debaillon a rare public forum. While the judge may have been speaking to the members of the newly impaneled jury, his unusually candid remarks were really directed to the general public, to his fellow citizens. He was keenly aware that what all the newspapers were reporting was true: "lynch fever" had reached epidemic levels in the parish. "In strong and clear language," the judge lectured his courtroom on "the evil effects of lynch law and its dangerous influence on society."

Thirteen cases were on the docket for consideration by the grand jury, but case number 1421, *State of Louisiana* v. *Ernest Blanc and Alexis Blanc*, was paramount. All grand jury proceedings are held in secret, but the names of witnesses called by the state are a matter of public record. That afternoon, the district attorney brought four witnesses in the matter of case 1421: Dr. A. R. Trahan, William Campbell, Isaac Broussard, and Simeon Begnaud. After hearing testimony from these four witnesses and after due deliberations, the grand jury issued a "true bill" signed by foreman Mouton. It was an indictment for murder: "That one Ernest Blanc and one Alexis Blanc at the parish aforesaid, on the 22nd day of April, A.D. 1896, wilfully, feloniously and of their malice aforethought did kill and murder one Martin Begnaud contrary to the form of the Statute in such case, made and provided and against the peace and dignity of the State of Louisiana." Three members of the jury that produced the indictment deserve mention. Desire Doucet, who had recently married Louise Cayret, was a resident of Scott Station and a close friend of Martin Begnaud. Simeon Begnaud did double duty, serving as a witness and as a member of the grand jury. Technically, Simeon was eligible to serve. He met all the legal requirements of law for membership, and there is no prohibition in the law against the relative of a victim in a grand jury proceeding serving on that same grand jury. Later, when asked by the press about his membership on the grand jury and his role vis-à-vis case 1421, Simeon Begnaud said that he had recused himself from all deliberations and discussions in that particular case. A third member of the grand jury with ties to Martin Begnaud was the victim's nephew Israel Prejean. No one seemed to notice the connection.

The grand jury did not complete its deliberations in the case until very late on Monday, and the indictment would not be officially filed until the next morning, Tuesday, February 9. But as soon as the panel adjourned on Monday night, Judge Debaillon was informed of the finding of a true bill. Wasting no time, the judge sent for the sheriff and directed him to have the Blanc brothers in his court for their arraignment at 10 A.M. Wednesday. The next few weeks would be the most important in the long law-enforcement career of Ike Broussard. Lafayette Parish was a powder keg, and the slightest spark could set off mob rule. During this tense period, Sheriff Broussard—under the critical glare of the press and public opinion—rose to the challenge, making several strategic decisions that enabled law and order to prevail and, at the same time, salvaged what was left of his reputation as a lawman. The first of these pivotal decisions was to bring the Blanc brothers back from New Orleans in daylight. Broussard knew that a lynch mob would never act in daylight, so those hours would give him time to secure the accused in the Lafayette Parish prison. That Monday night, on receiving instructions from Judge Debaillon, Broussard telegraphed William Uniacke, sheriff of Orleans Parish and master of Orleans Parish Prison, requesting that the Blanc brothers be made ready for travel early the next morning. Apprising no one in Lafayette of his plans and armed with a Winchester rifle, Broussard boarded the 2 A.M. train for New Orleans. He arrived in the Crescent City at 8:20 on the morning of February 9 and went immediately to the prison, where he found that Sheriff Uniacke had honored his request; the Blanc brothers were dressed and ready. They had been awakened by their guards at six, fed a hearty breakfast, and ordered to prepare themselves for travel.

The arrest and incarceration in New Orleans of the two young Frenchmen and the strained situation in the country parish where the crime had taken place were common knowledge in the city, for scarcely a day went by without a banner headline story in the local papers concerning this cause célèbre. And while no one back home in Lafayette Parish knew of Sheriff Broussard's plans for the return of his prisoners, everyone in New Orleans—at least at the prison and in the media—knew he was on his way. It was probably this knowledge that prompted Father Peter O'Neill, the prison chaplain, to drop by the brothers' cell on Monday night and offer to hear their confessions and administer Holy Communion. According to the *Daily Picayune*, the prisoners eagerly accepted the priest's offer and "prayed devotedly for the salvation of their souls and for forgiveness for their one and awful sin."

Broussard was in Orleans Parish Prison at the corner of Tulane and

Basin Streets only about five minutes, just long enough to handcuff his prisoners and escort them out of the building. Broussard was moving fast. He did not want to miss the morning westbound train; if he did, it would mean arriving in Lafayette after dark. Several guards, a group of reporters and a few curiosity seekers were waiting at the prison's Gravier Street entrance for Broussard and the Blancs. When they appeared, the guards said good-bye to the brothers and wished them luck; the two prisoners, in return, thanked the guards for their many courtesies. It was obvious that no one in the farewell party expected to see the two young men again. The entourage that hustled the half block to Baronne Street and boarded the Jackson Avenue streetcar totaled six: the sheriff, the prisoners, and three newspaper reporters. The brothers were in old-fashioned fetters, not only cuffed but also chained to each other at the wrists.

Individual bylines for newspaper reporters were not yet in vogue in American journalism, so the identities of Sheriff Broussard's traveling companions are unknown, but they remained inseparable from the lawman and his prisoners. It made for an unusual parade, even for New Orleans. All along the route people gathered in small groups to gawk at the famous captives. On the streetcar, several young ladies were seen casting furtive glances at the handsome duo. Some of them blushed and giggled when their looks were returned by Ernest Blanc, whose "long dark eyelashes" were especially attractive.

The six men nearly missed the ferry at the Tchoupitoulas Street terminal and had to run to catch it; after crossing the river to Gretna, they walked quickly the short distance to the Southern Pacific train station where they planned to board the San Antonio Express scheduled to depart at 9:45. Even though they had only about ten minutes to spare, word had spread that the celebrated "boy murderers" were at the Gretna station, and a large crowd of onlookers had assembled.

On board, the train's passengers were buzzing with excitement and could talk of little else but their chained fellow travelers. Sheriff Broussard and his charges occupied a first-class coach, and the lawman sealed off a section large enough to permit access for the three reporters, who carried on a constant conversation with Ernest Blanc. Alexis had little to say. Broussard's motives may have been self-serving here, for one of the scribes had shown the foresight to bring along a picnic basket. The sheriff had missed breakfast, and with no prospect for lunch he accepted the invitation of the reporter to help himself, promptly finishing off the contents of the basket. With some measure of regret, the owner of the basket wrote that "the person who exercised so much care in preparing the food found himself without anything to eat."

Despite their intense curiosity, none of the passengers on the crowded train tried to interfere or approach the prisoners, with one exception. Well into the journey, a woman entered the car and asked Sheriff Broussard for permission to speak with his prisoners. She would be getting off the train at the next stop and claimed she only wanted a moment with the boys. She was a mature woman, "matronly-looking" and well spoken. The sheriff voiced no objection and escorted the woman to the brothers. In the words of the *Daily Picayune*, "With an expression of well-meant sympathy, she asked the boys if they had a mother or father alive." Both replied negatively. She then asked if they had killed their victim on purpose. "Without thinking, Ernest answered that they had. Then, after a moment's reflection, he said that they had not." The woman observed how handsome they were, affectionately touched their shoulders, and returned to her seat, but not before telling them to be "good boys" when all this was over. Ernest replied, "We'll never get out of this scrape."

As the train approached Lafayette, one of the reporters asked if the brothers feared "any hostile demonstrations." They were indifferent. Surprisingly, Alexis spoke up and replied that they had accepted and were resigned to their fate. The train was scheduled to arrive at the Lafayette station at 3:15. Leaving the reporters in the first-class car, the sheriff moved the prisoners to the caboose. As soon as the train came to a halt, the three men disembarked and walked rapidly to the parish jail. The accused were secured in their cell and the sheriff called in all three of his deputies and established a round-the-clock guard. But word that the Blanc brothers were back in town spread rapidly—no doubt circulated by the reporters from New Orleans—and a small crowd began to gather near the courthouse. At dusk, it began to disperse, and by nightfall all seemed quiet. Sheriff Broussard, exhausted from forty-eight hours without sleep, left his infamous charges in the hands of the able chief deputy and went home for some much-needed rest. He got only about two hours' sleep. Around 11 P.M., he was awakened by one of his deputies, probably Gilbert Bienvenue, with news that a railroad man had brought reliable information that 150 armed men had left Scott Station headed for the Alexandria Road and that another 400 armed men from Carencro were marching south on that same road. (Running north and south about two miles west of Lafayette, the Alexandria Road was the main route connecting Lafayette and Carencro.) Martin Begnaud had many family members and friends in the Carencro area, so it was a scenario Sheriff Broussard could grasp readily.

Broussard dressed immediately, returned to the jail, chained his prisoners, and with Mouton and Bienvenue as armed escorts, headed east—in the opposite direction from the mob—in a hired, mule-drawn wagon driven by a black teamster. Aside from his rifle, the only thing the sheriff had time to throw in the wagon was a long coil of telegraph wire. The destination he had in mind was a swamp about five miles from Lafayette in the direction of New Iberia. When the group reached the swamp, the sheriff got off with the prisoners and ordered the driver to continue along the road to a safe distance and conceal the wagon from view. He posted his two deputies at key approaches to the swamp and then walked the Blancs deep into its murky interior. It was a very cloudy night with no moon, so dark that Broussard could barely make out the figures of the brothers. To guard against their escape, he tied one end of the telegraph wire securely around the captives' ankles and the other end around his own wrist. The weather was messy, with a steady drizzle, a low of forty-six degrees, and wind from the north at thirteen miles per hour. In the mud and amid the noises of hundreds of different swamp creatures, the three spent an altogether cold and miserable night. At daylight, they emerged from the swamp and the sheriff dispatched one of his deputies back to Lafayette to assess the situation. When the man returned with news that there was no sign of a mob and that all appeared calm, the lawmen and the outlaws headed back to Lafayette and got cleaned up. At 10 A.M., Sheriff Broussard, flanked by two armed deputies, presented his prisoners for their arraignment in Judge Conrad Debaillon's courtroom.

Book IV

THE FAMILY

11

New Orleans: August 1785

The treatment accorded the Acadian exiles in France was very different from the reception they received in Louisiana. With the end of the Seven Years' War, France moved quickly to repatriate those Acadians still alive in English prisons. The Treaty of Paris was signed in February 1763, and by May, thanks to the efforts of the French ambassador to the Court of St. James, the duke of Nivernois, 753 Acadians were transported in French ships to the Channel ports of Morlaix and St. Malo. On the one hand, the new arrivals were thrilled to learn that about two thousand fellow Acadians were living in French coastal cities; on the other hand, they had nothing they could call their own. The Acadians, independent, landowning frontiersmen, soon learned that a return to their yeoman way of life was impossible in the feudal economy of Europe, where virtually all land belonged to the crown, the nobility, or the church. Liberty, equality, and fraternity had not yet landed on French shores. Some learned trades as carpenters or cobblers, and a number turned to the sea and worked as fishermen or mariners, but for most Acadians in France, to work their own land remained their most cherished ambition.

Although the motives of the duke of Nivernois, the guiding hand behind the repatriation project, were not altogether altruistic, he genuinely sympathized with the plight of the Acadians. When news of his kindness to their countrymen imprisoned in England and his promise of resettlement in France reached America, many Acadians in the Thirteen Colonies, in the words of historian Oscar W. Winzerling, "escaped by devious ways to France." Ultimately, somewhere between 3,000 and 4,000 Acadians ended up in France, where their reputation as hard workers and good farmers had preceded them. Nivernois himself owned an entire island located off the central part of France's Atlantic coast, and he thought the Acadians uniquely qualified to develop its full potential. Plans were proceeding in that direction when the government made the duke a better offer: the crown would purchase the island for a small fortune and turn it into a fortress. Nivernois thus passed from the Acadian scene. The Acadians in France "reluctantly accepted the government's subsistence allowance of six *sous* per person until the anticipated day of restitution, but it soon became abundantly clear that the crown had neither the means nor the intention of compensating them." A once proud people was now living on the dole.

Life was hard for the Acadians in the French seaports. Most lived in poverty, with smallpox a frequent visitor. They were desperate to escape the seaport slums and grasped at every opportunity that even hinted at reunification or resettlement, no matter how ill conceived—and between wealthy landlords eager to lure the exiles to their own estates and a government eager to get them off public assistance, there were several such schemes. The next high-ranking Frenchman with plans for these industrious, agriculture-oriented people was the duke of Choiseul, France's foreign minister. He dreamed of a new French empire in the tropics of northern South America in Guiana, with its capital at Cayenne. It was a dream that turned into what Winzerling terms a "colossal failure." Fortunately, only a few Acadians agreed to take part; most who did so perished. The survivors were repatriated to France. (Eventually, France would come to realize that the only productive role for Guiana was that of a penal colony.)

As the years passed, other abortive attempts were made to settle the Acadians in Lorraine, in the Loire Valley, on Belle-Ile-en-Mer (a windswept island off the coast of Brittany), on the Falkland Islands in the south Atlantic, in Andalusia in Spain, in Flanders, in Limousin, on the island of Corsica in the Mediterranean, and on the islands of St.

Pierre and Miquelon, two "God-forsaken sand bars" off the coast of Newfoundland. For various reasons, the most common being barren soil, high taxes, harsh climate, and scarcity of fresh water, all of these schemes failed despite good-faith efforts on the part of the Acadians.

Increasingly desperate and with no one else to turn to, the refugees petitioned Louis XV for an audience. To what was probably their great surprise and delight, it was granted, and a delegation met with the penultimate Bourbon at Compiègne in July 1772. As one historian describes the meeting, "They humbly laid before him the circumstances of their wretched condition in France." The king was deeply touched, and he directed his ministers to integrate the Acadians into the agricultural life of France.

Louis XV's order resulted in the most serious attempt to resettle the Acadians permanently in France, a plan for transplanting them to the province of Poitou. (Ironically, this province had been the birthplace of many of the first settlers of Acadia more than a century and a half earlier.) Sponsored and financed by the crown, the plan called for the settlement of 626 Acadian families, 2,370 people, on the great Poitou estate of the marquis de Pérusse des Cars. Each Acadian head of household would be given ownership of two acres of land, and the government would build homes grouped together in a series of villages. French officials in charge of the project called it "La Colonie Acadienne du Poitou," but the Acadians called it "la Grande Ligne"—literally "the Great Road" but figuratively "the King's Highway"—in honor of their new patron, who built an access highway into the area to be developed. About 1,500 Acadians accepted the challenge, and they began to arrive in the fall of 1773. Among the first to reach la Grande Ligne, in October 1773, was the Jean Baptiste Doiron family of Le Havre. Jean Baptiste had been six years old in 1750, when his parents decided to leave Nova Scotia for Prince Edward Island, and fourteen in 1758, when his entire family was expelled from Canada. After his 1766 marriage to Blanche Bernard, he had found work as a seaman out of Le Havre. His young bride, nineteen at the time of the wedding, had tried to make a few extra pennies by spinning and knitting. At the time of their departure for the Poitou colony, they were the parents of two daughters: Marie Honorine, born in 1768, and Rose Lucile, born in 1772; two other daughters had died in infancy. During the family's residence in Poitou, which lasted almost three years, they attended mass regularly at St. John the Evangelist church in Chatellerault and were active in church affairs. Undoubtedly, one of their fondest memories of this period was the birth of a son, Jean Baptiste César Doiron, in 1775.

La Grande Ligne presented the young Acadian with an opportunity to become a landowner, like his father and his father's father before him, but problems surfaced immediately. Only a few cabins had been built on the site, and most families had to seek housing in the nearby towns of Poitiers and Chatellerault, paying rent with what little money they had. A more serious problem was the inadequacy of the soil. It was hopelessly unproductive: "crops germinated but, upon breaking the soil, yellowed and died." Much to the surprise of this people with farming in their blood, there were no harvests in 1774 or 1775. The marquis dealt the project its final blow by demanding the payment of rent in lieu of his share of the anticipated crops. Although the bureaucrats in charge of the administration of the colony objected, the nobleman still owned the land. Obviously, the Acadians had no money to pay rent. Near the end of 1775, by popular referendum, they voted to abandon the colony; by the middle of the next year, only 160 remained.

The once-again-displaced Acadians requested and received permission from the government to resettle in the larger port cities of western France: Rouen, Caen, La Rochelle, Bordeaux, and Nantes. After the great disappointment of la Grande Ligne, the Doiron family chose Nantes.

The collapse of the Poitou experiment did not cause the French government to give up on the Acadians; the king had spoken and his ministers would try again to integrate the exiles into the agricultural life of the nation. A previously scuttled plan to place the Acadians in Corsica was reactivated in 1777. Unlike the earlier Corsican proposal, this one was not meant to exploit the Acadians, but instead was a serious effort to place them on good land, with the government providing transportation and start-up assistance. The elders of the Acadian Nation, as the French officials referred to the exiles, warmed to this new project. But a rare dissension developed in the ranks, owing to the disillusionment and mistrust that now quite understandably joined despair and hopelessness in the emotional range of these unfortunate people. A minority of younger Acadians began talking about joining their friends and relatives in Louisiana, where from all accounts they were doing well. These young exiles enthusiastically followed news of the American Revolution. Their interest increased dramatically in 1778 when France signed a treaty of alliance with the United States and entered the war against England, and even more in 1779 when Spain also entered the war on the side of France. This meant the Louisiana Acadians were at war. Volunteering in large numbers to fight under the command of Spanish territorial governor Bernardo de Gálvez, they helped defeat the British at Baton Rouge in 1779, at Mobile in 1780, and at Pensacola in 1781. As Gálvez's biographer recounted these events, "The militia, particularly the Acadians, who had not forgotten the persecutions they had suffered at the hands of the English, behaved splendidly."

News of these triumphs against their old adversaries strengthened the cause of the young dissidents who wanted to go to Louisiana, resulting in a schism within the Acadian Nation in France. Unable to get a clear signal from the Acadian leaders, the French government dropped the Corsican project. And the possibility of France's paying to send the Acadians to Louisiana—and thereby enrich Spain—was not even worthy of consideration. Some Acadians who actually made such a proposal were dismissed as ungrateful. By 1783, when the Treaty of Paris ended the War of the American Revolution, the Acadian house was divided against itself and living conditions and morale were at their lowest point.

Just when the dream of reunification and a return to their traditional way of life seemed lost, Providence intervened on the side of the exiles. Henri Peyroux de la Coudrenière was a native of Nantes who had immigrated to America some years earlier. A pharmacist in France, he had forsaken his profession along with the land of his birth for the world of business in the Spanish colony of Louisiana. His success in the latter is unclear. One thing is certain: while in Louisiana, Peyroux befriended several Acadians and learned the details of their diaspora and their desire for reunification. Combining this knowledge with his own ambitions, Peyroux saw an opportunity and determined a course of action. He decided his ticket to prosperity in Louisiana was to obtain both an officer's commission in the Spanish army and a lucrative government post in New Orleans, appointments he would earn by presenting a blueprint for bringing to Louisiana—a colony desperately in need of settlers—hundreds of hardworking farmers, fishermen, and husbandmen with the potential for being good soldiers and loyal subjects. The best part of his plan was that they were all Catholic.

Peyroux returned to France and presented his idea to the Spanish ambassador in Paris, the count de Aranda, who endorsed it. The essence of the proposal was for Spain to underwrite and finance the transfer of approximately two thousand Acadians from France to Louisiana and, upon their arrival, provide them with land and the necessary items for their initial sustenance and subsequent agricultural production. Peyroux would coordinate the entire effort and be commissioned captain and commandant in the Spanish army in Louisiana when the project was completed. The ambassador urged Peyroux to begin recruiting interested Acadians residing in the western seaport cities of France. The count forwarded the Peyroux proposal to Madrid with a favorable recommendation, and on October 22, 1783, Charles III issued a royal order approving the plan of removing the Acadians in France to Louisiana.

Spain's favorable and generous response to Peyroux's idea owed much to the influence of Louisiana territorial governor Gálvez and of his uncle José de Gálvez, who held the post of minister of the Indies and was probably the most powerful man in Spain after the king. Providentially, Governor Gálvez and his wife, the young, beautiful, rich, and widowed New Orleanian Félicité de St. Maxent d'Estréhan, visited Madrid in 1783 for him to receive his commission as the new captain general of Havana, which post he would for the time being occupy simultaneously with the governorship. Gálvez knew from personal experience the value of the Acadians as farmers and militiamen. Moreover, his policy had taken on a new dimension with the Treaty of Paris, which mandated that England return all of Florida, both East and West, to Spain. Both banks of the Mississippi from Natchez to the mouth now belonged to Spain, and Gálvez wanted to move expeditiously with the settlement of loyal, Catholic subjects to counter the

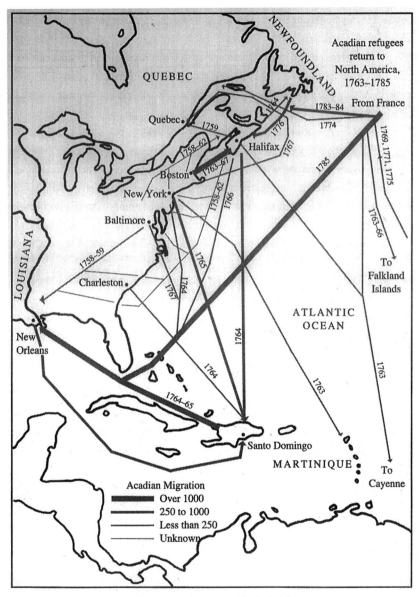

Acadian refugees
return to
North America,
1763–1785

From France

QUEBEC

NEWFOUNDLAND

Quebec

Halifax

Boston

New York

Baltimore

Charleston

LOUISIANA

New
Orleans

ATLANTIC
OCEAN

To
Falkland
Islands

Santo Domingo

MARTINIQUE

To
Cayenne

1759
1758–62
1763–67
1758–62
1766
1758–59
1765
1767
1761
1764
1764
1764
1764–65
1763
1763
1763–66
1769, 1771, 1775
1785
1767
1776
1784
1774
1783–84

Acadian Migration
▬▬▬ Over 1000
▬▬ 250 to 1000
—— Less than 250
—— Unknown

Acadian migration, 1755–1785

Courtesy Center for Canadian Studies, Mount Allison University, Sackville, N.B.

many Protestants who had moved into the area during the past twenty years of British rule. Louisiana was Spain's first line of defense in North America against an increasingly aggressive United States and its land-hungry citizens. If Louisiana were lost, Texas, California, and even Mexico could be threatened. Peyroux's plan thus coincided with Spain's strategic interest.

Several times during the delicate, complex negotiations that took place before the first Acadian boarded the first transport ship, José de Gálvez intervened to smooth the way. While Spain and its great minister were enthusiastic, however, problems with the Acadians and France remained. Many Acadians were skeptical, having been victimized by so many grandiose but vacuous schemes. Fortunately, though, Peyroux had enlisted a shoemaker from Nantes, an Acadian named Olivier Theriot, as his chief recruiter and propagandist. Persuasive and tenacious, Theriot traveled the western French seaports and managed to persuade a large percentage of the Acadians living there to take the Spanish proposal seriously. The question remained whether France would permit the Acadians to leave, and if so, how their many personal debts would be paid before they departed. Louis XVI, the new king, settled both issues by proclaiming that any Acadians who wished to leave his kingdom were free to do so, and he would pay all of their legitimate debts. While this was certainly a generous offer, it was also a financially sound one: a one-time payment in exchange for ridding France of a group of foreigners, many of whom had been supported by the government for years.

One further uncertainty remained: the fate of non-Acadian spouses of Acadians. There were not many of these, but a few Acadians had married outside the group, mostly to French nationals. Would Spain pay for their transportation to and support in Louisiana? Charles III, generally considered to be the most enlightened and progressive of the Spanish Bourbons, replied affirmatively. But what of non-Acadians merely betrothed to Acadians? Alas, that reply was negative.

One of the first families recruited by Olivier Theriot in Nantes to sign up for passage to Louisiana was the family of Jean Baptiste Doiron, now numbering five children. Joining Honorine (age seventeen) and Rose Lucile (thirteen), born at Le Havre, were Amable Ursule (six), Louis Toussaint (four), and Jean Charles (one), all born in Nantes. César, the young son born at Chatellerault, had died in infancy, as had Jean Louis, the first child born in Nantes. Jean Baptiste was now working as a carpenter, but it is safe to assume that Blanche was engaged in much less spinning and weaving, owing to the demands of raising the children.

The Doirons seem to have been a typically close-knit Acadian family—meaning that the entire family would leave for Louisiana together, or it would not leave at all. The Spanish position regarding Acadians engaged to non-Acadians likely caused much consternation for the family, particularly for Honorine, who—it appears—had fallen in love with and was betrothed to a Frenchman, a Breton seaman named François Begnaud. He was from St. Etienne de Montluc, a small town about ten miles northwest of Nantes.

The Doiron family did depart for America intact, sailing from Nantes aboard the *Beaumont* on June 11, 1785, after a two-week weather delay. The ship arrived at New Orleans on August 19. Its manifest had no listing for a François Begnaud, but the vessel carried two stowaways, unlisted and unnamed.

In all, seven ships sailed from Nantes and St. Malo to New Orleans. Their cargo consisted of about one-half of the Acadians living in France. Many more wanted to make the historic journey, but space was limited. Those who remained were, like their kinsmen stranded on the eastern seaboard of North America, eventually absorbed and assimilated into the national life of the host country. Nearly sixteen hundred Acadians arrived in Louisiana between July and December 1785 on the following ships (in the order of their arrival): *Le Bon Papa, La Bergère, Le Beaumont, St. Rémy, L'Amitié, La Villa de Arcangel,* and *La Carolina.* The surnames that appear with greatest frequency on the passenger lists are Dugas, LeBlanc, Doiron, Hébert, Trahan, Theriot, Richard, Granger, Guidry, Bourque, Boudreaux, Benoit, Landry, Doucet, and Gaudet.

In the absence of the governor, intendant Martín Navarro was in charge of the Louisiana colony. Navarro demonstrated much wisdom in his selection of an established, successful Acadian, Anselme Blanchard, to serve as the government's official liaison with the new arrivals. It meant a great deal to these wanderers to have one of their own officially welcome them to their new home in their native language. Navarro treated the colony's newest citizens with respect and dignity. He had two hospitals erected, one for men and one for women, where the ill and infirm could recuperate from the difficult transatlantic voyage. He had dormitories constructed where the newcomers could live for a month or so while their elected delegates surveyed available land for possible settlement. Each family received a small monetary grant to help them get started, along with supplies to meet their immediate needs. Most important, Navarro issued orders "to assist them in the choice of suitable lands, to guide them in the building of their new homes, and in every way to show the Acadians that it was the wish of the Spanish government that they should have full liberty in the selection of their future abodes."

If any of the new citizens had relatives or friends in already-established communities, such as in the Opelousas country or at the Attakapas Post, they were allowed to join them, and some did. Several hundred accepted the invitation of the colonial authorities for them to settle in the Baton Rouge and Manchac areas on the east and west banks of the Mississippi. But the largest number of the arrivals of 1785 settled in the LaFourche country, along Bayous LaFourche and Terrebonne about forty miles west of New Orleans.

Apparently through an intricate communications web that the Acadians maintained, the Doiron family knew of relatives living in the Attakapas country, and set out to join them in St. Martinville. Michel Bernard, Blanche Bernard Doiron's first cousin once removed, was one of the original pioneer Acadians who had settled the area in 1765. In 1771, the Spanish colonial government had awarded him a very large land grant on the west bank of Bayou Teche. By the time his relatives arrived from Europe, Michel Bernard and his son, François, had become well-established landowners and ranchers. Based on land records, it appears that the Bernards welcomed their long-lost relatives and provided them with land contiguous to their own. This was one of many family reunions that took place in Louisiana in 1785. But there may have been one participant in the Doiron-Bernard reunion who was not a family member, at least not yet.

On February 13, 1786, less than six months after her arrival at New Orleans, Honorine Doiron and François Begnaud were married in the church of St. Martin de Tours at St. Martinville. There is no record of the groom's journey to Louisiana or the date of his arrival. In a final report to Charles III on the Louisiana project, the count de Aranda stated that a total of twenty-eight stowaways had been discovered on board the ships that had landed in New Orleans. According to Winzerling, some of these were Frenchmen whom Navarro admitted as Acadians when they married their Acadian fiancées. Perhaps François Begnaud was one of them. One month after his marriage, Begnaud was permitted to purchase a parcel of land ten arpents in width that fronted on the west bank of Bayou Teche and extended westward to Bayou Vermilion, a distance of several miles. While this raw land was relatively cheap, it is quite possible that Begnaud borrowed the money to pay for it from his recent cousins by marriage, the Bernards. But it is also possible that the new husband had brought his life savings with him from France; eighteen years his wife's senior, he had worked for many years as a seaman out of Nantes.

Begnaud's purchase was part of an original grant from the French regime, the Ledée grant, of approximately twenty thousand arpents on both sides of Bayou Teche, centered on the site of present-day Breaux Bridge. The grant extended westward to Bayou Vermilion, a distance of about four to five miles depending on the location. Spanish officials encouraged the subdividing of this huge grant for the benefit of the Acadians. François Begnaud, now regarded as an Acadian as a result of his marriage, was one of those beneficiaries. Later he would sell to his father-in-law, Jean Baptiste Doiron, a three-arpent strip stretching from the Teche to the Vermilion for the princely sum of ninety-seven dollars. Clearly, these were family arrangements. The Doiron family, like many of their countrymen who arrived at New Orleans in 1785, had been in exile for nearly thirty years. They finally had come home to their New Acadia.

St. Martinville, Louisiana: April 1812

The removal of about one-half of the Acadian exiles living in France to Louisiana in 1785 ended the Acadian diaspora. In the Spanish colony they found a permanent place to settle that would allow them to live life as they chose to live it. The Acadians wanted to live together as a people, practice their Catholic faith unmolested, retain their French language and customs, and work their own land. In hindsight, especially considering what we know of life in the eighteenth century, the very idea of a group of semiliterate farmers, trappers, lumberjacks, and fishermen clinging to such a dream for so long and against such odds is remarkable. The fact that they succeeded was something of a miracle.

In this new subtropical environment, these exiles and their kinsmen who had preceded them began to carve out not only settlements, but ways of life. Those making their homes along the banks of the Mississippi or its tributary bayous became farmers; one can grow almost anything in the rich, alluvial soil found there. Most who chose to live near the shores of the Gulf of Mexico, with its marshes, swamps, inlets, and bays, became fishermen and trappers. And many who homesteaded west of the Atchafalaya Basin became ranchers on the broad savannas of the Attakapas Prairie.

Here in New Acadia, just as in predispersal times and during the difficult years in exile, the family was the strongest element in society.

Fathers and sons, brothers, and brothers-in-law sought to own neighboring lands, thus perpetuating the extended kinship phenomenon that forms such an important part of Acadian culture. For both pragmatic and spiritual reasons, that culture also admired and encouraged large families. Children were needed to work the fields, and the Church needed priests, nuns, and parishioners to maintain and spread the faith. Since the Acadians were a prolific, agricultural people, they constantly needed more and new land, but this need was thwarted by colonial Louisiana's forced-heirship laws, which divided an original land grant into progressively smaller tracts to each successive generation. In response, the Acadian population exhibited a gradual outward movement of settlement patterns.

Clearing the land, plowing the fields, tending the herds, harvesting the crops, and raising large families was hard work. In an effort to reduce these labors, the Louisiana Acadians took the first steps away from their long tradition of egalitarianism when they embraced slavery. At first only a few Acadians owned a few slaves, perhaps a wet nurse and a field hand, but the economic advantages were so obvious that others soon followed. By century's end, nearly every Acadian household in Louisiana had at least one slave, and sometimes two or three. So pervasive was the "peculiar institution" that even the priest usually owned at least one slave. Acadian historian Carl Brasseaux estimates that "within ten years most of the exiles attained a standard of living at least equal to that of predispersal Nova Scotia." The nineteenth century would witness even more changes in the lives of the Acadian people. The United States of America would come to them.

As set forth in the Treaty of Paris in 1783, the western boundary of the new country called the United States of America was the Mississippi River. The USA's neighbor on the west bank of the Mississippi, from Canada south to the Gulf of Mexico, was Spanish Louisiana. And from the Natchez Post on the east bank to the mouth of the river, both banks belonged to Spain. Thousands of Americans, formerly British subjects in the Thirteen Colonies but now citizens of a new republic and no longer hemmed in along the eastern seaboard by restrictions and policies imposed from London, poured over the Appalachian

Mountains to capture title to the lands now legally available to them, particularly in the fertile valleys of the Ohio and Tennessee Rivers. Almost overnight, the population of this entire region burgeoned, as did the products of their labors, mostly furs, lumber, and grain. And the fastest, cheapest, and safest way to market was downriver, by barge, to New Orleans, for shipment to domestic and international destinations. When, in 1795, Spain and the United States signed a treaty guaranteeing Americans the right of navigation and duty-free deposit at New Orleans, river traffic surged and hundreds of American flatboats could be seen floating down the Ohio, Tennessee, and Mississippi Rivers. The country that held New Orleans held the key to the economic well-being of the American frontiersmen living in the western portion of the new nation, and those citizens grew increasingly uncomfortable with the idea that Spain, or for that matter any foreign power, controlled their economic destiny. Their concern evolved into fear when the most powerful man in the world decided he wanted Louisiana.

The legacies of the French Revolution to Western civilization are legion and formidable and none more so than those attributed to Napoleon Bonaparte. A man of military genius and political vision, by 1799 he had become first consul of France and the most influential man on the European continent. That same year, he launched a series of military and policy initiatives with the goal of reestablishing the French colonial empire in North America. It would be centered in the French West Indies and governed from France's largest island in the Caribbean, Saint Domingue (Haiti). Bonaparte envisioned the new empire being supplied and reinforced from the mainland, from Louisiana. There were two major obstacles to the implementation of his plan: Louisiana belonged to Spain, and a black slave named Toussaint L'Ouverture had led an insurrection on Saint Domingue and had taken control of the island.

Neither obstacle served to deter Bonaparte. On October 1, 1800, by the Treaty of San Ildefonso, Spain ceded Louisiana to France in exchange for the return of the Grand Duchy of Tuscany in Italy to the duke of Parma, the brother-in-law of the king of Spain, Charles IV. The following year, Napoleon sent one of his favorite generals, his brother-in-law Charles Victor Emmanuel Leclerc, to Saint Domingue with a large expeditionary force to pacify the island and restore French rule. Once his Saint Domingue mission was accomplished, Leclerc and his army were to take official possession of Louisiana. General Leclerc, however, was unable to execute his orders. By November 1802, he and half his army were dead from yellow fever. The disaster of Saint Domingue served to dampen considerably the first consul's enthusiasm for a new colonial empire in North America.

Although the United States was not enthralled by the fact that New Orleans to belong to Spain, the idea of Napoleon as a next-door neighbor was downright alarming to President Thomas Jefferson and the leaders of Congress. Spain was regarded as a decaying power and a limited threat; Napoleon was regarded as precisely the opposite. Jefferson, while not dismissing the possibility of war with France over this issue, fervently hoped for a diplomatic solution. The last thing his fledgling nation needed at this point in its young history was war with a major European power. Jefferson directed the United States minister to France, Robert Livingston, to offer to purchase the Isle of Orleans, that small strip of land—not really an island—between Lake Pontchartrain and the Mississippi River that Bienville had chosen as the site of New Orleans more than eighty years earlier. If France would not sell, Livingston was instructed to try to purchase West Florida.

The American ambassador's initial offers were refused, but the president persisted. To reinforce the seriousness of the situation, Jefferson dispatched James Monroe as minister plenipotentiary and envoy extraordinary to France and Spain with authorization to offer a sum in excess of nine million dollars for the Isle of Orleans. Monroe arrived in early 1803 and was greeted with the happy news that Napoleon had changed diplomatic courses: the debacle in Saint Domingue had forced him to conclude that a successful defense of Louisiana against either the United States, with its advantages of men and geography, or Great Britain, with its powerful navy, would be impossible. In addition, another war with England was imminent and Napoleon's treasury needed to be replenished. With one diplomatic coup he could strengthen the enemy of his enemy and obtain a handsome purse in the process. Napoleon offered to sell all of Louisiana to the United States.

The dramatic proposal substantially exceeded the instructions and authorizations of Livingston and Monroe, but it was an offer they could not refuse. The United States bought Louisiana from France for about fifteen million dollars. Concerning the significance of this transaction, Napoleon prophesied, "This accession of territory affirms forever the power of the United States, and I have just given England a maritime rival that sooner or later will lay low her pride." All or part of fifteen states would eventually be formed from the Louisiana Purchase.

On November 30, 1803, Spain transferred possession of Louisiana to France, in implementation of the treaty three years before. Less than one month later, on December 20, representatives of the United States officially took possession of their new territory from France in ceremonies on the Place d'Armes in New Orleans. A short eleven years later, Napoleon's prophecy would be fulfilled. On January 8, 1815, an army composed primarily of frontiersmen from Kentucky and Tennessee, their ranks swelled by hundreds of Louisiana Acadian volunteers and commanded by General Andrew Jackson, crushed the British at the Battle of New Orleans.

The United States divided the land acquired in the Louisiana Purchase into two territories, the District of Louisiana and the Territory of Orleans. The latter comprised much of what is the present-day state of Louisiana, and the former took in everything north of the thirty-third parallel. Louisiana's Acadians found themselves residents of the Territory of Orleans. Nine years later, in 1812, Louisiana entered the Union as the eighteenth state of the United States.

Geographically situated in the deep southern section of the country, Louisiana took its historically predetermined place in the roll call of the states that would later be called the antebellum South. Prior to the Civil War, the South was the most affluent and politically powerful section of the country. Although its white population was considerably smaller than that of the North during these years, seven of the fourteen presidents elected between 1800 and 1860 were from the South. The region's political power was derived from its great wealth, which in turn was based on agriculture, chiefly the production of cotton. The only crop that could compete with cotton in terms of profitability was sugarcane, and nowhere did it grow better than in the dark, rich soil of south Louisiana. Blessed by nature with the ability to grow both cotton and sugarcane, and blessed with its great port city of New Orleans, Louisiana's planter class was the envy of the nation.

Many Acadians participated in the revolution that was taking place in southern agriculture. By the eve of the Civil War, some of the wealthiest Louisiana planters—owners of thousands of acres of land and hundreds of slaves—were descendants of the Acadian exiles. Egalitarianism, that quality forged in the Canadian wilderness and synonymous with Acadian culture, could not be sustained in a society based on slavery and capitalistic agriculture. But not all Acadians were rich planters. In fact, only a few dozen families attained such a standard. The great majority of Acadian heads of household were yeoman farmers and ranchers who owned few slaves, usually six or less, with whom they usually labored side by side in the fields and on the prairie. Some Acadians chose to leave life on the farm to become tradesmen and merchants. The more affluent sent their sons off to school in Europe or up East, or provided tutors, thereby supplying a growing class of professionals—doctors, lawyers, and educators. And, of course, some Acadians lived in poverty. These were farm and ranch laborers who worked for pennies a day as ditch diggers, cane cutters, cotton pickers, and cowboys.

The transformation from rule by a monarch to democratic self-government was an easy one for Louisiana's Acadians. They were no strangers to representative government. In Acadia/Nova Scotia, particularly under English rule, they had been regularly required to elect delegates to discuss issues of the day with colonial administrators. Those exiles who subsequently spent years in Europe were continually electing deputies to represent the Acadian Nation in negotiations with the French government or with private representatives of the numerous proposed resettlement schemes. Beginning in 1805 with the election of four Acadians to the first territorial legislature and continuing throughout the antebellum period, successive generations played an active role in the political life of Louisiana and the nation. Generally speaking, the greater the wealth of a public office seeker, the higher the office sought, and vice versa. Yeoman Acadians served as sheriffs, mayors, clerks of court, constables, assessors, police jurors (members of the parish administrative council), and justices of the peace. The Acadian plantation aristocracy achieved higher offices: the legislature, state-wide offices like governor and lieutenant governor, and national posts in Congress. From statehood to the Civil War, four Acadians served as governor of Louisiana: Henry Schuyler Thibodeaux from the LaFourche country (elected 1824), Jacques Dupré from the Opelousas country (1830), Alexandre Mouton from the Attakapas country (1843), and Paul Octave Hébert from the Acadian Coast (1853). Alexandre Mouton also served a term in the United States Senate. Two Acadians were elected lieutenant governor, Trasimond Landry of Ascension Parish in 1845 and Charles Homer Mouton of Lafayette Parish in 1856.

All of these Acadians helped to mold the administrative unit that would function first as a territory and later as a state of the American Union. French influence in local matters and interpersonal affairs prevailed; the territorial legislature determined that Louisiana would have parishes (not counties) and that French civil code law would be applied in all matters relating to property and family. The English common law system would be applied only in criminal cases.

By act of the territorial legislature in 1807, Louisiana was divided up into nineteen parishes. One of these, St. Martin Parish, encompassed roughly what had been the boundaries of the Attakapas Post: the Gulf of Mexico on the south, the Atchafalaya River and Grand Lake on the east, the Avoyelles District on the north and the Mermentau River and the chain of lakes through which it flows on the west. Thus it happened that, when Louisiana was officially admitted to the Union on April 30, 1812, François Begnaud, born in St. Etienne de Montluc, France, and his wife, Honorine Doiron, born in Le Havre, France, and the daughter of Acadian exiles, became citizens of the parish of St. Martin, state of Louisiana, in the United States of America.

The Begnauds and their progeny would follow a lifestyle consistent with Acadian traditions but adjusted for life in the American South. They became yeoman farmers and ranchers; they owned their land and a modest number of slaves, and they almost always married other Acadians and had very large families. The baptismal, marriage, and burial records of their parish churches indicate that the first Begnauds and their descendants were practicing Catholics. Whenever possible, their nearest neighbors were family members. Land records of the period indicate that François Begnaud's contiguous landowners were his in-laws, the Doirons, and their relatives the Bernards.

The family achieved a degree of prosperity, participated in the political and civic affairs of the parish, and were viewed as community leaders. François and Honorine had six children: Jean Pierre, François, Alexandre Narcisse, Marie Adèle, Marie Azelie, and Louise. All married other Acadians. A 1789 muster roll of the colonial militia of the Attakapas District lists Begnaud and Jean Baptiste Doiron as members. By 1792, Begnaud had been promoted to corporal. It is likely that his primary source of income came from ranching, since his cattle brand is one of the earliest registered in the parish. His agricultural pursuits must have been profitable, for he was able to purchase additional tracts of land. In addition to his large spread that fronted Bayou Teche to the east and Bayou Vermilion to the west, he evidently obtained land on the east bank of the Teche, because in 1809 he traded this east bank property for land on the west bank owned by Pierre Broussard. Begnaud retained the wood rights on both banks. This was an important supplemental source of revenue for the Begnauds, since wood rights in the eighteenth and nineteenth centuries were similar in value to subsurface mineral rights in the twentieth century. Wood was a precious commodity, needed for cooking year round and for heat in winter. The good fortune of the first Begnaud in America was shared with the extended family, for there is every indication that Honorine and her husband cared for and looked after her parents in their old age: Jean Baptiste Doiron died in 1809 at the age of sixty-six, and Blanche Bernard Doiron died in 1813, also at sixty-six, respectable ages considering the times and the many vicissitudes experienced by the couple during the course of their lives. Both are buried at St. Martinville.

By the time the lives of François and Honorine Begnaud came to a close, one fact stands out: they departed this world far better off economically than they had entered it. When Begnaud died in 1822 at seventy-two, his estate—excluding his home, livestock, and personal possessions—counted approximately two thousand acres of land and twelve slaves and was valued at $9,060. (The general rule for the value of raw land was $1 per arpent/acre; improved or cleared land was worth $1.25 per arpent/acre.) With the consent of all the heirs, Begnaud's widow retained ownership of the entire community, with the exception of seven slaves who were distributed among her children. When she died in 1830, the property and possessions of the first Begnaud family in Louisiana were distributed among the surviving heirs.

One year after François Begnaud's death, about half of the land inherited by his widow became part of a new parish. The nineteen parishes created by the territorial legislature were very large, and the lack of good roads made communication with the seats of parish government difficult. This very real inconvenience played into the hands of local political and business leaders eager to elevate their own areas to the status of separate parishes and their local villages or towns into new parish seats. Eventually, four new parishes were carved out of the original St. Martin Parish: St. Mary in 1811, Lafayette in 1823, Vermilion in 1844, and Iberia in 1868.

A historical coincidence gave Lafayette Parish its name. In 1823, the marquis de Lafayette, the great French general and hero of the American Revolution, announced his intention to accept the invitation of the United States government to be its honored guest and undertake a grand tour of the young nation to commemorate the forthcoming fiftieth anniversary of the signing of the Declaration of Independence. In his honor and in the hopes that the marquis would place Louisiana on his itinerary, the state legislature gave his name to the new parish just carved out of western St. Martin Parish. As the "Guest of the Nation," the French statesman made his triumphal tour during 1824 and 1825. The foresight of the legislature was rewarded when the general and his entourage arrived at New Orleans in April 1825. Alas, the marquis did not visit the new parish that carried his name, but he did stop briefly at Baton Rouge on April 16, en route to St. Louis on board the riverboat *Natchez*. It is entirely possible that a few citizens of the new parish named for the general were among the very large crowds that welcomed him to Baton Rouge. Regardless, the new boundary that separated St. Martin Parish and its new offspring, Lafayette Parish, divided almost in half the extensive landholdings of the heirs of François Begnaud.

St. Martin Parish is the cultural hearth of the Louisiana Acadians. It was populated early and the best lands taken by the first wave of pio-

neers. The newly created parish of Lafayette, on the other hand, was
sparsely populated, with large amounts of unclaimed, inexpensive public prairie land. The United States government, limited as it was in its
sources of revenue, was eager to sell its real estate to citizens at bargain
prices. This opportunity, together with the realities of forced heirship
and the fact that many Begnauds already found themselves residents of
Lafayette Parish, resulted in a gradual movement into the new parish
by many first- and second-generation Begnauds born in the United
States. In time, the family would number among the largest in the area
around Vermilionville, the small village that was selected as the parish
seat. Founded in 1822 by a group of Acadians headed by Jean Mouton,
the village took its name from Bayou Vermilion, which flows through
the center of the parish.

Alexandre Narcisse Begnaud, the third child of François and Honorine, and the family line that will be followed here, was born in 1791.
He married twice, first in 1814 to Fanolia Landry, who died in 1825, but
not before bearing five children, three of whom survived childhood:
Alexandre, the first and only son, Emelie, and Emilia. Begnaud's second marriage, in 1826 to Hortense Patin, produced fourteen children,
nine of whom survived childhood. A short time after the death of his
first wife, and probably about the time of his second marriage, this
first-generation American and his family became residents of Lafayette
Parish, with land and livestock on the west bank of Bayou Vermilion.
At the time of his death in 1849, Alexandre Narcisse Begnaud's two-
hundred-arpent west bank ranch was valued at $1,600 and his sixteen
slaves at $8,650. But his most profitable asset resulted from following
his father's practice of acquiring or retaining woodland. Alexandre
Narcisse never parted with his inheritance of fifteen arpents of woodland on the Sorrel Prairie in St. Martin Parish, and when his widow
died in 1861, those fifteen arpents were auctioned for $5,650, an impres-
sive sum for that time.

The differences between the wills of François Begnaud and his son,
separated by twenty-seven years, deserve comment. The former was
written only in French, but the latter was required by law to be written
in both French and English, a clear indication of the growing influence
of Anglo-Saxon culture. The value of land had increased considerably,

owing in part to simple supply and demand but also to the increasing profitability of cotton. And the son owned more slaves than the father, a sign of increased affluence, more widespread use of slave labor, and greater reliance on cash in the economy.

For many years after Louisiana and the rest of the states born of the Louisiana Purchase were admitted to the Union, they were visited by surveyors sent by the United States government to convert land measurements and maps from the French/Spanish system of water frontage and arpents to the American system of acres and sections. By the late 1820s, the federal government was ready to begin the sale of unclaimed preemptive lands in western Lafayette Parish. The price set by the government was $1.25 per acre.

In 1836, Vermilionville was officially incorporated as a village, and that same year Alexandre Begnaud, the eldest child of Alexandre Narcisse Begnaud and Fanolia Landry, only twenty-one years of age, was somehow able to raise, earn, or borrow fifty dollars to purchase forty acres of public land in Section 20 of Lafayette Parish about three miles northwest of Vermilionville. As a proud owner of a *vacherie*, young Begnaud did not remain a bachelor very long. In 1837, he married Eliza, *dit* Lise, Constantin, the eighteen-year-old daughter of a neighboring rancher, Jean Constantin, a native of Listrac-Medoc, France. Constantin had immigrated to Louisiana some years earlier and, in 1805, married an Acadian from the Opelousas country named Marie Sonnier. The practice of endogamy, which along with the phenomena of extended kinship and large families was so central to the culture of the Acadians, was alive and well in Louisiana, as demonstrated by the marriage alliances of the Begnaud and Constantin families. Two years prior to the marriage of Alexandre Begnaud and Lise Constantin, his sister Emilia had wed Pierre Constantin, Lise's brother. A few years later, Alexandre's half-sister Marie Alice married Ernest Constantin, another one of Lise's brothers. The circle was tightened when two of Alexandre's first cousins, François Terrance and Emile, the sons of his Uncle François—his father's older brother—married two more of Lise's sisters, Eugenie and Adelaide Constantin. All of these unions produced many children. Alexandre and Lise Begnaud's family was typical: fourteen children, ten daughters and four sons.

Here, in the first half of the nineteenth century, these Acadians had realized the dream of their exiled ancestors. They were prosperous landowners, and their culture, albeit with concessions to time and place, was intact; they enjoyed many decades of peace and prosperity. But shadows cast by the gathering clouds of war began to appear over the land.

Vermilionville, Louisiana: September 1859

Nearly one hundred years of peace and prosperity for the Acadians of Louisiana came to an end in the seventh decade of the nineteenth century. Slavery was the culprit.

In matters of race, events in the parishes carved out of the Attakapas country mirrored those of the greater South. Black Codes—or, in French Louisiana, the *Code Noir*—regulating the institution of slavery and relationships between the races were adopted by virtually every state, county (parish), and municipality in the South, and these laws became more restrictive with each passing decade, largely in response to several slave insurrections and northern abolitionist propaganda. Deviations by blacks—free or slave—from the *Code Noir* or from traditional customs were unacceptable. If legally constituted authority was unable or unwilling to enforce social conventions, self-appointed, respectable members of society undertook that responsibility, as distasteful as it might be. This is precisely what happened in the Acadian parishes west of the Atchafalaya River. The years 1858 and 1859 saw the organization of a formidable vigilante movement. The declared targets of the Committees of Vigilance were outlaws, mostly rustlers, thieves, and petty criminals, but the vigilantes were really playing to a greater audience: the large slave population of those parishes. If the vigilantes could deal decisively with free citizens who chose to violate tradition and custom and deviate from acceptable patterns of behavior, it would send a clear message to the servile population that to stray from the path brought grave consequences.

To be sure, this part of the world was still very much a frontier. Effective law enforcement was problematic, and a certain degree of lawlessness did exist. But the fact that many of the outlaws were free black and mulatto men, some living in open concubinage with white women ("the antebellum South's ultimate social taboo"), provided an added incentive to the vigilantes. The first committee was organized in the community of Côte Gélée, in the area of present-day Broussard on the eastern boundary of Lafayette Parish. It was founded by a wealthy planter, Major Aurelien St. Julien, a man greatly admired for his reputation of never allowing the law to interfere in any matter that he could handle himself. By 1859, with Major St. Julien as their inspiration, virtually every community in the parishes of St. Martin, St. Landry (the Opelousas country), Calcasieu (on the Texas border), Vermilion, and Lafayette had founded such a committee.

Generally, each committee had two tiers: a court that issued verdicts *in absentia* and the actual vigilantes who were charged with executing the sentences. Membership was separate or not, depending on the size of the committee. The structure of the Vermilionville Committee of Lafayette Parish was bifurcated. The judicial arm was called the Committee of Mutual Protection, and its president was the most influential Acadian of his day, former governor and United States senator Alexandre Mouton. The other committee members were mostly prosperous plantation owners like Colonel Aurelien Drozin Boudreaux, an officer in the state militia, who served as secretary. The administrative, or enforcement, arm of the committee was headed by a captain; serving in this capacity was Alfred Mouton, a brigadier general in the Louisiana Militia, a graduate of West Point, and the son of Senator Mouton.

In most communities, the captain of a committee was its only leader. A good example was the Breaux Bridge Committee of Vigilance of St. Martin Parish, whose captain was Joachim Begnaud, the son of Jean Louis Begnaud and the grandson of François Begnaud and Honorine Doiron. Sentences meted out by the committees were relatively evenhanded: five days to leave the state or at least the area; failure to abide by the banishment meant lashes, usually ten to twenty, depending on the condemned person's degree of contriteness; and finally, if the accused individual still refused to go, he or she was introduced to "Judge Lynch," as hanging was euphemistically referred to in those times. Sentences were always carried out in the middle of the night by ten to twelve committee members.

Major St. Julien may have been the titular leader of the Committees of Vigilance, but Alexandre Mouton was the real power behind this movement. His status as the elder statesman of the Acadians, his wealth, and his political connections, combined with his position as president of the Vermilionville committee, provided the Committees of Vigilance with the cloak of legitimacy. Sheriffs and other local law enforcement officers, even if they had had the inclination, would have found it very difficult to challenge his authority. Even the governor in Baton Rouge, Robert C. Wickliffe, was tentative in his response to the activities of the vigilantes, despite numerous complaints. But on May 28, 1859, the governor summoned up his courage and issued a proclamation in which he called for the Committees of Vigilance in the Acadian country to disband.

The governor's proclamation was ignored by the vigilantes, but it did offer encouragement to their opponents. The outlaws and the other fringe elements who had incurred the wrath of the Committees of Vigilance began to organize themselves into analogous paramilitary groups of antivigilantes, and they began to prepare for a major show of force by gathering large amounts of ammunition and arms and building a fortified encampment in a remote area of southwest St. Landry Parish near present-day Mire. It was in this large, fortresslike compound owned by Emilien Lagrange that most of those individuals who had been banished from St. Martin, Lafayette, and Vermilion Parishes gathered to plan their revenge while they waited for the governor to order in the state militia against the Committees of Vigilance. But the state militia never arrived, and the vigilante leadership had other plans.

At four o'clock in the morning on September 3, 1859, a force of 120 armed horsemen from St. Martin Parish, led by Major St. Julien, crossed the bridge at Bayou Vermilion; their destination was the plantation of François Terrance Begnaud in northwest Lafayette Parish, where they were to rendezvous with the rest of the Attakapas country Committees of Vigilance. Begnaud, a major in the state militia and a vigilante leader of Lafayette Parish, probably received a warm predawn greeting from his first cousin Joachim, captain of the Breaux Bridge Committee. Although there is no record to confirm his presence, it is almost certain that another first cousin, Terrance Begnaud's brother-in-law and neighbor Alexandre Begnaud, also took part in the impromptu family reunion.

Under the command of thirty-three-year-old Alfred Mouton, a column of perhaps six hundred armed horsemen crossed over into St. Landry Parish and laid siege to the fortified compound that housed between two and three hundred antivigilantes. In classic military fashion, Mouton opened the engagement with a show of firepower from the one piece of artillery in his possession, a cannon nicknamed Betsy. Frightened by either the potential destructive power of the cannon or merely its great noise, dozens of the antivigilantes tried to escape through the woods but were easily captured. Those remaining inside surrendered without a single shot being fired.

In a nearby grove of trees, court was held and sentences were handed out. Some leaders of the antivigilantes were given 120 lashes; the survival rate must have been low. The *Franklin Planters' Banner* noted that "several cadavers were [subsequently] found in the prairies." The provigilante *Opelousas Courier* also suggested that the death toll was heavy. One leader was said to have committed suicide. The remaining prisoners received twenty or forty lashes depending on the severity and notoriety of their past improprieties. Those who survived were permanently banished from the area. Those captives deemed deserving of special consideration were moved to an isolated area of the prairie in western Lafayette Parish about one mile west of Colonel A. D. Boudreaux's plantation. This site was part of several hundred acres owned by an absentee rancher, Dr. George Scranton, a physician who lived and practiced in Vermilionville. There, in a grove of perhaps two dozen beautiful live oak trees with limbs suitable for hanging, around eighty antivigilantes were lynched. The Committees of Vigilance achieved their dual purpose: they successfully removed from their parishes an undesirable element of the population, and they sent an unmistakable message to their slaves. One month later, in October 1859, when John Brown's raid at Harpers Ferry, Virginia, electrified the nation, peace and harmony reigned in the Attakapas country. But it was a deceptive peace and a false harmony. Nationally, more powerful players and higher stakes were at the table, and the forces of change were on the march.

Less than a year later, in April 1860, Alexandre Mouton, chairman of the Louisiana delegation to the national Democratic Party Convention in Charleston, South Carolina, led a walkout of the state's delegation over the issue of slavery and the candidacy of the primary contender for the party's presidential nomination, Senator Stephen A. Douglas of Illinois. No Democratic candidate could muster the necessary votes to secure the nomination, so Mouton and his fellow delegates returned in June to Baltimore, Maryland, where they would walk out again for the same reasons. The southern delegates then reassembled in Richmond, Virginia, where a rump convention selected John C. Breckinridge of Tennessee as its candidate on a proslavery platform. The remaining delegates in Baltimore nominated Douglas. With the Democratic field divided by two candidates, the candidate of the Republican Party was elected president of the United States in 1860 on a platform opposed to the extension of slavery. Not a single Louisianian cast his ballot for Abraham Lincoln in the national elections of 1860. The election of this gentle man to the presidency, this man whom southerners venomously referred to as the "Black Republican," meant war.

The Civil War and the political and social Reconstruction that followed were difficult times for all southerners, the Acadians of Louisiana included. With only a few exceptions, the South was the battleground, and numerous homes, farms, plantations, businesses, and entire cities and towns were destroyed throughout the region. The human cost was staggering: almost as many Americans were killed in the four years of the Civil War, 1861–1865, than in all the other wars fought by the United States put together, before or since. Southerners saw their property expropriated, confiscated, emancipated, or simply destroyed and the flower of an entire generation dead on the field of battle. William Ivy Hair has observed that the case of Louisiana is illustrative: "The Civil War and Reconstruction dislocated and severely depressed Louisiana's once-rich economy. In 1860 the state, with property valued at $602,118,568, ranked first in the South and second in the nation in per capita wealth. What followed was a generation of calamity. The first federal census after Reconstruction estimated the actual value of property at only $422,000,000, a plunge [to] thirty-seventh in wealth among all states and territories." It would be inaccurate to compare this experience in the history of the Acadian people of Louisiana with *le Grand Dérangement;* Acadians were not singled out for punishment, and the sheer horror of the events of 1755 and its aftermath (one can only hope) will never be equaled. As southerners, Louisiana's Acadians simply shared in the widespread misery that accompanied military defeat and the consequences of slavery.

Thousands of Acadians served in every theater of the war. Three attained the rank of general officer in the Confederate army; the most able of these was Brigadier General Alfred Mouton. In the fall of 1861, he founded the legendary 18th Louisiana Regiment and was commissioned its first colonel and commanding officer. The core of the 18th Louisiana was made up of Acadian volunteers from the Attakapas country. Mouton and his regiment fought at Shiloh, in the Teche and LaFourche campaigns, and at Red River. Few regiments suffered more casualties than the 18th Louisiana, and none more painful than the loss of its commanding officer. Fearless on the field of battle and always at the front leading his men, the "Acadian General" was seriously wounded at Shiloh and fatally wounded at the Battle of Mansfield in April of 1864.

After the first wave of enthusiasm for the war subsided, the number of volunteers dwindled on both sides and conscription became necessary. At first, in the South, only white men under the age of forty were subject to the draft, but by 1863, as rebel casualties began to mount and as the North's overwhelming advantage in manpower was becoming the clear determinant in battle after battle, the Confederacy was forced to call up able-bodied white men over forty. One of these was A. D. Boudreaux, the secretary of the Vermilionville vigilante committee, forty-seven years old in 1863 and a colonel in the state militia, who was commissioned a captain in the 2d Louisiana Reserve Corps. On the day he set out to join the 2d Louisiana, after bidding adieu to his large family, Boudreaux called together his six slaves. He told them that he was going off to war and that it was very unlikely he would return. He also told them that regardless of what happened to him, it was his opinion that in a relatively short period of time they would gain their freedom and that they must begin to prepare themselves for their new status. In what surely must have been a rare occurrence in the South, Colonel Boudreaux, eschewing Confederate money, gave each of his slaves a gold coin for use in their new life. Each slave buried his or her treasure in a secret location; a favorite hiding place was under a fence post where it would be easy to locate and recover. But Boudreaux's premonition proved false. He survived the war, was paroled at Washington, Louisiana, on June 17, 1865, and returned to Boudreaux Plantation. His crops and fields were in ruins, all of his livestock confiscated or slaughtered, and most of the outbuildings and a portion of the main house burned. He was welcomed home by his family and his six former slaves, now, as their former master had predicted, freedmen. In a gesture of equal, nay, greater magnanimity, each of the six former slaves returned his or her gold piece to Colonel Boudreaux in the belief that his need exceeded their own. They remained as servants and field hands on Boudreaux Plantation for the rest of their lives.

The colonel's neighbor Alexandre Begnaud was also called up. Although forty-eight in 1863 and the father of fourteen children, Begnaud served with the 18th Louisiana alongside his half brother Stanislas. Two other half brothers, Marcel and Felix, served with the 26th Louisiana Infantry. His first cousin Joachim, the vigilante leader from Breaux Bridge, served with distinction in the famous Yellow Jacket Brigade. Two other first cousins, Jean Lessin and Theogene, also fought for the "Lost Cause." And Lise Begnaud's nephew, the child of her sister Adelaide and Emile Begnaud, her husband's first cousin, was killed at the siege of Vicksburg. He was the namesake of the first of his line in North America, his great-grandfather, François Begnaud.

The American Civil War effectively ended on April 9, 1865, with the surrender of the Army of Northern Virginia and its commander, General Robert E. Lee, at Appomattox Court House, Virginia. One half of the nation had been virtually destroyed, and until it could rebuild, the other half was in control.

In the South, the Civil War was followed by "Reconstruction." This was the term used by the leaders of the Republican Party to describe their plans for the former Confederate states after the Civil War, but it did not refer to physical reconstruction; it referred to the political and, to a lesser extent, the social realignment of the South, which resulted in its becoming—for as long as Reconstruction was in effect—a bulwark of the Republican Party based on the vote of the freedmen. During Reconstruction, the South was occupied by United States armed forces, making it the only section of the nation ever subjected to military rule. The military governors of the southern states, political appointees and nearly all Republicans, were authorized to begin the process of reestablishing local and state civilian governments in the South with one very important caveat: no individual who bore arms against the Union or supported the Confederate cause was eligible to vote. Thus, with the entire white male population of the South effectively disenfranchised, all political power was vested in the hands of the freedmen, who could be counted upon to vote in overwhelming numbers for the party of Lincoln, the Great Emancipator.

Economically, the situation was grim. Southern whites had invested most of their capital in labor production—that is, slaves; they were thus ruined financially by emancipation. Lafayette Parish provides a good example of what happened throughout the South. The decennial census of 1860 reported personal property holdings for the parish valued at over six million dollars; the 1870 census for the same category was just over six hundred thousand dollars, a decrease of 90 percent. Similarly, real estate value declined by almost 20 percent over the same time period. Thousands of freedmen roamed the countryside, homeless, unemployed, and starving. Thievery and poaching were rampant. And while the motivation of the ex-slaves was usually survival with no malice intended, it made little difference to the white population, who in many cases were also only one step away from starvation. The white South wanted to fight back, but with large federal garrisons stationed in every southern capital and in most major cities of the region, there was little chance of success.

Reconstruction brought out the worst in men, both northerners and southerners. The initial response by southern whites to military domination, disenfranchisement, and economic chaos was terrorism, and their primary target was the freedmen. Several secret societies were organized across the South with the objective of preventing the freedmen from exercising their right to vote through the use of threats, intimidation, and murder, usually by lynching. The most infamous of the secret societies was the Ku Klux Klan, founded at Pulaski, Tennessee, in 1866. Despite the effective use of terrorism, the Klan and its fellow travelers failed to break the hold of the Republican Party in the South. They were simply no match for the military might of the United States Army and the power of government patronage in a depressed and downtrodden economy. The coup de grâce was administered in 1868 when most southern states—now firmly in Republican hands—adopted a Louisiana-inspired device called "Election Returning Boards," which had the power to invalidate the results of elections at every level of government. It therefore mattered little whether the freedmen voted or not, the Republican candidate was guaranteed victory. Southern whites yearned for "Redemption," the term coined by later historians to signify the overthrow of Republican rule.

In an epoch filled with irony, it was fitting that political and economic events in the North conspired to serve the interests of the white South and to undermine Reconstruction. President U. S. Grant's second term of office, 1872–1876, was wracked by scandals. With most of his attention directed at defending his administration, the president had little time to devote to southern issues. At the same time, many in Congress and in the northern press began to question the cost of the military occupation of the South; and as the price tag increased, the incongruence of one part of the nation imposing martial law on another part gained currency and the practice grew more and more indefensible. Most important of all, the Republican Party no longer needed the vote of the freedmen to sustain itself in power at the national level. The party of Lincoln, the party that freed the slaves and saved the Union, became the party of big business. The Republican Party abandoned its liberal social origins and embraced the conservative economic agenda of the nation's railroad, banking, shipping, and commercial interests. It was an extremely advantageous political alliance for the Republicans. By the mid-1870s, southern whites were mobilizing to fill the political vacuum left by the Republicans' reorientation, with the goal of regaining control of all levels of state and local government. In Louisiana, the White League led the way.

The first White League chapter was founded at Opelousas in April 1874, but new "clubs" were organized in almost every part of the state outside New Orleans. Unlike the Klan, the White League was not a hooded, covert society that employed secret handshakes, passwords, and symbols. White League members were proud of their stated goal: the restoration of white supremacy in Louisiana. Their methods varied by region, parish, and club, but like the secret societies, they used fear and intimidation as their ultimate weapons. While there is general agreement that the White League clubs in north Louisiana were more brutal in their methods than their south Louisiana counterparts, the lash and the rope administered by armed nightriders were common statewide. The clubs were immensely popular, and—at least in the Acadian country—resembled the vigilante movement of the late 1850s in their organization and membership. In Lafayette Parish, for example, there were fifteen clubs, with an estimated membership of eight hundred white men. Clubs were named for their organizer, their location, or the family that contributed the largest number of members. In the latter instance, the Begnaud family was unique; it had contributed so many members to the White League that two clubs carried its name: Begnaud No. 1 and Begnaud No. 2.

The president of Club Begnaud No. 2, formed on August 30, 1874, was Colonel A. D. Boudreaux, whose plantation was about four miles west of the village of Vermilionville. In light of the club's name, it is almost certain that Boudreaux's neighbor Alexandre Begnaud and Begnaud's four sons, Joseph (born in 1844), Martin (1850), Jean (1852) and Simeon (1854), were members. Colonel Boudreaux was the natural leader of these Acadian yeoman farmers and ranchers who had settled the prairies of western Lafayette Parish. Surrounded by *vacheries* that usually measured about forty acres, Boudreaux's 300-acre plantation stood apart because of its size. His leadership skills had been proved as secretary of the parish Committee of Vigilance in the late 1850s and as an officer in the state militia. He was a Confederate veteran, an officer, at a time when the tortured South bestowed an almost unnatural veneration on the soldiers of the Lost Cause, the higher the rank the higher the pedestal. Another connection between Colonel Boudreaux and Club Begnaud No. 2 was the marriage on the first day of November in that same year, 1874, of Alexandre Begnaud's eighteen-year-old daughter, Philomène, to the colonel's son Olivier, thus uniting these two large Acadian families.

Based on the available evidence, Club Begnaud No. 2 of the White League of the Parish of Lafayette was more interested in traditional political solutions than in intimidation. This club took a leadership role in creating a political organization for the entire parish. Its proceedings were all in French—written and spoken—and its stated strategy was to unite the White League membership of the parish behind consensus candidates for political office. The plan was simple yet pragmatic. By qualifying only one white Democratic candidate for each office, thus avoiding intraparty contests, the odds of victory would be considerably enhanced. The Club Begnaud No. 2 plan was effective up to a point and in ordinary times might have carried the day, but these were extraordinary times.

The White League's successful campaign combined economic and physical intimidation. By day, they urged all businesses and individuals to refrain from paying state taxes to the carpetbag administration of Governor William Pitt Kellogg in New Orleans. Next, anyone who voted for or supported a Republican was threatened with the loss of his job. This was a threat they could make good on, for virtually all landowners and businessmen of the area were members of the White League. By night, riders would periodically appear out of the darkness and crash into the cabins of African Americans looking for weapons; if any were found, they were confiscated and the unlucky owner was punished. The freedman was forbidden under pain of lynching to vote at any time, in any election. But the White Leaguers were most effective in dealing with local Republican officeholders. Out of fear for their own lives or for the lives of family members, they resigned by the hundreds and fled to New Orleans, where, like Governor Kellogg and the legislature, they enjoyed the protection of federal troops. These vacant offices were filled de facto by white Democrats. Federal troops, by now undergoing significant downsizing, were sent out to the Acadian country in an attempt to restore order, but when faced with the numerical superiority and firepower of the White League, they showed no inclination for confrontation.

The national and statewide elections of 1876 brought an end to Reconstruction and to the paramilitary, extralegal activities of the White League. In a disputed presidential election, the Republican candidate, Rutherford B. Hayes, was elected. For many reasons, but foremost in order to secure his own election, Hayes was forced to pledge that in exchange for clear title to the presidency, he would order the removal of all remaining federal troops from the South. In January 1877, a one-armed, one-legged former Confederate brigadier general, a Democrat named Francis Tillou Nicholls, was inaugurated governor of Louisiana. Reconstruction had ended.

Book V

THE ARRAIGNMENT

Lafayette, Louisiana: February 1897

As soon as Judge Conrad Debaillon declared court to be in session on the morning of Wednesday, February 10, District Attorney Gordy requested that case 1421 be taken up first on the court's calendar, and the judge concurred. Described by the *Times-Democrat* as "bespectacled and grave," Debaillon spoke to the Blanc brothers in their mother tongue, for it was his first language also. In fact, throughout the legal proceedings connected to the case, Judge Debaillon explained every significant procedure in French for the benefit of the accused. The judge was descended from French aristocrats, both his maternal and paternal grandparents having been French royalists who fled their native land during the Napoleonic era and settled in the Opelousas country. And he was educated in the French language, being an 1863 graduate of St. Charles College at Grand Coteau in St. Landry Parish, where the French Jesuits conducted all instruction in their native tongue. His French was therefore impeccable. He asked the defendants if they had engaged legal counsel; they replied no. He asked if they had the means to pay for legal counsel; again they replied no. Judge Debaillon then announced the appointment by the court of Joseph A. Chargois, R. W. Elliott, and Charles D. Caffery as counsel for the defense. Obviously, these appointments had been prearranged, and the three lawyers stepped forward to the bar and accepted their assignments. Clerk Voorhies then read the indictment. To the charges read, the judge asked the Blancs how they wished to plead. On their behalf, Mr. Chargois entered a plea of not guilty. The judge then asked if they wished to request a trial by judge or by jury. Mr. Chargois indicated a trial by jury. Judge Debaillon set the trial date for Wednesday, February 17, 1897, one week thence.

The judge had assembled an impressive legal team to defend the brothers. Joe Chargois was the senior of the three. He was experienced as both a criminal defense attorney and a prosecutor; he had served two terms as district attorney, from 1876 to 1884. (He had sought reelection to that post in April 1896 but had lost to Gordy.) Moreover, Chargois was intimately familiar with the case as a result of his previous representation of Hamp Benton. Charles D. Caffery was a former state senator and one of the leading citizens of the town, well connected in business circles and a highly regarded member of the local bar. Ralph William Elliott was the least experienced member of the defense team. Although forty years old, Elliott had only recently been admitted to the Louisiana bar and had decided to set up practice in the progressive railroad town on Bayou Vermilion. Perhaps he was searching for his roots. He was born in Lafayette, Louisiana—not the one in Lafayette Parish, but the first Lafayette, Louisiana, in Orleans Parish.

The three lawyers went right to work. The next morning, Thursday, February 11, they fired off a letter to Consul General Bosseront d'Anglade. Signed by all three members of the defense team, the letter asked for no assistance or intervention but simply notified the nearest official representative of the Blancs' native country of their troubles. The handwritten one-page letter contained a realistic evaluation of the situation and of the serious consequences of the impending legal proceedings:

> The undersigned beg leave to inform you that Ernest and Alexis Blanc, two young Frenchmen are here in jail under indictment for murder, in what we consider a very desperate case. We have been appointed by the Court to defend them but we have concluded, that as they claim to have neither relatives nor friends, the least we could do, would be to notify the nearest repre-

sentative of their Country. They were born and raised in Paris and have been here about three years. They are friendless and pennyless [*sic*] and we assure you are in a very desperate state. They are respectively 19 and 20 years of age, and, appear to have been well raised. Their case is fixed for Wednesday 17th inst, but may be deferred a few days.

D'Anglade replied the next day that he was quite familiar with the brothers' arrest from all the newspaper accounts and said he had followed the case with interest (for whatever reason, he neglected to mention that he had also visited the Blancs in prison). He acknowledged, however, that the state of Louisiana was exercising its proper legal jurisdiction in the matter. The diplomat closed his note diplomatically: "The attorneys appointed by the Court has [*sic*] given me confidence." The defense team spent the next few days consulting with their clients and preparing their strategy for the trial.

The efficiently functioning legal system and the fixed, near-at-hand trial date seem to have checked the epidemic of lynch fever, but the recovery proved only temporary. Rumors began to circulate that the defense would request a change of venue to move the trial out of the parish, and that they would put forth arguments aimed at preventing Alexis Blanc from receiving the death penalty, based on his tender age and the fact that he was not the actual murderer. On Monday morning when the court convened to hear other trials on the docket, District Attorney Gordy, as if to confirm the rumors, informed the judge of his wish that the defense not come forth with any dilatory motions that might result in delaying the trial of Ernest and Alexis Blanc. Their fears seemingly confirmed by the district attorney's observation, the people lost their patience. There is nothing published in any newspaper or any memoir about what transpired on Monday, February 15, but the aftermath was stunning. At 10 A.M. on Tuesday, February 16, one day before the trial of the century was scheduled to begin, Chargois, Caffery, and Elliott all withdrew as counsel for the defense. Debaillon was furious. In a rare fit of anger, he gave the three attorneys a tongue-lashing they probably never forgot. He then declared a recess. The official reason listed in the lawyers' motion of withdrawal was simple: the three lawyers claimed to "have been reliably informed and have good reason to believe that if a technical defense be made in behalf of said accused, and that the trial . . . be deferred, that the said defendants will be taken possession of and summarily executed." The "technical defense" was the contemplated change of venue motion. Although the defense lawyers' concern for their clients' safety was incontestably well founded, it was almost certainly paired with the realization that if they were to go through with the plan to seek a change of venue, they themselves might be lynched first, followed by the brothers Blanc.

The withdrawal of the defense team sent shock waves across the state. Predictably, the newspapers had a field day with this unexpected turn of events and made every attempt to create a polarized, adversarial conflict between Judge Debaillon and the three lawyers. No one was talking except Joe Chargois, but he held nothing back. Debaillon, according to Chargois, had no right to speak to him and his colleagues in such a strong manner, particularly in light of the fact that he—the judge—had once done exactly the same thing. Debaillon had first been elected to the district court bench in 1884, and was reelected in 1888, but resigned after only a few months in office. These were the peak years of regulator activity when violence was rampant in the parish. Debaillon had given as his reason for resigning the fact that "he would have possibly been under the painful necessity of sending a number of his friends to the state penitentiary." No one had any difficulty interpreting the judge's real reason for resigning in 1888 any more than they had difficulty understanding Chargois's and his colleagues' withdrawal from the murder case in 1897: all four men walked away from their professional responsibilities to protect their own lives and possibly the lives of family members.

Judge Debaillon was in a quandary. It was about 11 A.M. on February 16, the trial was scheduled to begin the following morning at ten, and the entire legal defense team had just resigned. The judge's dilemma was twofold: he had to keep the legal proceedings in the Blanc brothers' case moving at an orderly pace, since any undue delay might result in a victory for anarchy and a defeat for the rule of law, and he had to maintain the integrity of the judicial process. His first challenge was to find at least two replacements for the defense team, capable lawyers who could handle this very difficult assignment and who could not or would not be intimidated by threats of vigilante justice, and he had to find them right away. The judge knew of only two men who fit this template. Both possessed prestigious reputations, both were held in the highest esteem by the general population, and both were highly regarded longtime members of the Louisiana bar. If those qualifications did not deter the mob, then perhaps their advanced ages would; Debaillon hoped to exploit a strong Acadian tradition of profound respect for the elderly. While the senior status of these two men was an asset, it was also a problem, for both were semiretired and long past their professional apogees. But this was a bizarre situation and the law itself hung in the balance. Debaillon would have to appeal to them personally. The judge likely called for a public hack—a buggy—and set out with its driver for St. Martinville, about ten miles east of Lafayette. The St. Martinville road passed directly in front of Oakbourne Plantation, which would be his second stop, on the return trip.

Judge Debaillon's destination in St. Martinville was the home of his father-in-law. Charles Alexandre Homer Mouton had been, since the death of his uncle Alexandre Mouton in 1885, the senior statesman of the Acadians. Everyone in his family called him Homer; everyone else called him "Governor." He had been the first student to enroll in St. Charles College when it opened its doors in January 1838. He had graduated three years later at the age of eighteen. Before the Civil War, Homer Mouton had already served as district attorney, state senator, lieutenant governor, and district judge. When war broke out, he was serving in the latter capacity and continued to hold court until April 1863. In the first week of that month, Mouton's first cousin General Alfred Mouton issued a call for volunteers to fill the Confederate ranks in order to meet the threat posed by a massive Federal army that was moving up Bayou Teche. At the end of the day, Judge Mouton announced that he was closing down the district court until further notice. The next day he was in a Confederate uniform and reported for military duty. He served as aide-de-camp to General Mouton until the general's death one year later. After the war, Homer Mouton earned a reputation as one of the top criminal lawyers in the state. His first wife, whom he married in 1848, was Célimène Dupré, the granddaughter of Governor Jacques Dupré of Opelousas. She died in 1864, leaving Homer with eight children. In 1867, he remarried into an equally prominent St. Martin Parish family, the Oliviers, and relocated his residence and law practice to his wife's hometown of St. Martinville. He fathered seven more children with Emérenthe Olivier. Conrad Debaillon's wife was Louise Mouton, Homer Mouton's eldest daughter by his first marriage. Apparently considering this a family matter, the seventy-four-year-old veteran of many courtroom battles agreed to take the case.

It was early afternoon when Judge Debaillon and his driver turned off the St. Martinville road and pulled up in front of the large and beautiful main house at Oakbourne Plantation, the retirement home of Colonel Gustave A. Breaux. Debaillon knew that Colonel Breaux had never practiced criminal law, but he also knew that no one would dare challenge his qualifications: Harvard Law graduate, Civil War hero, state senator, and big-time railroad attorney. And if Jean Mouton was the father of Vermilionville, Gus Breaux, as we shall see, was its godfather. As expected, Colonel Breaux questioned his ability to adequately represent the defendants in this case in light of his total lack of experience in criminal law. Debaillon was ready for Breaux's excuse; would the colonel be willing to serve as cocounsel alongside Louisiana's premier criminal defense attorney, Homer Mouton? Having recently become a full-time resident of Lafayette Parish, Breaux was well acquainted with the difficulties confronting the court. The sixty-nine-year-old colonel agreed to serve.

At four o'clock that afternoon, Judge Debaillon was back on the bench and declared court in session. Governor Mouton and Colonel Breaux were present and the judge asked them to approach the bar. They were asked if they would accept appointment as counsel for the defense in case 1421, *State of Louisiana* v. *Ernest Blanc and Alexis Blanc.* Both responded in the affirmative. Governor Mouton then requested and received permission to address the court. The *Daily Picayune* reported, "He said he considered it his duty as an officer of the court to accept the charge and to defend the accused to the best of his ability. These young men were natives of a strange land, and even though guilty of the most damnable crime, yet they were entitled to receive all the rights and privileges accorded them under the law." The judge then ordered Sheriff Broussard to bring the Blanc brothers into court. Upon first entering the courtroom, they appeared apprehensive and confused, but Judge Debaillon, speaking in French quietly and reassuringly, explained everything that had transpired regarding their legal representation. The judge introduced the defendants to their new lawyers. He then outlined for the Blancs the impressive experience, ability, and accomplishments of their new advocates. Their fears calmed by the avuncular judge, the brothers seemed reassured. The judge announced that the trial was rescheduled for Thursday, February 25, and adjourned his court until ten the next morning. The sheriff then returned the prisoners to jail, where Colonel Breaux and Governor Mouton immediately began a consultation with their clients.

15

Lafayette, Louisiana: February 1897

On Wednesday, February 17, the original trial date, approximately a thousand spectators assembled in and around the courthouse square, and they were furious: first, because they had come for nothing, and second, they had come to see justice done—and for these Acadians the old saying "justice delayed is justice denied" was no mere platitude. Every Begnaud in Lafayette Parish over the age of twelve was present, and that was no small number. Many of Martin Begnaud's friends and neighbors were also in the parish seat that day, as well as hundreds of others drawn to the drama that was unfolding in their midst. Many of the men were heavily armed. The *Daily Picayune* headlined ANGRY MEN AT LAFAYETTE. Tension filled the air. Eyewitness newspaper accounts are illustrative: "The square of ground in which the courthouse, the parish prison and the clerk's office is situated was filled with groups of men earnestly discussing the turn which events had taken within the past twenty-four hours, and these discussions were anything but satisfactory"; and "Jeans suits of clothing and high-crowned, broadbrimmed white hats predominated, and the wearers of the clothing were in anything but an amiable mood"; and "There was every evidence of a latent disposition to precipitate matters should the least excuse be offered. The stern, set faces, the earnest conversations but too clearly betokened this, while the simple mention of the name of either one of the accused or their victim was the occasion of a crowd quickly form-ing." As the hours passed, the situation grew more tense. Sheriff Brous-sard, probably at the suggestion of William Campbell, approached Simeon Begnaud with an appeal that he help ease tempers. The mur-der victim's brother agreed to cooperate and spent most of the day urg-ing family members and friends and anyone who would listen to allow the law to take its course.

Simeon Begnaud's efforts helped, but there was another member of the family who had more influence. Country people versus town people was a quite divisive categorization in rural south Louisiana, even within families. This was particularly true of country people who har-bored a palpable distrust of townsfolk. Scott Station was not a town; in fact, it was not even much of a village—yet Simeon Begnaud had been labeled as one of "them," and as a result, his credibility with the country folk was compromised. But no one would ever mistake his older brother, Jean Begnaud, for a town dweller. In both age and size, Jean fell precisely between Martin and Simeon: he was two years younger than Martin and two years older than Simeon, not as tall as his older brother but bigger than his little brother. Jean was broad-shouldered and barrel-chested with a full, jet-black beard reaching to his waist, and he never went anywhere without a loaded double-barreled shotgun cra-dled in his arms. He was, simply put, a menacing sight. Like his father, he had married a Constantin, Emma, his double first cousin. By 1897, Emma had given birth to ten children, six living and four who lived less than a year. Before the end of the century, she would have three more children: two died and one lived; one of those infants, who died in 1899, was named Martin Begnaud. Jean Begnaud gave his people the word: "Allow the law to run its course, but if the law does not hang them, then we will." An echo of Jean's warning made the *Daily Pica-yune*'s front page: LAW WINS IN LAFAYETTE, UNLESS THE JURY FAILS TO DO ITS DUTY.

For most of the local country people, Jean's proviso was acceptable. By late afternoon on the seventeenth, most of the crowd had dispersed peacefully and were on their way home. But there remained in town a hard-core element, a group of about two dozen heavily armed trouble-makers bent on some kind of demonstration who had been drinking all afternoon and into the night. The sheriff and his deputies remained on full alert inside the prison. It was not until around midnight, when the malcontents had consumed enough liquor to reinforce their courage sufficiently, that they marched on the jail and demanded to speak with Sheriff Broussard. Their ploy was simultaneously original and transparent. They offered their services to the sheriff as prison guards. After all, the sheriff had only a few deputies and a lynch mob could materialize at any minute. Broussard quickly grasped the consequences should he refuse their offer: there would be a gunfight followed by two lynchings, for he was heavily outnumbered and outgunned. With profuse thanks and an outpouring of appreciation, the sheriff not only accepted the offer but welcomed it. In a very professional and serious manner, he placed his new volunteer, albeit inebriated, deputies all around the front and sides of the prison, but stationed none of them inside or behind it. When they were all in place and had been given their appropriately consequential duties and responsibilities, Broussard walked back into the prison, cuffed and chained the Blanc brothers, hustled them out the back door, and walked briskly to the train station just in time to board the westbound 1 A.M. train. The sheriff and his two prisoners spent the night in the Acadia Parish jail in Crowley, about twenty-five miles west of Lafayette. Broussard returned to Lafayette about one the next afternoon, alone. The new, unwelcome deputies were nowhere to be found, and the town had resumed normal activity.

The same afternoon that he returned from Crowley, Ike Broussard received a telegram from R. H. Snyder, Louisiana's lieutenant governor and acting governor. Any reasonable person who read the New Orleans papers on the morning of February 18 would have cause to believe that the chances of the Blanc brothers remaining alive long enough to be tried in a court of law were slim. Deeply concerned for the safety of the two French citizens jailed in the remote country parish, Consul General d'Anglade had telegraphed Governor Murphy J. Foster: "Ernest and Alexis Blanc two young Frenchmen are in jail at Lafayette and it appears in danger of being lynched. I beg your Excellency to give the proper instructions to prevent such an outrage." But Governor Foster was out of the state on business, and acting governor Snyder was at his home in St. Joseph, a distant village on the Mississippi River in north

Louisiana's Tensas Parish. In charge in Baton Rouge was T. G. Jones, the governor's private secretary. Jones telegraphed d'Anglade that he was sending the consul general's communiqué to the acting governor via telegraph and trains out of Vicksburg, Mississippi. He added, "Customary for local authorities to ask for troops, but your application may secure them." At 6:16 P.M. on February 18, d'Anglade finally received a telegram from Snyder: "Have wired Lafayette Sheriff to inform me of the situation and to use every effort to protect the prisoners." Perhaps influenced by Snyder's telegram, the sheriff let the Blanc brothers spend another night in the Acadia Parish prison. On Friday, February 19, he traveled to Crowley to fetch them and return them to their Lafayette jail cell.

Aside from the newspaper reports, only one other account of the atmosphere in Lafayette on February 17 exists, and it confirms the volatility of the situation and the influence of Jean Begnaud. Henriette Odéide Mouton was the sister of General Alfred Mouton and a resident of Lafayette. In a letter dated February 19, 1897, Henriette wrote to her son Alexandre, a New Orleans businessman:

> Everybody is on tip toe over the Begnaud murder trial, it is to take place next Thursday, the case was postponed last Wednesday to a week later; I presume the papers kept you posted with the reason why, matters for a while assumed a very threatening appearance, the village square was literally crowded, and grave fears were entertained that from one moment to another a mob would storm the jail; fortunately calm was restored, and all returned home quietly, to return next Thursday; they have vowed though, that if the prisoners escape sentence of death, that they will never see another sun set; there is not a *shadow of a doubt* that their promise will not be kept.

She underlined "shadow of a doubt."

16

Lafayette, Louisiana: February 1897

In open court on Thursday, February 18, Judge Debaillon issued two orders concerning case 1421. First, he entertained a motion from Governor Mouton and Colonel Breaux for a change of venue. It was the position of the defendants that they could not obtain a fair and impartial trial in Lafayette Parish. Without comment, the judge set a hearing on the change of venue motion for Saturday morning at ten. His next order, addressed to the clerk of court, Ed Voorhies, was a clear indication of the judge's feelings on the previous motion. He directed the clerk to assemble the members of the parish jury commission that afternoon for the purpose of selecting one hundred names for a fresh jury pool, from which twelve would be selected to serve on a petit jury for the trial of Ernest and Alexis Blanc. The judge's order further directed that a copy of all the names in the jury pool "be handed to each counsel representing said defendants." The jury commission completed its work, and on the following day, February 19, Lafayette Parish deputy sheriffs, armed with jury-duty notices, fanned out across the parish in search of the hundred men on the list. The notice directed each potential juror to "be in attendance at Court on Thursday Morning, February 25th 1897 at ten o'clock for service as *de talibus* Jurors in above cause (# 1421) and prosecution."

On Saturday morning, February 20, the courtroom was filled to capacity for the change of venue hearing. The crowd was an indication of things to come. Promptly at ten, Judge Debaillon called his court into session and the clerk read the motion under consideration:

> Before me, Ed G. Voorhies, the undersigned authority personally came and appeared Ernest Blanc and Alexis Blanc, the accused and defendants in the above entitled and numbered cause, who, after having been sworn according to law, upon the oaths, say: That they cannot go to trial and that they are entitled to a change of venue for the following reasons: Because they believe that by reason of prejudice existing in the public mind against them, created and formulated principally by publications and commentaries in newspapers in the parish and in the state of Louisiana, in circulation in said parish, and because, further, of repeated threats of violence made against them since their imprisonment, and because of the extensive circulation among the people of the parish of the pictures of said accused, accompanied by statements of circumstances uttered as ascertained facts calculated to excite the anger of the community against them; by reason of all of which they cannot obtain an impartial trial in the parish of Lafayette, where the indictment against them impending. This affidavit and application is not made for delay, but to obtain an impartial trial. The foregoing considered, the accused and defendants humbly pray that they be granted a change of venue, according to the law.

Upon completion of the reading, Governor Mouton and Colonel Breaux officially presented the motion and requested "a change of venue as prayed for." District Attorney Gordy and special counsel Campbell represented the state of Louisiana. In a very brief response, Gordy maintained that the Blanc brothers could receive a fair trial in the parish and that the state would bring forth witnesses to support that position. With opening statements completed, Judge Debaillon directed the sheriff to bring in the two defendants. After he did so and just as the state was about to call its first witness, in a highly unusual turn of events in an already sensational series of legal proceedings, Charles D. Caffery and Ralph W. Elliott rose, approached the bar, and asked to be recognized. They apologized to the judge for having withdrawn as counsel for the accused and asked to be reinstated. Speaking for both lawyers, Caffery said, "I feel now that this was an error, and make this public declaration in order that there may be no mistake as to my position." Various possibilities might explain this sudden change of heart: perhaps the lawyers had regained their courage, or perhaps they were secure in the knowledge that a change of venue would not be granted, or perhaps they simply wanted to be associated with figures like Mouton and Breaux. Nonetheless, it was an olive branch, and the judge accepted it and issued his own apology. His rather harsh remarks delivered from the bench earlier in the week had not been meant to impugn their motives in resigning, Debaillon said. He was only expressing "his sincere disappointment of the affair at so late an hour." (Considering his blunt words to the press, it came as no surprise that Joe Chargois did not take part in this reconciliation.) With the concurrence of the defendants, the judge reappointed Caffery and Elliott to the defense's legal team. He then asked the district attorney to call his first witness.

Gordy and Campbell had gathered fifty of the leading citizens of the parish in the courtroom that Saturday morning. Each was sworn in, each testified briefly, and each rendered an opinion that Ernest and Alexis Blanc could receive a fair and impartial trial in Lafayette Parish. The first two witnesses, both Catholic priests, were symbolic. The first was the Frenchman Father Forge, pastor of St. John the Evangelist Church in Lafayette, who had officiated at the funeral of Martin Begnaud. Father Forge testified that "an honorable and impartial man would always render a verdict according to the dictates of his conscience, regardless of outside influence or excitement." Next, Father F. A. B. Laforest, a French Canadian and pastor of St. Peter's Church in Carencro, offered these words: "The accused can certainly obtain a fair and impartial trial, notwithstanding the public excitement and actual state of affairs." Of particular interest was the testimony from the leading citizens of the Scott Station area, Martin Begnaud's friends and neighbors. Alcide Judice, Alexandre Delhomme, and Louis G. Breaux were called to the stand. It was during Louis Breaux's testimony that the defense team tried to make its only argument for a change of venue. It was probably Breaux's disingenuous statement, "I have heard little of this affair, as the people are not inclined to speak about it," that prompted Governor Mouton to ask Breaux, on cross examination, what would happen to the Blancs if they were not convicted. The district attorney objected to the question on the grounds that it called for speculation. In defense of the inquiry, "Mouton argued that he wanted to prove to the court there exists a purpose and intent on the part of the population to execute justice if the court fails to secure conviction." The judge sustained Gordy's objection, and there were no further questions from the defense table for the duration of the hearing. N. P. Moss, the merchant who had sold the Blanc brothers their pistols a year earlier, testified as to the fine impartiality of Lafayette Parish juries, as did Louis Deleglise of Carencro, who offered the following: "I am from France, a native. There is no prejudice that I know which would prevent a fair trial." H. A. Van Dercruyssen, the enterprising publisher of the *Lafayette Advertiser,* who had hawked photographs of the accused to disappointed spectators for ten cents apiece on the previous Wednesday, disagreed with the assertion by the defendants that his pictures had inflamed the crowds. Born in Belgium and a native French speaker, Van Dercruyssen swore, "I sold about 250 pictures of the Blanc brothers. Accused can get a fair trial in my opinion." The state rested.

The defense team called no witnesses; it either could not find or did not seek to find a single citizen of Lafayette Parish who would testify in favor of the change of venue motion. Before issuing his ruling, Judge Debaillon could not resist lecturing once more on the evils of mob rule. Referring to the arrests of Hamp Benton and Gustave Balin, he said, "What a fearful crime might have been committed under public furor had not the vigilance of the officers of the court, in the discharge of their duty, conveyed the suspected persons beyond danger." Looking directly into the eyes of his courtroom audience, the judge warned, "You, gentlemen, are to blame if the laws are not executed." Regaining his decorum, he thanked all those who had testified that day. As a result of their testimony, the judge said, it was now "very clear that the prisoners at the bar can and shall have a fair and impartial trial. The motion for change of venue is, therefore, overruled." He then declared court adjourned.

Book VI

THE VILLAGE

Royville, Louisiana: October 1877

The epoch between the end of the Civil War and the beginning of the twentieth century witnessed a country united politically but divided economically: one nation, but split into two very unequal parts, North and South; one prosperous, urban, and industrial and the other poor, rural, and agricultural. It would take decades for Dixie to overcome the legacy of military defeat and occupation. But the South was not a monolith. There were isolated examples of progress and economic change, and even in hard times there were always entrepreneurs. In the postbellum decades of the 1870s, 1880s, and 1890s, the best hope for the economic development of a particular region or locale in the South was the infusion of northern capital. A considerable number of parishes of south Louisiana managed to escape the grinding poverty experienced by many of their rural neighbors because a rich, visionary capitalist from New York decided to build a railroad through the heart of New Acadia.

Charles "Commodore" Morgan was a multimillionaire who had made a fortune in shipping along the eastern seaboard and the Gulf of Mexico; his ships had long plied the waters between New Orleans and other Gulf and Caribbean ports, particularly Galveston, Texas, and Havana, Cuba. He was a man of vision who understood the potential of the American transportation industry. New and great fortunes were

to be made in railroading. Morgan's goal was to link the southern me-
tropolises of New Orleans and Houston by rail. He vowed to "show the
people of New Orleans how to build a road."

From a business perspective, Charles Morgan believed that his project was conceptually sound; the missing element was the stable political environment necessary to inspire investor confidence. Northern investors, initially attracted to the business opportunities available in the
economically depressed South, were becoming increasingly disen-
chanted by the corrupt practices of carpetbag regimes in Louisiana and
the other states of the old Confederacy. Morgan's excellent business
and political contacts in New York City and Washington, D.C., led
him to the inescapable conclusion that Reconstruction was fast drawing to a close. The Commodore understood that once federal troops
were removed from Louisiana, the Democratic Party—white and conservative—would regain power, and he foresaw that this would provide
the more stable political setting necessary to promote investor confidence. To prepare the way for his railroad proposal, Morgan began to
ally himself with the emerging leadership of the state Democratic
Party. After Reconstruction ended, Morgan's Democratic friends, now
in control of the governor's mansion and the state legislature, granted
two exclusive charters, one in 1877 and one in 1878, to companies controlled by Morgan for the purpose of building a railroad between New
Orleans and Houston: the Louisiana Western Railroad, building east
from the Sabine River on the Louisiana-Texas border near Orange,
Texas, and the Louisiana and Texas Railroad, building west from Morgan City (formerly Brashear City but renamed in 1879 in honor of its
great benefactor, who had connected it to New Orleans by rail some
years earlier). Morgan was generously given five years from the passage
of each act to complete the projects, and his company was empowered
by the legislation to deviate from "such a course or route as may be
deemed by the Directors most expedient." A third Morgan company,
the Texas and New Orleans, chartered in Texas, was already laying
track east from Houston to Orange.

In this very different political milieu, willing investors were found
and construction proceeded at a steady pace, but not nearly fast
enough. Several strikes on all three lines caused delays. Morgan had a

reputation for paying fair wages, but this was extremely strenuous work, and labor discontent was probably unavoidable. Progress was further slowed when a yellow fever epidemic hit Morgan City. Many railroad hands died, and construction, which had reached almost to New Iberia, came to a screeching halt because suppliers, for fear of contamination, refused to deliver steel rail and other supplies to Morgan City, the company's construction headquarters. These delays caused the railroad company to reassess its construction schedule and reexamine the proposed route. It was rumored that the Louisiana and Texas Railroad Company had decided to save time and money by laying the track directly westward from New Iberia to near Abbeville rather than northwestward through Vermilionville as originally planned. Track was being laid at roughly one-half mile per day in good weather. By eliminating the fifteen or so miles of track between New Iberia and Vermilionville, a more direct, westward route could realize considerable savings. But a newly elected state senator from New Orleans whose hometown was Vermilionville had other plans.

In November 1878, voters of the Fifth Senatorial District of Louisiana, representing the First and Tenth Wards of New Orleans (present-day Central City and the Garden District), elected Gustave A. Breaux to the state senate. Few politicians commanded more respect and admiration. A decorated Civil War veteran, Breaux had served as colonel and commander of the 13th Louisiana Infantry Regiment, seeing combat at the battles of Vicksburg, Port Hudson, and Baton Rouge. He was a graduate of Harvard Law School and senior partner of Breaux, Fenner and Hall, one of the state's most influential law firms, with offices in New Orleans and Vermilionville. His Oakbourne Plantation was a beautiful estate near Vermilionville and his landholdings in the parish were substantial. Other members of his family owned considerable acreage in the western part of the parish. Louis Gustave Breaux, his nephew, had homesteaded and purchased land about five miles directly west of Vermilionville. The alternate route for the railroad ran about ten miles south of Vermilionville and would bypass all the Breaux family properties. Indeed, it would bypass Lafayette Parish completely. And if that were not motivation enough, this more southern route would deny Vermilionville the opportunity of becoming the nexus of Morgan's two railroad lines. Abbeville would be the more likely candidate. The economic potential of that link for his hometown did not escape Senator Breaux. Before the war, prior to going off to law school in Massachusetts, Breaux had spent a year as a clerk in the senate, so he was no stranger to its inner workings. Such knowledge, together with his personal reputation, served him well in his challenge to the railroad interests.

With the Morgan line threatening to choose the alternate route, the freshman senator moved quickly. On Monday, January 6, 1879, the first day of the regular session of the legislature, Colonel Breaux introduced legislation that required the Morgan company to build its railroad "to Vermilionville." To impress upon the company the seriousness of his purpose, Breaux crafted the bill to stipulate that Morgan had eighteen months to complete construction between Morgan City and Vermilionville and another eighteen months for the section between the Texas border and Vermilionville or lose the charter. The Breaux legislation was signed into law by Governor Nicholls on January 30, 1879, and there was no further talk of bypassing Vermilionville. With time limits now set, the pace of construction quickened.

It seems likely that the use of convict labor was an unwritten part of the agreement between government and business, because all along the line from Morgan City to Lake Charles, pinstriped convicts could be seen at work on the railroad. Louisiana operated no state penitentiary at the time. Instead, the state "leased" its convicts out to a private concern. Since 1868, Major Samuel L. James had held the lease, and his reputation for brutality and for loaning out convicts to do private labor was notorious. Moreover, James was dependent on the state legislature to continue his lease. The Morgan companies met Senator Breaux's deadline, but it would not have happened without extensive use of chain gangs. In order to avoid any future misunderstanding with the state, the Morgan lines engaged Breaux, Fenner and Hall to represent its legal interests.

Charles Morgan did not live to see the completion of his work; he died on May 9, 1878. Fortunately for Louisiana, Charles A. Whitney, Morgan's vice president and son-in-law, and a very able executive in his own right, took control of the Morgan interests and saw the project through to its end. By March 1880, the Texas and New Orleans had linked Houston and Orange; by early May, the Louisiana and Texas had reached Vermilionville, linking it with Morgan City and New Orleans; and later that month, the Louisiana Western Railroad laid the last section of track in Lafayette Parish, thus linking Orange with Vermilionville. Charles Morgan's dream had become a reality. As expected, there was much celebrating, but a great deal of touch-up work needed to be done, and it was not until 1881 that the big locomotives of the Morgan lines, with large white stars painted on their fronts and sides, began operating in earnest.

The importance of the railroad in the economic and cultural development of south Louisiana cannot be overstated. Small towns fortunate enough to be in its path, like Lafayette and Lake Charles, would eventually grow into regional centers for commerce, banking, transportation, and education. Even more dramatic was the creation of entirely new communities on the vast Attakapas Prairie, villages and towns that owed their very existence to the railroad. The precise locations of such towns were not accidental. Railroad executives and land speculators were the key players in this game, and they were almost all nonlocals and *Américains*. (Acadians referred to anyone who did not speak French as an *Américain*. This practice was inherited from their ancestors and originated with the influx of non-French-speaking Americans into the area following the Louisiana Purchase.) Business contacts between company executives and land speculators with advance knowledge of the railroad route were the key ingredients to winning a railroad facility for a particular location. Prior to public disclosure of the route, the speculators would purchase large blocks of cheap prairie land at strategic intervals along it, and then refuse to sell the right-of-way unless the company agreed to construct a facility on their land. While it might appear that this approach had the potential to cause interminable delays and force bitter negotiations, such was not the case. The landowners of south Louisiana had two factors working in their favor: Charles Morgan's liberal policy of providing reasonable market access wherever a critical mass of goods and services showed potential, and the company's need to complete construction in a timely manner in order to remain in the good graces of the shareholders and the state. And once the trains came, the demand for land for businesses and homes could and did reach boom proportions. Land prices skyrocketed.

James G. Parkerson, an agent for the Morgan interest, and land speculators such as Benjamin Rayne and the Duson brothers, C. C. and W. W., founders of Louisiana towns like Crowley, Eunice, Duson, and Rayne, became wealthy men in this business. But such was the size and scope of the railroad enterprise that a few members of the local gentry—men of modest financial resources willing to risk everything—also found a place at the table. Scott, Louisiana, was one of those towns founded during the building of the railroad, but unlike its sister communities, Scott was not the creation of *Américain* railroad executives and land speculators. Instead, it owed its existence to two farmers, one a French immigrant and the other an Acadian, from the Royville community in Lafayette Parish. Their names were Dominique Cayret and Alcide Judice.

Dominique Cayret was born on August 4, 1817, at Tabre in the department of the Hautes Pyrénées, a mountainous region on France's southern frontier with Spain; the family later settled in Bordeaux, the largest city in the region. In France, young Dominique apprenticed himself to a master furniture maker and learned the craft well. He arrived in America in the early 1840s and eventually made his way to Louisiana. When Cayret, now a master craftsman in his own right, met virgin Louisiana cypress, the result was extraordinary. From the soft, supple wood native to the coastal swamps, Cayret created beds and armoires of incomparable strength and grace, and his creations came to be in great demand among the plantation aristocracy of south Louisiana. He eventually settled in Lafayette Parish, where he fell in love with an Acadian girl, Hortense Duhon. They were married on February 8, 1853, in the church of St. John the Evangelist in Vermilionville; she was fifteen, and he was thirty-six.

Hortense and the Duhon family lived near Royville (present-day Youngsville), in the southeast part of the parish near the Vermilion Parish line, and it was there that the newlyweds settled. With money earned from his craft, Cayret gradually expanded his landholdings in the Duhons' area of the parish. By 1860, he owned 68 acres. In 1861, a unique opportunity presented itself and Cayret added to his holdings a beautiful 130-acre farm on the east bank of Bayou Vermilion near Royville, purchased from the estate of one Victor Herpin. The property contained a large Acadian cottage that became home to the Cayret family. Two tenant families worked the soil and tended the livestock, and Cayret settled down to live the life of a gentleman farmer. By 1870, his holdings had reached 450 acres; in that year, he paid $640 in wages, owned $800 worth of livestock, and his farms produced a hundred bushels of wheat, four hundred of corn, and sixteen bales of cotton.

Cayret supplemented his agricultural income by occasionally accepting commissions to build pieces of his exquisite furniture. There is no record of his having served in the Civil War, and he probably did not—as a French citizen, he could have claimed neutrality. While it is not known if he resorted to the practice, it was not uncommon to see the French tricolor flying in front of the homes of recent French immigrants to Louisiana in the hope of warding off both Union and Confederate raiding parties and recruiters.

During the course of their marriage, Dominique and Hortense had twelve children, nine girls and three boys. A girl and a boy died in infancy; ten children grew to maturity. In 1871, their eldest child, a daughter named Marie Anaïs, married a truly extraordinary young man, and he would have a profound impact on the lives of the entire Cayret family.

Alcide Judice, the only son among the nine children of Gustave Judice and Elizabeth Doucet, was born on January 14, 1852, in Lafayette Parish. During the Civil War, Gustave Judice was wounded and captured and served a long and difficult imprisonment in a Yankee POW camp. He returned from the war and, according to family history, was never quite the same. In 1870, Alcide was eighteen years old. The decennial United States Census of that year lists this young man as leasing eighteen acres of land, from which he harvested only three bales of cotton. He was struggling. The following year he married seventeen-year-old Anaïs Cayret. Anaïs went on to serve as the catalyst for the remarkable business relationship that developed between her husband and her father.

As was the custom for struggling young couples, it is very likely that Alcide and his bride moved in with the Cayrets of Royville, and he probably went to work for his father-in-law as an overseer or manager.

From an early age, Alcide Judice's ambition was to be a man of commerce. He had no formal education, but he was exceptionally well read and well informed of current events, and while he understood and appreciated the value of agriculture and husbandry—the primary pursuits of his part of the world—he also recognized that the economy of the nation was in transition and that somehow all of this was connected to the railroad. Alcide could read, write, and speak both French and English, although he always remained uncomfortable speaking the latter. He was a handsome man, his youthful good looks giving way to great dignity in middle age. A son, Leo, was born to Alcide and Anaïs in 1872, and when it appeared that there would be no further issue, Judice began focusing all of his energies on achieving his ambition. New Orleans, *la Ville* to the Acadians, was the business capital of the whole mid-South; any young man interested in serious business opportunities would have to familiarize himself with its commercial establishment. Alcide Judice understood this reality and was a frequent visitor, traveling by boat down Bayou Teche to Morgan City, and from there on board one of the new trains of Morgan's Louisiana and Texas Railroad. Upon returning from one of these trips, Judice presented a proposal to his father-in-law, a proposal based on certain information he had obtained in New Orleans.

The year must have been 1877. New Orleans was a hotbed of activity: federal troops were being withdrawn, Francis T. Nicholls, a Confederate veteran and Democrat, had been inaugurated governor in January, and a newly elected, Democrat-controlled legislature was passing bills of major consequence at a dizzying pace. One bill in particular, Act 37 of 1877, would have been of special interest to Judice. It was the act that gave Morgan exclusive rights to build a railroad from Morgan City to the Sabine River. Its passage, together with one or more important business meetings in New Orleans, provided the opportunity Alcide Judice had been seeking. Perhaps his meetings were with officials of the Morgan line, or perhaps he simply overheard a conversation or was shown a revealing document—but in whatever setting, Judice obtained advanced knowledge of the route of the new railroad through south Louisiana. To take advantage of this privileged information he would have to act quickly, before the route became general knowledge.

He also needed serious financial backing, for his resources were slim and credit was difficult to obtain. Judice had one hope. Upon his return to Royville, he laid out his proposal to his father-in-law and requested his assistance. Dominique Cayret said *oui*.

Dominique Cayret was an intelligent man. He could read and write both French and English, and although he either did not speak or chose not to speak English, he understood it perfectly. In 1877, he was sixty years old and his wife was pregnant with their eleventh child. (Louise was born on August 16, 1877.) He was a large landowner and a craftsman of considerable reputation. By the standards of his day, Cayret was successful, even prosperous. Why would a man in his position, at his station in life, put all of his worldly possessions and the economic security of his family in jeopardy by agreeing to participate in his son-in-law's venture? Dominique Cayret took his reasons with him to the grave, so we can only speculate. During all the years spent in the United States, Cayret maintained a lively correspondence with his relatives in Bordeaux, who kept him briefed on developments at home as well as in the rest of France. They almost certainly mentioned the transportation revolution sparked by the railroad and its concomitant economic benefits: France, particularly during the Second Empire, was a European leader in railroad construction; in time, her rail system would be the envy of the world. Aware of the French experience, Cayret must have had an appreciation for the business potential of the railroad.

And perhaps Cayret's motivation had something to do with his three sons: Lucien, Dominique Jr., and Jacques. Jacques died in infancy, and Dominique Jr. died as a young man, married but childless. Lucien was something of a disappointment. He was not a strong personality, and both his personal life and his attempts at business were marked by failure. He, too, died childless. Perhaps Dominique Cayret somehow knew that both the Cayret name and the Cayret sedulity would end with his death. The Frenchman from Bordeaux may have seen a younger version of himself in Alcide Judice. But for whatever reasons, a business alliance was formed.

The plan presented to Cayret by Judice was straightforward but quite risky. The stakes were particularly high for Cayret, for he would have to liquidate all of his holdings in order to capitalize the venture. Moreover, both families would have to be uprooted. The Louisiana Western Railroad was to be built east to west at latitude thirty degrees north. Judice's plan called for the identification and purchase of land along that route that met three criteria. First, because their capital was limited, the land must be cheap, which meant it would probably be raw, undeveloped prairie. Second, the property must be large enough to allow for the construction of a mercantile establishment with warehouses, with some left over for speculation purposes and some for cultivation and livestock—a provision insisted upon by Cayret as a hedge against failure and also because he wanted to continue to farm. The third criterion was the most important: the railroad route must run directly through the property. This provision was crucial, for it would enable the owner to deny a right-of-way to the railroad and halt or at least delay construction. The idea was to facilitate a bargain with the Morgan line, offering the right-of-way in exchange for the railroad company's construction of a depot.

Judice and his father-in-law were probably looking for a tract of about two hundred acres. Naturally, all the land acquired for the venture would be in Cayret's name, with the understanding that the father-in-law would eventually convey to the son-in-law sufficient property to launch his commercial enterprise. Contingent upon a generous cash advance from Cayret and credit agreements he had arranged with several large New Orleans merchants, Judice planned to build and stock a modern retail mercantile establishment to serve the needs of the railroad and area families and businesses; he would also serve as a broker between his customers and the railroad and act as a commodities speculator. While Judice would make money from commerce, Cayret would profit from land speculation by selling lots to the businesses and families sure to be attracted to the new railroad settlement. If the latter failed to develop, however, the Frenchman could still raise cattle and farm.

In all likelihood, Judice and Cayret began their search in the land records of Lafayette Parish in hopes of finding something nearby, thereby minimizing relocation costs and easing the strain on their families. As it turned out, visits to other courthouses in other parishes along the proposed railroad route proved unnecessary. They found what appeared to be an ideal location in their home parish. A quiet reconnoitering of the property in question served only to heighten their expectations, as it met or surpassed all of their requirements.

The land was about five miles due west of Vermilionville directly in the path of the proposed railroad route. The general tranquillity of this place was known to have been shattered only once in recent memory, on that day some twenty years earlier when vigilantes from the area parishes selected the site to hang about eighty of their captives. Pastoral and sparsely populated, it was owned by a physician practicing in the parish, Dr. George Washington Pierre Soulé Scranton. Dr. Scranton's father, George Washington Scranton, a Connecticut native and a graduate of Yale's medical school, had relocated to Louisiana in 1840 seeking a warmer climate for health reasons. The senior Scranton established a medical practice in Lafayette Parish. In 1851 and 1852, he purchased several large blocks of public land in the western part of that parish at $1.25 per acre, probably for investment purposes. Following in his father's footsteps, the younger Scranton graduated from the University of Louisiana Medical School (later Tulane University) and went into medical practice in Lafayette Parish. Upon his father's death in 1853, the son inherited the land in question. Over the years, he had disposed of a few small tracts, but in 1877 he still owned 360 acres of undeveloped prairie, presumably leased to his neighbors for pasture. Typical of the Attakapas Prairie, Scranton's land was flat, interrupted only by an occasional majestic live oak. And there was one grove of about two dozen of those centuries-old, magnificent trees, the same trees that had attracted the vigilantes.

It did not take much imagination for Alcide Judice to envisage this site as the location of either a future business establishment or a residence or both. Scranton's land was bounded by three large ranches: Alexandre Delhomme's on the west and north, Colonel A. D. Boudreaux's on the east, and to the south, across a public road, Louis Gustave Breaux's. In the twentieth century, that public road would be proclaimed the "Old Spanish Trail," but in the 1870s it had no such pretensions. It was simply a public dirt road, muddy and impassable much of the year. Yet Cayret and Judice, being men of vision, may have grasped its potential as a complementary transportation artery, thus adding value to the Scranton site. All three of Scranton's contiguous neighbors were grizzled Civil War veterans with large families, and all had managed to survive the economic vicissitudes of Reconstruction and retain ownership of at least most of their land. They were not wealthy men, but they were respected and industrious. Judice was probably impressed by the fact that these men and their neighbors supported a school for local children. It was called the Begnaud School and located on the *vacherie* of Alexandre Begnaud, about two miles northeast of the Scranton property. The little one-room cypress schoolhouse was originally built by Begnaud to provide a place where his fourteen children might be instructed in the basics, but the school was soon adopted by most of the white families of the area. Elementary grades one through six were usually taught by an itinerant teacher four to six months a year; instruction was in French. The teacher, always a male, boarded with Alexandre and Lise Begnaud, while the remaining families of the children attending the school paid his salary. A champion of education all of his adult life, Judice may have had a personal interest in the little school: his five-year-old son, Leo, was the perfect age to be a prospective student.

It was not necessary for Cayret to purchase all of Dr. Scranton's land west of Vermilionville, but it was absolutely essential that he gain ownership of those tracts through the center of which the proposed railroad route ran, plus a little more for development. Cayret and Judice would approach Scranton and hope for the best. No one knows for certain what took place during the negotiations, but on October 13, 1877, at Royville, Louisiana, in the offices of Francis P. Parent, notary public, and witnessed by two citizens, Jacques Bommissien and Pierre Duffon, two legal documents were simultaneously executed. In one transaction, Dominique Cayret sold a tract of land to George W. Scranton "in this parish of Lafayette, State of Louisiana, on the eastern side of Bayou Vermilion and containing one hundred and thirty acres and edifices together with all improvements, buildings and fencing for the price and sum of three thousand and two hundred dollars." This was the farm acquired by Cayret in 1861 from the succession of Victor Herpin. In the other transaction, George W. Scranton sold to Dominique Cayret four contiguous tracts of land: "1st a certain tract of land situated in this parish . . . containing two hundred and forty-five (245) acres, more or less. 2nd a piece of land . . . in this parish containing forty 27/100 acres more or less. 3rd a certain tract of land situated in this parish containing thirty-five acres, more or less. . . . The said George W. Scranton further sells . . . a certain tract of land containing forty acres, more or less . . . for the price and sum of three thousand dollars." Cayret thus acquired all of Scranton's land west of Vermilionville, a total of 360 acres. Some money changed hands, but the deal was fundamentally a land swap.

It is interesting to note that the parcels exchanged were not equal in size or monetary value. Dr. Scranton paid Cayret two hundred dollars more and received fewer acres in the exchange. Obviously, Scranton thought he was getting the better of the deal, and on the surface he was. He was now the proud owner of a productive farm located in the rich, alluvial soil along Bayou Vermilion, a comfortable home with barns and fences and two established tenants to do all the work. Scranton would probably earn more in two or three years from this acquisition than the total earnings produced from his western prairie lands since their acquisition. Also, the doctor may have been thinking of the future, for Vermilionville's city fathers had long talked of deepening the channel and turning Bayou Vermilion into a reliable year-round navigable stream with an outlet to the Gulf of Mexico. Scranton had to have calculated the potential real estate value of Cayret's east bank property when he agreed to the land swap. But the future of economic development, at least in this part of the world, was by land and not by sea, and the real winners in the deal were Dominique Cayret and Alcide Judice. They moved immediately to implement the next phase of their plan: the relocation of their families to the Scranton site.

18

Scott Station, Louisiana: February 1881

Dominique Cayret eventually sold all of his Royville-area farms and deployed his accumulated capital to the development of his new holdings. Soon after he closed the deal with Scranton, he had work begun on a new home on the prairie. Cayret had no wish to live too near a railroad track or too near any neighbors. He enjoyed the country life.

The site he chose for his family's new residence was located on the northeasternmost part of his property, approximately one-half mile from the cluster of live oak trees where the tracks were expected to be laid and where his son-in-law planned to build his mercantile store. It was a beautiful location. The site was on a slight rise and contained two grand live oak trees, and the house was built facing south under the shade of their giant limbs. The home was a large, stately two-story raised cottage made of cypress, large enough to be a comfortable dwelling for the very young and very feminine Cayret household. There were galleries or porches on all four sides, and the front or south side faced the Old Spanish Trail. The first floor consisted of three bedrooms, a parlor or living room, a large kitchen, and a dining room, with fireplaces in the parlor and kitchen. The ceilings were ten feet high. The upstairs consisted of one spacious bedroom, probably assigned to the six single Cayret daughters. In the Acadian fashion, the stairs leading to the second story were located outside on the west gallery. The front door was flanked by sidelights with a transom above. The house was painted dark green, with full shutters on its many windows, which were opened and closed as dictated by Louisiana's extreme weather conditions; cypress shingles covered the roof. The outhouse, barns, tool sheds, and corrals were located behind the house. At the end of 1878, in residence at the new Cayret home on the Attakapas Prairie were—in addition to Mr. and Mrs. Cayret—baby Louise and her five sisters, two brothers, married sister Anaïs, her husband Alcide, and their son Leo. This arrangement lasted only a short time, for as soon as the house was finished, Cayret had begun building a dwelling for the Judices. Similar in style and construction but much smaller, only one story, it stood about a quarter mile west of the Cayret residence; from the porch that spanned the front of her house and faced east, Anaïs Judice had a clear view of her parent's abode. The Judice's raised cottage had two bedrooms, a living room, and a combination kitchen/dining room with a fireplace. All these rooms had twelve-foot ceilings. In a short time, the Cayret women had worn a distinct path between the two houses. By early 1879, both families were comfortably established in their new surroundings.

Alcide Judice's plan for prosperity was not foolproof. Many things could go wrong. The greatest threat, of course, was that the railroad would not come their way, and as we have seen, that almost happened in late 1878. The anxiety experienced by the two entrepreneurs must have been palpable when they learned that the railroad might bypass their property in favor of a more southern route. We do not know the degree to which they lobbied Senator Breaux for his assistance in preventing this catastrophe, but it is almost certain that Cayret and Judice shared the closely held knowledge of the proposed railroad route with their new neighbor, the senator's nephew Louis Gustave Breaux, for the value of his property would also be enhanced by the coming of the iron horse. And even though the senator needed little or no persuasion, it is also highly probable that his friends and relatives in the western part of the parish made their wishes known to him in forceful and unmistakable fashion. His success in mandating the routing of the Morgan line through Vermilionville—and, as a result, through their lands—must have been greeted with great relief.

On the other hand, the same legislation made it easier for railroad companies to obtain rights-of-way by expropriating now and paying later. The law did not prevent Dominique Cayret from playing his trump card, however; in early 1879, when the Louisiana Western Railroad approached him for a right-of-way through his property, he refused—but was quick to add that he would gladly grant a right-of-way on the most favorable terms if the railroad company agreed to construct a depot on his land. Perhaps the Morgan line was favorably disposed, perhaps it was Senator Breaux's influence, perhaps it was Alcide Judice's contacts with railroad company executives, or perhaps it was a combination of all of these and other factors, but for whatever reason, the Louisiana Western Railroad acceded to Cayret's demands. A depot would be built on his property. The deed was consummated on May 10, 1879. Dominique Cayret sold the Louisiana Western Railroad a right-of-way through his land for the grand sum of $1:

> Be it known, that whereas the Louisiana Western Railroad Company are now locating and about constructing their Railroad between Vermilionville, Louisiana, and the Sabine River, to connect with the railroad running to Houston, Texas; and the said road is to pass through my property and, it is believed, will increase its value; in consideration thereof, and of the payment to me of one dollar, which I acknowledge to have received, I hereby sell a tract of land through my property one hundred feet wide . . . to be used by said company for their track or for any other purpose connected with the building or maintaining said road.

It is justifiable to say that both the Louisiana Western Railroad and Dominique Cayret made good deals. Now the pace of activity quickened as the railroad moved to meet its state-imposed and self-imposed deadlines. On December 6, 1879, the *Lafayette Advertiser* reported that "track is sixteen miles east of Lake Charles." On May 4, 1880, the *Daily Picayune* reported, "All track is laid to a point six miles from Vermilionville," and on May 17, 1880, "All work is done." These dates seemingly indicate that track was laid through the Cayret property on or near the anniversary of the sale, May 10. One can imagine Delhommes, Boudreauxs, Breauxs, Begnauds, Judices, Cayrets, and the other adults and children of the area as spectators, cheering the workmen as they laid each section of rail. The center of attention was probably the construction superintendent in charge, G. P. Scott.

A few months later, sometime during the summer of 1880, the Morgan company informed Cayret of some unexpected but very welcome news. The L.W.R.R. would establish on his land not just a depot but a full-blown railroad station, complete with a section house for a section foreman and his crew, a home for the stationmaster and his family, and a depot offering full passenger and freight service. The company wanted to begin construction immediately. The station would be the first stop on the Louisiana Western Railroad line for westbound traffic. The station in Vermilionville was the western terminus of the L.W.R.R.'s sister company, the Louisiana and Texas Railroad; all traffic going farther west would be on track owned by the Louisiana Western. A different carrier meant that additional freight and passenger charges would be imposed. People and produce traveling west from Vermilionville were required to pay the "western" rates at Scott Station, the name chosen for the new railroad stop. (The choice of a name was made by area residents, who had been requested to come up with one by the L.W.R.R.) Until consolidation of the railroad lines some years later, Scott Station was the western gatekeeper for the L.W.R.R. Because Scott Station was thus synonymous with western tolls, the citizens of Vermilionville began referring to the little station as "where the West begins." The motto remains alive today.

The section house on the north side of the track was built first, followed by the depot directly across from the section house. But there was a problem. The hundred-foot-wide right-of-way sold to the railroad by Cayret for one dollar was inadequate to encompass the full-sized station. More land was needed on both sides of the track. Additional buildings were also needed, as well as a sidetrack about four hundred yards long on the depot (south) side to permit loading and unloading of cargo from the depot's docks and adjacent commercial warehouses without interrupting traffic on the main line. Would Cayret allow the railroad to proceed with the necessary construction with the understanding that fair compensation would be forthcoming when the company's land agents could arrange for the actual purchase? Cayret readily agreed. While all of this activity was taking place, Alcide

Judice was not idle. He had already started building his store and ware-houses. On June 2, 1880, just three weeks after the railbed was laid through Cayret's property, Judice purchased from his father-in-law the acreage that contained the beautiful grove of live oaks that now ran along the track just east of the new depot:

> Mr. Dominique Cayret of said Parish and State does . . . sell . . . unto Mr. Alcide Judice also of said Parish and State . . . a certain tract of prairie land situated in said Parish and lying ten arpents running East and West by three arpents North and South and is [*sic*] bounded on the South side of the Louisiana Western Railroad near the switch of said Road and where the buildings of the present Vendee are being erected. Vendor also sells to the present Vendee a roadside enough so that two vehicles may pass beside the other with safety, on the North side by said rail road to run in an East-erly direction. This sale made and accepted for and in consideration of the price and sum of one hundred and twenty-five dollars.

The Judice Store opened its doors for business in early 1881. On February 21, Cayret and the railroad company legalized their land deal of the previous year. For "ninety-five dollars cash," Cayret sold two strips of land, one on the north side of the track for the completed sec-tion house and one on the south side for the side track and depot which was "being erected." In this transaction, Cayret also granted "a servitude to the public over my said lands for reaching said depot building for the shipping and receiving of freights and embarking of passengers."

The third and final edifice that would complete Scott Station, the stationmaster's residence, was built either during or shortly after this flurry of construction activity of 1880 and 1881. Because it was to be the home of the highest-ranking company official in residence, the railroad company wanted the house to reflect that status. Cayret agreed to build a suitable home at his expense and on his land, near the other railroad facilities, in exchange for a long-term lease of the house by the Louisiana Western Railroad. Stationmasters assigned to Scott Station might have found reasons to dislike their posting, but the quality of their living quarters was not one of them. The home was vintage Dom-inique Cayret. He constructed the stationmaster's house, as he had his own, in a picturesque setting between two magnificent live oak trees. The site was about a hundred yards south of the depot, across the road deeded by Cayret to Alcide Judice as part of their June 1880 conveyance. A large, one-story, raised and very handsome Victorian cottage, it faced north, and from its spacious front porch the stationmaster had a clear view of the track, the depot, and the section house. A large parlor, entered from the front porch, occupied the center of the house, giving way to a dining room that could seat twenty comfortably. The dining room opened into a back gallery and a moderate-sized kitchen. The east wing was taken up by two large bedrooms and a small water closet, while a large front bedroom made up the west wing. (Later, the west wing was enlarged into a master bedroom suite with a dressing area and a spacious water closet.) Behind the house was a carriage shed that could accommodate two vehicles; a storeroom was attached to the shed. In the backyard another giant live oak provided shade on hot summer days. There were no neighbors to the west, only flat, open prairie land; but next door to the east was the emerging business complex of Alcide Judice. As far as the L.W.R.R. was concerned, Scott Station was now fully operational.

Amid an atmosphere of excitement and anticipation, Scott Station became a reality in 1881. But business activity and railroading were not the only factors contributing to the festive atmosphere; there were also some exciting events in the personal lives of the two founding families of the fledgling hamlet. Mother and daughter, Hortense Duhon Cayret and Anaïs Cayret Judice, were both pregnant, probably unexpectedly. Julie Nita Cayret was born on July 10, 1881, the twelfth and last child of Dominique and Hortense Cayret. Anaïs Bella Judice was born on October 2, 1881. She and her nine-year-old brother Leo would be the only children born to Alcide and Anaïs Judice. Since the Cayrets considered themselves residents of the "country" and the Judices were considered "town" folk, family history claims Bella Judice as the first child born in Scott Station, Louisiana.

19

Scott Station was a company town, a railroad company town. The stationmaster was the highest-ranking railroad official in residence. His job was a midlevel, white-collar management position; a stationmaster (or station agent) was usually in charge of a small or medium-sized station. He and his family, if he had one, lived in a home provided by the company. If he was single—and many of these young men were—the section foreman, the number two company man in the line of authority, might also reside in the home assigned to his boss.

The duties of the stationmaster at a small station were demanding: sell passenger tickets, make change, answer and send telegraph messages, keep the books, tend the switches, handle baggage, make certain that all commercial freight was loaded and unloaded properly, and collect freight charges. A vigorous physical condition was an obvious prerequisite for the job, but a stationmaster also needed a certain amount of diplomatic skill. In the words of one railroad historian, "He must be ready, like the conductor, to submit to some abuse from ill-bred customers, and should be the peer of the businessmen of his town." Occasionally, laborers might be available to help with the heavy lifting, but there were no clerks. If business increased to a level sufficient to warrant the employment of an assistant, that post was usually filled by a young woman to help with the telegraphing and ticket sales. If the stationmaster was unmarried, it was not uncommon for a love interest to develop between these two; as we shall see, this may have been the case in Scott Station.

Once a railroad was completed, it was common industry practice in the 1880s to have a section foreman in charge of maintaining track in his section, usually five to eight miles in length, with a crew of four to twelve laborers under his supervision. They were required to ride the rails twice daily in handcars to make certain that every joint of the track was firmly in place. They removed obstructions, restored downed telegraph lines and poles, drained standing water from the ditches that ran on either side of the raised rail bed (wet ground could undermine the gravel below the track), and inspected and, if necessary, repaired all bridges and trestles in their section.

The section foreman at Scott Station and his crew lived in the section house on the north side of the track, across from the depot. It was a big one-story house made of rough-hewn cypress timbers. A deep porch ran across the entire front of the house, where the men sat, chewed tobacco, spit, played cards or dominoes, and gossiped on warm southern nights. Inside were three communal rooms: a bunk room for sleeping, a kitchen, and a large combination recreation/living/dining room. Heat was supplied by one immense fireplace, which was also used for cooking. In the backyard, a four-seater outhouse serviced the residents.

The center of railroad activity in Scott Station was the depot. In design and size it was like most others of its kind built by railroad companies throughout the United States in the second half of the nineteenth century: rectangular in shape, high-pitched roof, loading docks on two sides, and painted unmistakable railroad yellow. The primary entrance was on the north side of the building that faced the main track. Inside was a large room filled with benches for passengers waiting for their trains. This room ended at the ticket office, where all business was transacted; the ticket office doubled as the telegraph office and the office of the stationmaster/agent. A side door led into a cavernous warehouse containing all manner of freight awaiting shipment. Massive sliding doors provided easy access to the loading platforms.

Around the turn of the century, railroad consolidation caused Scott

Station to be downsized from a fully operational station to a whistle-stop. During the brief twenty years before that happened, the village was a beehive of commercial activity, and Alcide Judice led the way. In only a few years he became one of the wealthiest, most respected, and most admired men in Lafayette Parish.

In addition to the credit due his own foresight, Judice owed his success to Scott Station's overnight transformation into a magnet for virtually all the commercial, business, transportation, and financial activity in the entire western part of the parish. *Le Magasin de Judice,* the Judice Store, was the only mercantile establishment in the area. The place was swarming with people with money in their pockets: railroad men, from executives to laborers; farmers and ranchers bringing cotton and cattle and other produce and livestock almost daily for storage in Judice's warehouses until they could be loaded onto the trains; these same men needing plows, harnesses, wagons, or buggies; their wives and families shopping for everything from shoes to Sunday bonnets; and the ever-increasing number of travelers boarding and disembarking from the passenger trains.

There was no organized bank in the parish in the 1880s, but a farmer or rancher or railroad man of good reputation could always obtain a loan or credit at fair interest from Alcide Judice. His large black steel safe, five feet high, was quite a conversation piece. It was admired by the patrons and gave an air of professionalism and security to the establishment. Even the purchase of a stamp or the posting of a letter required a visit to the Judice Store: on May 21, 1883, the United States Postal Service established a post office at Scott Station; Alcide Judice became the first postmaster and the actual post office was located in a corner of his big mercantile store.

But Judice was more than just a middleman. He understood the economic benefits and potential of a vertical monopoly, a concept one of his contemporaries, John D. Rockefeller, was pioneering in the oil business on a much grander scale. Judice began his own brand of vertical monopoly by investing his money in farms. By 1895, he owned a total of fourteen producing farms or ranches, all in the Eighth Ward of Lafayette Parish. (All parishes in Louisiana are subdivided into wards.) Worked by tenants and sharecroppers, the average Judice farm measured about forty-five acres; his total acreage in production in that year was 638. Scott Station south of the railroad track, including Judice's store and warehouses, was (is) in the Eighth Ward. Thus, within three to four miles extending south, east, and west throughout the ward, Judice owned not only the principal retail and storage operations but also numerous production facilities that could trade only with him and would plant crops determined by him to be the most profitable in any given year. He was a voracious reader and kept au courant of business trends and commodity prices. If cotton prices were depressed, as they often were in the second half of the nineteenth century, sugarcane could be planted instead. If federal sugar support subsidies—always a favorite of Louisiana politicians in Washington—were endangered, the cultivation of rice was an option. And the proximity of his Scott Station operation to his numerous agricultural properties made for easy supervision and fast farm-to-market delivery.

For strictly speculative purposes, Judice had also acquired large blocks of cheap swampland in Calcasieu and St. Martin Parishes, which in the twentieth century became the sites of major oil and gas discoveries. His stock portfolio, heavily concentrated in fledgling Louisiana-based oil and banking companies, was impressive. It was not surprising that when the first bank in Lafayette Parish was organized in 1891, the People's State Bank and Trust Company, Alcide Judice was a charter member of its board of directors. In 1895, when the bank was granted a federal charter and reorganized as the First National Bank of Lafayette, Judice was one of its largest shareholders and a founding member of its board of directors.

A naturally inquisitive man, Alcide Judice kept abreast of national and world affairs. He and two friends from Scott Station may have been the only residents of the area to attend the 1893 Chicago World's Fair, officially called the Columbian Exposition. Originally planned to open the previous year to commemorate the four-hundredth anniversary of Columbus's voyage, the fair turned out to have so many exhibits that its opening had to be postponed for a year. Of the huge fair's many themes, the power of electricity was probably the most impressive. Although the power source was not yet in practical use and was years away from rural America (not reaching Scott, Louisiana, until 1926), the Westinghouse Company set up the world's largest electric lighting plant and generated enough electricity to light up the entire fair. Not to be outdone, Westinghouse's chief competitor, General Electric, broke the night sky with the largest light ever built, a six-thousand-pound searchlight. Its ray could be seen for miles. Buildings at the exposition displayed the latest locomotives, kitchen appliances, farm equipment, and everything imaginable from the mundane to the extraordinary. While at the fair, Judice may have ridden on a new invention designed by George W. G. Ferris, who obtained a concession from the exposition to construct a giant ride for the public; the Ferris wheel was an instant success. And Judice and his friends almost certainly took in a performance of Buffalo Bill's Wild West show, which had just returned to America after a spectacularly successful four-year tour of Europe. This World's Fair was the experience of a lifetime, and Judice never tired of regaling his family and friends and business associates with stories about it.

It was journalistic practice in the nineteenth and even the early twentieth century, particularly in small towns, for newspapers to inform their readers of important out-of-town personages who were visiting or had recently visited the community. Two weeklies were published in the parish seat of Lafayette, the *Gazette* and the *Advertiser,* and if either editor was aware of the presence of Alcide Judice within the corporate limits, it made the news. He was regularly identified by the two newspapers as "the big merchant from Scott Station."

As the 1880s unfolded, others sought to establish businesses in the village. Whether several acres for a cotton gin or a single lot for a home, the land had to be purchased from Dominique Cayret. In October of 1882, two brothers, Martin and Simeon Begnaud, formed a partnership and purchased one-fourth of an arpent of land from Cayret for fifty dollars. This large lot was located north of and alongside the railroad track. The two bachelors, ages thirty-two and twenty-eight respectively, were the sons of Alexandre and Lise Begnaud, born and raised on their father's *vacherie* about two miles northeast of the new railroad station. Although their father was a modestly successful farmer and rancher, there were fourteen siblings to consider, and given Louisiana's forced heirship laws, inheritance was not a promising career option for Martin and Simeon. Besides, the world of business and commerce they saw emerging at Scott Station was far more inviting than the drudgery of farm labor. They reached the conclusion that all of those railroaders with time on their hands and money in their pockets, to say nothing of the local farmers and ranchers, needed another place to spend their money besides the Judice Store. What Scott Station needed, the brothers decided, was a saloon.

Begnaud's Tavern, the community's second business enterprise, opened its doors in the spring of 1883, and it was very successful. The saloon faced south, its front door about thirty yards from the railroad track. The two Begnaud brothers were very different in both appearance and personality. Martin was tall—over six feet—gaunt, soft-spoken, courtly, and gentle; Simeon was short and stocky, self-assured, aggressive, and extroverted. Simeon loved the bar business and Martin did not. Martin believed the partnership should diversify and Simeon agreed; the younger brother would continue running the saloon while his big brother would run their new venture: a general store. The phenomenal success of their neighbor across the tracks, Alcide Judice, served as a model for Martin Begnaud. In March of 1887, the Begnaud partnership purchased another parcel of land from Dominique Cayret for fifty dollars, this time half an arpent. It was adjacent to and east of the lot occupied by Begnaud's Tavern.

By January 1888, Begnaud's General Store was ready to open its doors. It was not as large as the Judice Store, but the Begnaud brothers built a warehouse behind the store to handle excess inventory and to lay up commodities, hence the need for a larger piece of real estate. Like Begnaud's Tavern, the new business faced the railroad track. It was first and foremost a dry goods store, selling most—but not all—of the sundries and hardware items available across the track at *le Magasin de Judice*. A practical man, Begnaud knew that he did not possess the resources or the experience to compete head-to-head with Alcide Judice. Instead, he decided to specialize in two less competitive commodities: rice and eggs.

Cotton was the biggest cash crop in Lafayette Parish. Almost overnight, the prairie land in the western section now served by Scott

Station became the top cotton-producing area of the parish. Cotton gins sprang up like mushrooms in the village. By the mid-1890s, there were five gins at Scott Station turning out between three and four thousand bales of cotton a year, roughly a quarter of the parish's entire output. (The much larger town of Lafayette was home to only three gins.) Bales of cotton are enormous and heavy and require much warehouse space as well as labor for loading and unloading. With limited space and capital, Martin Begnaud decided to bypass the cotton market altogether and concentrate on the growing market for rice. Beginning in 1887, depressed cotton prices resulted in many area farmers planting rice as an alternative. After making arrangements with rice brokers in New Orleans, Begnaud set out to convince the rice growers that he possessed the contacts and the ability to obtain top dollar for their staple. The race to gin the first bale of cotton of the year in the parish had always been a newsworthy event greeted with much anticipation by the entire population. So too was the race to ship the first consignment of rice. The August 23 edition of the *Advertiser* announced the 1890 winner: "Martin Begnaud shipped last week to W. B. Thompson and Co., 20 sacks of rice, weighing about 3,671 lbs. This is the first shipment from the parish."

Begnaud also knew that the demand for eggs by the housewives of New Orleans and Houston was substantial and held the potential for providing a steady source of customers and income. Having grown up on a farm, Martin knew the nutritional value of eggs, and he also knew that the person on most farms in charge of gathering and selling eggs was the lady of the house. Using all of his considerable charm, he traveled over the countryside persuading farmers and their wives and daughters to raise more chickens in order to produce more eggs, and to sell their surplus to him. Begnaud had a built-in head start: his eight sisters (two had died by 1888) all lived in the area and all were married to farmers and ranchers. In April 1889 the *Advertiser* reported, "There are two crops that never fail at Scott in the Springtime—eggs and babies." The following spring the same paper proclaimed, "Martin Begnaud has a corner on eggs . . . he has been shipping a large number of dozens of eggs each week. Scott has always been a great egg center."

The Begnaud brothers' partnership was doing well. In 1889, Simeon expanded the tavern, adding a restaurant and oyster bar. In 1895, Martin purchased 150 acres of land about two miles north of Scott Station. Following the example set by Alcide Judice, Begnaud planned to grow his own produce, probably rice, for his own business purposes. It was about this time, too, that the Lafayette papers began to mention that Martin Begnaud had reportedly been seen in town. He was tabbed by the local press as "the enterprising merchant" from Scott Station.

In addition to the five cotton gins, the Judice and Begnaud stores, and Begnaud's Tavern, the obvious economic opportunities unfolding at Scott Station attracted the attention of other entrepreneurs. Cayret did a brisk business in land sales. In late 1888, Jules Guidry opened Scott Station's third mercantile store. The following year saw the opening of the first "Coffee House," which seems to have been a saloon that also served coffee. As such, it provided Begnaud's Tavern with its first competition. Peck's Coffee House was owned and operated by Alphonse Peck and was located on the north side of the track and facing it, just west of and next door to Begnaud's Tavern. Also in 1889, Marcel Sonnier opened a sugar mill to take advantage of the increased production of sugarcane in the area as farmers continued to diversify as a result of depressed cotton prices. Sonnier's mill produced only syrup and remained in successful operation for many years. But it was the opening of the Hotel St. Paul that brought real cohesion and community spirit to the village. Built by Jules Guidry, the hotel was a huge two-story wooden structure located next door to the section house on the east, almost directly across the track from the depot. It opened in 1889 and was greatly welcomed by the many Southern Pacific executives visiting Scott Station on railroad business who had previously been forced to bunk in the section house.

In 1890, Guidry converted the upstairs into a dance hall, which soon became the major social gathering place of the community. Three hundred people attended the first ball, in January of 1890. Both the upstairs and the downstairs of the Hotel St. Paul had two wide galleries that extended the full length of the building on both the south side, facing the railroad track, and the east side. Several large rocking chairs were available for hotel guests on the downstairs gallery, while the upstairs gallery was popular as a promenade for strolling and courting during dances and other social engagements. The Hotel St. Paul and its large dance hall provided a venue for the emergence of a society and culture in the community. In addition to the regularly scheduled dances sponsored by the hotel and held four times a year, one every calendar quarter, the big second-story hall was the scene of wedding receptions, political meetings, concerts, performances of the Scott Drama Association, celebrations (Mardi Gras, the Fourth of July, and Bastille Day were the three biggest) and benefits like the annual dinner for the Catholic Knights.

Possibly the form of entertainment most enjoyed by the citizens of Scott Station was the baseball games played on Sunday afternoons in the spring and summer by the Scott Station Hard-to-Beats, all of whom were African Americans. Their stiffest competition came from the teams from Frogtown (Rayne) and Breaux Bridge. The games, played on a diamond north of the village in a pasture owned by Alexandre Delhomme, were characterized by amazing plays and high scores. Every game was a sellout and spectators and fans, black and white, cheered for the home team. The winning team was usually presented with a keg of beer provided by "Miyon," as Simeon Begnaud was known except during Mardi Gras, when he donned a mask and costume and became the "Count of Mixology."

Understandably, the quest for economic advancement was paramount for the businessmen of Scott Station, but they did not lose sight of the commonweal. The first civic activity undertaken by the village leaders was in the field of education, and their approach to this endeavor was singular. The first school built in the village, in 1889, was a "colored" school. It was almost certainly a one-room schoolhouse with several grades taught simultaneously, because it had only one teacher, a Mr. A. B. Johnson. It was located about one-half mile northwest of the depot on land donated by Alexandre Delhomme. The school was privately built and operated through the generosity of the leading citizens of the community, but open to the public; all black children were invited to attend. While it is true that white students could attend the old Begnaud School, the fact that a group of white men in the Deep South of that time would come together to underwrite the education of black children bespeaks a degree of enlightenment. Education was clearly the village's top priority. By 1895, white families clustered in and around

Scott Station counted more than seventy-five children of educable age. A new, larger school, more centrally located, was needed for them. On land donated by Louis G. Breaux on the south side of the track facing the Old Spanish Trail, about a quarter of a mile directly south of the depot, the Lafayette Parish School Board built a new Scott School. Grades one through eight were offered, the standard for that time, by a staff of two teachers. The Begnaud School was closed down.

In the nineteenth century, the single most serious impediment to education in rural America was transportation: how to get children from the farm to school and back again. Even where roads were passable—and most were not—a majority of farm families simply could not afford to divert wagons and horses or mules needed for plowing and harvesting, or to expend the personal time required to convey their children to and from school. Alcide Judice solved that problem for the families of Scott Station and the entire surrounding area. Every morning and every afternoon along designated routes fanning out in every direction, teams of covered wagons owned by Judice and driven by teamsters employed by him provided free transportation to and from the Scott School. It has been suggested that this effort may have been the first organized school transportation system in the United States. Judice's simple yet eloquent epitaph is certainly appropriate: "Educate the Child."

No one in Scott Station ever lost sight of the fact that the Southern Pacific Railroad was the backbone of the village's economy. In addition to day-to-day operations and maintenance and an incredible amount of freight activity, passenger service and mail delivery continually increased. In rural nineteenth-century America, roads were few and unreliable, and anyone seeking to journey any considerable distance traveled by train. Scott Station was on the San Francisco and New Orleans line of the Southern Pacific Railroad Company. Four passenger trains, two heading east and two heading west, stopped daily to load and unload travelers. The eastbound trains, final destination New Orleans, arrived at the Scott Station depot at 5 A.M. and 12:40 P.M. The westbound Sunset Limited arrived at 4:05 A.M., final destination San Francisco, and the other westbound passenger train, final destination San Antonio, Texas, arrived at 11:16 P.M.

The man responsible for the safety of these passengers, as well as for every other phase of the railroad operation at Scott Station, was the stationmaster. Although the record is unclear, it appears that Scott Station had several different agents from its inception in 1881 until 1888. But in 1888 a new stationmaster arrived and remained for ten years. He was a career railroad man who fell in love, literally, with his new Acadian neighbors. His name was James Thomas Mulkern, and he had been known by his initials, J. T., before he came to Scott Station, where he was promptly tagged "Muldoon," after a popular fictional character in Irish jokes of the day. For the Acadians of south Louisiana, there is no clearer sign of acceptance and affection than to be given and called by a *petit nom*, a nickname. Mulkern's quick entrance into this status was quite extraordinary in light of the fact that he was a Yankee, born in Milford, Ohio, and raised in Dubuque, Iowa. His father, John Thomas Mulkern, had been born in Ballinasloe, Ireland, and had immigrated to the United States as a teenager. In exchange for citizenship, he had served four years with the 29th Illinois Infantry during the Civil War. After the war, he had remained in the Midwest, eventually settling in Dubuque, where he entered the cooperage business and was active in the local chapter of the Grand Army of the Republic.

The senior Mulkern was not only a patriot but also a devout Roman Catholic, two traits he passed on to his son, who was born in 1865. J. T. graduated from Baylies Commercial College in Dubuque in 1884 and went to work for the Southern Pacific. He progressed up the employment ladder, and in 1888 was given his first independent posting, as stationmaster at Scott Station. He was wiry, strong, and very short, barely five feet. He worked hard, played hard, and—probably unlike his predecessors—was Catholic, three traits that made him instantly popular with his Acadian neighbors.

One of Mulkern's best friends was fellow bachelor Martin Begnaud. They enjoyed each other's company and took great delight in teasing and playing practical jokes on each other and on others. During the Fourth of July celebration of 1889, at a ball and fireworks display at the St. Paul Hotel, Begnaud, in earshot of all, proclaimed that the Fourth of July was a Yankee holiday and should not be celebrated by "good Confederates." Muldoon, his Irish up, rose to the bait and challenged

Begnaud to back up his insult with his fists. It was quite a sight, the big merchant and the little stationmaster standing toe-to-toe preparing for battle. But just at that moment, above the noise of the crowd, came an announcement that no self-respecting Frenchman or Irishman could ignore: the bar was open for business. "Blue and grey were once more united," and the two friends sauntered off together in great jocularity in the direction of the bar.

The gay bachelor days came to an end, however, on September 15, 1891, when J. T. Mulkern wed the most eligible maiden of Scott Station, Cecile Cayret, daughter of Dominique and Hortense Cayret. Although no hard facts are available, it is at least possible that their romance blossomed, like so many others in railroad lore, while Cecile worked part-time at the ticket window of the train station. The Cayret girls were reputed to have a lot of spunk.

Whatever the particulars of the romance, the wedding was a "beautiful and impressive" ceremony in the church of St. John the Evangelist at Lafayette. The bride was married in her slippers so as not to be taller than her groom; with that adjustment, they were exactly the same height. The Catholic rites were followed by a reception from which the guests accompanied the newlyweds to the station, where Mr. and Mrs. Mulkern boarded the midnight train "for an extended bridal tour." The local paper observed, "Judging from the quantity of rice and old shoes fired after the young couple, there is no failure in the rice crop and the shoemakers will be busy this Fall." Following the honeymoon, the couple returned to live in the beautiful home that had been built ten years earlier by the bride's father for the stationmasters of Scott Station.

The year 1891 provided the founding family of Scott Station with still another cause for celebration: the completion of the village's first and only mansion. Alcide and Anaïs Judice, together with their children, Leo and Bella, moved out of the cottage provided by Dominique Cayret that had served as their home for ten years and into their own home on their own property, about five acres directly across from the Judice Store and surrounded by ancient live oaks. In an interesting innovation for the time, a giant windmill on the grounds provided running water, including what is believed to be the first residential indoor plumbing in the parish. The two-story Victorian-style mansion faced west. Its first floor consisted of a screened front porch, a living room, a dining room with a large bay window, a kitchen that opened onto a screened back porch, a master bedroom suite, and a library with floor-to-ceiling bookshelves with sliding ladders. The library held an estimated thousand volumes, equally divided among French and English titles, although French was the only language spoken in the home. Upstairs comprised a screened porch and three large bedrooms, each with its own fully equipped water closet with stained glass windows. The bedroom on the north side had a balcony that looked out over a rose garden that was always in bloom, if not with roses then with other seasonal flowers. Every room in the house had a fireplace. Behind the mansion on the south side was a carriage house with space for three large vehicles. On its top floor was a fully furnished apartment for guests. The entire estate was surrounded by a wooden fence ten feet high that effectively blocked out the view of the railroad track, provided privacy, and served as an enclosure for the large flock of peacocks that freely roamed the grounds. In its day, the Judice mansion was deservedly regarded with awe and admiration.

Although 1891 was in many ways a good year in Scott Station, it closed on a somber note. On December 31, Dominique Cayret died at the age of seventy-four. Frightened to live in the country without male protection, the widow Cayret and her five unmarried daughters moved in with the newlyweds in the stationmaster's home, in what proved to be a permanent arrangement. (History is silent as to how "Muldoon" felt about this transformation in his domicile.) Cayret was buried on his land in a grave along the little path that had been worn out by his younger daughters going back and forth between his home and the cottage he had built for Anaïs and her husband. A small iron fence was built to enclose the tomb and enough surrounding ground to form the family's private graveyard. The burial ground remains so today.

20

Scott Station, Louisiana: April 1896

Thanks to the railroad, the economy of Scott Station and its environs in the 1880s and 1890s was in better shape than that of much of the rural South, which was still struggling to overcome the disastrous economic consequences of the Civil War and Reconstruction. Nevertheless, the area's politics mirrored those of the majority of whites throughout the South. The voters were solidly Democratic, the legacy of Republican-imposed Reconstruction.

The citizens of the village maintained a keen interest in politics. Regular elections every four years for local and statewide offices, especially sheriff and governor, generated the most debate, but national issues were not ignored. The most influential political power broker in Scott Station was Alexandre Delhomme, a contemporary of A. D. Boudreaux and Alexandre Begnaud, and one of the pioneers of the area. A prosperous farmer and rancher before the arrival of the railroad, Delhomme was now best known for operating one of the largest cotton gins in town. The Lafayette papers called Delhomme "the old Democratic warhorse." He was a permanent fixture on the Lafayette Parish Democratic Executive Committee, and no candidate for any office, no matter how high or how low, could expect to carry the box at Scott Station without his endorsement.

The community boasted an active chapter of the Farmers Alliance and Industrial Union, an offshoot of the Populist movement then sweeping the agricultural states of the South and Midwest. Dedicated to improving the quality of life of farm families and reversing the decline in prices for the staples they produced, the Alliance held many rallies and meetings at Scott Station under the leadership of Louis G. Breaux.

The village was also a pro-silver stronghold. The fight for the free and unlimited coinage of silver was the most controversial national issue of the 1890s. Farmers, ranchers, and those businessmen who made their living from agriculture held firmly to the belief that the minting of silver as well as gold would stimulate the economy and result in higher crop prices. Alcide Judice and Martin Begnaud were among the founders of the Lafayette Parish Bi-Metallic League.

On the national level in the 1890s, the Republican Party stood for high tariffs, the gold standard, and civil rights for blacks; the Democratic Party stood for low or no tariffs and the unlimited coinage of silver. In the area of civil rights, the national Democratic Party was forced to downplay and otherwise obfuscate its position in order to mollify its powerful southern wing, for whom any mention of the subject was anathema. In Louisiana—alone among the southern states—a high tariff position was acceptable among Democrats as long as it was applied only to sugar imports. But all of these contentious issues were overshadowed in the Pelican State by the controversial Louisiana Lottery. No other issue, before or since, has so divided the people. You were either for the lottery or against it; there was no middle ground. Scott Station was a hotbed of antilottery activity. Alexandre Delhomme, a political disciple of Governor Francis T. Nicholls, rallied the opposition.

The Louisiana Lottery Company had been granted a twenty-five-year charter in 1868 by a carpetbag governor and a Republican-controlled legislature. The company enjoyed the incredibly advantageous condition of paying no state taxes. In reality this was a national lottery; tickets were sold in every state in the Union through the mail, and most of the players were outside Louisiana. The lottery was a phenomenal financial success, taking in an annual revenue estimated at twenty to thirty million dollars and returning less than fifty percent in prizes. Many state officials, legislators, newspaper reporters, and editors received bribes in the form of regular payments for favorable treatment and publicity.

With the return of Democratic rule in 1877, the lottery merely switched sides, allying itself in a mutual aid pact with the Democratic Party, particularly with a New Orleans political machine known as the Ring. The corrupt practices continued unabated. Often the company bought its own tickets and won its own prizes. It manipulated public sentiment by employing revered ex-Confederate generals to appear at drawings to add an air of respectability to the process. Both P. G. T. Beauregard and Jubal A. Early worked for the Louisiana Lottery and served as legislative lobbyists for the company.

Disagreement about the lottery resulted in the division of the Democratic Party into three factions: the prolottery Ring and two antilottery factions labeled by historians the Bourbons and the Patricians. The Ring, with its base in New Orleans and some statewide support, especially among African Americans, was the most powerful of the three. While not always able to elect the governor of its choosing, the Ring had a lock on the legislature. The Bourbon faction was composed mostly of wealthy plantation owners united by their unanimous support for high protective tariffs on sugar and their opposition to taxes of any size, shape, and variety. The reason for the name Bourbon is that they, "like the French royals restored to power after the fall of Napoleon, were said to have 'learned nothing and forgotten nothing.'" Although the group had definite Republican leanings, memories of Reconstruction and their vehement opposition to racial equality precluded most—but not all—Bourbons from embracing the GOP. As for the Patricians, their label was not based on any exalted status, though some wealthy planters could be counted among their ranks. Rather, it was because in the area of race relations they tended to exhibit the traditional patrician quality of noblesse oblige: they were willing to permit blacks a modicum of civil rights and minimal participation in the political process. Most yeoman farmers, ranchers, and their agribusiness neighbors were in this Democratic camp, whose leader was Governor Nicholls. During his first term (1877–1881), Nicholls witnessed with increasing dismay the corrupt influence of the lottery and his inability to do anything about it because of the Ring's solid control of the legislature and the lottery's twenty-five-year lease. The company's influence reached new heights during the two terms of Governor Samuel D. McEnery of Monroe (1881–1888), who was owned by the lottery. Corruption rose to such levels that many people referred to the governor as McLottery, and Nicholls was elected to a second term in 1888 with a mandate to end the lottery's reign. Under the leadership of Alexandre Delhomme, the Patrician Democrats of Scott Station held numerous pro-Nicholls and anti-lottery rallies. Delhomme's closest political allies during these years were the Begnaud brothers, his colleagues on the Lafayette Parish Democratic Executive Committee: Martin in the 1880s and Simeon in the 1890s. Their efforts and those of their political allies across the state accomplished little, however, and Governor Nicholls was no more successful in curtailing the lottery's activities in his second term than he had been in his first.

The twenty-five-year life of the lottery was scheduled to expire in 1893, and the company sought a new twenty-five-year charter. Passage of a legislative act followed by a favorable vote of the electorate was required for rechartering. With the blessing of Governor Nicholls, a group of men led by state senator Murphy J. Foster of St. Mary Parish formed the Anti-Lottery League in an effort to fight rechartering, which was scheduled to come up before the legislature in the 1890 session. The Anti-Lottery League suffered a crushing defeat in round one when the legislature voted by a more than two-thirds majority to renew the charter. A gubernatorial veto was useless, for the two-thirds margin of victory was enough to override.

The second—and last—chance for the antilottery forces was the popular vote, scheduled to take place at the same time as the gubernatorial elections of 1892. McEnery was seeking reelection as a prolottery Democrat and Murphy Foster was running as an antilottery Democrat. Two Republican candidates (on opposite sides of the lottery issue) joined the field, but they were not factors. Campaigning was vigorous and the race appeared to be too close to call. But then, seemingly out of nowhere, fate intervened, in the form of the United States Supreme Court.

For many years, other states had complained about their inability to regulate the Louisiana Lottery operating within their borders via the United States Postal Service. Responding to such concerns, the 1890 Congress enacted a statute prohibiting all lotteries from using the mail. The Louisiana Lottery Company moved quickly to challenge the new law's constitutionality in the federal courts. Two years passed and the issue was almost forgotten by the general public when, two months before the Louisiana gubernatorial election of 1892, the Supreme Court upheld the law's constitutionality and ordered the Louisiana Lottery to cease use of the U.S. mail immediately. The effect of the ruling was that the lottery could operate only within the boundaries of the state of Louisiana, and even there only through retail or other nonpostal outlets. The party was over. The Louisiana Lottery Company abandoned its recharter fight, withdrew all financial support from McEnery and other prolottery candidates, emptied its bank accounts, and moved its operations to Honduras. The vote on rechartering failed, and Foster was elected governor.

The demise of the Louisiana Lottery meant a decline in the Ring's influence, and the other two factions of the Democratic Party moved to fill the vacuum. By all indicators Governor Foster, a wealthy sugar planter, should have been a Bourbon, and in many ways he was one, but his long fight against the lottery had helped forge an alliance among his followers with the considerable political organization of Francis T. Nicholls. As he planned his reelection campaign for 1896, Governor Foster moved to bring the Democratic Party together under his leadership. He took two key steps that strengthened and unified his position. First, he appointed Nicholls chief justice of the Louisiana Supreme Court, thus ensuring himself of the support of the still formidable Nicholls organization. Second, with the lottery now out of the picture, Foster made his political peace with the power brokers from New Orleans and secured the endorsement of what was left of the Ring.

Foster's opponent in 1896 was Republican John N. Pharr. Under normal conditions, Pharr would not have been given much of a chance in this solid Democratic state, but these were uncommon times and Pharr was able to put together an unusual coalition that gave his candidacy substantial momentum; many observers even believed he was going to win. Pharr brought his own considerable assets to the race; he was one of the richest men in the state and did not mind spending his own money. He was a rare free-silver Republican, and this brought him the backing of the People's Party. Known as the Populists and particularly strong in north Louisiana, these small farmers, tenants, and sharecroppers chafed under the economic domination of the Bourbons and longed for a political alternative. Pharr's bi-metallic stand enabled the Populists to support a Republican. Moreover, in 1894 a Democratic Congress had passed, and Democratic president Grover Cleveland had signed, the Wilson-Gorman Act, which ended federal price supports for Louisiana sugar. Furious, nearly every sugar planter along the Mississippi River and Bayou Teche rallied to the Pharr banner. Meanwhile, in New Orleans, a reform movement called the Citizens' League had been launched in an effort to clean out City Hall and the legislative members of the old Ring, now allied with Foster. The Citizens' League had little choice but to support Pharr. And, finally, the most significant vote of all, that of the African Americans, would stand with the party of Lincoln in overwhelming numbers. Made up of so many disparate interests, Pharr's candidacy was known as the Fusion ticket.

In this election, as in all southern elections of the 1890s, white supremacy was the pivotal issue. Of course, dating from the end of the Civil War, keeping the Negro "in his place" and the violence that stance provoked played a role in virtually every important election in the South, but in the last decade of the century the violence reached new levels. Night riders, imitators of the Ku Klux Klan—sometimes hooded, sometimes not—roamed the countryside lynching, burning, beating, and otherwise intimidating African Americans in an effort to prevent their participation in the political process. By 1896, these terrorists had a name: they were called Regulators, and they contributed to making the elections of 1896 one of the most violent and corrupt in Louisiana history.

The elections were scheduled for Tuesday, April 21. At the state level, candidates for governor, lieutenant governor, secretary of state, attorney general, state treasurer, auditor of public accounts, and superintendent of public education would be on the ballot, with the race for governor the most important and the most hotly contested. And that race was nonpareil in that both candidates were from the same parish and had the same occupation; both Foster and Pharr were successful sugarcane planters from St. Mary Parish. Locally, there were races for sheriff, judge, and district attorney for the Seventeenth Judicial District, which encompassed Lafayette and Vermilion Parishes, state senator from the Eleventh Senatorial District (Lafayette, Iberia, and St. Martin Parishes), state representative from Lafayette Parish, and, for Scott Station only—where Jules Guidry's Dance Hall served as the polling place—a police juror, a constable, and a justice of the peace. Of these, the office of sheriff was the most powerful and influential, not just in the parish or in the state, but throughout the American West. Isaac A. Broussard, the popular "cowboy" sheriff of Lafayette Parish, was seeking a third term; he had first been elected in 1888, then reelected in 1892. His opponent was the young mayor of Lafayette, William Campbell, who was seeking to advance his political career. Both Broussard and Campbell were Democrats.

Ike Broussard owed his "cowboy" sobriquet to his origins in Calcasieu Parish, the southwesternmost parish of Louisiana; bordering Texas, it was known for its big cattle ranches and many cowboys. At the age of thirteen, Ike and his widowed mother had moved to Lafayette Parish, where his father had family. Raising livestock was Broussard's lifetime avocation and he carefully cultivated his image by wearing western garb and practicing a tough brand of law enforcement. Yet despite his apparent popularity and his eminent Acadian surname, his elections could never be taken for granted because in this heavily Catholic region, Ike Broussard was a Baptist. He had been raised in his mother's church, and his wife was also Protestant.

It was not easy for a man who did not drink or dance to be a successful politician in south Louisiana in those years. But Ike played his politics well, and while he may have abstained from "John Barleycorn" and the two-step personally, he made it clear that he had no objection to these enjoyments. The sheriff was a regular visitor to the balls held at the St. Paul Hotel, where he quite visibly encouraged his kinsmen to "pass a good time." On the other hand, he had little tolerance for lawbreakers. He hated Regulators and hunted them down with a vengeance, not so much because of what they were doing, but because they were doing it outside the limits of the law. Broussard was unre-

lenting in his pursuit of criminals. When he felt it necessary, the cowboy sheriff did not hesitate to use strong-arm and even brutal methods
in his police work—nor was he above using the letter of the law to help
his own political fortunes. His most controversial use (or abuse) of his
office for political advantage occurred on April 13, 1896, at Falk's Opera
House in Lafayette, where Pharr and his supporters had scheduled a
rally. The fact that "400 white persons were in attendance" probably
sent shivers down the spine of local Democratic Party leaders. Broussard and his deputies raided the opera house and dispersed the crowd
on the pretext of calling a fire drill. Pharr was humiliated, and his supporters were furious. The raid, in the heat of a bitterly fought campaign, endeared the sheriff to Democrats, made him a pariah among
Republicans, and gave others cause to reassess their opinion of Ike
Broussard.

Broussard's opponent in 1896 was a man of a very different personality. If Ike Broussard was a cowboy, William Campbell was a scholar.
His grandfather John, a surveyor, had immigrated to south Louisiana
from Scotland by way of Pittsburgh in the early nineteenth century and
had settled in Vermilionville. His son, William's father and namesake,
had married Acadian Alida Guidry, and William Campbell the
younger was brought up in the faith and language of his mother's people. He graduated from St. Charles College, the Jesuit college at Grand
Coteau, in 1876 and went to work as a deputy sheriff, but after a few
years enrolled in Tulane University, where he received his law degree in
1889. He then returned to his hometown of Lafayette and opened a
legal practice.

Campbell was an extremely well-read man with broad intellectual
interests and was also considered something of an authority on the
Bible. Eager for public service, he was elected mayor of Lafayette in
1893. But the young attorney had two problems that he had to overcome in order to be successful in parishwide politics: his name and his
flirtation with Freemasonry. A Scottish name was not politically advantageous in south Louisiana, but that was simply a matter of birth. A
candidate's religion was a different issue. Raised in a strict Catholic
home, but intellectually curious about world religions and varying biblical interpretations, Campbell had at one time left the church and

joined a Masonic lodge. He remained a member for only a short time, perhaps a year or two, before returning to the faith of his childhood. Although Campbell would remain a devoted Catholic for the rest of his life, this act of conscience was not a political asset.

Campaigning almost entirely in French, Broussard and Campbell waged a vigorous contest. But the race for sheriff of Lafayette Parish in 1896 was overshadowed by the greater drama being played out state-wide in the rancorous race for governor. Democrats were on the defensive across the state. It seemed their only chance of victory was to employ one of three stratagems: steal the election through fraud, physically prevent blacks from voting through force and intimidation, or shame whites into voting Democratic with a warning that a Republican victory would mean an end to white supremacy. As the stakes were high, they did all three. A racist press did its best to plant racial fear among whites. Henry J. Hearsey, editor of the *New Orleans Daily States,* labeled the Fusion ticket—with its combination of north Louisiana Populists, south Louisiana sugarcane planters, and African Americans—"hayseed, canejuice . . . and malodorous nigger wool." Democrat-controlled newspapers constantly referred to Pharr, whose middle initial was N., as "John Nigger Pharr." Particularly irksome to the Regulators was that the Pharr platform contained an antilynching plank. Twenty-one lynchings, roughly a fifth of all such killings in the United States for the year, were reported in connection with the 1896 Louisiana elections. And that was only the number reported; the actual number was probably higher, and no one counted beatings, burnings, and other acts of violence.

On election day, Tuesday, April 21, the combination of voter fraud and intimidation proved successful. In certain remote rural parishes where Democrats were in firm control of the courthouses, the results were conspicuously false. A typical but not isolated example was East Carroll Parish; although the rolls listed 275 registered white voters and 3,250 registered black voters, the election results were 2,635 for Foster and 0 for Pharr. The vote counters in West Feliciana Parish were more generous. There, white registration numbered 575 and black registration 2,771; on election day, Foster received 3,093 votes to Pharr's 1. State-wide, the vote was 116,216 for Foster and 90,138 for Pharr. Foster, who lost his home parish by a wide margin, lost every Acadian parish except St. Martin and Lafayette. He carried the latter 1,509 to 654, with his strongest showing being the 217-38 victory in the precinct, or "box," as it was called then, at the dance hall in Scott Station.

In the race for sheriff, William Campbell did far better than anyone expected; Ike Broussard was reelected to a third term by a slim margin of 1,218 to 1,024. Campbell's strength was largely owing to a rare divergence of political views between the two largest families of Scott Station, the Begnauds and the Boudreauxs. The Boudreauxs had supported the incumbent and the Begnauds the challenger. In other important parochial races, Conrad Debaillon, the incumbent district judge, and Ed Voorhies, the incumbent parish clerk of court, were both reelected.

Newspaper sketch of Martin
Begnaud, the murder victim

Martin Begnaud's bed,
on which he was killed
*Courtesy Marie Therese
P. A. Begnaud; photo by
Patsy Arceneaux*

Eliza Constantin Begnaud, Martin Begnaud's mother. This picture is believed to have been taken on the afternoon of April 24, 1896, the day of her son's funeral.
Courtesy Noelie M. Provost

Sheriff's Isaac "Ike" Broussard, who devoted much of his energy on the Begnaud case to preventing the suspects he arrested from being lynched. Newspaper sketch.

Sheriff I. A. Broussard.

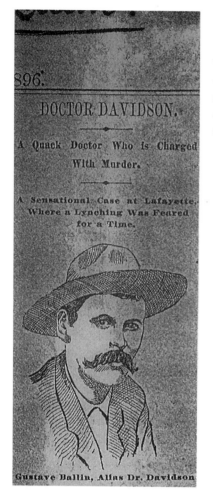

896.

DOCTOR DAVIDSON.

A Quack Doctor Who is Charged With Murder.

A Sensational Case at Lafayette, Where a Lynching Was Feared for a Time.

Gustave Ballin, Alias Dr. Davidson

Gustave Balin (here misspelled "Ballin"), alias "Dr. Davidson," a con artist and French army deserter already indicted for murder, was quickly arrested as one of the killers of Martin Begnaud.

Hampton "Hamp" Benton Jr., notorious local figure who was with Gustave Balin in suspicious circumstances on the night of the Begnaud murder. He too was arrested for the crime.
Courtesy Cynthia Benton Prevost

The home built 1880–1881 by Dominique Cayret for the stationmasters of Scott Station. It was from this house that J. T. Mulkern set out on the morning he discovered the corpse of Martin Begnaud.
Photo by Patsy Arceneaux

The core of this house (awninged entrance) was once Martin Begnaud's general store and residence, in which he was killed. The building was purchased in 1902 and moved by the new owner about 200 yards north of its original location. A private residence, it has undergone numerous additions over the years.
Courtesy the author

Alcide Judice, the force behind the founding of Scott Station, and reported to be the next target for robbery and murder.
Courtesy Bella N. C. Abramson

Anaïs Bella Judice, daughter of Alcide and Anaïs Cayret Judice, and said to be the first child born in Scott Station.
Courtesy Bella N. C. Abramson

Alexis (left) and Ernest Blanc, confessed killers of Martin Begnaud. The Blancs almost certainly would never have been apprehended if they had not returned to Lafayette Parish.

Courtesy the author

BOUDREAUX PLANTATION, c. 1896

The plantation of A. D. Boudreaux, where the Blanc brothers lived and worked in the months leading up to the murder. Their cabin, near which they buried the murder weapon and other evidence, is depicted at the upper right.

Drawn by Patsy Arceneaux from a sketch by Laurent Boudreaux, courtesy Francis S. LeBlanc

Newspaper sketches of the legal principals in the Blanc brothers' trial: Special prosecutor William Cambell (top left), District Attorney Minos T. Gordy (top right), Judge Conrad Debaillon (middle left), and defense counsel Charles Homer Mouton (middle right) and Gustave Breaux (left).

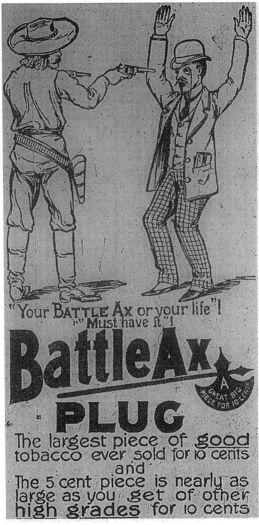

From the *Lafayette Advertiser* a few weeks before the Blanc brothers committed their crime. Even in France the Blancs had been avid readers of Wild West novels—a form of literature that Ernest Blanc publicly blamed for his ruin. Perhaps this ad helped to fan the brothers' plans for robbery.

Simeon Begnaud, saloon keeper, brother of Martin, and the last to see him alive except the killers. *Courtesy Lucien Martin*

Acadian Gothic: Jean Begnaud, ca. 1902, holding his ever-ready shotgun and the reins of his favorite horse. His wife and double first cousin, Emma Constantin Begnaud, is at his right side. On the horse is Theo Begnaud, their youngest child (born 1900). The other adults are their daughter Emma and her suitor Henri Pellesier. Henri and Emma were married in 1903. *Courtesy Francis S. LeBlanc*

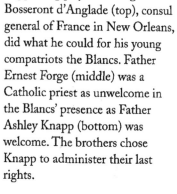

Supporting players: Georges Bosseront d'Anglade (top), consul general of France in New Orleans, did what he could for his young compatriots the Blancs. Father Ernest Forge (middle) was a Catholic priest as unwelcome in the Blancs' presence as Father Ashley Knapp (bottom) was welcome. The brothers chose Knapp to administer their last rights.

Newspaper reproductions of drawings made by Ernest Blanc while in prison

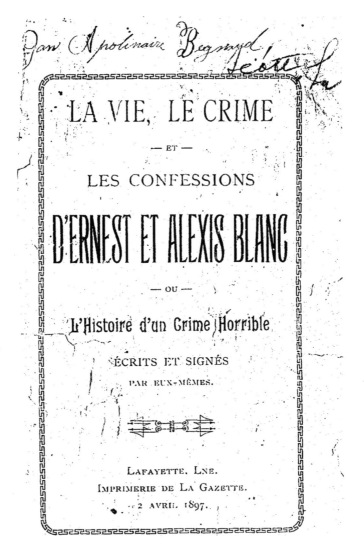

LA VIE, LE CRIME

— ET —

LES CONFESSIONS

D'ERNEST ET ALEXIS BLANC

— OU —

L'Histoire d'un Crime Horrible

ÉCRITS ET SIGNÉS

PAR EUX-MÊMES.

LAFAYETTE, LNE.
IMPRIMERIE DE LA GAZETTE.
2 AVRIL 1897.

Title page of *The Life, Crime, and Confessions of Ernest and Alexis Blanc,* actually consisting almost entirely of Ernest's prison writings. This copy of the book, in its original hide cover, belonged to Jean Apolinaire Begnaud, brother-in-law of Martin Begnaud and one of the official witnesses to the execution of the Blancs. The book is dated April 2, 1897, the day of the hangings, and actually appeared on April 3.
Courtesy the author

DEATH WARRANT.

EXECUTIVE DEPARTMENT--STATE OF LOUISIANA.

Baton Rouge, La., *March 18th* 189 7

TO *the Hon. J. A. Brown, esq.*

Sheriff of the Parish of *[illegible]*

Whereas, it appears from the annexed duly certified copy, that at a session of the Honorable the *17th*

Judi Dist Court and held on the *24th* day of *February* 1897, *Ernest Blanc and Alexis Blanc* *was* tried and convicted of the crime of

Murder

and for said offense w *as*, by judgment of said Court, rendered on the *4th*

day of *March* 1897, sentenced by his Honor the Judge of said Court to be hanged by the neck until *he* be dead.

Now, therefore, I, MURPHY JAMES FOSTER, Governor of the State of Louisiana, do hereby direct and require you, the said *J. A. Brown,* Sheriff, to cause the execution to be done on the body of said *Ernest Blanc and Alexis Blanc*

, so convicted and condemned, in all things according to the judgment and sentence of said Court and the law in all such cases made and provided, on *Friday* the *second* day of *April* 189 7, between the hours *12* o'clock *M.* and *2* o'clock *P. M.*, within the inclosure of the parish jail of your parish, in your presence and that of at least four and not exceeding fifteen witnesses, "one or more of whom shall be a practicing physician," residents of your parish, who shall duly attest the same, under oath, which attestation shall be returned by you together with the annexed copy of the proceedings had in said case, to said Court, and for which this will be your warrant and authority.

Given under my signature and the Seal of the State of Louisiana, at the City of Baton Rouge the same day, month and year first above written.

Sig. Murphy J. Foster

Governor of Louisiana.

By the Governor :

Sig. John T. Michel

Secretary of State.

The death warrant for the Blancs' execution, signed by Governor Murphy James Foster and Secretary of State John T. Michel. Foster steadfastly refused to consider clemency in the case.

The Blanc brothers on the scaffold. Drawing by Floyd Sonnier, Cajun artist, from a photograph that appeared in the November 13, 1955, edition of the *Lafayette Daily Advertiser,* and from written accounts of the execution. The photograph itself is in too poor a condition to be reproduced.

Top: The Begnaud family plot in the St. John the Evangelist Cathedral Cemetery, Lafayette. The four wrought-iron grave markers within the enclosure are those, from left to right, of Simeon Begnaud (d. 1906), Eliza Constantin Begnaud (d. 1898), Martin Begnaud (d. 1896), and Alexandre Begnaud (d. 1883). Bottom: The grassy area, in the same cemetery as the Begnaud plot, is the suspected location in which Ernest and Alexis Blanc are buried.

Courtesy the author

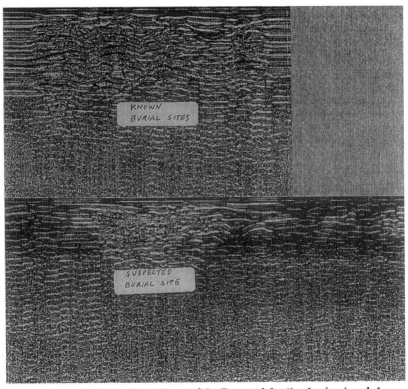

Ground-penetrating radar readings of the Begnaud family plot (top) and the suspected grave of the Blanc brothers (bottom). The wavy patterns clearly indicate the bodies of the four Begnaud family members in the former, and suggest the presence of one or more bodies in the latter.

Book VII

THE TRIAL

best seats for viewing were located; those not so fortunate crowded together tightly on the ground floor.

Two brief yet anxiety-inducing incidents occurred before the trial began, one outside the courthouse and one inside the courtroom. The first occurred when sheriff's deputies tried to disarm Jean Begnaud as he attempted to enter the courthouse with his loaded double-barreled shotgun. Aside from the guns belonging to the law enforcement officers of the court, no weapons of any kind were permitted inside the courtroom. Begnaud was adamant, refusing to surrender his weapon. A heated argument took place, but the deputies eventually persuaded the farmer to hand over his shotgun on the condition that it would be returned at the end of the day. Inside the courtroom, the crowd cleared an aisle through which Jean Begnaud walked; he entered the bar and sat in the chair reserved for him at the prosecution's table next to District Attorney Gordy. His brother Simeon sat on the other side of Gordy, and William Campbell, as special counsel for the state, sat next to Simeon. Under armed guard, the defendants had been brought in through a back entrance and were seated at the defense table, flanked by their impressive legal representation: Governor Mouton, Colonel Breaux, and the reinstated Caffery and Elliott. The sheriff and two deputies, heavily armed with side arms and rifles, as well as the clerk of court, were also inside the bar. Just as he was about to bang the gavel calling the court to order, Debaillon saw smoke rising from the middle of the courtroom. The threat of fire in nineteenth-century America, where virtually all buildings were constructed mostly of wood, was a constant fear. The Lafayette Parish Courthouse, all wood, very old, and grossly overcrowded, was a virtual tinderbox. The judge immediately directed Sheriff Broussard to examine the situation. The source of the smoke was a blazing coat jacket worn by one of the spectators, which had caught fire from a still-lit cigar that had been placed in one of the pockets. The gentleman in question had obviously hoped to rekindle his stogie at another time. The smoldering spectator was quickly hustled outside and, finally, Judge Debaillon called court into session and announced that the jury selection process would begin.

Normally, the hundred members of the jury pool would be in the courtroom awaiting questioning by the respective attorneys, but on this day there was no space for them, and they had been assembled across the street at the parish jail. The judge directed Ed Voorhies to draw thirty slips of paper from the *de talibus* list, each slip containing the name of a prospective juror. The thirty slips were then given to the sheriff, who walked across the street and returned with the first group of potential jurors in tow. It was necessary for Judge Debaillon to direct the spectators to open an aisle in order for the sheriff and the jury candidates to pass through. Before the day was over, Ed Voorhies would pull thirty more slips of paper and Ike Broussard would make another trip to the parish jail to fetch another contingent of prospective jurors. Fifty-eight men would be called before TWELVE MEN, GOOD AND TRUE, as the front-page headlines of the *Daily Picayune* announced, were seated.

Under the Louisiana Code of Criminal Procedure in force in 1897, any potential juror in a capital murder case could be excused for appropriate cause by either the state or the defense, subject to the approval of the presiding judge; as for peremptory challenges, the removal of a potential juror without cause, the state was allowed six and the defense twelve challenges per defendant. In case 1421, the prosecution would thus have a total of twelve peremptory challenges and the defense would have twenty-four. Debaillon's prediction that jury selection would be completed by noon proved to be overly optimistic. At the midday "dinner" break, only four jurors had been seated. The state made no secret of the fact that it would seek the death penalty in this case, and every potential juror was asked by the prosecution if he opposed the death penalty. Under Louisiana criminal law, opposition to capital punishment in a capital murder case was automatic grounds for dismissal for cause.

Emile Romero was the fourth prospective juror called that morning, and during his examination a heated and time-consuming debate occurred between the defense and the prosecution. Motions were made, soliloquies delivered, and numerous lawbooks and revised statutes consulted by the judge before the proceedings could continue. It was during these exchanges that the attorneys for the accused first revealed their legal strategy: they would seek a "qualified verdict." In response to the question concerning capital punishment, Romero had replied that he was "not opposed." District Attorney Gordy had then asked Romero if he was aware that he could qualify his verdict. Governor Mouton immediately objected, and there ensued a learned and vigorous exchange between the advocates.

The attorneys for the Blanc brothers were under no illusions: they knew their clients would be found guilty, but they hoped to avoid the death penalty. In a murder trial in Louisiana, a jury verdict of guilty was punishable by hanging, unless the jury returned a qualified verdict, in which case the person convicted was sentenced to life in prison. A qualified verdict usually meant that the jury had found extenuating or mitigating circumstances. The evidence against their clients was so overwhelming that the defense team would not seek to disprove the brothers' guilt; rather, they would try to persuade the jury to spare the lives of the defendants because of their youth (eighteen and nineteen at the time of the crime), their origin (foreigners in a strange land), and their family situation (orphans). The defense did not want the option of a qualified verdict to surface during the jury selection process. They sought to tender twelve men for the jury who they felt could be persuaded to bring in a qualified verdict, and they did not want to allow the prosecution to ferret out those so inclined. But Judge Debaillon overruled his father-in-law's motion, and the state was allowed to continue its line of questioning.

Nonplussed by his son-in-law's ruling, Governor Mouton immediately served notice to the court that the defense reserved a bill of exception, thereby revealing the defense's plan to appeal the conviction of its clients, if necessary. A bill of exception was used as the basis for an appeal of a conviction to the Louisiana Supreme Court; for each such bill reserved by the defense during trial, the attorneys would submit to the supreme court a written petition claiming that the presiding judge had erred in his ruling on a particular point of law or procedure. The presiding judge, in turn, was given the opportunity to respond in writing to each petition. The supreme court would then consider all arguments and decide whether to sustain the verdict, reverse the verdict, or order a new trial. The state did tender Emile Romero, but the defense used one of its peremptory challenges to have him excused.

Jury selection continued until 7 P.M., when the twelfth and final juror was seated. A total of twenty-six potential jurors had been dismissed for cause: one for illness, one on a legal technicality (the wrong person with a similar name had been served), two because they were no longer residents of the parish, four because they had already formed an opinion in the case, five because they were opposed to capital punishment, and thirteen because they did not understand English. Twenty peremptory challenges were used, four by the state and sixteen by the defense. The Blancs appeared nervous but quite interested in all of the proceedings. Ernest was far more comfortable with English than was his younger brother, but Alexis appeared to be more assertive and animated than in the past, and whispered suggestions to his lawyers in French. In fact, it was Alexis who informed the attorneys that two of the potential jurors were related by marriage to the victim. Alexandre Martin was Martin Begnaud's brother-in-law, being married to Azema Begnaud, Martin's youngest sibling, and Pierre Bacque was married to one of Martin's nieces. The defense used two of its peremptory challenges to excuse the in-laws.

The jury that was finally chosen to hear *State of Louisiana* v. *Ernest Blanc and Alexis Blanc* consisted of Clarence Avant, William Beadle, Cleopha Broussard, William Burke, W. P. Butcher, George A. De-Blanc, William R. Foote, Ignace Hulin, George R. McCoy, Leonard Miller, Joseph Spell, and Tillman Spell. Except for a few businessmen, all were farmers. A little after 7 P.M., Colonel Gus Breaux rose and moved to recess the proceedings until the following day at 10 A.M. There were no objections and the motion was granted. Judge Debaillon declared court adjourned and ordered the courtroom cleared.

At one o'clock the next morning, Sheriff Broussard was awakened by the sound of gunfire—serious gunfire. It could only mean one thing. He grabbed his rifle and raced, half-dressed, the several blocks to the jail. All was calm. The cause of the alarm turned out to be a fire at an oil storage facility on the outskirts of town. Since there were no sirens or fire bells, the customary method for sounding a fire alarm in small towns like Lafayette was to fire gunshots into the air. Every male over the age of sixteen, when made aware of a fire, was expected to empty his weapon into the sky. The fire was not severe, and the relieved sheriff returned home to bed.

22

Lafayette, Louisiana: February 1897

Friday, February 26, was another cool, clear morning, and the number of people streaming into Lafayette was at least equal to and perhaps exceeded that of the previous day. In order to curtail the pushing and shoving, Judge Debaillon directed that the courtroom doors be opened at nine, one hour before court was scheduled to convene. By 9:15, every seat and every place a person could stand had been taken. The judge was also hoping for a little more decorum from the spectators; on Thursday two benches had collapsed under the weight of the multitude. When court convened promptly at ten, he issued a stern warning that the slightest disturbance would result in immediate expulsion from the courtroom. The same lineup of players was inside the bar. Ernest Blanc appeared "confident" and Alexis "smiled." The jury was polled—all twelve were present—and the state was directed to call its first witness.

Dr. Alphonse Gladu took the stand, was sworn in, and was asked to identify himself and state his connection with the case. After giving his name, he attested: "I am a practicing physician. In April, 1896, I was the coroner of this parish and held the autopsy on the body of Martin Begnaud. I found the body in bed, tied hand and foot, gagged and bloody. He was stabbed in fifty-two places from the throat to the lower portion of the breast." Dr. Gladu then proceeded to give additional, technical details of the autopsy and its findings. He concluded his statement with the following: "The wound that penetrated the heart was made with a triangular instrument." District Attorney Gordy then attempted to show the witness a three-sided file for the purpose of asking Dr. Gladu if the file could have produced wounds such as those found on the body, but Governor Mouton objected. The file had not been properly introduced into evidence, it had not been identified as the murder weapon, and it had not been found on the premises. Gordy countered that he was only trying to ascertain if the wounds could have been inflicted by such an instrument. The objection was overruled and the defense reserved a bill of exception. Cleared to respond, Gladu said that "the instrument shown him would produce a wound exactly like the ones found on Begnaud."

On cross-examination, Gus Breaux asked numerous questions about the wounds, such as their width, depth, and location and whether Dr. Gladu could say which had been inflicted first, the deep ones or the shallow ones. The physician responded that he was not able to make such a judgment. The witness was then shown a stiletto and asked if the wounds could have been made by such a weapon. Gladu replied in the affirmative. On redirect, the doctor explained that he and the team of physicians who conducted the autopsy had opened the chest cavity of the victim to confirm that the stab wounds to the heart, each measuring from four to five inches in depth, would have been fatal, and found that they would have been.

The state's second witness was Dr. John D. Trahan, one of the physicians present at the autopsy. Beginning with "I am a practicing physician for thirty years in this parish. I assisted in the inquest of Martin Begnaud," his testimony closely tracked his colleague's. Trahan did add that the wounds to the neck, as well as those to the heart, were lethal; any one of them could have produced death. Dr. Trahan identified the blood-soaked clothing worn by the victim the night of the murder, the rope used to tie him up, the punctured calico cloth in which he had been encased, and the strips of cloth used to gag and blindfold him. All of these were entered into evidence. In probably the most dramatic moment of the trial, the old doctor lifted the calico cloth and slipped the file through one of the many holes, demonstrating that it was a perfect fit. On cross-examination, Trahan admitted that no weapon was found at the murder scene and that there were no signs of a struggle. Dr. Trahan, who had known the victim, was asked to describe him physically, "Mr. Begnaud in his life was a very strong and muscular man. He was a man of courage." How, then, could the physician explain the absence of a struggle? "My opinion as to why he did not resist was that he must have been overpowered by some weapon presented at him which checked him."

The third witness for the prosecution was Dr. Anatole R. Trahan, the son of the prior witness and another member of the inquest team. His testimony was brief, but he did make two significant points, one a forensic detail and the other a personal opinion. Martin Begnaud had been dead ten to twelve hours at the time of the autopsy, and his hands were purple. The tight ropes that bound his hands prevented the blood in them from circulating—conclusive proof, in the physician's medical opinion, that the victim was helpless at the time of the murder. On the subject of the absence of a struggle, the younger Dr. Trahan said, "The only way that I can account for Mr. Begnaud failing to defend himself was that a revolver was placed at his head." The next witness for the state was William B. Stansbury, a *Times-Democrat* reporter who had interviewed the Blanc brothers in Orleans Parish Prison on the night of January 4. In that interview, Ernest Blanc had given a detailed, lurid account of the murder and had recounted the brothers' subsequent international travels. The state sought to enter Stansbury's January 5 *Times-Democrat* article into evidence, for it was tantamount to a confession. Governor Mouton objected based on the fact that the so-called confession had been made under duress and that the reporter had used an interpreter. It was now near midday and Judge Debaillon declared a recess.

When the Court reconvened for the afternoon session, the jury was not present. Since the defendants had pleaded not guilty and had not signed a binding confession, the newspaper reporter's testimony of a voluntary confession would carry enormous weight with the jury. Debaillon therefore did not want the twelve to hear opposing arguments on the admissibility of Stansbury's testimony until he had heard them himself and was prepared to make his ruling. Governor Mouton main-

tained that the young Frenchmen had been terrified at being placed in
Orleans Parish Prison and that the reporter had used "promises, threats
and inducements" in order to get them to confess. The old lawyer further maintained that because the reporter did not understand French,
any testimony he might give would amount to hearsay. Stansbury was
indignant. He insisted that the interview had been totally voluntary. In
fact, Ernest Blanc had already given a similar account to reporters from
the *Daily Picayune*. And while Stansbury may have used an interpreter,
Ernest Blanc had spoken in English when he described the actual murder. Again, the judge overruled his father-in-law's objection and allowed the state to proceed with its witness. The defense gave notice
that it reserved another bill of exception. The jury then returned to the
courtroom and listened to Stansbury read, verbatim, his long and
highly descriptive account of the murder of Martin Begnaud as related
by Ernest Blanc. On cross-examination by Colonel Breaux, Stansbury
testified that Ernest Blanc had made clear that he and he alone had
killed the merchant, and that "Alexis had not struck a blow at Begnaud."

The next witness for the prosecution was William Campbell. Already inside the bar, he had to walk only a few feet to the witness stand
from the chair he occupied as special counsel for the state. Homer
Mouton asked that the jury again be removed from the courtroom during the debate on motions concerning the admissibility of Campbell's
testimony. With the jury out of the room, Campbell testified that the
Blanc brothers had confessed to the murder of Martin Begnaud twice
in his presence, once in Lafayette on January 4 and again in New Orleans on January 9. "Eloquently," according to the *Daily Picayune*, Governor Mouton argued that the Blancs had been in mortal fear for their
lives in the Lafayette jail on January 4 and that Campbell used the
threat of a lynch mob in order to obtain a confession. Campbell responded that he had never asked the brothers about the murder but
had only inquired about the stolen money. As to threats or promises,
Campbell said that he had made only one promise to Ernest and Alexis
Blanc: if they would explain what happened to the money, he would re-
locate them to a safe place. The confession in New Orleans, Campbell
added, where there was no threat of a lynch mob, was given voluntarily.

That interview had produced a detailed account of the murder, and Sheriff Broussard, Simeon Begnaud, and several other onlookers had been present as witnesses. And all of his extended conversations with the accused, swore the special counsel, had been conducted in French. Judge Debaillon sustained the defense's objection concerning the Lafayette confession but overruled the one regarding the New Orleans confession. He decided that the Blancs had been under no threat of a lynch mob in Orleans Parish, and that their confession had been given freely.

The jurors were brought back in, and William Campbell proceeded to relate to the jury what he had been told by the defendants in New Orleans on January 9. His testimony was essentially a corroboration of Stansbury's story. In response to questioning from his cocounsel, Campbell explained that on the January trip to New Orleans he had taken with him the file unearthed by sheriff's deputies next to the Blancs' cabin on Boudreaux Plantation. He had shown the file to the Blanc brothers in their jail cell and they had identified it as the murder weapon.

The next witness for the state was Sheriff Isaac Broussard, who began by assuring everyone present that he spoke French. The district attorney thanked him for volunteering that information and then went ahead with his questioning. The sheriff's testimony basically confirmed that of Stansbury and Campbell. The next witness, Simeon Begnaud, described how he had accompanied Chief Deputy Thomas Mouton and another deputy to Boudreaux Plantation and personally witnessed the excavation of the area around the Blanc brothers' cabin, including the discovery there of the file and a cash box that had belonged to his brother. He had also found a key to his brother's store in the nearby grass. At this point, the state offered the file in evidence. There was no objection. Begnaud also validated the testimony of Campbell and Broussard, stating that he spoke French and had been present when the two previous witnesses questioned the brothers in Lafayette and New Orleans.

The last witness called by the state was Valery Boudreaux, the son of Colonel A. D. Boudreaux. He had been born and raised on Boudreaux Plantation and was intimately familiar with all of its buildings and grounds. He testified that he had been present with Mouton and Begnaud during the digging and was an eyewitness to the discovery of the file and the cash box. When Mr. Boudreaux completed his testimony, the state rested its case.

The defense called only two witnesses, L. Leo Judice and Camille Sperafico. Judice was a young merchant from Scott Station in business with his father, Alcide Judice, and Sperafico was a farmer from the same area. Each spent only a short time on the witness stand. Both testified that they had known the defendants for about two years and that, to the best of their knowledge, the young Frenchmen enjoyed a "reputation for quiet, industry and good behavior." There was no cross-examination of either witness by the prosecution. With the completion of Mr. Sperafico's testimony, the defense rested.

It was a little past seven in the evening. Judge Debaillon informed both teams of advocates that following a brief recess he would call for closing arguments.

Court reconvened about 7:30, and William Campbell began the prosecution's closing. Addressing the jury, Campbell made four points: the Blanc brothers were guilty; each juror had sworn that he had no qualms about imposing capital punishment; nothing in the evidence warranted a qualified verdict; and if the jury brought in a qualified verdict, the accused might at some time in the future either escape from the penitentiary or be pardoned and released. They must be sentenced to hang: "the people demand their punishment." The district attorney followed, concentrating on the enormity of the crime: "It was unparalleled in the annals of civilization, and was without doubt the most damnable in its atrocity of any that could disgrace the history of barbarism." Gordy told the jury that the defense might try to argue that Alexis Blanc deserved a more lenient sentence since he was not the "cutter," to use Ernest's words; the D.A. contended that as "they were united in the perpetration of the crime, then they should be united in death." He closed by reminding the jury that the defendants had not taken the stand in their own defense.

For the defense's closing, Colonel Breaux began with tangential comments in praise of "Mr. Begnaud," the victim's brother, for "his magnanimous and noble stand" in preventing mob rule in the parish.

There were two Mr. Begnauds inside the bar and the colonel did not specify which one he was referring to, but he almost certainly meant Simeon, whose efforts in this regard were well known; Jean's contributions had been more subtle. Suave and impeccably attired despite the late hour, Breaux turned his attention to the fate of his charges. They had received a fair trial and now it was up to the jury, "twelve men good and true and honest," as the defense attorney reformulated the traditional description. He would not try to excuse the crime but asked the jury to remove all thoughts of vengeance from their hearts: "Vengeance is mine, saith the Lord God of hosts, and vengeance has no place in the laws of the state." He then carefully explained the law regarding capital murder cases and the fact that it allowed them to bring in a "qualified verdict," which he implored them to do: "Look at these two young men and ask yourself if you can find it in your hearts to hang them." Ralph Elliott followed Colonel Breaux, delivering a brief but eloquent appeal for mercy. It was the only time in the course of the trial that either of the brothers displayed any emotion: when the advocate described the Blancs as "motherless, fatherless and friendless," Alexis Blanc began to cry. The younger brother regained his composure as Elliott relinquished the floor to Caffery, who launched into a scathing attack on capital punishment, which he described as "cruel and a relic of barbarism."

Governor Mouton was the last member of the defense team to address the jury, and when he rose, a new silence filled the courtroom. The hour was now approaching 9 P.M.; it had been a long day. Obviously very tired, disheveled, and looking much older than his seventy-four years, Homer Mouton delivered a plea for mercy that demonstrated his sincere compassion for the two young men whose very lives had been placed in his hands. He asked the jury to bring in a qualified verdict, and closed the defense's case powerfully: "If you shut your ears to the cry of mercy from these boys, beware when you face the eternal judgment; beware that the Judge of all judges does not say to you when you ask for mercy: 'You showed it not, but yielded to public clamor and took life.'" None of the defense attorneys tried to bifurcate the verdict, to persuade the jury that Alexis should receive a more lenient sentence than his brother. The district attorney had the option to close for the state, and he did. Minos Gordy appealed to the manhood of the jurors and ask them to "stand up for Louisiana." Mob rule, he argued, was only encouraged when the law failed to act in the manner prescribed. He urged them to bring in an unqualified verdict of guilty. Judge Debaillon then charged the jury.

The judge's charge focused on the Louisiana laws applicable in a murder case, both for assigning the death penalty and for bringing a qualified verdict. He explained that the brothers had been charged together as principals, and that "if the jury was satisfied that one was present, aiding and abetting the other, although he did not inflict a wound himself, he was equally guilty." He added that "a confession, when voluntarily made, was . . . the highest kind of evidence." After reading to the jury its duties and responsibilities directly from the Louisiana Revised Statutes, he turned the case over to them. It was 10:45 P.M. The jury was out fifteen minutes. At 11 o'clock they filed into the crowded courtroom. George A. DeBlanc, who had just been elected foreman, read the verdict: "Guilty as charged in the bill of indictment." Governor Mouton asked that the jury be polled, and each individual member responded with the word "guilty." Ernest Blanc's lips quivered, and he turned to his elderly lawyer and said, in French, "Well, I guess it's only a matter of a few days now." Homer Mouton did not answer, he simply wept.

Judge Debaillon thanked the jury for its work and complimented the advocates on both sides for the professional manner in which they had conducted themselves and the case. He then declared court adjourned and ordered the courtroom cleared. Ernest and Alexis Blanc shook hands with each of their attorneys and thanked them for their efforts and their kindness. After the prisoners had been returned to their cell, one of the lawyers informally asked the judge why he had not set a date for sentencing, a common practice at the end of trials yielding guilty verdicts. Debaillon replied that he had chosen not to announce the sentencing date in order to save his courtroom from further destruction. That day, a third bench had crashed under the weight of the crowds. A public announcement would only have guaranteed another overflow audience. Also during these informal posttrial conversations, William Stansbury asked the defense attorneys why they had not made a plea to save the life of Alexis Blanc. An unidentified member of the defense team replied that, yes, such an appeal to the jury had been part of the original strategy, but sometime during the course of the trial the clients had directed the team not to pursue it. The brothers had decided that they would either be freed together or they would die together. The *Daily Picayune* speculated that the case would undoubtedly be appealed to the Louisiana Supreme Court.

The most sensational murder trial in the history of south Louisiana was over. The next morning, the aggressive correspondent of the *Daily Picayune* parked himself outside the window of the ground-floor jail cell that housed the convicted killers and conducted a lengthy, in-depth interview with them. His report appeared as a front-page lead story in the Sunday, February 28, 1897, issue of the paper. In many ways it is an interesting piece, for it provides additional insight into the character of the condemned brothers. The Blancs appeared to be in "splendid health and spirits." They had just had a great breakfast, a special treat from the sheriff, and they were looking forward to another visit from a group of nuns from the Mt. Carmel Convent in Lafayette—apparently the nuns had visited them in the parish prison sometime before the trial. Expecting to find the brothers despondent, the reporter found instead "great good humor." Alexis in particular had undergone a transformation. Whereas before he had been quiet and absorbed in his thoughts, the scribe now found him "talkative and full of questions." The writer attributed the brothers' attitude to the great load having been lifted from their shoulders. The two expressed much gratitude to Sheriff Broussard and William Campbell, who they believed had saved their necks—literally—from the hands of several lynch mobs, and they had high praise for their attorneys. But they reserved special praise for Thomas Mouton, the chief deputy, for whom they obviously felt particular affection.

Probing questions into the Blancs' personal life prior to arriving in the United States, however, yielded little. Their mother, they said, had died in 1893, and their father, a banker, in 1889. When the reporter inquired as to the first name of their father, neither could remember. "A strange admission," wrote the correspondent. Nonetheless, he admiringly observed the deep "fraternal affection" the brothers had for one another. The interview ended in late morning when Governor Mouton and Colonel Breaux arrived for a consultation with their clients. The attorneys were eager to begin developing a strategy for an appeal based on the several bills of exception they had reserved during the trial. But there would be no appeal. Apparently the Blanc brothers that morning vetoed the recommendations of their legal advisers. Later, in response to another reporter's question as to why no appeal was made, Ernest replied emphatically, "Why should we? It will only prolong our troubles."

In preparation for writing a story with a very different ending, the *Daily Picayune* reporter had mingled freely with the throngs of people who had converged on the courthouse square during the trial and had interviewed several of the "rough-looking men" who had surrounded the courthouse and crowded into an already overcrowded courtroom just as the jury retired for its deliberations at 10:45 Friday night. The men spoke candidly. Their plan, had the jury brought in a qualified verdict, was to hang the jury first, and then bring the Blanc brothers to Scott Station and hang them from a tree near the scene of the crime. Most of these men, who numbered in the hundreds, were from the Scott Station and Carencro areas. When asked to comment on the conspiracy, Ike Broussard said he had been fully aware of the plan and had "provided for all emergencies." The entire budget for the sheriff's department of Lafayette Parish in 1897, as appropriated by the parish police jury, was $2,300, which covered the salaries of the sheriff and the three deputies plus all operating expenses for the office. (Fortunately for the sheriff, the costs of feeding prisoners in the parish jail did not have to come from this allotment; the prison warden who doubled as the chief deputy billed the police jury on a monthly basis for such expenses.) If the sheriff employed special or auxiliary deputies, he had to depend on an agreeable police jury to appropriate additional funds after the fact, not always a foregone conclusion when a rival political faction had a majority vote on the parish administrative council. It is almost certain that Ike Broussard engaged several special deputies over the many tension-packed days during the trial of Ernest and Alexis Blanc. But even with several dozen special deputies, the sheriff's ability to "provide for all emergencies" is open to question. The *Daily Picayune* article of February 28 ended with the reporter's assessment of the post-trial atmosphere in Lafayette: "The verdict, however, settled everything and today everything is as quiet as usual."

On Monday, March 1, Judge Debaillon decided on the sentencing date—it would be Thursday, March 4—but he told no one except the officers of the court and the attorneys for the Blanc brothers. The judge requested that they be in his courtroom at midafternoon on that date. As requested, all parties were present at the appointed hour, and the sheriff was instructed to retrieve the prisoners. There were only a few visitors in the courtroom that afternoon. At 3:30 P.M., Ernest and Alexis Blanc stood before Judge Debaillon. The judge asked Ernest in English if he had anything to say. He replied in English that he had nothing to say. The same question was put to Alexis, and he gave the same response. Debaillon then told them that they had been ably defended by eminent counsel and that the facts in the case justified the findings. He then pronounced sentence. Ernest was sentenced first:

> In this case, after trial, the Jury having returned a verdict of guilty; the defendant Ernest Blanc and his counsel being now present in open Court, said Ernest Blanc was asked by the Court if he had anything to say why the sentence of the law should not now be pronounced upon him and having declared that he had nothing to say or offer, it was by the Court considered that Ernest Blanc here present in Court be taken hence and to the common Jail of this parish or to some other lawful place of confinement and there detained in sage and sure custody until his Excellency the Governor of the State of Louisiana shall fix the day of his execution, and on the day so fixed by his Excellency, the said Ernest Blanc be taken thence and within the four walls of the Parish Jail of the Parish of Lafayette or within the enclosures of said Parish Jail, or in an enclosure about or near said Jail and the said Ernest Blanc then and there suffer the punishment of death by being hung by the neck until he be dead, as provided by act No. 79 of the General Assembly of this State approved July 10th 1884.

The pronouncement for Alexis was identical, the court order differing only in the substitution of his name for Ernest's.

Both brothers were sentenced to hang.

23

New Orleans: March 1897

The recently concluded winter session of the Seventeenth Judicial District Court had left Ike Broussard with nine convicted criminals in his jail scheduled to begin prison terms on March 10 in the state penitentiary in Baton Rouge. It was Broussard's responsibility to transport these convicts to their new residence. For several reasons, the sheriff decided to use this opportunity to move the Blanc brothers back to Orleans Parish Prison. Their status had changed. They were no longer simply accused of a crime; they were now convicted and condemned to death. No one had to tell Broussard that a condemned man is a desperate man. Special precautions were called for. Lynch fever had cooled considerably in the parish, but it would not take much to trigger a relapse, and rumors were circulating in Lafayette that the consul general of France in New Orleans was busy at work on behalf of his fellow countrymen.

Another consideration was that Broussard's little jail was in the process of undergoing much-needed and long-deferred repairs and renovations. The recent threats of mob rule in the parish had underscored the need to shore up security at the jail, and the police jury had appropriated funds for that purpose. Workmen continually going in and out of the jail and hammering and sawing would simply offer too many opportunities for two desperate men.

Complicating matters further was the necessity for additional construction to comply with Louisiana law as contained in Judge Debaillon's court order that the hanging must take place "within the four walls of the Parish Jail of the Parish of Lafayette or within the enclosures of said Parish Jail, or in an enclosure about or near said Jail." There had not been a legal hanging in Lafayette Parish since before the Civil War. Back then, "enclosures" were unnecessary; executions took place outdoors under a tree. Progress and modernity as manifested in the laws regulating hanging demanded an enclosure, and since conducting the execution inside the jail was not even an option, the sheriff ordered that a wooden fence eighteen feet high be constructed adjacent to the jail in a large empty lot on the north side. The fence would encircle a small area that would hold the gallows and allow enough room for about fifty spectators.

The exact date of the executions was still unknown. Once an accused person had been duly tried and convicted and all appeals had been exhausted, the governor could legally set the date. Since there was no appeal in this case, Ed Voorhies, the parish clerk of court, was responsible for compiling the necessary paperwork and forwarding it to the governor's office for consideration by the state's chief executive. It was a new experience for Voorhies. It marked the first time in his long career that the documents he had to complete were a matter of life and death, and he wanted to make certain that all was in order. He proceeded carefully. Governor Foster's practice was to set an execution date within two weeks of receiving the appropriate documentation. Construction of the enclosure would not begin until the date of execution was set, but Broussard knew that Voorhies was nearly finished with his phase of the process and that, from that point on, events would move quickly. Late on the afternoon of Tuesday, March 9, Broussard walked to the cell housing the Blanc brothers and told them to be prepared to travel that night. He would come for them at 2 A.M. and they would board the night train for New Orleans. To assist him in the prisoner transfer, the sheriff engaged the services of two strong, dependable young men as auxiliary deputies: L. Leo Judice and Aurelian Olivier. Broussard himself would be in charge of the Blancs, while Chief Deputy Mouton and the two special deputies would guard the other prisoners.

In the days following the trial, the Blanc brothers received a steady flow of visitors, mostly curiosity seekers. The young men were celebrities. Their most welcome visitors were the sisters of the Mt. Carmel Convent, who came almost every day. The most unwelcome was Father Forge, whom the Blancs refused to see. (No doubt they remembered the priest's disingenuous testimony at the change of venue hearing.) And a new cast of reporters had replaced the members of the New Orleans press corps. With a hiatus in the legal proceedings, the city papers had recalled their correspondents, but they had been succeeded by reporters from the local weeklies: the *St. Landry Clarion*, the *Opelousas Courier*, the *Abbeville Meridional*, the *Crowley Signal*, the *Weekly Iberian*, and the two Lafayette papers. No new revelations appeared in the posttrial articles published in these journals. The condemned brothers continued to lament the fact that they had been done in by their own words but seemed to accept the outcome of the case. As Alexis Blanc told a reporter from the *Courier*, "We burned the last bridge of hope when we made our confession and the verdict was a just one."

For some time, Chief Deputy Mouton had been encouraging the Blancs to write an account of their extensive travels and adventures. Perhaps realizing that time was running out, Ernest Blanc began to write the day after they had been found guilty. By sunlight during the day and candlelight at night, it took him four days to complete *Meurtre de Martin Begnaud*, "Murder of Martin Begnaud." It is a record of their travels in Europe and the United States in 1893, a blow-by-blow account of the gruesome events of April 22, 1896, at Scott Station, and another travelogue of their international voyages following the murder. The ten-page memoir is thus a written confession. On March 3, when the writing was completed and the dedication to Thomas Mouton inscribed, first Ernest and then Alexis affixed their signatures to the document. The prisoners then presented the piece to their beloved jailer.

If Ernest needed further inspiration to continue writing, he received it the next day when Judge Debaillon sentenced him and his brother to hang. The very next morning he began writing *La Vie Humaine*, "Human Life," six pages of reflection on the miserable and hopeless mess he had made of his life, the unrealistic and immature influence resulting from his exposure to the novels of Gustave Aimard (a French novelist who wrote on the subject of the American West and Mexico), and the two hard but not unpleasant years he and his brother had spent on Boudreaux Plantation. Completed on March 8, *La Vie Humaine* was also dedicated and presented as a gift to Thomas Mouton.

These compositions seem to have been cathartic for Ernest Blanc. On Tuesday, March 9, he had begun work on his third literary effort when he was interrupted from his musings by the sheriff's announcement that he and his brother were being moved to New Orleans. It was the news the brothers had been waiting to hear. Over the last several days, in the quiet, dark hours of the night, they had concocted a plan of escape. They knew that it represented a desperate attempt with little chance of success, but they were desperate men. They had nothing to lose.

The scheme was simple, but it required the participation of both brothers. During exercise or outhouse breaks, only one prisoner was allowed outside his cell at a time. But if they were being moved to New Orleans, both brothers would have to be let out of their cell at the same time, or at least that was their hope. The fact that their transfer was going to take place at night was an added bonus. Inside the dark jail, with only candles and lanterns to provide minimal light, the chances for the successful execution of their plan would be enhanced. Sheriff Broussard's weapon of choice for travel was a Winchester rifle, but in his jail he always wore a holstered revolver. The Blancs saw that revolver as their ticket to freedom. At 2 A.M., the only light in the Blanc cell would come from one candle. Ernest would stand back in one corner of the cell with the lit candle, leaving Alexis in the other, dark corner. With Ernest in view, an assault on the sheriff by the gentle Alexis would be unexpected. Alexis's assignment was to take advantage of the element of surprise by grabbing the sheriff's side arm, with Ernest right behind to assist in the subjugation of the lawman. And they had a weapon. Over the last several nights when all was quiet, the brothers had worked loose an iron bar from between the mortar and bricks of the little chimney in their jail cell. Its purpose was for use as a club. Once armed and in control, with the sheriff as a hostage, they would make their escape.

At the designated hour, as Sheriff Broussard prepared to enter the barred corridor where the cell housing the Blanc brothers was located, he lifted his revolver out of its holster and gave it to his chief deputy to hold. This was very uncharacteristic behavior. Perhaps it was the almost total darkness in the corridor that prompted this added bit of precaution on Broussard's part, but in any event, Thomas Mouton took the gun from his boss. When Ernest heard the sheriff coming, he lit the candle and stood off to one side. Broussard unlocked the cell door and as he walked in, he was jumped by Alexis Blanc. The sheriff was, indeed, surprised, but not as surprised as Alexis when he reached down and found an empty holster. In the meantime, just as Alexis made his move, Ernest reached down to grab the iron bar, but in doing so, he dropped the lighted candle. Now the entire cell was pitch-black, which served to even the odds. Quickly, Broussard pushed Alexis hard into his brother, causing both to go crashing down along with the sheriff, who ended up on top of them. In complete darkness, Broussard quickly handcuffed Alexis first, threw him aside, and then handcuffed Ernest. The entire episode lasted less than a minute. Later that morning, on the train to New Orleans, the Blanc brothers and Sheriff Broussard held a frank discussion of the escape attempt; there appeared to be no hard feelings on anyone's part.

The New Orleans dailies had coined a new epithet for the infamous Blanc brothers: the "Boy Murderers." When the big-city papers learned that the brothers were being moved, correspondents were sent to cover the transfer. Two major stories resulted. One dealt with the attempted escape, which was covered in every detail. The sensational nature of the stories written about the abortive escape attempt served to further darken in the public mind the already dismal image of Ernest and Alexis Blanc. They were portrayed in these newspaper accounts as truly desperate, vicious criminals, or in the words of the *Times-Democrat*, "young demons."

The other story to emerge from press coverage of the prison transfer concerned the existence of a second murder weapon. Almost as an afterthought, in casual conversation on the train ride to New Orleans in the early morning hours of March 10, Alexis Blanc mentioned that he and his brother had forged a second file into a dagger. He had carried it on his person the night of the robbery and murder, but had never used it. Both files had been buried behind the little cabin on Boudreaux Plantation, about six feet apart. Alexis wondered aloud to the sheriff whether the file that had been found was in fact the true murder weapon. In response to Broussard's inquiry as to which of the files was the actual murder weapon, neither Alexis nor Ernest could remember. The following week, when he returned from depositing his prisoners in New Orleans and Baton Rouge, Sheriff Broussard invited Simeon Begnaud to join him and a deputy in the search for the second weapon. With Colonel Boudreaux's permission to dig on his property, a second file, a twin to the first, was found. Of this discovery, a reporter given to hyperbole wrote, "It can be seen that this pointed file which was taken out of the ground today played an important part in this awful drama whose last act will soon conclude by the death on the scaffold of two of the youngest but most inhuman murderers that have darkened the criminal history of Louisiana."

One other noteworthy event transpired on that predawn train ride. In New Iberia, Robert F. Broussard, newly elected congressman from Louisiana's Third Congressional District, boarded the train. A former district attorney, he was very interested in the recent trial and—like everyone else in Louisiana—was very well acquainted with the story of the murder of Martin Begnaud. He was thrilled to meet the famous Blanc brothers and gave them each five dollars, suggesting they use the money to buy champagne. The Blancs did not follow Congressman Broussard's recommendation; instead, they used the money to buy extra food in Orleans Parish Prison.

When the Blanc brothers were escorted into their former New Orleans residence at the corner of Tulane and Basin Streets at 9 A.M. on Wednesday, March 10, it was like a homecoming. Captain Thomas Fulham, the prison warden, and turnkey Jack Villere were happy to see the inmates once again, but the Blancs were anything but happy. On instructions from Sheriff Broussard, they were placed in separate cells. After his recent experience, it was the judgment of the Lafayette Parish sheriff that keeping the brothers in different cells would seriously impede their ability to conspire in future escape attempts. They were housed on the same tier but not in the same cell. Each day of their confinement in Orleans Parish Prison, the brothers begged their jailers to allow them to share a cell together. Captain Fulham went so far as to intervene on their behalf with Sheriff Broussard, but to no avail. The headlines of one paper read, THE BLANC BROTHERS ARE MORE GRIEVED ABOUT THEIR SEPARATION THAN APPROACHING DEATH.

Ernest resumed his writing and completed the third and final piece of his trilogy. The third installment consisted of four essays, untitled, covering seven pages and dated March 9, 18, 19, and 20. Like his other writings, these were dedicated to Mr. Thomas, as the essayist called Deputy Mouton, and consisted of rambling thoughts on Ernest's life, his predicament, and the necessity to "pay his debt in order to obtain mercy and the forgiveness of God." When not writing, the elder Blanc brother read a catechism book, *The Last of the Breton Kings,* and demonstrated his considerable artistic talent by drawing a number of pen-and-ink sketches of animals and romantic figures from history. Alexis spent most of his time lying in his hammock absorbed in *Camille,* the Alexandre Dumas *fils* classic tale of love and tragedy. And the brothers continued to have many visitors, most welcome but some unwelcome. Certainly three of the latter arrived the night of March 24.

Ed Voorhies had completed all the paperwork required by Louisiana law for two legal executions to take place in his parish and had forwarded this documentation to the governor's office on March 17. Murphy Foster acted immediately. On March 18, the governor telegraphed Sheriff Broussard of his decision to set the date of execution for two weeks thence, Friday, April 2, 1897. The sheriff ordered work to begin immediately on the fence to enclose the gallows.

Because the governor made his decision on a Thursday and both his and the Louisiana secretary of state's signatures were required on the death warrant, it is probable that Broussard did not receive official delivery of the document until the following week. It was his duty as sheriff to personally serve the warrant on the Blanc brothers, and after receiving it himself he wasted little time. On his trip to New Orleans to deliver the message of death, the sheriff was accompanied by two other public officials, coroner A. R. Trahan and state senator Romuald P. "Rom" LeBlanc. The three arrived unannounced at Orleans Parish Prison at 8 P.M. Wednesday, March 24. Captain Fulham, unprepared for his visitors, was surprised when he learned of the purpose of their call. And Broussard, likewise, may have been surprised to learn that the Blancs—thanks to Georges Bosseront d'Anglade—already knew that a date had been set for their execution. Nonetheless, the letter of the law must be carried out, and the warden ordered several deputies to bring the two prisoners to a large room. There, Ernest and Alexis Blanc found the three officials from Acadian country waiting for them. It was now only 8:30, but the jailhouse information network had done its work and the place was swarming with newspapermen. Standing in front of the Blancs, the sheriff pulled a document from his pocket. All conversation ceased and silence filled the room. Broussard read the following:

DEATH WARRANT.

EXECUTIVE DEPARTMENT—STATE OF LOUISIANA.

Baton Rouge, La., March 18, 1897

To the Honorable I. A. Broussard

Sheriff of the Parish of Lafayette,

Whereas, it appears from the annexed duly certified copy, that at a session of the Honorable 17th Judicial District Court and held on the 26th day of February 1897, Ernest Blanc and Alexis Blanc were tried and convicted of the crime of Murder and for said offense were, by judgment of said Court, rendered on the 4th day of March 1897, sentenced by his Honor the Judge of said Court to be hanged by the neck until they be dead.

Now, therefore, I, MURPHY JAMES FOSTER, Governor of the State of Louisiana, do hereby direct and require you, the said I. A. Broussard, Sheriff, to cause the execution to be done on the body of said Ernest Blanc and Alexis Blanc, so convicted and condemned, in all things according to the judgment and sentence of said Court and the law in all such cases made and provided, on Friday the second day of April 1897 between the hours of 12 o'clock M and 3 o'clock PM, within the enclosure of the parish jail of your parish, in your presence and that of at least four and not exceeding fifteen witnesses, one or more of whom shall be a practicing physician, residents of your parish, who shall duly attest the same, under oath, which attestation shall be returned by you together with the annexed copy of the proceedings had in said case, to said Court, and for which this will be your warrant and authority.

Given under my signature and the Seal of the State of Louisiana, at the City of Baton Rouge the same day, month and year first above written.

Sig Murphy J. Foster

Governor of Louisiana

Sig John T. Michel

Secretary of State

When the sheriff had finished reading the warrant, Ernest Blanc was the first to speak: "We are ready anytime now." Sheriff Broussard asked if there was anything he could do for them. Surprisingly, they did not ask to be placed in the same cell, perhaps because they already knew the answer. But Ernest did request corridor privileges, and Broussard said he had no objections provided Captain Fulham gave his permission. "I see the French consul is trying hard to get your sentence commuted," observed Broussard. "Yes, but it is too late now," replied Ernest. "Yes, too late," added Alexis. Cigars were passed all around. Alexis declined, but Ernest lit up.

Book VIII

THE BROTHERS

24

New Orleans: March 1897

L'Abeille de la Nouvelle-Orléans was almost certainly the daily newspaper of choice for French officials in New Orleans. The Saturday morning edition of March 19, 1897, contained a bulletin noting that Governor Foster had signed the *arrêt de mort*, death warrant, for Ernest and Alexis Blanc, setting April 2 as the execution date. Early the following morning, Orleans Parish chief deputy sheriff Ben Tiller was in his office in the Criminal District Court Building drinking coffee and reading the Sunday papers. Tiller was surprised to look up from his reading and see three well-dressed, distinguished-looking gentlemen standing before him. They introduced themselves as Consul General d'Anglade, his deputy Henri Dessommes, and E. J. Meral, an attorney-at-law. The consul general requested that he and his colleagues be escorted to Orleans Parish Prison and be allowed to interview the Blanc brothers. His request was granted without delay.

The three were taken first to the cell of Alexis Blanc. After taking down copious notes of a personal nature, such as birth date, schools attended, date of departure from France, parents' names and dates of death, d'Anglade turned to questions about the trial. For the first time, Alexis expressed the opinion that he and his brother had not received a fair trial. According to the *Daily Picayune,* "He was satisfied in his own mind that the jury was prejudiced and had determined its verdict before being sworn in." The consul general's interview with Ernest followed the same pattern with the same results; Ernest, too, did not feel they had received a fair trial. It was d'Anglade, during the course of these interviews, who informed the brothers that the governor had set the date for their execution. This distressing news was at least somewhat offset by the French official's genuine concern for his two young countrymen and his promise to "see what I can do for you."

Outside, d'Anglade went out of his way to make it abundantly clear to the press that he was acting "not as an official representative here of the French government," but "as an individual." But Sheriff William Uniacke was not happy with the turn of events. He had planned to keep the news of the execution date from the Blancs for as long as possible. After d'Anglade's disclosure, the sheriff placed the brothers under a deathwatch for which he had to hire three new deputies, and he vowed to send the bill to Lafayette Parish.

Born in Paris in 1858, Marie Gabriel Georges Bosseront d'Anglade was the son of a high-ranking official in the French foreign ministry. Both he and an older brother had followed in their father's footsteps and become diplomats. D'Anglade had received his first posting at the tender age of seventeen to Montevideo, Uruguay, with the rank of *consul suppléant*, assistant consul. This was followed by promotions and new assignments to London and Honolulu, and in 1893 he was sent to New Orleans as consul general. By spring 1897, d'Anglade knew this was to be his last year in the Crescent City; in January 1898 he would become consul general in Milan, Italy. Yet his last year in Louisiana would be one of the most memorable in a long and distinguished diplomatic career, encompassing as it did the Blanc brothers affair as well as his own courtship of and marriage to Alice Macmurdo Yuille, a beautiful New Orleans widow. In a letter to the Quai d'Orsay informing his superiors of this new development in his personal life, d'Anglade emphasized that "Mrs. Yuille is of American nationality but she comes from an old Creole family established in Louisiana for nearly 200 years and by her language, her education and her habits, she is essentially French."

It is probable that d'Anglade and his fiancée had many discussions on the subject of his humanitarian efforts on behalf of his two young countrymen. Of course, the consul general was well acquainted with the Martin Begnaud murder case from his dealings with Gustave Balin, but he had remained in the background; lawyers engaged by his office had shielded his involvement. Thus far, his only direct entanglement in this affair had been his telegram forwarded to acting governor Snyder expressing concern for the safety of the Blanc brothers in the Lafayette Parish prison. His decision to come to their aid now probably stemmed from a genuine feeling of compassion for the two young orphans, as well as doubts cast as to the fairness of their trial.

On March 7, d'Anglade had received a disturbing letter from H. L. Falk, president of the Louisiana Mutual Benevolent Association, a New Orleans insurance company. Born and raised in Lafayette Parish and well acquainted with its people and customs, Falk had the credentials of a credible commentator, and his letter must have been enlightening to d'Anglade. On the subject of the law, Falk wrote, "There is not an iota of proof that these Boys Commited this Crime beyond there own Confession. Which is no proof of there Guilt, The Law of this state does not permit any man to give evidence against himself, Consequently there is no proof that these boys are Guilty." In an effort to help the Frenchman understand the situation accurately, he went on, "I was borne in that town and I am fully aware the way that Justice is adminsterd there. If you have friends and money you are safe, If you have nether friends or money, you are indeed doomed." He closed with a threat: "It is your Duty to bring this mater before the Abbassodore in Washington, or before your Goverment. Should I not get any answer from you i will write direct to Washington, D.C." Falk's family was prominent in Lafayette, where they owned Falk's Opera House, a popular theater for traveling and local productions, political rallies, and various other gatherings. The family was also active in the Republican Party. Thus Falk certainly had insight into the criminal justice system of his home parish as it was administered by the Democratic power structure. D'Anglade sent him a handwritten one-sentence reply thanking him for his interest in and sympathy for the plight of d'Anglade's "compatriots." It is not known if the diplomat met personally with Falk to obtain more information, but he may have.

Falk's letter and the Blanc brothers' assertions that they had not received a fair trial seem to have convinced d'Anglade that he must do whatever he could—within his self-imposed limits "as an individual"—to save the lives of his countrymen, and time was running out. His only hope was for the governor to issue a reprieve or a commutation of sentence. D'Anglade knew that given Foster's reputation for law and order, it was entirely possible that the governor would refuse to consider either of these options under any conditions, but he was determined to make the effort nonetheless. Consultations with several attorneys produced four avenues identified as having some potential for success. The first was a personal appeal by d'Anglade to Foster, one humanitarian to another. A second possibility was an effort to tilt the tide of public opinion in favor of mercy for the two young, poor, orphaned foreigners. The third was a petition signed by an overwhelming number of the state's citizens urging the governor to grant clemency to the condemned Frenchmen. Finally, if all else failed, d'Anglade would try to organize a petition out of Lafayette Parish aimed either at persuading Foster to save the lives of the Blanc brothers through a commutation of sentence or at getting the presiding judge in the case to make such a recommendation to the governor or to the state board of pardons. The last approach grew out of d'Anglade's lawyers' having informed him that regarding criminal cases, local public opinion and the views of the sitting judge were influential with state officials.

The consul general made his personal appeal to the governor in a handwritten letter dated March 25. After notifying Foster that a petition sponsored by the French societies of New Orleans and signed by a "large number of the residents of this city" was on its way to the governor's desk, d'Anglade made his plea: "I am aware that the brothers Blanc have confessed to the crime but they are orphans, without a friend, in a foreign land, and so young, that, confident in your high sense of humanity and your well known sentiments, I will ask you two favors. First, to grant a reprieve of execution, sufficient for the petition in favor of the Blanc brothers to be thoroughly examined by the board of pardons. Second, that the Blanc brothers be kept in the Parish Prison of New Orleans to prevent the possible consequence of public animosity in Lafayette. I am confident that your Excellency will grant me these two favors asked in behalf of my countrymen."

Murphy J. Foster was touched by d'Anglade's letter. His reply, dated March 27, is a thoughtful four-page letter written in his own hand. No copies were made, for the letter is not in the Murphy J. Foster Papers or the Louisiana State Archives. The consul general had the only copy and kept it. The text of the governor's letter in its entirety:

I have the honor to acknowledge receipt of your communication of the 25th instant, concerning the reprieve of the Blanc brothers, and have carefully considered its contents.

Superadded to a natural desire to temper justice with mercy, the appeal of the citizens of France residing in New Orleans, coming through the official representative of that great Republic, must have profound weight in my determination of the grave question of executive clemency to the Blanc brothers.

These parties, by their own confession, are guilty and were convicted of a crime, for brutality and cruelty, which scarcely finds a parallel in the criminal annals of this or any other civilized country.

There is absolutely no doubt of their guilt. Nor is any alleged.

There is no question of the fairness and impartiality of their trial and since their conviction, there are no developments, even suggested, going to show any mitigating or extenuating circumstances connected with this crime. On the contrary, their conduct, since conviction, in attempting to take the life of Sheriff Broussard, fully establishes the fact, in my mind, that they are most dangerous and desperate criminals.

The grounds set forth, in your appeal, for my interference is that they are youthful strangers.

These young men have fully reached the age of accountability for their acts. Indeed, they are men, in physical development and far above the average in intelligence. While friendless strangers, in a foreign land, must command our sympathies, these parties, in the legal proceedings leading up to their conviction, had all the benefits and privileges extended our own citizens, and there is no claim of bias or prejudice on account of their foreign citizenship.

They were defended by the ablest members of the bar, appointed by the Court before which they were tried and to the credit of the legal profession, these attorneys ably and conscientiously discharged their duty.

To interfere with the regular, fixed and proper course of the law in this case, would be to invite a disregard for the law. And convinced, as I am, that the Blanc brothers, after a fair trial, have been convicted of a most revolting crime, I am compelled to decline to interfere with the administration of law and justice in this case.

With assurances that this determination is from a full sense of my official duty and responsibility, I have the honor to remain, with great respect, Murphy J. Foster, Governor of Louisiana.

Even before receiving Foster's reply, d'Anglade set his second option into motion. Statewide sentiment against the Blanc brothers was fundamentally due to the sensational nature of the reporting of all aspects of the case by the New Orleans dailies. If these same newspapers could somehow be persuaded to mount a publicity campaign for clemency, public opinion might be swayed. To lead this effort, the French diplomat turned to the most influential and respected man in the city—and the only man who might perform such a miracle—the archbishop of the Roman Catholic Diocese of New Orleans, Francis Janssens. Like the consul general, Janssens was a strong opponent of capital punishment, and he agreed to help, but unofficially, behind the scenes, and under conditions of strict confidentiality. Janssens would approach his close friend Thomas G. Rapier, publisher of the *Daily Picayune.* Rapier was a devout Catholic and a Knight of St. Gregory, one of the highest honors the pope can bestow on a Catholic layman, signifying deep devotion and high service to the Church.

Under normal circumstances, the archbishop would wield substantial influence with Rapier, but not on this occasion. There is no known record in the United States of the discussions or correspondence that took place between the prelate and the publisher concerning this matter of manipulating public opinion, but fortunately, d'Anglade filed away the confidential letter he received from Janssens, to which the archbishop had attached Rapier's equally confidential reply to Janssens's request to launch a public appeal for clemency for Ernest and Alexis Blanc, and both letters are in the French Diplomatic Archives in Nantes, France. They reveal that Rapier killed the idea in no uncertain terms: "Your Grace, I have this to say=1st The Picayune would oppose a commutation and I think the Times-Democrat would do the same=2nd I am satisfied the general public would oppose a commutation and think it probable that any strong effort in that direction would cause a great deal of bad feeling if not have worse consequences."

Thus rebuffed by the press, d'Anglade now shifted his focus to the chief legal officer of Louisiana, the attorney general. Although Baton Rouge had been reinstated as the state capital in 1879 as part of the Democratic backlash against Reconstruction, the attorney general was still located in New Orleans with offices at the Cotton Exchange. On the afternoon of March 22, the consul general paid a visit to the current attorney general, Milton J. Cunningham. The French official sought advice on how to proceed with a petition drive on behalf of the Blanc brothers. Cunningham, from Natchitoches in northwest Louisiana, was in his third term and knew the process well. He explained the form the petition should take and the procedure for placing it before the state Board of Pardons, after first procuring a recommendation from the presiding judge in the case. Cunningham was gracious but not optimistic. He did not discourage d'Anglade's efforts in New Orleans, but offered a bit of advice, advice that d'Anglade had already been given by his own attorneys: a petition for clemency would carry the greatest weight with the Board of Pardons if it originated in and was signed by the citizens of Lafayette Parish. There was no meeting of the Board of Pardons planned before April 2, but one could be called if the petitions generated enough interest among the general citizenry and among members of the board, or if it received a recommendation of clemency from Conrad Debaillon. The consul general and his advisers decided to mobilize their forces in New Orleans first.

Emil Joseph Meral and J. Numa Augustin, highly respected members of the Louisiana bar, both served from time to time as attorneys for the French consulate; both were also leaders and members of the many French societies active in New Orleans during the second half of the nineteenth century. D'Anglade hoped that the members of these organizations, influenced by Meral and Augustin, would serve as the core group of signatories for his petition. On March 23, an emergency meeting of the presidents of the fourteen active French societies was held for the purpose of reviewing a draft of the petition, prepared by Augustin and directed to the governor. A final draft was agreed upon, and the presidents made plans to circulate copies throughout *la Ville* in hopes of obtaining thousands of signatures.

Beginning with the Louisiana Purchase in 1803 and continuing for the remainder of the century, each year witnessed a decline in French influence in Louisiana and a concomitant decline in the number of Francophones as the region became more and more Americanized. This process was more rapid in New Orleans than in the Acadian country as a result of immigration—mostly Irish, German, and Italian—and the cosmopolitan, commercial nature of the city. By the end of the century, the forces mobilized to preserve the French language in the daily and business life of New Orleans were fighting a rearguard action. Yes, there were still enough Francophones to support a bilingual daily newspaper, *L'Abeille de la Nouvelle-Orléans,* but just barely; it would cease daily publication in 1917 and, after surviving five more years as a weekly, close its doors forever in 1923. The most visible remnants of French influence in the Crescent City were intellectual, charitable, musical, and social societies committed to preserving the French language and culture. The most prestigious of the fourteen active in 1897 was *L'Athénée Louisianais,* a learned society dedicated to the study of scientific, literary, artistic, and international affairs. By and large, the remaining societies were essentially social clubs interested in good food, good wine, and good times, all in French. *La Société du 14 Juillet, La Société Française de Bienfaisance, La Société Française de Jefferson, Les Bouchers,* and *Les Orphéon* were among the largest. As organizations, their political clout was minimal, but their membership rolls contained men of great influence and position.

The petition these people were being asked to sign consisted of two and a half typed pages and emphasized the youth of the Blancs and their status as "both strangers, without relations or friends" who, "being orphans, have been deprived of the benefits of a moral and family education." "In the spirit of clemency and pity," it requested Foster to "commute the death sentence of Alexis and Ernest Blanc to imprisonment in the State Penitentiary for Life." Over the next few days, signatures to the petition were solicited, but with disappointing results. The petition sent to Governor Foster on March 26 contained only seven hundred signatures, d'Anglade's not among them. As he said in his cover letter, "I do not consider that in my official capacity, it would be proper for me to sign that document, but endorse it most heartily." The next day, March 27, d'Anglade received Foster's reflective letter and knew that there would be no reprieve. On March 29, however, a small glimmer of hope appeared in the form of a personal note from the governor: "I have received your favor inclosing petitions for clemency in the case of the Blanc brother [sic] and handed the same to Attorney General Cunningham, of the Board of Pardons, in person." Was Governor Foster shifting responsibility in this matter to the attorney general's office? Could it be that Foster might reconsider his position if the Board of Pardons acted favorably on the petition?

D'Anglade had not forgotten Cunningham's recommendation that a petition from Lafayette Parish would have considerable impact before the board. Toward that end, the diplomat telegraphed the only Frenchman he knew in Lafayette Parish and implored him to circulate a petition on behalf of the Blanc brothers. It was a waste of time. Mincing no words, Father Ernest Forge replied that "no one in the parish would sign such a petition." Running out of time and options, d'Anglade sent his friend and lawyer, Numa Augustin, to consult with Attorney General Cunningham. Cunningham was candid. The law must be followed, and he would not call a meeting of the Board of Pardons unless he received a recommendation for clemency from Judge Debaillon. But Cunningham had obviously given the matter some thought, and he offered Augustin some friendly advice: approach Debaillon through his father-in-law, Homer Mouton. Cunningham knew that Mouton felt a deep personal affection for the brothers and that he had struggled valiantly under adverse conditions to try to save them from the hangman's noose.

Upon learning of Cunningham's suggested avenue of approach from Augustin, d'Anglade could not believe his good fortune. That very day, March 29, d'Anglade had received—via messenger—the following letter: "Having been one of the counsels who have defended Ernest and Alexis Blanc, by appointment of the Court, I desired to see you concerning the case of these unfortunate young men. I came to the city yesterday on business and I regret that my business compels me to leave in the morning for home. If I can do anything to obtain a commutation of their sentence I would be happy to do so. I am stopping at Fabacher's Restaurant and will be there at 7 P.M." It was signed "C. H. Mouton, St. Martinville, La."

That night, the French diplomat and the old Acadian met, and

Mouton agreed to intercede with his son-in-law on behalf of the Blanc brothers. Mouton left New Orleans the morning of March 30 armed with several copies of the petition and pledged to make a forceful case for clemency before the judge. The next day, however, d'Anglade received by personal messenger an envelope from the attorney general's office. In it was a Western Union telegram sent that day from Lafayette, Louisiana, and directed to Attorney General Cunningham. It contained one sentence: "I refuse to recommend commutation in Blanc Brother [sic]." It was signed "C. Debaillon." Cunningham had scribbled a note in the margin, "As the Judge declines delay would seem to be useless."

In Lafayette Parish, news of d'Anglade's efforts on behalf of Ernest and Alexis Blanc was greeted with anger and bitterness. It must also be observed that in the election for district judge in April 1896, Conrad Debaillon had failed to carry Lafayette Parish, being defeated there by Julian Mouton, 1,227 to 1,010. His victory was the result of an 864-vote majority in Vermilion Parish, where according to the *Lafayette Advertiser* of May 2, 1896, he received the "nigger votes." When Debaillon was reelected district judge in 1900, however, he carried Lafayette Parish by a two-to-one margin.

25

_____

New Orleans: March 1897

As was now his usual practice, Sheriff Isaac Broussard telegraphed his Orleans counterpart on Tuesday, March 30, to have his prisoners ready for travel first thing the following morning. Broussard and his chief deputy arrived a little before eight Wednesday morning, and Orleans Parish deputies were sent to retrieve the Blanc brothers. The Frenchmen were escorted into the prison bullpen, where the two Lafayette lawmen, Orleans Parish sheriff Uniacke, and prison warden Fulham were waiting. The presence of these powerful officials, obviously gathered for a final farewell, produced a jolt of reality in the two young men, like cold water being splashed in their faces. Uniacke and Fulham shook hands with the brothers, then Broussard and Mouton secured their wrist irons and marched them out of the big prison. New Orleans then witnessed its second parade headed by Ike Broussard, only this one was larger than the first. The press corps following closely on the sheriff's heels had grown considerably, and Uniacke had assigned three Orleans Parish deputies, Albert Blouin, John M. McDonald, and John McGivney, to shepherd the procession as far as the train station across the river in Algiers. All along the route, crowds gathered to watch the group go by. On board the transfer ship *Endeavor*, the brothers asked Broussard if they could remain on deck and view the river. It was a gloomy day with intermittent rain, but Broussard agreed; he stood with them near the guardrail. It was a short ride. Once on board the west-bound train, the lawmen added shackles to the prisoners' legs.

The RIDE TO THEIR DEATH, as a headline in the *Times-Democrat* cried out, was relatively uneventful. Except for occasional small talk with the sheriff and the deputy, the prisoners were alone with their thoughts. Even the members of the fourth estate seemed to respect their need for solitude; so did all passengers on the train, although they continually walked in silence up and down the aisle of the car containing the "Boy Murderers" in order to steal a glimpse of the famous pair. Ernest asked Broussard if he planned to protect them in the event of a reprieve from the governor as a result of the efforts of Monsieur d'Anglade. "I will protect you with my life," replied the sheriff.

After much time had gone by, Alexis, with tears welling up in his eyes, asked Broussard, "Are you going to hang us yourself?" "Yes," he answered. "It is my duty and I don't think a man ought to get another to perform his own duty." The question was the consequence of specu-lation in the press as to whether the sheriff or the unofficial state hang-man, known only as "Taylor," would conduct the execution. Other parishes had used Taylor over the years, and he had let it be known that he was available for the Lafayette job. Sheriff Broussard's decision to conduct the proceedings himself drew much praise from the local newspapers as a cost-saving measure. The subject under discussion ended with a request from Alexis: "When we get up there do it as quick as you can." When the Southern Pacific train reached New Iberia, Dis-trict Attorney Gordy came on board. He had ridden over from Abbe-ville to say good-bye; the accuser and the accused shook hands and declared no hard feelings all around.

En route, Broussard had surmised that a fairly large crowd would greet the brothers at their final destination, but even he was surprised by the size of the welcoming party. About three hundred people were gathered at the Lafayette railroad station to watch the sheriff and the deputy step off the train with Ernest and Alexis Blanc. The throng was quiet and orderly, more curious than anything else, and made way for the lawmen and the prisoners before following them to the jail. Once the group was inside the Lafayette Parish prison, the crowd slowly dis-persed. The brothers were taken to their old cell on the ground floor of the jail, where they received another jolt of reality: the window of the cell presented them with a full view of the gallows. As they stood in shock, staring out the window, the sheriff directed local blacksmiths Louis Lacoste and his son Leopold to do the job for which they had been paid five dollars by the parish. They had fashioned two leg irons connected by a ten-foot-long iron chain, and they now riveted one shackle to Ernest's left ankle, then passed the chain through the bars of the window and riveted the other shackle to the Alexis's right leg. Once these restraints were secured, Sheriff Broussard removed the brothers' wrist irons, freeing their hands. The long chain would allow the prisoners just enough room to move about the cell to eat, drink, visit, and use *le pot de chambre*.

Two other, more welcome visitors had been patiently waiting to see the Blancs: a pair of Catholic priests, neither of whom was Father Forge. They were admitted to the cell with the Blancs' consent. Father Ashley Henry Arthur Albert Knapp was a white-and-black-robed Dominican missionary assigned to that religious order's North American headquarters in St. Hyacinthe, Canada. Born in London in 1866 to a prominent English family whose business pursuits required them to move to France, he had received his education in that country. A convert, he was "received into the Catholic Church by the bishop of Bayeux and Lisieux in his eighteenth year, and three years later, in 1886, entered the Dominican Order at Corbara in Corsica . . . and was admitted to profession on 22 October, 1887." Father Knapp was assigned to Canada in 1895 and was serving as an itinerant missionary to the Francophone population of North America. He may have been drawn to Lafayette by the incredible amount of publicity surrounding the Martin Begnaud murder case. A bond was immediately forged between the condemned men and the monk, who at thirty-one was relatively close to them in age and who spoke their native language. The other priest, Father Julien Ravier-Boulard, was also a Frenchman, and may have been sent by Archbishop Janssens, who was probably aware of the ill will that existed between the local pastor and the Blancs. After talking and praying for a considerable time, the clergymen left, but not before Father Knapp and the Blanc brothers agreed that the missionary would administer to them the last rites of the Roman

Catholic Church, the sacrament of Extreme Unction, on the day of their execution.

When the priests were gone, Alexis, who could not take his eyes off the scaffold, explained to his brother his conception of the mechanics of the gallows and how far he thought their bodies would fall. Alexis estimated that the scaffold stood about twenty feet high with two trap-doors. One reporter explained: "The doors are worked open by an iron lever on the left side. The trap door to the right has an iron eye, which is termed a staple, and this goes through a cut in the other trap. A bar of iron, which is hinged to an upright lever, passes through the eye and holds the doors firm, but as soon as the lever is pulled it flies from the staple and the traps open." The gallows, which had never been used, had been built several years earlier in Lake Charles to hang Sylvester Atchler, who had been tried and convicted of murdering a deputy sher-iff of Calcasieu Parish, but Atchler had been granted a commutation and sentenced to life in prison. Some years later it was moved to Crow-ley to hang Octave Thibodeaux, convicted of damaging a section of Southern Pacific track at Eunice and thereby causing the death of a fireman, but he had escaped while awaiting execution. (He was eventu-ally recaptured but secured a new trial and was acquitted.) Ike Brous-sard had found the instrument of death gathering cobwebs in the Acadia Parish prison, brought it to Lafayette, and mounted it on a twenty-foot scaffold. As Alexis and Ernest were discussing the func-tioning parts of the gallows, Sheriff Broussard was hosting a press con-ference inside the wooden fence that served as the enclosure. He was in the process of giving the large number of reporters a guided tour of the gallows and a lecture on its design and operation when Alexis called out from his cell window to the sheriff to let two of the reporters test its reliability. The *Daily Picayune* noted that "everybody laughed."

At the conclusion of the press conference, Sheriff Broussard in-formed the newsmen that everything was in place for an orderly and tasteful double execution. Since the boys weighed between 150 and 175 pounds, the sheriff said that it was his "intention to give the boys a fall of about 6½ feet, which will insure a broken neck." An anonymous lady of the community had made and donated two black hoods that would be placed over the convicts' heads, and William Lewis, a carpenter and "transfer agent," had donated two pine coffins. Lewis would transport the coffins in one of his wagons the short two blocks to the paupers' section of the church cemetery, directly behind St. John the Evangelist church, where the brothers would be buried one on top of the other in a single unmarked grave, also dug by Lewis. Separated in life over the last few weeks, the Blanc brothers would have unlimited intimacy in death. They would be attired in two brand new black wool suits, white shirts, and black slippers, both pairs size nine, that Broussard had purchased from local merchant Leon Plonsky. (The next month, Broussard submitted an invoice totaling $38, with appropriate receipts from Leon Plonsky, Inc., to the Lafayette Parish Police Jury for reimbursement.) The ropes for the hanging had been greased and stretched to ensure their dependability. In deference to the family of the victim and according to custom, Ike Broussard asked Jean Begnaud—in his role as the head of the family—if he would like to provide volunteers to man the night shift of the deathwatch he had placed on the brothers. Jean Begnaud himself and his eldest nephew, Israel Prejean, the son of sister Azelie, would handle the night shift for March 31; Simeon Begnaud and J. W. Broussard, a close friend of Martin Begnaud, would take the night of April 1. Then the sheriff asked Jean Begnaud if the family wanted the privilege of tying the hangman's knot. Jean awarded that honor to his brother-in-law Alexandre Martin, perhaps in compensation for his having been excluded from the trial jury, the victim of a peremptory challenge by the defense. The husband of Martin Begnaud's youngest sister, Azema, would thus have the rare opportunity of tying two hangman's knots.

Around dusk on March 31, Simeon Begnaud called on the brothers and asked if there was anything he could get for them. Alexis, knowing Simeon's penchant for fine wine, said they would appreciate a good bottle of white wine. The tavern keeper sent over his best bottle of French white, which was served with dinner and consumed with great relish. By 10 P.M., the brothers were fast asleep on their mattresses under the watchful eyes of the Begnaud family.

Thursday, April 1, was relatively quiet for Ernest and Alexis Blanc. Early that morning, Father Knapp and Father Ravier-Boulard administered Mass and Holy Communion to the brothers. The sheriff ordered a special breakfast consisting of "steak, potatoes, plenty of browned onions and bread." After breakfast, slices of cake made especially for the prisoners by Mrs. Anatole R. Trahan, the coroner's wife, were served with glasses of wine, courtesy of the sheriff. Simeon Begnaud came by for a brief chat, and William Campbell dropped by for a visit, but the condemned men spent most of the day reading and meditating. About seven in the evening, when Sheriff Broussard dropped by to say goodnight, the brothers inquired as to the exact time of the execution, for they knew that it must occur between the hours of noon and 3 P.M. to conform with the governor's death warrant. The sheriff said one o'clock. Alexis asked if he could wait until three, and Broussard had no objection. In the last recorded conversation of the day, Alexis, who seemed to have matured over the last few weeks, emended his request, saying, "Well, will you wait not later than 2 o'clock; that will do? If the governor intends to give us a respite, he will do so around that time. Should no word come at 2 o'clock let us hang." Without hesitation, the sheriff said, "Agreed."

All day on April 1, trains arrived in Lafayette from all directions, delivering spectators from as far away as New Orleans. The gathering numbers exhibited much grumbling and dissatisfaction upon learning that, in addition to the sheriff and his deputies, only visiting sheriffs, physicians, members of the press, and the fifteen witnesses permitted by law would be allowed within the enclosure. Some of the out-of-town onlookers had traveled great distances and wanted to be as close as possible to the execution scene. There was general agreement that the fence surrounding the gallows would not survive the morrow. Throughout the day, dozens—perhaps hundreds—of people came to the jail asking to view the prisoners. Probably to avoid confrontation, Thomas Mouton agreed to permit viewing under strict conditions: if they agreed to be searched for concealed weapons, the thrill seekers would be allowed to walk, in small groups without loitering, through the jail and by the cell containing the Blanc brothers, but quietly and in silence.

As for Ernest and Alexis, they seemed amused by their notoriety. After a light supper, Ernest lit up one of the cigars that had been left for them by Sheriff Broussard, and the brothers chatted with some of the folks in the parade of onlookers, which continued well into the night. Around 10 P.M. they were served coffee, and they continued to speak to each other in hushed tones until about 2 A.M., when they seemed to go to sleep.

26

Lafayette, Louisiana: April 1897

Who were Ernest and Alexis Blanc? Who were these two young Frenchmen, arrested, tried, convicted, and condemned to death in a remote, rural town in the southern United States? What little information is available on their early years comes from two sources: Ernest Blanc's writings and the numerous interviews printed in the New Orleans newspapers. And the elder brother, having done most of the talking as well as all of the writing, is the fount of both sources.

From the beginning of the brothers' incarceration, Ike Broussard had given his chief deputy the task of making certain that nothing happened to them. Given the incredible amount of publicity surrounding all aspects of the case, the fact that the prisoners were foreign nationals, and the constant threat of "Judge Lynch," Broussard was taking no chances. Thomas Mouton thus became for all practical purposes the Blancs' personal jailer. Mouton was fifty-three years old, the father of six grown children, and a widower. He had the time and the temperament to become a surrogate father to these two orphan boys, and he did. When the Blancs were imprisoned in New Orleans, Mouton made regular trips to make certain they were being cared for properly. In the Lafayette jail, he was a constant presence outside their cell.

As previously noted, Mouton had suggested that the brothers write about their lives, and had offered to provide pen and paper. Ernest had taken advantage of the offer and completed several brief compositions, all in French and all dedicated to Mouton. Written in the beautiful penmanship so admired by the people of Scott Station, *Meurtre de Martin Begnaud* was a confession. The memoir deals mostly with events the night of the murder and the Blancs' subsequent travels in the United States and Europe. Ernest took three days to write it, and it contains a small amount of information about the brothers' lives prior to their arrival at Scott Station in the spring of 1894. His second composition, *La Vie Humaine,* is philosophical in tone and somewhat spiritual in subject matter, and provides only snippets of information on the author's childhood and adolescent years. In the four short pieces written between March 9 and March 20, Ernest reminisces about growing up in Paris and being in love with a young girl named Amélie, whom he never met but loved from afar. Taken together, these writings provide glimpses into the Blancs' early lives. The newspaper accounts form a less valuable source of biographical information. Ernest Blanc was a reporter's dream interview, always having something to say, but regarding personal matters he was vague and spoke only in general terms. A salient omission in both his prison compositions and press interviews—perhaps inadvertent, perhaps purposeful—is the names of his parents. Nevertheless, a sketch of the brothers' lives, bare though it may be, does emerge from a careful analysis of these sources. When placed in the context of history, in the context of time and place, some aspects of their biography can be deduced.

Ernest and Alexis Blanc were born in Paris in 1876 and 1877, respectively. They lived in the St. Germain-des-Prés section of the city, in those days a petit bourgeois or blue-collar neighborhood. Their father was a clerk/accountant in a bank and their mother a seamstress. Whatever the income level of the family, the Blancs said they had lived comfortably and had been thoroughly exposed to life in the Paris of the Third Republic, considered by many of that epoch to be the most exciting and vibrant city in the world. The Third Republic came into being in 1871 in the aftermath of France's disastrous defeat in the Franco-Prussian War of 1870 and the soul-wrenching experience of the Paris Commune. The country was united in its determination that such calamities must never be repeated. The democratically elected Third

Republic would endeavor to bring all Frenchmen into the life of the nation, a stance that ushered in an era of creativity rarely seen in the history of any country, in any time: in medicine and science, Pasteur, Curie, Broglie, and Poincaré; in music, Debussy and Ravel; in literature, Flaubert, Mallarmé, Sand, and Anatole France; in art, Cézanne and Degas; on the stage, Sarah Bernhardt; and in the convent, St. Thérèse of Lisieux, the "Little Flower." The reforms of the Third Republic opened the doors to a political, economic, and cultural explosion that propelled France into the modern world and placed her, once again, among the foremost nations of the globe.

By far the most important of these reforms occurred in the field of education, and the Blancs were among the beneficiaries. It was abundantly clear to anyone who met the brothers that they were well educated, and that Ernest was possibly a borderline genius. He wrote prose beautifully and possessed an extensive vocabulary. He was also considerably artistic, and while in prison enjoyed making pencil drawings and sketches of imaginary subjects with supplies provided by Thomas Mouton. The Third Republic had introduced France's first system of "lay, obligatory, free schools." This was truly a revolutionary achievement, accomplished in the face of bitter opposition from the Roman Catholic Church. Not wanting to give up their monopolistic control of French education, the clerics had "feared more good than evil might come from general literacy."

If the Blancs were, in addition to their academic prowess, fine physical specimens—and Ernest certainly was—it was probably because Pierre de Coubertin had successfully championed the mandatory teaching of physical fitness in all the nation's schools. (Coubertin was the organizer of the first modern-day Olympic Games, held in Athens in 1896.) And without a doubt the young Blancs had each had a bicycle, because Paris and all of France went bicycle-crazy in the 1880s and 1890s, thanks to two brothers named Michelin who developed a rubber tire that made bike riding a pleasure rather than a pain. Ernest and Alexis were probably too young to ride by the huge open-air warehouse where Frederic Auguste Bartholdi was building the Statue of Liberty in 1884. But they were just the right age in 1889—twelve and thirteen— to take regular rides around the great field in the center of Paris called the Champs de Mars, where Alexandre Gustave Eiffel was building the tallest edifice in the world. La Tour Eiffel was the centerpiece of the World's Fair of 1889, a celebration of the hundredth anniversary of the French Revolution. According to the Blancs, the death of their father that year did not cause undue economic hardship, and their life in Paris continued to be comfortable. Thus Mme Blanc was presumably able to afford three tickets to the most popular attraction of the fair, the Buffalo Bill Wild West show, or as the French called it, *L'Ouest Sauvage de Buffalo Bill.*

President Sadi Carnot of France, accompanied by his wife and entire cabinet, joined twenty thousand other spectators for the first performance of *L'Ouest Sauvage* on May 18. Buffalo Bill's Wild West—Colonel William F. Cody never called it a "show," disliking the circus aspect of the term—occupied thirty acres "on the edge of the Bois de Boulogne in the Parc du Neuilly within sight of the Arc de Triomphe." The U-shaped riding arena had as its background a gigantic mural of the Rocky Mountains. The show opened, as was its custom, with a parade of riders, stagecoaches, and Indians, led by Buffalo Bill himself. In the United States, this spectacle always drew wild applause and yells from the audience. Much to the riders' surprise and chagrin, the French spectators remained absolutely silent. The next event, a mock attack on the Deadwood stagecoach, also elicited little reaction. Buffalo Bill and his troupe had unknowingly encountered their first sample of culture shock. Cody and his manager began to fear that their decision to tour the Continent had been a terrible mistake, an apprehension that only grew when crack shot Annie Oakley entered the arena and the men in the stands began snickering about her diminutive stature. But Oakley then performed a series of shooting tricks that had the crowd on the edge of their seats. By the end of her act, the audience thundered, "Vive Annie Oakley! Vive Annie Oakley!"

From that moment, the French became wrapped up in the spirit of the Wild West, and the show became a must-see attraction. It played to sellout crowds for the next six months. "In Paris, everything, from buckskin suits to western sunbonnets, was bought and worn after Cody's first summer there. The stetson hat, first made popular by Cody, became the fashionable headgear for women, and children took whatever was at hand to imitate the dress of cowboys and Indians. That same year popcorn was introduced by the Wild West, and five tons of it was sold on the grounds." The sultan of Turkey, the shah of Persia, and the king of Senegal traveled long distances to see the spectacle. The latter offered Buffalo Bill one hundred thousand francs for Annie Oakley so she could clean out the lion population of his kingdom. Like other members of the show, most of the American Indians came and went as they pleased, and Parisians marveled at seeing them wandering about the city in full headdress.

In all probability, the entire experience constituted an introduction to the American West for young Ernest and Alexis Blanc, who undoubtedly marveled at the whole affair as did other children their age. For Ernest, it gave birth to a lifetime obsession. It is no surprise that his favorite writer was Gustave Aimard. Charles Breaux's gift of the book on Jesse James was by no means the brothers' introduction to frontier life.

During one of his Orleans Parish Prison interviews, Ernest Blanc mentioned that he had read all the great French classics, and referred to Alexandre Dumas in particular. This was most likely true, for Third Republic teachers would have exposed their students to the great writers and literature of France. But Blanc admits in *La Vie Humaine* that it was Aimard's novels that had stimulated his interest in the American West. Aimard sought to emulate the Leatherstocking Tales of James Fenimore Cooper, the nineteenth-century novelist of the North American frontier, but in style and content, the Frenchman's works were more akin—albeit in an inferior manner—to a later novelist of the West, Zane Grey. Aimard penned more than ninety titles between 1858 and 1883, most of them on the subject of the American West and Mexico, and his own life was an inspiration to an adventurous and impressionable boy like Ernest Blanc. Aimard had signed on as a ship's cabin boy at the age of twelve and for ten years traveled all over the world leading a life of adventure and discovery. He later lived in Mexico and traveled throughout the western United States before returning to France to write fiction based on his travels. His first novel, *The Trappers of Arkansas*, in 1858, was a best seller and was reprinted fourteen times. His subsequent books, such as *The Law of the Lynch* (1859), *The Outlaws of Missouri* (1868), *Gold Fever* (1875), and *The Bandits of Arizona* (1882), sold well but never matched the success of the first volume.

Aimard portrayed the USA's western frontier as a place of excitement, opportunity, and riches. The stories had little or no plot beyond the standard quest for gold or a woman's heart, but the descriptions of the West, with its horses, saloons, gunfights, covered wagons, and especially Indians, were vivid and exotic. These books captured Ernest Blanc's imagination: "All this reading struck my impressionable mind to such a point that nothing could hold me back, I was resolved to emigrate to America with my brother, and to settle in the Far West. The desert, with all its splendors and charm, its grandiose nature, attracted me like a magnet attracts iron." Sadly, it was the death of his mother in 1893 that presented him with the opportunity to realize his lifelong dream. Both Blanc brothers appear to have been devastated by their loss, and as Ernest explained, "Considering our position, we decided to leave France, where nothing kept us anymore." They liquidated the property and possessions of their deceased parents and boarded a steamer at Antwerp, Belgium, destination America. Eight days later, on August 24, 1893, the teenagers arrived in New York.

Once in America, the Blancs began preparations for their westward journey and their new lives as soldiers of fortune. Each purchased a rifle, a revolver, a hunting knife, a supply of ammunition, and a railroad ticket to "Omaha City," one of the most interesting places described by Aimard. Disaster struck in St. Louis, where their train had a one-day layover. They lost everything. Exactly what happened is unclear, but it seems the brothers were robbed. They would certainly have been easy marks: two inexperienced teenagers, loaded down with weapons they had no idea how to use or carry, dressed in strange clothes, and unable to speak English. They resorted to living in an abandoned cabin on the outskirts of St. Louis, subsisting on a few kernels of roasted corn, until they were rescued by a band of gypsies. The gypsies gave them food, water, shelter, and jobs caring for their herd of horses. Knowing less about horses than they did about guns, the Blanc brothers were both injured in the performance of their new duties. The gypsies took them to a hospital in St. Louis, where they stayed for about one month. While it must have been a hospital for the indigent, they were well cared for and upon their release were fully recovered. The boys had not wanted to be discharged, for winter was approaching and they had nowhere to go.

Fortunately, a local farmer offered them a job that paid no money but provided food, shelter, and clothes; they eagerly accepted the offer and spent a hard-working, but not uncomfortable, winter. With the coming of spring, they requested a change in the status of their employment; they wanted to be paid. The farmer said no, and the brothers decided to head for "New Orleans where our language was spoken." With only three dollars in their pockets, they road the rails down to New Orleans, but "finding nothing to do there," they headed west in a boxcar pulled by a locomotive of the Southern Pacific Railroad. For no particular reason, they jumped off the train at Scott Station. Perhaps they asked one of the village merchants where they might find work. In any event, they ended up at Boudreaux Plantation, where Colonel A. D. Boudreaux hired them at $25 per month and gave them a place to live. The month was April 1894.

27

Lafayette, Louisiana: April 1897

In 1880, the population of the village of Vermilionville was 888. Only seventeen years later, thanks to the railroad, the population of the town of Lafayette had quadrupled to well over 3,000. But in spite of this impressive growth, Lafayette was not ready for the mass of humanity that descended upon it on Friday, April 2, 1897. Between four and five thousand people arrived to witness the execution of Ernest and Alexis Blanc. Men and boys predominated, but many women and some girls were also present, and all were dressed in Sunday attire. It was a beautiful, clear spring day, with a low of 62 degrees at dawn that would only reach a high of 71 by noon: a perfect day for a hanging.

Every road leading into town was jammed with horses, mules, oxcarts, wagons, buggies, and pedestrians. All the Southern Pacific lines in the region were offering excursion rates, and every train that came in brought hundreds of visitors. The "Doodle Bug" was a commuter train that operated between Crowley and Lafayette. Consisting of an engine and one passenger car, it left Crowley early each morning and returned from Lafayette late every afternoon. For ten cents, the Doodle Bug could be flagged down anywhere along the route. But it made no stops that morning. When it left Crowley, it was already filled to capacity. Scott Station was deserted. Carencro looked like a ghost town. Every hotel and boardinghouse in Lafayette had been filled to capacity the night before, and every spare room in town had been rented. The saloons, all hosting packed houses, had remained open all night; business was too good to close, and besides, most customers had nowhere to go. Owing to the fence encircling the gallows, rooftops and trees were prime viewing sites, and by early morning hundreds of people had staked out claims for the available lookouts. Upon arising and assessing the view from his cell window, which revealed hundreds of roof and tree dwellers, Ernest remarked sardonically that his neck would not be the first one broken that day. In fact, the only known photograph of the double execution was taken from a treetop; an intervening branch can be detected interfering with the cameraman's view.

Most families came with picnic baskets filled with fried chicken, bread, pies, and other delicacies, and they claimed every vacant piece of ground where they could spread blankets and lay out the food. Enterprising vendors were omnipresent, the most popular being black women offering hot coffee, cakes, gingerbread, boudin, pralines, and *oreilles de cochon,* i.e., pig's ears, flat, square, fried donuts—without the holes—with a corner curled down to resemble their namesake and served with syrup. It was a festival, a celebration of justice delivered. The only sour note circulating among the multitude was their disappointment with the high fence surrounding the gallows. It would prevent many from getting a clear view of the execution. They wanted to get as close as possible, but Sheriff Broussard had spread the word that he would kill any man who tried to tear down the fence.

The Blanc brothers awoke about 5 A.M. and requested coffee and wine. It was brought to them. Father Knapp and Father Ravier-Boulard arrived at six. Together they celebrated Holy Mass and prayed with the brothers. Before leaving, the Dominican monk assured the condemned men that he would return later to administer the last sacraments and remain with them until the end.

At seven, Deputy Mouton brought in breakfast and the prisoners ate heartily. In spite of everything, Alexis had not lost his sense of humor; he jokingly suggested to his brother that it was not necessary to save any food for the next day. In Mouton's presence as he served the meal, the Blancs made an oral bequest of their possessions, asking the jailer to carry out their wishes. The sum total of their earthly posses-

sions consisted of three Bibles that had been given to them over the last
several months. One was to go to Sheriff Broussard, one to Deputy
Alexandre Billeaud, and one to Thomas Mouton, but only after their
benefactors had departed this world. Thomas Mouton thanked the
brothers and promised to follow their instructions.

At 9 A.M., the press corps was allowed in for a last news conference
with the doomed convicts. Little was said that was newsworthy. Many
of the reporters had spent hundreds of hours with the two young
Frenchmen and were on a first name basis with them. It was a time for
adieus. The consensus of the newspapermen was that the Blanc brothers faced the ultimate sanction with "coolness" and "resignation."

At ten-thirty, Sheriff Broussard climbed the scaffold to fasten the
two ropes to the gallows. The sheriff made one adjustment to his calcu-
lations from the previous day. For good measure, the six-and-a-half-
foot drop was increased to seven and a half feet. Ike Broussard was not
taking any chances.

When he had completed his preparations on the scaffold, Broussard
walked over to the courthouse to see Ed Voorhies swear in the fifteen
men the sheriff had invited to be the official witnesses to the execution.
Each was a family member, friend, or business associate of the victim.
The law mandated that at least one of the fifteen must be a physician,
and that role was filled by Dr. P. M. Girard, Martin Begnaud's personal
doctor. Three close friends of the "enterprising merchant," all from
Scott Station, were part of the group: J. T. Mulkern, L. Leo Judice, and
Desire Doucet. Martin's two surviving brothers, Jean and Simeon,
along with two brothers-in-law, Esteve Breaux and Jean Apolinaire
Begnaud, were included. The list was rounded out by Adam Bourgeois,
Aymer Comeaux, V. E. Dupuis, Ludovic Billeaud, Henry Church, P. B.
Roy, and—in recognition of his important role in the drama—William
Campbell. When the ceremony was over, Sheriff Broussard then swore
in nine carefully chosen volunteers to serve as special deputies to help
with crowd control and any unforeseen developments.

At noon, carrying the clothes he had purchased for the brothers,
Broussard returned to the jail, where he found blacksmiths Louis and
Leopold Lacoste waiting for him as instructed. He led them to the cell,
where the sheriff first handcuffed Alexis and then directed the black-

smiths to unshackle his leg irons. The same protocol was followed with Ernest. As Louis Lacoste and his son left the cell, two large basins of warm water were brought in for the brothers to bathe in private. When they had finished their *toilette*, the basins were removed from the cell and the chief deputy removed their handcuffs in order for them to dress. The new black alpaca wool suits fit perfectly, as did the white socks and black slippers. When Sheriff Broussard returned to check on their progress, he noted that they had not attached the collars to their white shirts. (In those days men's shirts and collars were sold separately.) Alexis, once more either demonstrating his courage or deflecting his fear with humor, replied that the collar would only interfere with the rope's work. When the brothers were thus properly dressed for the occasion, the handcuffs were returned to their wrists.

Father Knapp arrived at 1 P.M., and Sheriff Broussard ordered the Blancs' cell and the entire area around it cleared of all persons save for the clergyman and the prisoners. The condemned men were left alone with their spiritual adviser.

At 1:25, Broussard and the fifteen witnesses entered the jail cell and the sheriff—for the second and last time—read Governor Foster's death warrant.

Precisely at 2 P.M., a procession "led by Father Knapp in his white and black robes of the Dominican order" walked the short distance to the gallows. With bowed head and raised crucifix, chanting an invocation, the monk was followed by Alexis Blanc, escorted by Sheriff Broussard, Ernest Blanc, escorted by Deputy Billeaud, and the fifteen official witnesses to the execution. As the procession made its way to the gallows, soft, feminine cries of "Adieu Ernest, Adieu Alexis" could be heard above the crowd. The only woman allowed in the small enclosure was Odéide Benton, who stood next to her husband near the foot of the scaffold. As the prisoners passed, Alexis looked at Hamp Benton and said, "I'm sorry." Ernest exchanged looks with Benton but said nothing.

Only the priest, the two prisoners, and the two lawmen mounted the steps to the top of the scaffold. From that vantage point, a sea of humanity stretched as far as the eye could see, and there was extreme pressure on the tall fence from the push of the crowd. On the ground directly below the gibbet, like invitations from the Grim Reaper, were two open coffins. The faces of the brothers were pale, but firm and without emotion. They knelt down at the feet of their confessor and, with heads bowed, offered a short prayer. A crucifix cradled in his left arm, the Dominican raised his right hand and blessed the two men. When he had finished the blessing, Father Knapp presented them with the crucifix and each kissed the foot of the Savior "in a reverent manner." The priest then stepped aside and the brothers stood up. It had been previously agreed upon that Ernest would speak on behalf of both brothers, and the sheriff informed the elder brother that the time had come. Ernest took a step forward and Alexis took a step back. A silence fell over the crowd. Ernest Blanc addressed the throng quietly and clearly in his native tongue:

> Friends—We will soon satisfy the law, and pay with our lives its tribute. Before we die I want to say a few words to you all. We are young men, and it is hard to quit this life at so early an age, especially in this manner. For what we did we offer no excuse, and again admit the justice of the sentence, though we had hoped that our years would plead for us, and serve to have this method of expiation pass from us. To one and all of you, we desire to say that we bear no ill-will. No spark of malice rests within us, and we hope that now we are about to face our God we will receive your pardon. Our death by hanging is to our minds directly attributable to our failure to practice our religion. We had been unmindful of our obligations in this respect, and lost sight completely of our God and the care of our souls. The reading of bad books, sensational stories and the character of literature to which we took a fancy is responsible for our commission of the murder. It is a practice that cannot be too strongly condemned, and if the words of men soon to die are entitled to any weight, give heed to the warning which our presence on this scaffold furnishes to you young men and you boys. Let our hanging be a lesson and a deterring example. Avoid bad books. Quit them, if you, too, read them, and pay more heed to your souls' salvation than we did. We have nothing else to say in addition to this poor advice and can only bid one and all au revoir.

Ernest Blanc then stepped back and Alexis stepped forward, placing them side-by-side in the center of the trapdoors. As Sheriff Broussard bent down to tie their legs, Ernest turned to Alexis and said, "Good-bye." Reciprocating the look, Alexis responded, "Good-bye." In a low voice, Alexis turned slightly to the sheriff and said, "You have been kind to us, and we are grateful." In response, Broussard said, "Good-bye, boys." The process moved quickly now. "With celerity the sheriff slipped the nooses over the heads of the boys, the knots striking the right ears; then the black caps were drawn over their heads." Broussard jerked the handle of the lever forcefully and the bodies fell through the air at approximately 2:10 P.M. Several women swooned and fainted. At almost the same moment, the fence collapsed and the crowd surged in around the gallows. The bodies hung for twelve minutes until the twitching and struggling stopped, which occurred first for Ernest. The coroner, Dr. Trahan, felt the wrists and pronounced the two dead at approximately 2:22. He had Dr. Girard confirm his findings, then deputies unlocked the handcuffs, untied the feet, removed the hoods, gently lifted the ropes from around the necks, and carefully laid the bodies in the coffins. The lids were set in place, and the sheriff asked for twelve volunteer pallbearers to carry the coffins into the courthouse so the physicians could examine the bodies more closely.

There was no shortage of volunteers, and the coffins were carried across the street, where Dr. Trahan, Dr. Girard, and the other physicians present confirmed that Ernest and Alexis Blanc had each "died from a dislocation of the vertebra." The coffins remained opened in the courthouse for about an hour, and thousands filed by for a last look at the "boy murderers." While the medical examination was taking place at the courthouse, Sheriff Broussard, following custom, had cut the ropes used in the hanging into pieces roughly six inches in length to give to the members of the Begnaud family as mementos. The few remaining segments of rope were thrown into the crowd, and a mad scramble ensued for these highly coveted souvenirs. When the public viewing was over, the lids to the coffins were replaced and a new set of volunteer pallbearers carried them out to the waiting wagon of William Lewis. Many of these pallbearers had been drinking and some were drunk, and, regrettably, they dropped one of the coffins as they attempted to lift it on to the wagon and one of the bodies rolled out. No one was certain which one of the brothers it was, since he was quickly put back into his pine casket for the ride to the church. Handled more carefully this time, the coffins were brought into the church for a brief burial service read by Father Knapp, assisted by the pastor, Father Forge. Following the service, the coffins were put back on the wagon and driven around the church to the cemetery in back. They were stacked one on top of the other in a single grave, in the same cemetery that contained the grave of Martin Begnaud. In the Burial Record Book of St. John the Evangelist church, Father Ernest Forge wrote in pen the date, April 2, 1897, the names of Ernest Blanc and Alexis Blanc, and two words, "*pendu aujourd'hui,*" "hung today."

28

New York City: May 1897

The execution of Ernest and Alexis Blanc for the murder of Martin Begnaud received international news coverage. Every paper in the state, major or minor, carried a story on the hanging of the young Frenchmen. The newspaper in greatest demand was a weekly, the *Lafayette Gazette,* whose April 3, 1897, special edition contained an English translation of *Meurtre de Martin Begnaud,* the confession written by Ernest Blanc from prison and signed by both brothers, a literary prize courtesy of Thomas Mouton, who either gave or sold the gift from his prisoners to the paper. It caused quite a sensation. Apparently, Mouton had kept the existence of the document and his deal with the *Gazette* a secret. The enterprising weekly also obtained from the chief deputy the rights to all the remaining prison compositions of Ernest Blanc.

Published in their entirety in pamphlet form, the writings formed a twenty-three-page booklet bearing the title *La Vie, le Crime, et les Confessions d'Ernest et Alexis Blanc; ou, L'Histoire d'un Crime Horrible.* The cover page noted, "Ecrits et Signés par Eux-Mêmes" ("Written and Signed by Themselves"). Hitting the streets on April 3 at a price of twenty-five cents, the booklet quickly sold out. Meanwhile, the New Orleans dailies, for whom the saga had filled so much newsprint, used up even more in mega-articles retelling the entire chain of events from beginning to end.

Two common themes emerged from this incredible amount of commentary on the execution of the Blanc brothers. First, it marked a turning point for the legal justice system in Louisiana. That these two men could have been arrested, tried by a jury, sentenced in a court of law, and executed for their crime, all according to law, was a major accomplishment considering the climate of violence that existed in the American South of that era. Typically, lynch law would have prevailed in such a case. Whenever the press mentioned that the execution had been the first legal hanging in Lafayette Parish since the Civil War, the emphasis was on "legal" rather than "hanging," and parishes like Lafayette were the rule and not the exception in Louisiana and the South. The New Orleans public was duly impressed with the triumph of the rule of law and the legal justice system in Acadian country. A second area of consensus among observers of the drama was that Ernest and Alexis Blanc had died like men, with courage and dignity. The April 3, 1897, editions of the *New York Times* and the *Houston Post* contained articles on the execution, as did the April 18 edition of the *Courrier des Etats-Unis*, a French-language weekly published in New York but having a primarily Canadian circulation. Several Paris newspapers, including *Le Temps, L'Evénement, Le XIXe Siècle,* and *Petit Parisien,* carried accounts of the crime and punishment in their April 19 editions.

On May 6, 1897, a little more than a month after the execution of the Blanc brothers, Father Ernest Forge received a letter that, without exaggeration, must have given him the shock of his life. He responded without delay because the letter came from a fellow priest, but upon reflection he decided to share it with local authorities who, in turn, passed it on to the press. Written in French, it read:

New York, May 2, 1897.
   Reverend Sir—Permit me to ask of you the details relative to the death of two young men, Ernest and Alexis Blanc, who it appears were executed in your parish in expiation of a crime committed by them. It is the mother of the two young men who requests me to write to ascertain if her sons were really guilty, and under what circumstances, and in what spiritual condition they died.

Thanking you in advance, believe me, etc.
Theo. Wucher,
Priest of St. Vincent de Paul
120 W. 24th street, New York.

The letter became front-page headlines in Louisiana on Saturday, May 8.

Father Forge responded promptly and without elaboration to Father Wucher: yes, the Blanc brothers had been guilty and, yes, they had been given the last rites of the Church and a Christian burial. The *Daily Picayune* also responded promptly, putting a correspondent on the night train to New York with an appointment to meet with the priest. Theophile Wucher, born in Strasbourg, France, in 1860, was a member of a religious order called the Fathers of Mercy and had been ordained in 1883. Founded in France, the Fathers of Mercy was a missionary order of priests dedicated to diocesan work, which meant that the members served under a bishop rather than under the head of a religious order. Wucher had come to the United States in 1885 and founded several churches in the New York City and New Jersey area, as well as a home for immigrant women, a children's home, and a home for the elderly. A great builder and leader of the Roman Catholic Church in the New York metropolitan area, Wucher had become pastor of St. Vincent de Paul in 1895. This large and important parish would serve as his base for the rest of his life, and he would remain its pastor until his death in 1933.

The Alsatian priest's interview with the reporter from the *Daily Picayune* led nowhere. Father Wucher had received a letter postmarked Paris, France, dated April 21, 1897, and signed by a woman who claimed to be "a warm personal friend of Mrs. Blanc, the mother of the boys." She requested Father Wucher to inquire as to the circumstances surrounding the manner and cause of the brothers' deaths. Because the letter was marked "secret," Wucher would not share it or the name of its writer with the reporter, but he did agree to read the paragraph that summed up its purpose: "Their family refuses to believe that they committed such an atrocity, and their poor mother is almost crazed with despair, not knowing what to believe. If she only could know some of the circumstances of their last days; if they died in a Christian way, it would console her in some way." Wucher said that the boy's mother learned of her sons' unfortunate demise and of "their alleged trip to France" from reading an article concerning the execution in a Paris newspaper. In response to the reporter's inquiry, the priest claimed that he did not know the Blanc brothers and "did not remember the mother of the boys, though he said it was quite possible she had attended his church here." (Wucher's use of the word *here* is puzzling and perhaps represents a misunderstanding, since there is no evidence suggesting that Mme Blanc ever came to America; the Church of St. Vincent de Paul has no records which indicate that she was a parishioner.) When the reporter learned that the letter did not contain the name or address of the mother, he asked Wucher if the letter might be a hoax, an attempt on the part of the woman writing the letter to obtain whatever money or property the Blanc brothers may have left. "Father Wucher answered positively in the negative." In his opinion, those pieces of information were omitted in order "to shield the mother and the rest of the family from any unnecessary publicity."

Epilogue

―――

Baton Rouge, Louisiana: December, 1998.

The origins of Ernest and Alexis Blanc have proved to be elusive. Based on the information they provided, Ernest would have been born in 1877 and Alexis in 1878, but since specific dates are unknown, a margin of error of at least two years must be considered in any attempt to confirm those as the years of their birth. The city of Paris, then and now, is divided into twenty wards or districts called *arrondissements;* the St. Germain-des-Prés section, where the Blanc brothers said they were born and raised, falls primarily within the boundaries of the sixth arrondissement. A careful examination of the birth records in the Archives de Paris for this district for the years 1875 to 1880 uncovered no record of the birth of either brother. The search was then expanded to include the years 1873 to 1882 and the birth records of all twenty arrondissements. There was still not a single Alexis Blanc listed. Of Russian origin, the given name Alexis was not common in Third Republic France. Several Ernest Blancs were found, but cross-referencing these listings with subsequent death, marriage, and military records eliminated all but one. The remaining Ernest Blanc was apparently an illegitimate child, since the father's name is not recorded. He was born in 1877 to Emilie Blanc, a cook. But there is no record of an Alexis Blanc born to an Emilie Blanc in Paris in the decade of the 1870s. On the off chance that the brothers were born outside the city, the birth records of the major Paris suburbs were also examined, with equally disappointing results. Likewise, baptismal records from the churches in the St. Germain-des-Prés area turned up nothing.

As to the fate of their mother, the Blancs were uncharacteristically specific: they said she died in July 1893. Indeed, it was her death that prompted their decision to journey to America. The records of the Bureau des Mairies and the Bureau des Cimetières, however, which together contain all the death and cemetery records for every arrondissement of Paris, have no listing for a Mme or Mlle Blanc who died that month. (Although the brothers never mentioned it, she could have remarried and been listed under another name at the time of her death.) Concerning the death of their father, the brothers Blanc gave conflicting accounts. In a January 7, 1897, interview with the *Times-Democrat*, Ernest Blanc said that he was seven years old when his father died. This would have been 1883 or 1884. But in the February 28, 1897, *Daily Picayune* interview in which the Blancs claimed they could not remember their father's Christian name, they said he died in 1889. Again, a thorough search of the death records of the city of Paris for a M. Blanc for the years 1883, 1884, and 1889 produced no leads. On the chance that the father of Ernest and Alexis Blanc might have been a property owner, tenant, or registered voter, selected property records and voter registration lists for the sixth arrondissement for the years in question were examined, but no connections could be identified. Neither did a search of succession (will) records for 1882–1894.

There are many possible explanations for this lack of documentation on the background of our young protagonists. The most obvious is that they were not born in Paris. They could have been born elsewhere in France and moved to the capital as young children, so that Paris was the only home they had ever known. Another explanation is that their mother may have returned to her parents' home—perhaps somewhere in the provinces—to give birth. She also may have returned to her parents' home to die, whenever that may have been. It may be that Ernest and Alexis Blanc were illegitimate sons of either the same mother and father or the same mother and different fathers. Another possibility is that one or both of the Blancs were traveling under assumed names. And one cannot discount the opinion of André Boudreaux, Alexis's friend, that the Blanc brothers were not really brothers at all.

Two other documented events that might shed some light on the mystery took place in 1897. On Sunday, March 19, before Georges Bosseront d'Anglade had decided to seek a commuted sentence for the condemned brothers, he visited them in Orleans Parish Prison and, as mentioned previously, took extensive notes of an in-depth personal interview he conducted. Records on the life and times of the consul general can be found in two depositories in France. His personal file is located in the Archives du Ministère des Affaires Etrangères in Paris, and his diplomatic file is located in Le Centre des Archives Diplomatiques in Nantes. Both are filled with useful information, but d'Anglade's notes of March 19, 1897, or copies thereof, are not included. Nor do these files contain any other information that might serve as a clue to the origin of the Blancs. The French diplomat seems to have been quite serious when he issued the disclaimer that he was acting "as an individual" and "not as an official representative here of the French government." The other lead from 1897 is the mysterious letter posted from France and received by Father Theophile Wucher in New York in May of that year; perhaps it would prove useful—if only it could be found. The archives of the Fathers of Mercy are located in the Archives Nationales in Paris. Each item in the dossier, including those on the life and work of Father Wucher, is indexed, but the letter in question is not part of the file. Nor is it to be found in the archives of St. Vincent de Paul Catholic Church in New York. (Incidentally, today, New Yorkers and visitors to the city who wish to celebrate Holy Mass in French may still do so every Sunday at St. Vincent de Paul on West 24th Street.)

There was still one other piece of information left by the Blanc brothers that warranted investigation. Writing from his cell in the Lafayette Parish prison, Ernest Blanc claimed that he and Alexis had first arrived in the United States on August 24, 1893, at the port of New York, on board an unidentified steamer that had sailed from Antwerp, Belgium. Ernest's memory was off by only one day. The passenger lists for vessels arriving at the Port of New York in the last century are located in the National Archives in Washington, D.C. The SS *Noorland*, of Belgian registry, docked at New York harbor on August 23, 1893, with 467 passengers, including two boys from France named Blanc, ages seventeen and sixteen, in steerage, i.e., third class. Actually, Ernest was technically correct as to the date of their arrival in America. In those days, first- and second-class passengers were allowed to disembark at the Hudson Street Pier; there, no inspections or papers of entry were required. But third-class passengers were required to pass through Ellis Island, where health inspectors conducted examinations and barred sick or diseased persons from entering the country. The Ellis Island protocol took an extra day. Apparently the Blanc brothers passed their physicals and were allowed to enter the United States on August 24, 1893.

This inquiry into the details of their voyage to America yielded an unexpected discovery with a direct impact on the search for the origins of the Blanc brothers. The names of the two French citizens, ages seventeen and sixteen, listed in the SS *Noorland*'s manifest were not Ernest and Alexis Blanc. They were Emile and Jean Blanc. Clearly, these were the same two people executed for murder in Louisiana: the dates, the country of origin, the ship's registry, their ages, and the family name all fit. And the difference in first names is completely explainable, according to historian Jean Maurin of the University of Paris VIII. It has long been and still is the French custom, Maurin explains, to give two, three, four, or even five Christian names to children. The Blanc brothers simply had more than one given name each, and the ship's registration officer listed only one, probably the first. All passengers listed on the SS *Noorland*'s manifest, regardless of class, are identified by single given names. Of course, this discovery necessitated a return to the Paris birth records, this time in search of Ernest Emile (or Emile Ernest) Blanc and Alexis Jean (or Jean Alexis) Blanc. But the results of this research proved as futile as the first effort. In fact, the other name of the one Ernest Blanc who showed some promise was not Emile, but Albert.

For passenger ships sailing to the Western Hemisphere from Europe, the last port-of-call to board passengers is customarily Southampton, on the southern coast of England, and records of all ships arriving and departing that port can be found in the Public Records Office in London. For 1893, there is no record of the SS *Noorland* docking at Southampton in August—a finding consistent with Ernest's account of their transatlantic voyage of that year. According to the Blancs, however, this was not their last oceanic voyage; they supposedly returned to Europe in May 1896 via New York and Southampton, and then sailed back in July via Southampton and New York. The archival record does not support this claim: the Southampton port records indicate no persons named Blanc who passed through the harbor between May and August 1896. On the chance that the Blancs may actually have landed at Plymouth rather than Southampton, those records were also examined, but with equally negative results. Neither is there any record of their arrival at New York for the entire period from June 15, 1896, to January 1, 1897. And there is no evidence that they entered the Port of New Orleans from July 1 to January 1. Again, there are explanations for this absence of substantiating data. The two most obvious are, first, that the brothers traveled under assumed names, and second, that they never really left American shores. The latter possibility cannot be overlooked in light of the puzzling reference by the author of the mysterious Wucher letter to "their *alleged* trip to France" (emphasis added). The statement appears to suggest that had the Blanc brothers really returned to France in 1896, the writer and/or their putative mother would have had some knowledge of their presence in the country.

Finally, what of the boy murderers' travels in America? This question presented still another avenue of research that might lead to their location on significant dates, confirming their movements in the United States and verifying their whereabouts. The brothers carefully identified the many cities and towns that they had visited on their railroad treks across the North American continent in 1893 and 1896. In every case, local librarians and archivists were contacted in writing and asked for any information or indication that the Blancs might have visited the area on the dates in question. Most responded, all in the negative. Similarly, custodians of court records in these cities and towns were contacted on the remote possibility that the brothers had a run-in with the law. All these efforts proved fruitless, as did passenger train records for the decade of the 1890s.

There remained one concrete piece of evidence to be examined. This evidence was the bodies of Ernest and Alexis Blanc. The burial records of St. John the Evangelist Church in Lafayette give no precise indication of where in the indigent section of the cemetery this unmarked, shared grave might be located. In recent years, the Cathedral of St. John the Evangelist—the Diocese of Lafayette was carved out of the Archdiocese of New Orleans in 1918, and the Lafayette church became the seat of the new bishop and, thus, a cathedral—has surveyed and mapped out its cemetery. For obvious reasons, however, only known—that is, marked—sites were identifiable. To further complicate matters, the "potter's field" section of the cemetery has moved around over the last hundred years, so that there is no one area where the indigent are buried. Thus, there is no record of the location of the grave of Ernest and Alexis Blanc.

Mary Attwood, the curator of the St. John the Evangelist cemetery, was vaguely familiar with the story of the murder of Martin Begnaud. She indicated that, from time to time, she had heard elderly visitors to the cemetery discussing the story of the Scott merchant and the fact that his assassins were buried in an unmarked grave in the cemetery. These senior citizens remembered visiting the cemetery as children with their parents and grandparents, who would point out the spot where the infamous Blancs were buried. Ms. Attwood agreed to make inquiries on our behalf. Through the information gleaned from those queries, she determined that the most likely spot is located about forty yards almost directly behind the church. A raised, grassy knoll, the site is part of a walking path that separates rows of marked graves. The earth there has the appearance of a grave, but it could just as easily be where gravediggers, over time, disposed of surplus dirt from the surrounding grave sites. (Ironically, the knoll is only a few yards from the grave of Jean Begnaud, who died of natural causes in 1917.)

At this point, the nationally recognized forensic anthropologist Mary H. Manhein of Louisiana State University was consulted. Manhein, a veteran of many other digs in Catholic cemeteries, visited and examined the site and reached several conclusions. First, the dig would not be a difficult one. There was ample ground to work with and the excavation could be undertaken and completed without disturbing any neighboring graves. Second, through carbon dating and other tests, it would be possible to determine the approximate age of whatever—if anything—might be found buried there. If human remains were found, it might also be possible to discern whether the burial site contained more than one body. Third, provided sufficient human remains were found, DNA testing could determine if one or more persons occupied the grave, and if so, whether they were related—and specifically, if they could be brothers. Finally, Manhein gave assurances that whatever the results of this undertaking, the area would be restored to its original condition following the completion of the excavation.

The next step was to use noninvasive means to ascertain if anything at all was buried at the site. At Mary Manhein's suggestion, two graduate-student geologists from Louisiana State University, Roberta Zenero and David Seng, visited the graveyard and reached the conclusion that ground-penetrating (GPR) profiles could make such a determination. As Zenero and Seng describe this technology, "GPR is a non-intrusive, shallow geophysical instrument that images the subsurface. An electromagnetic pulse is transmitted into the earth and reflected back to a receiver. Reflections are generated when the electrical properties of the subsurface change." For comparative purposes, the geologists tested two sites: the suspected site and a known burial site of approximately the same age and in the same kind of soil. The known site is located about fifty yards south of the suspected site; it is the grave of Martin Begnaud, dating, of course, from 1896. The murder victim's grave is enclosed by a wrought-iron fence that also encompasses the graves of his father, Alexandre, who died in 1883; his mother, Lise, who died in 1898; and his brother Simeon, who died in 1906. Given the proximity of these four graves, it was convenient for the geologists to profile the entire area within the iron fence. Based on their findings at the Begnaud site, Zenero and Seng concluded that "four distinct high amplitude disturbances can be seen in the record that correspond with the placement of headstones." For the suspected site of the Blancs' grave, they concluded, "The configuration and amplitude of these reflections are consistent with observations at the known burial site. Ground penetrating radar records from a suspected unmarked burial site within this cemetery indicate that the mound in question is in fact a burial site. Data suggests that the mound may contain the remains of more than one burial. It is not possible to determine conclusively the orientation of the remains."

Under present Louisiana law, in order to perform a legal excavation of a burial site in a church-owned cemetery, two prerequisites must be met. The first is that the appropriate court must issue an order permitting the exhumation. On January 12, 1995, the Fifteenth Judicial District Court, Parish of Lafayette, State of Louisiana, Docket: 95-0035 3-B, authorized the disinterment of the suspected site in the St. John the Evangelist cemetery. Second, the "cemetery authority," in this case the church, must also grant permission. A letter addressed to the pastor of St. John the Evangelist requesting such permission was referred to the parish cemetery commission. At a meeting of that commission on January 15, 1996, Ms. Manhein, Ms. Zenero, Mr. Seng, and the author, with numerous charts and graphs in tow, presented the scientific findings and requested permission to undertake the project. Our request was denied. Aside from the value of setting the historical record straight, there were several sound reasons for our belief that it was in the best interest of the Cathedral of St. John the Evangelist to allow our project to proceed. First, the cemetery is a very old and historic one. Famous pioneers, generals, governors, ambassadors, statesmen, and leaders of every stripe can be counted among its lodgers. To identify the actual burial site of two of Louisiana's most famous murderers could only add to the cemetery's litany of historic figures-in-residence and enhance its reputation as one of the most interesting graveyards in the state. Second, Ernest and Alexis Blanc's grave—or somebody's grave—is in the middle of a walking path. Hundreds, perhaps thousands, of visitors to the cemetery each year stroll over this grave unaware that they are walking over the bodies of the dead. These remains could be moved to a more appropriate location. Third, the brothers Blanc were administered and received the sacraments of the church, were given a Christian funeral, and were buried in consecrated ground. They were guilty of a horrible crime, but they accepted responsibility for their actions, and they paid the price demanded by society and the law. Against the advice of their own legal counsel, they refused to allow their case to be appealed. At a minimum, an appeal would have prolonged their lives. They made peace with their God, and they looked death squarely in the face and did not blink. Do they not deserve a marked grave?

Americans—and Acadians are certainly no exception—have always been enthralled by famous murders and murder trials. The communications revolution of the twentieth century turned the most celebrated of these events into national *causes célèbres*. Leopold and Loeb, the Lindbergh baby, O. J. Simpson, and the English au pair are a few examples. Make no mistake, the murder of Martin Begnaud and the trial of the Blanc brothers was as big an event in the lives of the people of south Louisiana as any of the aforementioned crimes have been in modern times. Like the people alive at the time of the assassination of Abraham Lincoln, or those who can remember Pearl Harbor or the day John F. Kennedy was killed, the Acadians of the 1890s found that their lives were forever marked by what they were doing when those events occurred. All of these tragedies, of course, produced victims, villains, and heroes; William Campbell and Simeon Begnaud emerged as the heroes of our story. Campbell's shrewd, professional handling of the case and of himself won the admiration of the entire parish and the political loyalty of its citizens for a lifetime. He was elected district attorney in 1900 and 1904, and beginning in 1908, he was elected to the district court bench every four years until his death in 1928. Simeon Begnaud, the tavern keeper from Scott Station, became a celebrity almost overnight as a result of the horrible murder of his brother and business partner. Even before the Blancs were executed, he began building a large saloon on the courthouse square in Lafayette, just one block from the gallows. When construction was completed, he closed up his tavern in Scott Station and transferred its liquor stock to his new saloon. Overnight, it became the most popular watering hole in the area and a stunning financial success. When Begnaud died in 1906, his nephew Rousseau Dugas inherited the business and kept it going for many, many years.

In an interesting turn of events, in 1925, the Begnaud and Campbell families were united when Milton Campbell, William Campbell's son (the one whose birth he almost missed because he was taking the confessions of the Blanc brothers in Orleans Parish Prison), married Louise Mouton, Jean Begnaud's eldest grandchild. Ike Broussard was reelected sheriff in 1900, but it would be his last term. After being defeated in 1904, Broussard sought reelection several more times, but without success. Apparently his enemies and his brand of law enforcement caught up with him. Gustave Balin enjoyed a brief moment of fame and was able to apply his artistic talents to the building of Mardi

Gras floats. But Balin would always operate on the fringes of the law and, within a few months of his release from prison, he was in trouble again. He was charged with two counts of attempted murder. Balin, probably drunk, tried to kill two "working girls" employed by Madame Baptiste, the proprietress of one of the parish's most respected bordellos. There is no record of any official follow-up to these charges, and Balin seems to have faded from the Acadian scene. Few of us would have survived what Hamp Benton experienced; his great physical strength and mental toughness probably saved his life during his torturous incarceration. Benton spent most of his remaining days telling his story in local saloons in exchange for drinks. It was such an incredible story that there were always takers.

The murder of Martin Begnaud was not the first uncommon tragedy to strike the Begnaud family; nor would it be the last. The first incident occurred seventeen years before the murder and the most recent almost a century later. In the first case, the casualty was Martin's sister Regina, and in the second, his niece. In 1879, Regina was bitten by a rabid dog. Rabies, what the historian Christina Vella called the "leprosy of the nineteenth century," is fatal even today unless the victim is quickly inoculated with a series of shots that can check the spread of the disease in humans. Louis Pasteur's discovery of the vaccine for rabies in 1885 was six years too late for Regina Begnaud. Once a person is bitten, death comes in anywhere from two to twelve days and is preceded by madness, foaming at the mouth, and a violent, aggressive disposition. If the infected individual bites or scratches someone else, then that person will likely contract the disease. Regina Begnaud's family was thus faced with the terrible dilemma of how to deal humanely with a loved one faced with such an agonizing, inevitable demise.

Regina's father, Alexandre, and her four brothers, Joseph (who died in 1893), Martin, Jean, and Simeon, together with her young husband, Joe Dugas, very slowly and very carefully approached her with two thick mattresses, three men to a mattress. When the signal was given, they rushed Regina from two different directions, crushed her between the mattresses, threw her to the ground, and—with plenty of rope— bound the mattresses so tightly together that she could not move, much less escape. In this manner she was prevented from harming others and herself. Maintaining a twenty-four-hour watch, the family listened to Regina's muffled moans and groans and screams until she died on May 6, 1879. She was twenty-one years old and the mother of a six-week old baby boy named Rousseau. It is said that she was the prettiest of the ten Begnaud girls.

All of Alexandre and Lise Begnaud's fourteen children, except bachelors Martin and Simeon, produced large families of their own, making for a total of ninety-one grandchildren for Alexandre and Lise. Their last surviving grandchild, Laurence Arceneaux, died on February 16, 1991, six months shy of her ninety-fourth birthday. Laurence was the younger sister of Carmen Arceneaux, the godchild of Martin Begnaud; they were the daughters of Jacques Arceneaux and Martin's sister Alexandrine. There are striking parallels between the death of Laurence and the death of her uncle Martin. Laurence was a lifelong resident of Duson, Louisiana, a small village five miles west of Scott in Lafayette Parish, a village that also began as a railroad settlement. Like her uncle, Laurence Arceneaux never married, and lived on the north side of the track. Like her uncle, she was murdered by two men sometime in the hours between 9 P.M. and 3 A.M. She, too, was found by a neighbor the next morning in a pool of dry, caked blood. But unlike her uncle, she was not killed with a sharpened, foot-long, three-sided file with a wooden handle. Instead, she was "brutally beaten to death with a number of objects including a television set, telephone, lamp, stool, glass punch bowl, flashlight and vase." Also unlike her uncle, Laurence apparently put up a hell of a fight, and her money was safely deposited in a local bank. Two men, Kevin Touchet and Shane Michael Thomas, were arrested for the killing and indicted on charges of first-degree murder. Touchet, a convicted felon who had already served time in prison, entered a plea of "no contest" to manslaughter on August 1, 1996, and was sentenced to twenty-one years at hard labor with credit for time served. He had been in jail for over five years by the time he entered the plea and will thus be eligible for parole in 2001. Thomas entered a plea of "no contest" to accessory after the fact to manslaughter on November 25, 1996. He was sentenced to five years at hard labor with credit for time served. Thomas had been in jail for over five years by the time he entered his plea, so he was immediately released. The criminal justice system in the United States of America has changed dramatically in the last one hundred years.

I make one final observation with some trepidation because it is almost certainly totally unrelated to this saga. Yet it intrigues me. On September 10, 1898, two years after the murder of Martin Begnaud and one year after the execution of Ernest and Alexis Blanc, in Geneva, Switzerland, Empress Elizabeth of Austria, the wife of Franz Joseph, emperor of the Austro-Hungarian Empire, was assassinated by an Italian anarchist named Luigi Lucheni. He stabbed her through the heart. According to historian Barbara Tuchman, "Lucheni tried to buy a stiletto but lacked the necessary 12 francs. In its place he fashioned a homemade dagger out of an old file, carefully sharpened and fitted to a handle made from a piece of firewood." I could find no connection between Luigi Lucheni or the anarchist movement and Ernest and Alexis Blanc.

NOTES

ABBREVIATIONS

Bee	*L'Abeille de la Nouvelle-Orléans/New Orleans Bee*
CADN	Le Centre des Archives Diplomatiques de Nantes, Nantes, France
DP	*New Orleans Daily Picayune*
GBC	*Généalogie de la Famille d'Alexandre Begnaud et Lise Constantin,* by Philip Martin. Lafayette, La.: n.p., 1902
LA	*Lafayette Advertiser*
LG	*Lafayette Gazette*
LPCCR	Lafayette Parish Clerk of Court Records
LSU	Louisiana State University
OCP	Octavie Cayret Papers, Scott, Louisiana. In possession of Mrs. J. Allen Mouton.
PI	Personal Interviews (followed by initials of person interviewed; see Bibliography)
TD	*New Orleans Times-Democrat*
USL	University of Southwestern Louisiana
Vie	*La Vie, le Crime, et les Confessions d'Ernest et Alexis Blanc; ou, L'Histoire d'un Crime Horrible, Ecrits et Signés par Eux-Mêmes.* Lafayette, La.: Imprimerie de la Gazette, 1897
WR	Weather Reports, United States Department of Agriculture, Weather Bureau Monthly Observations at New Orleans

PROLOGUE

2. PI-MAD; *TD*, April 24, 1896; *DP*, April, 24, 1896; LPCCR, 1892 Map of Scott, Notary Records Book #18864.

I: The Murder
CHAPTER I

5. *sixty-seven degrees:* WR, April 23, 1896.

5. *raised horses and cattle:* The Attakapas Prairie received its name from the small tribe of American Indians that inhabited this area of southwest Louisiana (Griffin, 7).

6. *developed around them:* Dormon, 64–65; Millet, 172–73; *DP,* May 4 and May 7, 1880; *LA,* July 24, 1879; Griffin, 33–37.

6. *Louisiana Western Railroad: LA,* December 7, 1878, July 5, 1879, October 26, 1889.

6. *G. P. Scott:* Griffin, 74; Kenneson, 207. The sources are in disagreement over the initials of Mr. Scott. A 1960 history of Scott, Louisiana, reports the superintendent's name as S. P. Scott, but no documentation is given to support that claim (Toups, 27). Subsequent newspaper articles used the "S. P." initials, though contemporary accounts refer to the man only as "Mr. Scott" (OCP).

6. *unable to agree on any other:* OCP.

6. *stationmaster and his family:* ibid.; PI-ELDM.

6. *Southern Pacific Railroad Company:* Hoffsommer, 153.

6. *hotel/boardinghouse: LA,* November 2, 1889, January 18, 1890.

6. *a blacksmith shed, two taverns:* ibid., December 7, 1889.

6. *three large mercantile stores:* ibid., November 2, 1895.

6. *it only made molasses:* ibid., November 2, 1889.

6. *five steam-powered cotton gins . . . several homes:* ibid., November 14, 1896, March 29, 1890, August 19, 1893.

6. *one for blacks and one for whites:* ibid., April 6, 1889, October 19, 1895.

6. *small cemetery:* PI-ELDM, JAM.

6. *two hundred people: LA,* December 7, 1889, November 14, 1896.

7. *handguns were rare:* PI-HNS, CL, EB.

7. *Roads . . . in terrible condition : LA,* January 26, 1889.

7. *no one knew of any:* PI-HNS, CL, EB.

7. *changed its name to Lafayette:* Griffin, 37, 288.

7. *mass was celebrated:* Toups, 9; PI-CL, EB, HNS.

7. *its one telephone: LA,* March 28, 1896.

7. *indoor plumbing:* PI-BNCA.

7. *dominoes or checkers:* PI-JB, EB.

7. *Two taverns: LA,* January 18, 1890, October 19, 1895.

7. *enough English to communicate:* PI-HNS, CL, EB.

7. *everyone had a nickname:* PI-HNS, CL, EB.

7. *statewide elections had taken place:* Hair, 256–67; *DP,* April 21, 1896.

8. *interest ran high:* Hair, 256–67; *DP,* April 21, 1896; *LA,* April 4, 1896, April 18, 1896.

8. *The store faced south:* LPCCR, 1892 Map of Scott, Notary Records Book # 18864; PI-ELDM, JAM.

8. *living quarters . . . in the rear: DP,* April 24, 1896; *TD,* April 24, 1896.

8. *Begnaud's bed:* Identified by J. Parrot Bacot, director of the Louisiana State University Art Museum. The bed in which Martin Begnaud was murdered was inherited by his youngest sister, Azema (Mrs. Alexandre Martin). At her death, the bed was handed down to her oldest daughter, Honorine (Mrs. Maurice Pellessier). At her death, the bed went to her daughter, Marie Therese (Mrs. Mayo Begnaud), and remains in her possession.

8. *made into a blindfold:* TD, April 24, 1896; DP, April 24, 1896.

8. *appeared like red roses:* PI-ER, CL.

8. *stabbed more than fifty times:* TD, April 24, 1896; DP, April 24, 1896.

8. *cut from ear to ear:* TD, April 24, 1896.

8. *MARTIN BEGNAUD ASSASSINÉ:* Bee, April 24, 1896.

CHAPTER 2

9. *News of J. T Mulkern's . . . :* TD, April 24, 1896; DP, April 24, 1896.

9. *The sheriff's office in Lafayette:* DP, April 24, 1896; Bee, April 24, 1896.

9. *"on the ground":* DP, April 24, 1896.

9. *New Orleans press in the 1890s:* Gill, 145–74.

9. *MURDER MOST FOUL. . . . :* TD, April 24, 1896; DP, April 24, 1896; Bee, April, 24, 1896.

10. *The entire parish was in shock:* ibid.

10. *at the crime scene . . . ten o'clock:* TD, April 24, 1896.

10. *Dr. Alphonse Gladu:* ibid.

10. *Dr. Fred Mayer:* LA, April 13, 1889.

10. *Drs. Trahan:* TD, February 27, 1897; Fortier, 3:436–37; *Mayors of Lafayette,* 13; Mamalakis, 165–67.

10. *1,053 for Gladu:* LA, April 25, 1896.

10. *a coroner's jury:* TD, April 24, 1896.

10. *fully clothed in the same attire:* DP, February 27, 1897.

10. *in the shape of a stiletto:* TD, April 24, 1896.

11. *the jugular vein severed:* ibid.

11. *no signs of a struggle:* DP, April 24, 1896.

11. *bled to death:* ibid.

11. *wounds . . . in the shape of a necklace:* ibid.; TD, April 24, 1896.

11. *slit from ear to ear:* TD, April 24, 1896.

11. *residents who saw the body:* ibid.

11. *prepared the body for burial:* ibid. The official coroner's report of the examination of Begnaud's body could not be located, and it probably no longer exists. Fortunately, the newspapers of the time published a detailed account. For more on the duties of the office of parish coroner in Louisiana in the last half of the nineteenth century, see Olcott, 12–26, 202–206.

11. *J. T. Mulkern and Simeon Begnaud, . . . no signs of forced entry:* TD, April 24, 1896; DP, April 24, 1896.

12. *"Woe unto the guilty wretches":* DP, April 24, 1896.

12. *impossible for the bloodhounds to find a solid trail:* TD, April 24, 1896; DP, April 24, 1896.

12. *telegraphed . . . New Orleans police for help:* DP, April 25, 1896.

12. *"just . . . sheriff's request":* ibid.

12. *"secure a competent negro . . .":* ibid.

12. *Lynchings and race riots:* ibid.; Gill, 145–54.

13. *"the enterprising merchant":* LA, August 23, 1890.

13. *"It is no . . . in the State":* TD, April 25, 1896.

13. *an occasional boarder . . . down on his luck:* LA, April 25, 1896, May 2, 1896.

13. *record their purchases using the honor system:* PI-JB, HLB, RBA.

13. *"Mr. Begnaud was . . . his friend":* TD, April 24, 1896.

13. *the bells of St. John:* Funeral Record Book, 1896, St. John the Evangelist Church, Lafayette, La.

14. *hundreds more mourners outside:* DP, April 25, 1896.

14. *Father Ernest Forge:* LA, November 1, 1905; Forge Letters, Archives of the University of Notre Dame, Hesburgh Library; St. Bernard Church Parish Brochure, 1972.

14. *"This large assemblage . . . of midnight assassins":* LA, May 2, 1896.

14. *congregation was in tears:* ibid.

14. *overcome with emotion:* DP, April 25, 1896.

14. *"Religion . . . the next world":* LA, May 2, 1896.

14. *preceded in death by his father:* GBC, 9.

14. *survived by his mother:* ibid., 11–37.

14. *Carmen Arceneaux:* PI-AJB, CBP; GBC, 35.

15. *taken time for his widowed mother:* PI-JB, HLB.

15. *the bereaved mother would join her husband:* LA, May 2, 1896; GBP, 5, 27.

15. *No one shed more tears:* PI-RBA, RBB.

CHAPTER 3

16. *Gustave Ludovic Balin:* d'Anglade File, CADN.

16. *moved to Louisiana from Florida:* ibid.

16. *posing as a "Dr. Davidson":* Abbeville Meridional, May 16, 1896; DP, May 20, 1896.

16. *the people of the town . . . discovered the formula:* Abbeville Meridional, May 2, 1896.

16. *a Spanish portrait painter:* LA, May 2, 1896.

16. *for which he did possess some talent:* PI-AJB, FSL.

16. *"about 40 years old . . . active as a cat":* DP, July 29, 1896.

16. *hand-crafted Italian stiletto:* DP, April 3, 1897.

17. *dragnet of telegraph messages:* LA, May 2, 1896.

17. *a remote cabin:* Abbeville Meridional, May 16, 1896.

17. *had lived with Martin Begnaud:* LA, May 2, 1896.

17. *under intense pressure:* DP, April 3, 1897.

17. *they began making inquiries:* ibid.

17. *Balin's fate was sealed:* ibid.

17. *a defiant personality:* Benton Papers, Slidell, La.; PI-AJB.

17. *back down to no man:* DP, May 20, 1896; PI-AJB, CBP.

17. *listed his occupation as farming:* DP, April 3, 1897.

18. *showered her children with love:* PI-AJB, CBP.

18. *returned a "no true bill":* DP, May 20, 1896, April 3, 1897. For more on the murder of B. J. Pope, see LG, June 9, 1894.

18. *carrying a concealed weapon:* LA, October 16, 1893.

18. *total population of 15,964:* U.S. Census, 1890, Population Schedule, Lafayette Parish, La.

18. *no one had worked harder:* PI-AJB, CBP.

18. *one had already been engaged:* DP, April 3, 1897.

18. *asked the owner to leave the equipment:* ibid.

18. *"in a low, earnest conversation":* ibid.

19. *Benton denied any knowledge:* ibid.
19. *spent the night at home:* ibid.
19. *substantial traces of blood:* ibid.; d'Anglade File, CADN.
19. *Irish houseguest named Kenly:* DP, April 3, 1896.
19. *he had been drunk:* ibid.
19. *placed under twenty-four-hour guard:* ibid.
19. *A SUSPECTED ITALIAN ARRESTED:* TD, April 24, 1896.
19. *immigrants were lynched in the city:* Gill, 145–54.
20. *he was a Frenchman:* d'Anglade File, CADN.
20. *deserted them for good:* DP, April 3, 1897.
20. *acted as the actual assassin:* ibid.
20. *he would kill the sheriff:* ibid.
20. *Broussard rejected the idea:* ibid.
20. *a stakeout of Benton's home:* ibid.
21. *pistols cocked and pointed:* ibid.
21. *Handcuffed and escorted . . . to Lafayette :* ibid. It should be noted that newspaper accounts differ as to the exact date of Benton's arrest. Some claim that Sheriff Broussard arrested Benton a few days after the murder, while others report that the arrest took place two or three weeks later.
21. *the one the mob wanted:* ibid.
21. *lived . . . near the Lafayette train station:* ibid.; Guaranty Bank, *Lafayette,* 21; PI-AJB, CBP.
21. *children would always remember:* PI-AJB, CBP.
21. *Jefferson Parish jail:* DP, May 22, 1896.
22. *the only person authorized:* PI-AJB, CBP.
22. *dispersed sometime after midnight:* DP, May 21, 1896.
22. *Orleans Parish prison:* ibid.
22. *Benton maintained his innocence:* PI-AJB, CBP, LBDD.

CHAPTER 4

23. *would not confess:* DP, April 3, 1896.
23. *severely beaten and tortured:* PI-AJB, CBP, LBDD, BH, MMMS.
23. *His fingernails were pulled out . . . only source of protein:* PI-AJB, CBP, LBDD, BH, MMMS.
23. *the sheriff refused:* PI-AJB, CBP, LBDD, BH, MMMS.
23. *bail was never granted:* LPCCR, Seventeenth Judicial District Court Minute Book, 1896, pp. 380, 384.
24. *approach his interrogation with caution:* DP, May 20, 1896.
24. *he was a Frenchman:* d'Anglade File, CADN.
24. *his diet . . . was the same as Benton's:* ibid.
24. *no memory of the events:* DP, April 3, 1897.
24. *a chicken thief:* ibid.; d'Anglade File, CADN.
24. *renting a sulky:* DP, April 3, 1897; d'Anglade File, CADN.
24. *he did not own a stiletto and he was innocent:* DP, April 3, 1897; d'Anglade File, CADN.
24. *forbade . . . contact with the outside world:* DP, April 3, 1897; d'Anglade File, CADN.
24. *rumors about a lynch mob:* DP, April 3, 1897; d'Anglade File, CADN.

24. *Lafayette Parish grand jury:* LPCCR, Seventeenth Judicial District Court Minute Book, 1895, pp. 294, 329.

24. *Martin Begnaud had been on the list:* ibid.

25. *Calcasieu Parish jail:* DP, April 3, 1897.

25. *a "true bill" of indictment:* LPCCR, Seventeenth Judicial District Court Minute Book, 1896, p. 330.

25. *Benton and Balin would be placed on trial:* ibid.

25. *allow Balin to write his letters:* d'Anglade File, CADN.

25. *a flurry of correspondence:* ibid.

25. *they lynched people in this part of the world:* ibid.

25. *He pleaded that a lawyer be provided:* ibid.

26. *His uncle . . . a respected veterinarian:* ibid.

26. *to avoid court-martial:* ibid.

26. *"If he is guilty . . . be released":* ibid.

26. *kept this knowledge to himself:* ibid.

26. *d'Anglade reluctantly agreed:* ibid.

26. *But October came and went without a trial:* LPCCR, Seventeenth Judicial District Court Minute Book, 1896.

26. *an unwritten political agreement:* LA, June 21, 1890.

26. *Gordy of Vermilion Parish:* LA, April 25, 1896.

27. *the money . . . failed to surface:* DP, April 3, 1897.

27. *the Tulane University Law School graduate:* Fortier, 3:181–82.

27. *Armed with the promise . . . his intransigence stiffened:* d'Anglade File, CADN.

27. *Benton . . . was unyielding:* PI-AJB, CBP, LBDD, BH, MMMS.

27. *speculation . . . the guilty parties were still at large:* PI-JB, RBA.

27. *"to any person . . . Martin Begnaud":* LA, November 21, 1896.

27. *Simeon had deposited $1,000:* ibid.

27. *"S. R. Parkerson, Cashier":* ibid.

28. *the family . . . had secured the services of an attorney:* LA, January 9, 1897.

28. *William Campbell:* Fortier, 3:86–87; *Mayors of Lafayette*, 7; Perrin, ed., 212; LA, June 23, 1908.

28. *strong faction of the Democratic Party:* LA, March 4, 1896, April 11, 1896, April 25, 1896.

28. *reviewing every aspect of the case:* PI-JB, RBA.

28. *interviewed each member of the Begnaud family:* PI-JB, RBA.

28. *found one scenario particularly intriguing:* GBC, 31.

28. *allowed them to live . . . at Boudreaux Plantation:* Lafayette Daily Advertiser, December 7, 1980. A portion of the original big house still stands today. It is located on Debonaire Street in Scott, Louisiana. Mamalakis, 28–30.

28. *given his age as seventeen, and Alexis, sixteen:* DP, April 3, 1897.

28. *Vallena . . . distrusted them:* PI-FSL.

29. *their spare time in the village:* PI-JB, HLB, RBA, RBB.

29. *the brothers' tales of . . . Europe and the United States: Vie,* 11–15.

29. *polite, well mannered, and educated:* ibid.

29. *could draw . . . with uncanny accuracy:* DP, March 26, 1897.

29. *one hand wrote in French while the other wrote in English:* PI-JLR, CL.

29. *Philomène . . . persuaded her husband:* PI-FSL.

29. *sharing a room with their son André:* PI-FSL, MPBR.

29. *a special bond between nurse and patient:* PI-FSL, MPBR.

29. *devastated by the death of her brother:* PI-RBA, RBB.

29. *"traveling money":* DP, April 3, 1897.

29. *the sale of a painting:* ibid.

30. *their intention . . . to return to France :* ibid.

30. *no family and no possessions:* ibid.

30. *like losing two members of his own family:* ibid.

30. *Vallena had been Olivier's nurse:* PI-JLR, FSL.

30. *Good riddance, Vallena declared:* PI-JLR, FSL.

31. *he seemed uneasy:* PI-JLR, FSL.

31. *to confirm her suspicions:* DP, April 3, 1897.

31. *but William Campbell did not:* PI-JB, RBA.

31. *gone . . . eight months: Vie,* 9–10.

31. *investigation . . . discovered nothing:* DP, April 3, 1897.

31. *postmasters . . . could not recall:* ibid.

31. *the Blancs had come into some money:* ibid.

31. *stuffed money bags around their midsections: Vie,* 9.

31. *wanted for murder in Louisiana:* DP, January 5, 1897.

31. *"five feet, eight inches . . . and gentle as a woman":* ibid.

31. *dragnet of telegrams . . . turned up nothing:* ibid., April 3, 1897.

II: THE PEOPLE

CHAPTER 5

36. *"I do not know . . . of Acadia":* Bancroft, 2:434.

36. *four ships set sail:* Arsenault, *Histoire,* 16; Brebner, 19; Clark, 78; Griffiths, *Contexts,* 3; Griffiths, *Creation,* 3–4.

36. *The land of* Acadie: The origins of the name of the colony are unclear. Some scholars speculate that *Acadie* was the French pronunciation for one or more American Indian names for the region. For further discussion and alternate theories, see Clark, 7n. For more on the fishermen and the land itself, see Arsenault, *Histoire,* 15–19; Balesi, 3; Brebner, 18; Clark, 11–55, 75; Griffiths, *Creation,* 3.

37. *Pierre du Gast, sieur de Monts:* Arsenault, *Histoire,* 21; Brebner, 19; Clark, 78–79; Griffiths, *Creation,* 3–5.

37. *they christened Ile St. Croix:* Clark, 78, 79; Griffiths, *Creation,* 4.

37. *Louis Hébert:* Clark 79, 79n; Arsenault, *Histoire,* 21.

37. *Port Royal:* Clark, 79, 79n; Brebner, 19–20; Arsenault, *Histoire,* 22–23.

37. *The Micmacs taught the French:* Bird, 9; Clark, 68–70.

37. *"From the very first . . . Acadian home":* Bird, 9. For more on marriages between Acadian men and Micmac women, see D'Entremont.

38. *Samuel de Champlain founded Quebec:* Parkman, 333–38; Kennedy, 21–22.

38. *"a good sized herd . . . of sheep":* Griffiths, *Contexts,* 26.

38. *"Land ownership . . . agrarian life-style":* Brasseaux, *New Acadia,* 4.

39. For more information on individual Acadians and their families in the seventeenth and eighteenth centuries, see DeVille, *Church,* 2–27, and *Families,* 8–22. Hebert, *Acadians,* contains the census reports for Acadia for the years 1671 (p. 456), 1686 (p. 472), and 1714 (p. 522).

39. *the waters . . . were frozen solid:* Balesi, 2.

39. *New England farmers cast envious eyes:* Sauer, 252; Greene, 238; Current et al., 26–33; Brebner 53–56.

39. *three military excursions against Acadia:* Current et al., 29–33, 64; Brebner, 53–56, 108–109; Clark, 144, 148, 157, 184.

39. *Argall . . . succeeded in torching Port Royal:* Brebner, 49–50; Clark, 81.

40. *These years . . . were generally tranquil:* Winzerling, 7.

40. *sole purpose of looting . . . lucrative government post:* ibid., 8; Brebner, 20; Clark, 113.

40. *Treaty of Ryswick:* Brebner, 52–53; Winzerling, 8.

41. *Champlain . . . never gave up searching:* Parkman, 345. As late as 1803, U.S. president Thomas Jefferson was still searching for the Northwest Passage. His specific orders to Meriwether Lewis and William Clark read: "The object of your mission is single, the direct water communication from sea to sea formed by the bed of the Missouri & perhaps the Oregon" (Ambrose, 116).

41. *The Society of Jesus:* Clark, 75–77; Griffiths, *Contexts,* 10–11; Jennings, *Empire,* 217–18, 96–97; Parkman, 344.

41. *he proved to be a master diplomat:* Jennings, *Empire,* 217–18; Parkman, 342–45.

41. *All official expeditions:* Balesi, 9, 17–20; Kennedy, 38.

42. *a new governor of New France:* Balesi, 12–14.

42. *"great water":* Beckwith, 4.

42. *did it flow west or south?:* Kellogg, 223.

42. *In the first week . . . departed Quebec:* Balesi, 14.

42. *Their destination was the Jesuit mission:* ibid., 15.

42. *one of North America's most important historic trips:* ibid., 18.

42. *the great water did not flow west, but south:* ibid., 23.

42. *Primitive living conditions:* ibid., 29.

43. *After wintering . . . Jolliet reached Quebec:* ibid., 25.

43. *Several major findings were revealed:* ibid., 23.

43. *The "El Dorado" of furs:* ibid., 71.

43. *Count de Frontenac's choice . . . La Salle:* ibid., 36–43.

43. *a number of years building forts . . . La Salle's expedition :* Terrell, 140.

43. *Jacques de la Metairie, a royal notary:* Balesi, 57–58.

44. *a hero's welcome:* ibid., 67–74.

44. *La Salle set sail once again:* ibid., 83.

44. *This voyage was a calamity:* Davis, 29.

44. *fewer than a dozen survivors:* Balesi, 86.

44. *An immediate follow-up . . . was precluded:* ibid., 32, 36; Hero, 51; Crouse, 162–63.

45. *Construction was completed:* Curtis Joubert to author, May 27, 1997; Brasseaux, *Comparative,* 40–41.

CHAPTER 6

46. *Philip's claim was certainly defensible:* Palmer and Colton, 185–91, 264–75; Current et al., 60–69; Beard, 17; Balesi, 254.

46. *the fourth and final invasion:* Brebner, 55; Clark, 186–87; Griffiths, *Creation*, 19–21; Winzerling, 8.

47. *renamed it Nova Scotia:* Arsenault, *Histoire*, 113; Brasseaux, *New Acadia*, 6; Brebner, 22; Clark, 83n; Griffiths, *Contexts*, 35–36.

47. *the "Golden Age" of the Acadians:* Griffiths, *Contexts*, 61.

47. *the right to practice their religion:* Arsenault, *Histoire*, 111–27; Brebner, 64; Griffiths, *Creation*, 20–25; Griffiths, *Contexts*, 35; Clark, 187.

47. *Louis XIV emptied France's prisons:* Brebner, 64–65.

47. *"to continue our subjects, to retain . . . remove elsewhere":* Bradshaw, "Remembering," 11.

48. *On their farms . . . :* Brebner, 41; Clark, 158–76, 230–44; "Tour of Inspection," 1–172; Arsenault, *Histoire*, 91–96.

48. *the great prize was the farmland:* Clark, 144, 222, 358, 264, 326–28.

48. *low infant mortality:* Griffiths, *Contexts*, 60–61.

48. *the Acadian population of Nova Scotia:* Clark, 211–12.

48. *loss of the Acadian peninsula:* Gaxotte, 12–17.

49. *Louisbourg was deemed impregnable:* Allain, 46; Giraud, 1:19.

49. La Nouvelle Orléans: Giraud, 1:14; Crouse, 159n; Gaxotte, 12–17; Taylor, *Reconstructed*, 9.

49. *The founder of Louisiana:* Giraud, I, 30–54; Allain, 49.

49. *most preferred prison in France:* Taylor, *History*, 9.

49. *relied on downriver grain shipments . . . to survive:* Allain, 50; Giraud, 1:40–80; Balesi, xii–xiii, 152–86; Dawson, 8; Wall, 38–49, 405; Hero, 89–109; Davis, 52–62; Taylor, *History*, 8–10.

50. *"witty, charming . . . to excess":* Gaxotte, 15.

50. *The proximity . . . was of genuine concern:* Brebner, 45; Jennings, *Empire*, 134.

50. *an unconditional oath of allegiance:* Arsenault, *Histoire*, 117–27; Brasseaux, "Scattered," 3–6; Brebner, 220–21; Griffiths, *Creation*, 27.

50. *the Board of Trade . . . pursued the issue:* Brasseaux, "Scattered," 3; Griffiths, *Contexts*, 38–39; Griffiths, *Creation*, 29.

51. *paid a high price for their refusal:* Brasseaux, "Scattered," 1; Brebner, 203; Griffiths, *Contexts*, 62–94; Griffiths, *Creation*, 52–67.

51. *"managed simultaneously to . . . all parties":* Brasseaux, *New Acadia*, 15.

51. *The first real test:* ibid., 16–17; Current et al., 66; Clark, 186–95.

51. *abbé Jean Louis LeLoutre . . . raids:* Brasseaux, *New Acadia*, 17; Brebner, 119–21; Griffiths, *Creation*, 47.

51. *Acadians were not impressed:* Brasseaux, *New Acadia*, 180; Griffiths, *Creation*, 45–48.

52. *a few young Acadians undeniably fought:* Griffiths, *Creation*, 45; Winzerling, 12.

52. *Philipps served as an absentee administrator:* Brasseaux, *New Acadia*, 14.

52. *the real chief executive . . . Major Mascarene:* Griffiths, *Contexts*, 76, 78; Griffiths, *Creation*, 30.

52. *Mascarene was a Huguenot:* Brebner, 189; Brasseaux, *New Acadia*, 18; Griffiths, *Contexts*, 79–80; Griffiths, *Creation*, 4.

52. *"Gibraltar of New France":* Eccles, 150.

52. *treaty of Aix-la-Chapelle:* Jennings, *Empire*, 65–75; Balesi, 254–55.

54. *The plan had three components:* Brasseaux, *New Acadia,* 17–18.

54. *Colonel Edward Cornwallis:* ibid.; Arsenault, *Histoire,* 127; Griffiths, *Creation,* 40.

54. *intended to serve as a barrier:* Brasseaux, *New Acadia,* 17; Brebner, 166.

54. *The Annapolis Royal garrison:* Brasseaux, *New Acadia,* 23; Brasseaux, *"Scattered,"* 3–4; Brebner, 176, 183.

54. *Cornwallis began the process:* Clark, 339; Griffiths, *Contexts,* 80; Arsenault, *Histoire,* 151.

55. *He demanded that every Acadian take the . . . oath:* Brasseaux, *New Acadia,* 17–18; Griffiths, *Creation,* 40, 42.

55. *They countered Cornwallis's demands:* Brasseaux, *New Acadia,* 20.

55. *They chose to migrate:* Brasseaux, *"Scattered,"* 2–3; Brebner 184–85.

55. *These Acadian émigrés settled . . . Quebec:* Brasseaux, *"Scattered,"* 2–3; Brebner 184–85.

55. *One family . . . chose to leave:* Stephen White to author, March 9, 1995, October 24, 1995. Dr. Stephen White of the Centre for Acadian Studies at the University of Moncton, New Brunswick, Canada, searched church records and census reports unavailable in this country and determined, "about 1750, they took refuge on what is now Prince Edward Island." Also, the 1752 Census of Ile St. Jean reported that "Paul Douaron" and his family have "been in the country two years" ("Tour of Inspection," 86). For maps of the movements, see Hebert, *Exile,* 654, 658.

55. *The Doirons' destination was Ile St. Jean:* 1752 Census of Ile St. Jean; Arsenault, *Histoire,* 159–60.

55. *Cornwallis seemed to acknowledge . . . Neutral French:* Arsenault, *Histoire,* 154; Brebner, 176.

55. *Cornwallis was recalled:* Arsenault, *Histoire,* 162.

55. *Colonel Peregrine Thomas Hopson:* ibid.

56. *Governor Hopson's political independence:* Brasseaux, *New Acadia,* 18; Brebner, 189; Griffiths, *Creation,* 48; Griffiths, *Contexts,* 79–80.

56. *"he emphasized . . . their wrongs":* Brebner, 189.

56. *"live stock . . . fowls or chickens":* "Tour of Inspection," 86.

56. *Hélenne joined her eight older siblings:* ibid.

56. *Hopson was forced to return:* Brebner, 190.

CHAPTER 7

57. *The Acadian diaspora began:* Brasseaux, *"Scattered,"* 11–69, esp. 55.

57. *the French and Indian War began:* Jennings, *Empire,* 65–68, 157–59, 405–25; Balesi, 265; Hero, 112–13; Williams, *Wars,* 68.

58. *Braddock approved a plan:* Jennings, *Empire,* 135–38.

58. *both were rather easily overwhelmed and surrendered:* ibid.,157–59.

58. *Lawrence issued orders for the expulsion:* Brasseaux, *New Acadia,* 23–24.

58. *His orders were specific:* Brasseaux, *"Scattered,"* 8, 34–61; Winzerling, 19.

58. *Le Grand Dérangement:* Griffiths, *Contexts,* 96.

59. *Without consulting Governor Shirley:* Brasseaux, *"Scattered,"* 6.

59. *an army of over 2,000:* ibid., 5; Brebner, 204, 217–18; Winzerling, 15.

59. *By November, 1755, a large segment . . . deported:* Griffiths, *Contexts,* 89.

60. *Lawrence was . . . named governor:* Brebner, 220–30. To fully grasp the cruelty of *le Grand*

Dérangement, the reader may wish to examine Charles Lawrence's original orders to British troops for the expulsion and treatment of the Acadians. These are found in Jehn, 1–9, 31.

60. *Lawrence's civilian coconspirators:* Brebner, 222–23.

60. *Each . . . had committed his financial fortune:* ibid.

61. *Council . . . received a petition:* ibid., 195.

61. *Six families . . . were readmitted:* ibid.

61. Evangeline: A Tale of Acadie: Brasseaux, *Evangeline,* 7.

61. *Hundreds of Acadians died of smallpox:* Arsenault, *Histoire,* 217–18; Brasseaux, *"Scattered,"* 9, 22; Griffiths, *Contexts,* 92.

62. *Unsanitary conditions. . . . too weak to survive:* Arsenault, *Histoire,* 195–206; Brasseaux, *"Scattered,"* 11, 22; Winzerling, 19–20.

62. *some examples of charity:* Brasseaux, *"Scattered,"* 16; Winzerling, 19.

62. *ferried across the Atlantic:* Brasseaux, *"Scattered,"* 11, 35; Winzerling, 21.

62. *released when the war ended:* Winzerling, 41.

62. *moved to expel the entire Acadian population:* Brasseaux, *"Scattered,"* 29; Bumsted, 10–11.

62. *In that number was the Paul Doiron family:* White to author; "Tour of Inspection," 86.

62. *The colonial governors were not pleased:* Brasseaux, *"Scattered,"* 28–30.

62. *new exiles be transported directly to Europe:* ibid., 34–35.

62. *There were 27 survivors:* Winzerling, 20.

62. *3,000 remaining . . . 1,300 did not survive:* Brasseaux, *"Scattered,"* 34–35.

62. *The survivors . . . were put ashore:* White to author, October 24, 1995. For the history of these particular exiles, see Hebert, *Exile,* 75–76. General Jeffery Amherst was in charge of deporting the Acadians from Ile St. Jean and Ile Royale. His zeal in undertaking this effort was extraordinary: "The French inhabitants all to be sent to France, except such as you may like to continue in the town of Louisbourg. Some may be of service. I would have the settlements in the different parts of this Island absolutely destroyed" (Warburton, 90).

63. *five thousand New Englanders had settled in Nova Scotia:* Rawlyk, 221.

63. *"We did, in my opinion . . . to extirpate":* Winzerling, 17.

63. *From 1756 . . . war raged:* Jennings, *Empire,* 426–28.

63. *The Seven Years' War:* ibid., xx.

63. *England agreed to return:* Davis, 97.

63. *Louis XV made France's exit:* ibid.

65. *René Bernard and his wife:* Brebner, 68; Clark, 220–23; Winzerling, 9; White to author, October, 24, 1995.

65. *the Bernards escaped:* White to author, October 24, 1995. For the history, see Blanchard, 46–52.

65. *they were unable to escape:* White to author, March 9, 1995, October 24, 1995; Gerard-Marc Braud to author, January 27, 1995. Mr. Braud of Nantes, France, is a noted authority on Acadian exiles in the French ports. Also see Hebert, *Exile,* 75–76; and for the history, see Warburton, 89–90.

65. *the entire Bernard family survived:* White to author, October 24, 1995.

65. *they found life . . . hard:* White to author March 9, 1995, October 24, 1995.

65. *What was left of these two families was united:* ibid.

65. *At the war's end:* ibid.; Arsenault, *Histoire,* 311; Winzerling, 21; White to author, October 24, 1995.

66. *seek a new life . . . El Dorado of Furs:* Balesi, 71; Brasseaux, *New Acadia,* 34.

66. *Broussard and 193 followers sailed:* Brasseaux, *New Acadia,* 74.

66. *They offered to provide the exiles with foodstuffs:* ibid.

66. *This first group of Louisiana Acadians:* ibid. For more on the subject, see DeVille, *Attakapas.*

66. *they set about to build a church:* Pourciau, 2. For more on Beausoleil Broussard, see Segura, 147-53.

67. *many of their relatives . . . landowners in Louisiana:* Brasseaux, "Phantom," 124-32.

67. *the Opelousas country:* The area was so called for the Opelousas Indians.

67. *1,500 exiles had resettled:* Brasseaux, *New Acadia,* 73.

III: The Return
CHAPTER 8

71. *no feasts . . . no celebrating:* PI-EB, JB, RBA, CL, FSL.

71. *a visit from "Papa Noël":* PI-EB, JB, RBA, CL, FSL.

71. *homemade toys:* PI-EB, JB, RBA, CL, FSL.

72. *lasted until past suppertime:* PI-EB, JB, RBA, CL, FSL. Mrs. A. D. Boudreaux, née Azema Martin, died on August 2, 1894. *LA,* August 11, 1894.

72. *temperatures would drop:* WR, January 4, 1897.

72. *made its regularly scheduled stop: Southern Pacific Railroad Schedule Book,* 464.

72. *it was never reported:* Given the publicity surrounding the activities of the Blanc brothers, a sighting of their arrival would have been reported; none was.

72. *Ernest and Alexis Blanc were standing before him: TD,* January 5, 1897; *LA,* January 9, 1897.

72. *talked into the early morning hours: TD,* January 5, 1897; *LA,* January 9, 1897.

73. *few were stirring about:* PI-JLR, CL.

73. *eager to see his old friend, André:* PI-JLR, MPBR.

73. *alone in the house:* PI-JLR, CL, FSL.

73. *She did not respond to repeated knocks:* PI-JLR, CL, FSL.

73. *notify William Campbell immediately:* PI-JLR, EB.

73. *Campbell would notify the sheriff in the morning:* PI-JLR, EB. Among the descendants of Colonel A. D. Boudreaux, there are two versions of how Sheriff Broussard was notified of the Blancs' return. Laurent Boudreaux, a grandson, had remained to spend the night with his grandfather. The next morning, he rode on horseback to his father's house near Rayne, Louisiana, about fifteen miles west of Scott Station, bringing news of the return of Ernest and Alexis. His father, Valery Boudreaux, saddled up and rode the twenty miles back to Lafayette and alerted the sheriff (PI-FSL). The version that appears in the text was used because it is more consistent with published accounts at the time.

73. *A student of the Bible:* PI-ECCR, FR.

73. *Intellectual affair with Freemasonry:* PI-ECCR, FR. William Campbell's Masonic prayer book, *The Freemason's Companion: A Ritual,* is in the possession of his granddaughter, Ellen Cecile Campbell Resweber.

73. *King James Version:* PI-ECCR, FR.

74. *meet his lawyer at Boudreaux Plantation: DP*, January 5, 1897.

74. *agreed to follow Campbell's strategy:* PI-JLR, EB.

75. *Simeon Begnaud had already arrived: DP*, January 5, 1897.

75. *Arrested them for the murder:* ibid.; *St. Landry Clarion*, January 9, 1897; *Abbeville Meridional*, January 9, 1897.

75. *escorted . . . by the two lawmen and Campbell:* Benton Papers; *TD*, January 5, 1897; *DP*, January 5, 1897; *LA*, January 9, 1897.

75. *Ernest Blanc . . . in the corporate, or city, jail:* Benton Papers.

75. *the rain had stopped:* WR.

75. *"tramped" back to New Orleans. . . . fifty dollars:* Benton Papers; *TD*, January 5 and February 27, 1897; *DP*, January 5 and February 27, 1897; *LA*, January 9, 1897.

75. *"Lies":* Benton Papers.

76. *Campbell offered . . . protection: DP*, February 27, 1897; *TD*, February 27, 1897.

76. *"Have you seen my brother?":* Benton Papers.

76. *interrogators left the jail cell. . . .marched him across the street to the courthouse:* ibid.; *TD*, January 5 and 27, 1897; *DP*, January 5 and 27, 1897; *LA*, January 9, 1897.

76. *"We have just . . . confessed to everything":* Benton Papers; *Lafayette Daily Advertiser*, November 13, 1955.

76. *"He promised me he never would":* Lafayette Daily Advertiser, November 13, 1955.

76. *journeyed to Paris before returning:* ibid.; *Vie*, 6–9.

77. *transport his prisoners to safety: Lafayette Daily Advertiser*, November 13, 1955; *Vie*, 6–9.

77. *"When Alexis was told . . . had taken Begnaud's money": Lafayette Daily Advertiser*, November 13, 1955.

77. *confirmed that they had visited Paris:* Benton Papers; *TD*, January 5 and February 27, 1897; *DP*, January 5 and February 27, 1897; *LA*, January 9, 1897; *Vie*, 6–9.

77. *According to the Blancs, both items had been buried. . . . It was empty:* Benton Papers; *TD*, January 5 and February 27, 1897; *DP*, January 5 and February 27, 1897; *LA*, January 9, 1897; *Vie*, 6–9.

CHAPTER 9

78. *The Blancs gave countless interviews: TD*, January 5, 1897; *DP*, January 5, 1897.

78. *friend and neighbor Charles Breaux: TD*, January 5, 1897; *DP*, January 5, 1897; *LA*, January 9, 1897.

79. *each purchased a pistol: LA*, April 4, 1896; *Vie*, 6.

79. *they began to fashion a homemade version: Vie*, 6; *DP*, January 5, 1897; *TD*, January 5, 1897.

79. *kept large sums of money in his safe: TD*, January 5, 1897; *DP*, January, 5, 1897.

79. *hide out in the ditch: TD*, January 5, 1897; *DP*, January, 5, 1897.

79. *It was election eve:* Hair, 256–67.

79. *They returned the next night: TD*, January 5, 1897.

79. *It was election day: LA*, April 25, 1896.

79. *Martin Begnaud in animated conversation: TD*, January 5, 1897.

80. *faster than they had anticipated:* ibid.

80. *"Who's there?":* ibid.

80. *Begnaud opened the door:* ibid.

80. *they lost their nerve:* ibid.

80. *"We are hungry . . .":* ibid.

80. *the merchant did as ordered:* ibid.

80. *"We wrapped him up. . . to make sure": Vie,* 7.

80. *"looked liked a well-strung sausage":* ibid.

80. *"I own all; I tell you all . . .": TD,* January 5, 1897.

81. *into sacks and put the sacks in a box:* ibid.; *DP,* January 5, 1897.

81. *A total of $3,100: TD,* January 5, 1897; *DP,* January 5, 1897.

81. *They made $25 a month: Lafayette Daily Advertiser,* April 22, 1984.

81. *the dogs turned away: Vie,* 8

81. *"After having suffered . . . at our bodies":* ibid., 9.

81. *"buy suitcases . . . unload our burden":* ibid.

81. *"We stayed a few days there . . .":* ibid.

82. *"In the California . . . in St. Louis": TD,* January 5, 1897.

82. *safe for them to return: DP,* January 5, 1897.

82. *denied having their sights set on another victim:* ibid.

82. *their next target . . . Alcide Judice: TD,* February, 10, 1897.

82. *J. A. Chargois . . . to defend Hampton Benton Jr.: DP,* January 6, 1897.

82. *Alexis was openly remorseful; Ernest was not:* ibid.; *DP,* January, 5, 1897.

82. *based on circumstantial evidence:* ibid.

82. *a jailhouse visit:* d'Anglade File, CADN.

83. *Balin . . . was innocent and must be released:* ibid.

83. *Broussard boarded the westbound train: Bee,* January 9, 1897; *DP,* January 9, 1897.

83. *On January 9, Broussard boarded: DP,* January 13, 1897.

83. *dismissed all charges . . . and set them free:* ibid.

83. *celebrity status:* PI-AJB, CBP, FSL.

83. *a designer and builder of Mardi Gras floats: Opelousas Courier,* March 6, 1897.

83. *"he was never the same":* PI-AJB.

83. *follow-up interviews. . . . official interrogation: TD,* February 27, 1897; *DP,* February 27, 1897.

83. *The four men had all read . . . the voluminous accounts: TD,* January 5, 1897; *DP,* January 5, 1897.

83. *far more detailed . . . than the original admissions:* Benton Papers.

83. *the Blancs freely confessed again: TD,* February 27, 1897; *DP,* February 27, 1897.

83. *Milton Campbell, born on January 17, 1897:* PI-ECCR.

CHAPTER 10

84. *the Honorable Conrad Debaillon presiding:* LPCCR, Seventeenth Judicial District Court Minute Book, 1897, p. 386.

84. *At 10 A.M., court was officially declared open:* ibid.

84. *"cause to come":* ibid.

85. *a jury commission: Acts Passed by the General Assembly . . . ,* Act 99 of 1896, Sections 5 and 7.

85. *the names of fifty "discreet" citizens:* ibid.

85. *The four members of the Lafayette Parish Jury Commission: DP*, February 19, 1897.

85. *that cold morning:* WR, February 8, 1897.

85. *The first order of substantive business:* LPCCR, Seventeenth Judicial District Court Minute Book, 1897, pp. 386–87.

85. *J. Edmond Mouton to serve as foreman:* ibid., 386; *DP*, February 9, 1897.

85. *to draw fifteen names:* LPCCR, Seventeenth Judicial District Court Minute Book, 1897, p. 387.

85. *"I [name] do solemnly swear . . . so help me God":* ibid.

85. *"The Judge . . . to the Grand Jury":* ibid.; *TD*, February 10, 1897.

86. *"lynch fever":* TD, February 10, 1897; *New Orleans Daily States*, February 17, 1897; *DP*, February 18, 1897.

86. *"In strong and clear . . . influence on society":* DP, February 9, 1897.

86. *Thirteen cases were on the docket:* LPCCR, Indictment Book, 1897, pp. 85–89

86. *the district attorney brought four witnesses:* ibid., 88.

86. *"That one Ernest Blanc . . . the State of Louisiana":* ibid.

86. *Desire Doucet, who had recently married:* OCP.

86. *Simeon was eligible to serve: Louisiana Code of Criminal Procedure*, Article 401.

86. *Begnaud said that he had recused himself: DP*, February 11, 1897.

86. *the victim's nephew Israel Prejean:* Israel Prejean was the son of Martin Begnaud's sister Azelie (*GBC*, 19).

87. *the judge sent for the sheriff: DP*, February, 10, 1897.

87. *dressed and ready:* ibid.

87. *Father Peter O'Neill, the prison chaplain:* ibid.

87. *"prayed devotedly . . . one and awful sin":* ibid.

87. *Broussard was in Orleans Parish Prison:* ibid.

88. *people gathered . . . to gawk:* ibid.

88. *"long dark eyelashes":* ibid., February 26, 1897.

88. *nearly missed the ferry:* ibid., February 10, 1897.

88. *"boy murderers": TD*, March 31, 1897.

88. *a constant conversation with Ernest Blanc: DP*, February 10, 1897.

89. *"the person who exercised . . . without anything to eat":* ibid.

89. *"With an expression . . . a mother or a father alive":* ibid.

89. *"Without thinking, Ernest answered . . . they had not":* ibid.

89. *"good boys":* ibid.

89. *"We'll never get out of this scrape":* ibid.

89. *"any hostile demonstrations":* ibid.

89. *a small crowd began to gather near the courthouse:* ibid.

89. *all seemed quiet:* ibid.

90. *he was awakened: TD*, February 10, 1897.

90. *mule-drawn wagon driven by a black teamster: DP*, February 11, 1897.

90. *conceal the wagon from view:* ibid.

90. *he tied . . . around his own wrist:* ibid.

90. *steady drizzle: TD*, February 11, 1897.

90. *forty-six degrees and wind:* WR, February 10, 1897.

90. *no sign of a mob:* DP, February 11, 1897.

90. *headed back to Lafayette:* ibid.; LPCCR, Seventeenth Judicial District Court Minute Book, 1897, p. 390.

IV: THE FAMILY

CHAPTER II

93. *the duke of Nivernois:* Winzerling, 27.

94. *"escaped by devious ways to France":* ibid., 22.

94. *Nivernois thus passed from the Acadian scene:* ibid., 58.

94. *"reluctantly accepted . . . them":* Brasseaux, *New Acadia,* 59.

94. *a "colossal failure":* Winzerling, 59.

94. *other abortive attempts were made:* ibid., 59, 60, 65.

95. *"God-forsaken sand bars":* ibid., 64.

95. *"They humbly laid . . . in France":* ibid., 66.

95. *The king was deeply touched:* ibid., 67.

95. *Louis XV's order:* ibid., 56; Arsenault, *Histoire,* 314; Brasseaux, *"Scattered,"* 36; Brasseaux, *New Acadia,* 63.

126. *Sponsored and financed by the crown:* Arsenault, *Histoire,* 313–14; Winzerling, 68.

95. *"la Grande Ligne":* Winzerling, 75.

95. *the parents of two daughters:* White to author, October 24, 1995; Hebert, *Exile,* 113, 114; Rieder and Rieder, *France,* 1:56; Robichaux, *Chatellerault,* 61.

96. *one of their fondest memories:* Robichaux, 35.

96. *"crops germinated but . . . died":* Brasseaux, *New Acadia,* 63.

96. *no harvests in 1774 or 1775:* Winzerling, 76.

96. *they voted to abandon the colony:* ibid., 78.

96. *received permission . . . to resettle:* ibid., 79.

96. *the Doiron family chose Nantes:* Robichaux, *Chatellerault,* 35; Robichaux, *Nantes,* 57.

96. *A previously scuttled plan . . . was reactivated:* Winzerling, 65.

97. *joining their friends . . . in Louisiana:* Brasseaux, "Phantom," 129.

97. *"The militia, particularly the Acadians . . . behaved splendidly":* Caughey, 163. For more, see Brasseaux, *New Acadia,* 79.

97. *the possibility . . . was not even worthy of consideration:* Brasseaux, *New Acadia,* 69–70.

97. *A pharmacist in France:* Braud, 93.

98. *appointments he would earn:* ibid.

98. *Peyroux would coordinate the entire effort:* Brasseaux, *New Acadia,* 66.

98. *issued a royal order. . . to Louisiana:* Winzerling, 97.

98. *his policy had taken on a new dimension:* Wall, 53.

100. *Peyroux's plan thus coincided:* Brasseaux, *New Acadia,* 66–69.

100. *José de Gálvez intervened:* ibid.

100. *Peyroux had enlisted . . . Olivier Theriot:* ibid., 67.

100. *The question remained:* Braud, 94; Winzerling, 100.

100. *Louis XVI, the new king:* Brasseaux, *New Acadia,* 70.

100. *Charles III . . . replied affirmatively:* ibid., 70–71.

100. *Alas, that reply was negative:* Winzerling, 105.

100. *One of the first families:* Robichaux, *Nantes,* 57; Rieder and Rieder, *France,* 98.

101. *He was from St. Etienne de Montluc:* Begnaud, "Generations," 3, 4.

101. *sailing from Nantes aboard the* Beaumont: Winzerling, 137, 202; Braud, 99; Rieder and Rieder, *Expeditions,* 28; Chandler, 73–81.

101. *a two-week weather delay:* Winzerling, 137.

101. *two stowaways:* Voorhies, 521.

101. *Nearly sixteen hundred Acadians arrived:* Brasseaux, *New Acadia,* 72; Braud, 97–103; Winzerling, 130–53.

102. *"to assist them . . . their future abodes":* Winzerling, 132.

102. *Several hundred accepted the invitation:* Brasseaux, *New Acadia,* 108–109.

102. *the largest number . . . settled in the LaFourche country:* ibid., 112.

102. *Michel Bernard:* ibid., 206; White to author, October 24,1995.

102. *a very large land grant. . . .well-established landowners:* Conrad, *Domesday,* 1:7; DeVille, *Post,* 14.

102. *land contiguous to their own:* Conrad, *Domesday,* 1:105; Sanders, *Records,* 3.

103. *Honorine Doiron and François Begnaud were married:* Begnaud, "Generations," 5.

103. *Navarro admitted as Acadians when they married:* Winzerling, 155.

103. *a parcel of land ten arpents in width:* Conrad, *Domesday,* 1:14.

103. *the new husband had brought his life savings:* Begnaud, *"Generations,"* 6.

103. *twenty thousand arpents on both sides:* Conrad, *Domesday,* 1:14.

103. *Later he would sell . . . a three-arpent strip:* ibid., Vol. 2, Part 1, 49.

CHAPTER 12

105. *forced-heirship laws:* ibid., 1:xiii.

105. *they embraced slavery:* Brasseaux, *New Acadia,* 188; Sanders, "Slaveholders," 84–91; Baker, 144–47.

105. *every Acadian household had at least one slave:* Baker, 144.

105. *priest usually owned . . . one slave:* Brasseaux, *New Acadia,* 169.

105. *"within ten years . . . Nova Scotia":* Brasseaux, *New Acadia,* 121.

105. *the Treaty of Paris:* Wall, 79.

105. *Americans . . . poured over the Appalachian Mountains:* Allen, 28–57.

106. *fastest, cheapest, and safest way to market:* ibid.

106. *right of navigation and duty free deposit:* ibid.; Wall, 79.

106. *a series of military and policy initiatives:* Richard, 20.

106. *envisioned the new empire:* ibid., 28–29.

106. *Napoleon sent one of his favorite generals:* ibid., 28; Wall, 82.

107. *he and half his army were dead:* Haggerty, 212.

107. *regarded as a decaying power:* Ryan, 2; Richard, 20. For more on the Saint Domingue revolution, see James, *The Black Jacobins.*

107. *Jefferson . . . hoped for a diplomatic solution:* Current et al., 197; Richard, 18.

107. *offer to purchase the "Isle of Orleans":* Richard, 21.

107. *Jefferson dispatched James Monroe:* ibid., 25.

107. *successful defense . . . would be impossible:* ibid., 29.

108. *fifteen million dollars:* ibid., 31.

108. *"This accession . . . lay low her pride":* ibid., 29.

108. *All or part of fifteen states:* ibid., 45.

108. *Napoleon's prophecy would be fulfilled:* Wall, 111.

108. *divided the land . . . into two territories:* ibid., 91–106.

108. *seven of the fourteen presidents:* Brasseaux, *Transformation,* xiii.

109. *the envy of the nation:* Hair, 34; Taylor, *History,* 62–69.

109. *Egalitarianism . . . could not be sustained:* Brasseaux, *Transformation,* 14–19.

109. *the election of four Acadians:* ibid., 45–48.

110. *four Acadians served as governor:* Dawson, 96–98, 106–108, 118–22, 130–34.

110. *Two Acadians were elected lieutenant governor:* Brasseaux, *Transformation,* 53.

110. *French influence in local matters:* Wall, 94.

110. *divided up into nineteen parishes:* ibid.

110. *St. Martin Parish:* Bradshaw, "St. Martin Parish," 4.

111. *Begnaud's contiguous landowners:* Conrad, *Domesday,* 1:105.

111. *six children:* Begnaud, "Generations," 5.

111. *A 1789 muster roll:* ibid.

111. *promoted to corporal:* Sanders, *Records,* 47.

111. *his primary source of income:* Begnaud, "Generations," 5.

111. *he traded this east bank property:* Conrad, *Domesday,* Vol. 2, Part 1, p. 177.

111. *Both are buried at St. Martinville:* Hebert, *Southwest,* 1:175; White to author, October 24, 1995.

111. *valued at $9,060:* St. Martin Parish Courthouse Records, Succession of François Begnaud, #5888, August 16, 1826.

112. *The property and possessions . . . were distributed:* St. Martin Parish Courthouse Records, Succession of Honorine Begnaud, #2470, November 12, 1830.

112. *four new parishes were carved out:* Bradshaw, "St. Martin Parish," 3; Pourciau, 5; Griffin, 23.

112. *the marquis de Lafayette:* Loveland, 3; Thom, 1–3.

112. *state legislature gave his name to the new parish:* Griffin, 23.

112. *"Guest of the Nation":* ibid.

112. *the marquis did not visit:* ibid.

112. *the new boundary . . . divided almost in half:* Conrad, *Domesday,* 1:xv, 87.

113. *gradual movement into the new parish:* Brasseaux, *Transformation,* 11; U.S. Censuses, 1820, 1830, 1840, 1850, Population Schedules, St. Martin Parish, La.; U.S. Censuses, 1840, 1850, Population Schedules, Lafayette Parish, La.

113. *Founded in 1822:* Griffin, 22–25.

113. *Alexandre Narcisse Begnaud:* Begnaud, "Generations," 6; GBC, 5.

113. *Fanolia Landry:* Begnaud, "Generations," 9–10.

113. *Ranch was valued at $1,600 . . . slaves at $8,650:* GBC, 9; LPCCR, Succession of Alexandre Narcisse Begnaud, #627, July, 1849.

113. *never parted with his inheritance:* LPCCR, Succession of Hortense Patin, #4101, December 28, 1861.

114. *visited by surveyors:* Conrad, *Domesday,* 1:3–5.

114. *the price set by the government:* Conrad, "Public Land," 18 (1983): 58.

114. *Vermilionville was officially incorporated:* Taylor, "Land Settlement," 120. Glenn Conrad lists the year of Alexandre Begnaud's land purchase as 1838 (Conrad, "Public Land," 19 [1984]: 68). It is likely that the actual claim and purchase were made in 1836, and the official registration of same in 1838.

114. *In 1837, he married Eliza:* Hebert, *Southwest,* 1:144.

114. *Constantin had immigrated to Louisiana:* ibid., 1:521.

114. *Emilia had wed Pierre Constantin:* ibid., 2:213; Begnaud, "Generations," 9, 11.

115. *Alexandre and Lise Begnaud's family:* GBC, 9; Begnaud, "Generations," 92–93.

CHAPTER 13

116. *Deviations by blacks . . . were unacceptable:* Fredrickson, 3, 203–204.

117. *This is precisely what happened:* Brasseaux, *Transformation,* 55, 115.

117. *"the antebellum South's . . . taboo":* ibid., 117.

117. *The first committee:* Barde, 15.

117. *founded by a wealthy planter:* ibid., 19.

117. *Committee of Mutual Protection:* Brasseaux, *Transformation,* 118.

117. *Alfred Mouton:* Barde, 197.

117. *Breaux Bridge Committee of Vigilance:* ibid., 198.

118. *"Judge Lynch":* Brasseaux, *Transformation,* 122.

118. *His status . . . cloak of legitimacy:* ibid., 118.

118. *he called for the Committees . . . to disband:* ibid., 123.

118. *paramilitary groups of antivigilantes:* ibid., 56.

119. *gathered to plan their revenge:* ibid., 123.

119. *a force of 120 armed horsemen:* Barde, 233.

119. *Begnaud, a major in the state militia:* ibid., 197.

119. *laid siege to the fortified compound:* Brasseaux, *Transformation,* 120–21.

119. *a cannon nicknamed "Betsy":* Arceneaux, *Mouton,* 30.

119. *120 lashes:* Barde, 250.

119. *"several cadavers . . . in the prairies":* Brasseaux, *Transformation,* 122.

119. *captives deemed deserving . . . were moved:* ibid.

120. *a deceptive peace:* Potter, 370.

120. *a walkout of the state's delegation:* Brasseaux, *Transformation,* 59–60.

120. *No Democratic candidate could . . . secure the nomination:* ibid.

120. *a rump convention selected John C. Breckinridge:* McPherson, 216

120. *Democratic field divided:* ibid., 220–21.

120. *The election of this gentle man . . . meant war:* Wall, 171.

120. *The human cost was staggering:* McPherson, 854; *Baton Rouge Morning Advocate,* May 25, 1998.

121. *"The Civil War . . . states and territories":* Hair, 34.

121. *Fearless on the field of battle:* Arceneaux, *Mouton,* 132.

121. *only white men under age forty:* McPherson, 430.

121. *A. D. Boudreaux . . . commissioned a captain:* Booth, 1:31.

122. *called together his six slaves:* PI-FSL.

122. *He survived the war:* Booth, 1:31.

122. *returned his or her gold piece:* PI-FSL.

122. *Alexandre Begnaud, was also called up:* Booth, 1:155.

122. *the 26th Louisiana Infantry:* ibid.

122. *Yellow Jacket Brigade:* ibid.

122. *He was the namesake:* ibid.

123. *"Reconstruction":* Foner, xix, 276, 525–82.

123. *the South was occupied:* ibid., 276.

123. *military governors:* ibid., 61.

123. *Economically, the situation was grim:* Barry, 101.

123. *Lafayette Parish provides a good example:* Brasseaux, *Transformation,* 155–57.

123. *The white South wanted to fight back:* Current et al., 463; Foner, 294; Davis, 270.

124. *the Ku Klux Klan:* Taylor, *Reconstructed,* 145.

124. *"Election Returning Boards":* ibid.,181.

124. *Southern whites yearned for "Redemption":* Current et al., 468.

124. *Grant's second term of office:* ibid., 483.

124. *many in Congress . . . began to question:* ibid., 487.

124. *Republican Party no longer needed the vote:* ibid., 477.

125. *the White League:* Taylor, *Reconstructed,* 279.

125. *restoration of white supremacy:* ibid.

125. *fifteen clubs . . . membership of eight hundred:* Griffin, 65–71.

125. *two clubs carried its name:* ibid., 68–69.

125. *In light of the club's name . . .:* ibid; *GBC,* 9.

125. *Surrounded by* vacheries: Tax Assessment Roll, Parish of Lafayette, 1880; U.S. Census, 1880, Agricultural Schedule, Lafayette Parish, La.

126. *Another connection . . . was the marriage:* Begnaud, "Generations," 93.

126. *more interested in traditional political solutions:* Griffin, 69.

126. *refrain from paying state taxes:* Taylor, *Reconstructed,* 274.

126. *forbidden under pain of lynching to vote:* ibid., 299.

126. *they resigned by the hundreds and fled:* ibid., 297.

127. *Federal troops . . . were sent out:* ibid., 299.

127. *Rutherford B. Hayes, was elected:* Current et al., 487.

V: THE ARRAIGNMENT
CHAPTER 14

131. *the judge concurred:* TD, February 11, 1897.

131. *in French for the benefit of the accused:* DP, February 11, 1897; Debaillon Papers.

131. *Judge Debaillon then announced the appointment:* LPCCR, Seventeenth Judicial District Court Minute Book, 1897, p. 390.

132. *the judge asked . . . how they wished to plead:* ibid.

132. *set the trial date for . . . one week thence:* ibid.

132. *had lost to Gordy:* Conrad, ed., *Biography,* 1:352.

132. *Charles D. Caffery:* U.S. Census, 1900, Population Schedule, Lafayette Parish, La.; *Mayors of Lafayette,* 11; Anders, *Early Families* (Caffery Family).

132. *the first Lafayette, Louisiana:* In 1884, the first Lafayette, Louisiana, was absorbed into New Orleans's corporate limits. That same year Vermilionville was authorized to change its name to Lafayette. Residents of Vermilionville had long wanted to change the name of their town to reflect that of their parish (Griffin, 37; Fortier, 3:149–50).

132. *"The undersigned beg . . . but may be deferred a few days":* Joseph A. Chargois, R. W. Elliott, and Charles D. Caffery to Georges Bosseront d'Anglade, February 11, 1897, d'Anglade File, CADN.

133. *quite familiar with the brothers' arrest:* Georges Bosseront d'Anglade to Joseph A. Chargois, R. W. Elliott, and Charles D. Caffery, February 12, 1897, d'Anglade File, CADN.

133. *"The attorneys appointed . . . given me confidence":* ibid.

133. *he was not the actual murderer: DP,* February 15, 1897.

133. *dilatory motions . . . delaying the trial:* ibid.

133. *all withdrew as counsel for the defense:* LPCCR, Seventeenth Judicial District Court Minute Book, 1897, p. 399.

133. *In a rare fit of anger . . . declared a recess: DP,* February 17, 1897.

133. *"have been reliably informed . . . summarily executed":* ibid.

134. *newspapers . . . adversarial conflict: DP,* February 18, 1897.

134. *Debaillon . . . had no right to speak to him:* ibid.

134. *"he would have . . . state penitentiary":* ibid.

135. *the home of his father-in-law:* Debaillon Papers; Conrad, ed., *Biography,* 1:588.

135. *The first student to enroll:* ibid.

135. *one of the top criminal lawyers in the state:* ibid.

135. *Célimène Dupré:* Mouton, 32.

135. *Louise Mouton:* ibid.

136. *Oakbourne Plantation: Images de Lafayette,* 23.

136. *Debaillon knew . . . his qualifications: Biographical and Historical Memoirs of Louisiana,* 315; Conrad, ed., *Biography,* 1:105.

136. *recently become a full-time resident:* ibid.

136. *Both responded in the affirmative:* LPCCR, Seventeenth Judicial District Court Minute Book, 1897, p. 399.

136. *"He said he considered it his duty . . . under the law": DP,* February 17, 1897.

136. *The Judge then ordered . . . the Blanc brothers into court:* ibid.

137. *Their fears calmed:* ibid.

137. *trial was rescheduled:* LPCCR, Seventeenth Judicial District Court Minute Book, 1897, p. 399.

137. *returned the prisoners to jail: DP,* February 17, 1897.

CHAPTER 15

138. *a thousand spectators assembled: DP,* February 18, 1897.

138. *Every Begnaud . . . was present:* PI-JB, HLB.

138. *ANGRY MEN AT LAFAYETTE: DP,* February 18, 1897.

138. *"The square of ground . . . anything but satisfactory":* ibid.

138. *"Jeans suits of clothing . . . but an amiable mood":* ibid.

138. *"There was every evidence . . . crowd quickly forming":* ibid.

139. *Begnaud's efforts helped:* ibid.

139. *palpable distrust of townfolk:* PI-JB, HLB.

139. *one of "them":* PI-JB, HLB.

139. *Jean Begnaud, for a town dweller:* PI-JB, HLB.

139. *a menacing sight:* PI-JB, HLB. A photograph of Jean Begnaud with his ever-ready shot-gun cradled in his arms appears among the illustrations to this book.

139. *Emma had given birth to ten children:* GBC, 29.

139. *she would have three more:* ibid.

139. *"Allow the law . . . then we will":* PI-JB, HLB.

139. *LAW WINS IN LAFAYETTE:* DP, February 11, 1897.

140. *they marched on the jail:* ibid., February 18, 1897.

140. *hustled them out the back door:* ibid.

140. *spent the night in the Acadia Parish jail:* ibid., February 19, 1897.

140. *Broussard received a telegram:* Western Union telegram, R. H. Snyder to G. B. d'Anglade, February 18, 1897, d'Anglade File, CADN.

140. *"Ernest and Alexis Blanc . . . prevent such an outrage":* d'Anglade to Murphy J. Foster, February 18, 1897, d'Anglade File, CADN.

141. *"Customary for local authorities . . . may secure them":* Western Union telegram, T. G. Jones to G. B. d'Anglade, February 18, 1897, d'Anglade File, CADN.

141. *"Have wired Lafayette Sheriff . . . protect the prisoners":* Western Union telegram, R. H. Snyder to G. B. d'Anglade, February 18, 1897, d'Anglade File, CADN.

141. *fetch them and return . . . to their jail cell:* DP, February 19, 1897.

141. *"Everybody is on tip toe . . . will not be kept":* Henriette Odéide Mouton to Alexandre Mouton, February 19, 1897, Lucile Mouton Griffin Collection.

CHAPTER 16

142. *he entertained a motion . . . for a change of venue:* LPCCR, Seventeenth Judicial District Court Minute Book, 1897, p. 401.

142. *the judge set a hearing:* ibid.

142. *He directed . . . assemble the members:* ibid., 402.

142. *"be handed to each counsel . . . said defendants":* ibid.

142. *"be in attendance . . . and prosecution":* ibid.

142. *Courtroom was filled to capacity:* DP, February 21, 1897.

143. *"Before me, Ed G. Voorhies . . . according to the law":* ibid.

143. *"a change of venue as prayed for":* ibid.

143. *District Attorney Gordy and special counsel Campbell:* ibid.

143. *Charles D. Caffery and Ralph W. Elliott rose:* ibid.; LPCCR, Seventeenth Judicial District Court Minute Book, 1897, p. 402.

143. *They . . . asked to be reinstated:* DP, February 21, 1897.

143. *"I feel now that . . . as to my position":* ibid.

144. *"his sincere disappointment of . . . so late an hour":* ibid.

144. *reappointed Caffery and Elliott:* ibid.

144. *"An honorable and impartial man . . . influence or excitement":* ibid.

144. *"The accused can . . . state of affairs":* ibid.

144. *"I have heard little of this . . . speak about it":* ibid.

144. *The district attorney objected:* ibid.

145. *"Mouton argued . . . fails to secure conviction":* ibid.

145. *"I am from France . . . a fair trial":* ibid.

145. *"I sold about 250 pictures . . . in my opinion":* ibid.

145. *Called no witnesses:* ibid.

145. *"What a fearful crime . . . persons beyond danger":* ibid.

145. *"You, gentlemen, are . . . not executed":* ibid.

145. *"very clear that the prisoners . . . overruled":* ibid.; LPCCR, Seventeenth Judicial District Court Minute Book, 1897, p. 404.

VI: The Village
CHAPTER 17

149. *build a railroad through the heart of New Acadia:* Baughman, 208; "Morgan Whitney's Louisiana"; Ayers, 112.

149. *Charles "Commodore" Morgan:* Baughman, 154.

150. *"show the people . . . build a road":* ibid.

150. *project was conceptually sound:* Carter, 11–28.

150. *granted two exclusive charters: Acts Passed by the General Assembly . . . ,* Act 37 of 1877, pp. 37–49, and Act 21 of 1878, pp. 258–68; Baughman, 177.

150. *"such a course . . . most expedient": Acts Passed by the General Assembly . . . ,* Act 37 of 1877, p. 38.

150. *A third Morgan company:* Baughman, 210–18.

150. *Several strikes on all three lines: LA,* October 11, 1879, November 22, 1879.

151. *Many railroad hands died:* ibid.

151. *laying the track directly westward: LA,* April 27, 1878, September 20, 1879.

151. *elected Gustave A. Breaux: Official Journal of the Proceedings of the Senate . . . ,* 1879, 4.

151. *Few politicians commanded more respect: Biographical and Historical Memoirs of Louisiana,* 315; Conrad, ed., *Biography,* 1:105.

151. *His Oakbourne Plantation:* Conrad, ed., *Biography,* 1:105.

151. *had homesteaded and purchased land:* Taylor, "Land Settlement," 121.

152. *a clerk in the senate: Biographical and Historical Memoirs of Louisiana,* 315.

152. *"to Vermilionville": Acts Passed by the General Assembly . . . ,* Act 12, 1879.

152. *Morgan had eighteen months:* ibid.

152. *The Breaux legislation:* ibid.; *LA,* January 11, 1879.

152. *the use of convict labor: LA,* May 31, 1879, July 5, 1879, July 24, 1879, August 9, 1879.

152. *engaged Breaux, Fenner and Hall: Biographical and Historical Memoirs of Louisiana,* 315.

152. *died on May 9, 1878:* Baughman, 218.

153. *Charles A. Whitney . . . took control:* ibid. "Marie Louise Morgan Whitney used the proceeds from the sale of her father's railroad empire to provide the financial backing to her sons, Charles and George, to start Whitney National Bank" ("Morgan Whitney's Louisiana").

153. *the Texas and New Orleans had linked:* DP, May 17, 1880, August 28, 1880.

153. *operating in earnest:* DP, May 30, 1880; Carter, 11, 54.

153. *The importance of the railroad:* Griffin, 37; Goins and Caldwell, xvi–xvii; Hoffsommer, 153; Baughman 230; Millet, 374–79.

153. *Small towns . . . would eventually grow:* Dormon, 64–65.

153. *two factors working in their favor:* Baughman, 177.

154. *James G. Parkerson, an agent:* Fontenot and Freeland, 1:123, 244, 264; LA, March 8, 1879.

154. *Dominique Cayret was born:* Mulkern-Cayret Papers.

154. *the family later settled in Bordeaux:* PI-ELDM, JAM.

154. *Dominique apprenticed himself:* PI-ELDM, JAM. Examples of the craftsmanship of Dominique Cayret are in the possession of his great-granddaughter, Elia Louise Doucet Mouton of Scott, Louisiana. They are a bed and an armoire. The grace in the design of the bed and the incredible size of the armoire are unique.

154. *in great demand:* PI-ELDM, JAM.

154. *settled in Lafayette Parish:* OCP.

154. *he owned 68 acres:* U.S. Census, 1860, Agricultural Schedule, Lafayette Parish, La.

155. *130-acre farm:* LPCCR, Sheriff's Sale No.3928, February 6, 1861.

155. *Two tenant families:* U.S. Census, 1870, Agricultural Schedule, Lafayette Parish, La.

155. *holdings had reached 450 acres:* ibid.

155. *occasionally accepting commissions:* PI-ELDM, JAM.

155. *the French tricolor flying:* Edmonds, 34.

155. *twelve children:* OCP.

155. *Alcide Judice, the only son:* Taylor, "Judice," 98–116; Anders, *Early Families* (Judice Family).

155. *He returned from the war:* Anders, *Early Families* (Judice Family).

155. *leasing eighteen acres:* U.S. Census, 1870, Agricultural Schedule, Lafayette Parish, La.

155. *he married . . . Anaïs Cayret:* Taylor, "Judice," 115; OCP.

156. *a man of commerce:* PI-BNCA, ELDM, JAM.

156. *speak both French and English:* Lafayette Daily Advertiser, Progress Edition, January 30, 1963.

156. *A son, Leo, was born:* PI-BNCA, ELDM, JAM.

156. *presented a proposal:* PI-BNCA, ELDM, JAM.

156. *One bill in particular: Acts Passed by the General Assembly . . . ,* Act 37, 1877.

156. *advance knowledge of the route:* PI-BNCA, ELDM, JAM.

157. *Dominique Cayret said oui:* PI-BNCA, ELDM, JAM; OCP; *Lafayette Daily Advertiser,* September 7, 1986.

157. *write both French and English:* PI-ELDM, JAM.

157. *Louise was born:* OCP.

157. *a lively correspondence:* PI-ELDM, JAM.

157. *the transportation revolution:* Elwitt, 103–136.

157. *his three sons:* OCP.

157. *Jacques died in infancy:* OCP.

157. *not a strong personality:* PI-ELDM, JAM.

158. *Railroad was to be built east to west:* Goins and Caldwell, Map 2; U.S. Geological Survey on line.

158. *three criteria:* PI-BNCA, ELDM, JAM.

159. *an ideal location: Lafayette Daily Advertiser,* September 9, 1984, September 7, 1986.

159. *Dr. George Washington Pierre Soulé Scranton:* Anders, *Early Families* (Scranton Family).

159. *The senior Scranton established a medical practice:* ibid.

159. *several large blocks of public land:* Taylor, "Land Settlement," 120–21.

159. *the younger Scranton . . . went into medical practice:* Anders, *Early Families* (Scranton Family).

159. *bounded by three large ranches:* Taylor, "Land Settlement," 120–21; PI-SLP, PMPG, CL, JLR.

159. *"Old Spanish Trail":* Weber, *Spanish,* 345; *Louisiana Trails Advisory Council Report,* 45, 55. For more on the Old Spanish Trail, see Anding, 9–15.

160. *All three of Scranton's contiguous neighbors:* Tax Assessment Roll, Parish of Lafayette, 1880; U.S. Census, 1880, Agricultural Schedule, Lafayette Parish, La.; PI-HNS, CL, EB, SLP, JLR.

160. *The Begnaud School: GBC,* 1; Begnaud, *Superintendents* (A. Edgar Martin).

160. *taught by an itinerant teacher: GBC,* 1; PI-CL, JB, ER, MNMP.

160. *two legal documents:* LPCCR, Land Sale No. 8791, recorded January 29, 1878, and Land Sale No. 9538, recorded August 1, 1879.

160. *"in this parish . . . two hundred dollars":* ibid.

161. *"1st a certain . . . three thousand dollars":* ibid.

161. *talked of deepening the channel:* Griffin, 85–87.

CHAPTER 18

162. *The site he chose:* Elia Louise Doucet Mouton to author, August 14, 1996; PI-ELDM, JAM.

162. *large, stately two-story:* PI-ELDM, JAM.

163. *in residence at the new Cayret home:* PI-ELDM, JAM; OCP

163. *Similar in style and construction:* Elia Louise Doucet Mouton to author, August 14, 1996.

163. *established in their new surroundings:* The Dominique Cayret home was torn down sometime in the 1950s. The site is presently occupied by a strip shopping center appropriately called the Twin Oaks Shopping Center. At this writing, only one of the oaks is still standing. The cottage of Anaïs and Alcide Judice was also demolished in the 1950s, and the land has become the grounds of the Louis Leo Judice Elementary School in Scott, Louisiana. If it were still standing, this house would be directly across the street from Saints Peter and Paul Catholic Church (PI-CL, ELDM, JAM).

163. *The greatest threat: LA,* September 20, 1879.

164. *legislation made it easier . . . to obtain rights-of-way: Acts Passed by the General Assembly . . .* , Act 21, 1879.

164. *he refused:* PI-ELDM, JAM, SLP.

164. *if . . . agreed to construct a depot:* PI-ELDM, JAM, SLP.

164. *"Be it known . . . maintaining said road":* LPCCR, Land Sale No. 9400, recorded May 21, 1879.

165. *a full-blown railroad station:* LPCCR, Land Sale, recorded February 24, 1881.

165. *"where the West begins":* PI-ELDM, JAM, CL.

165. *Cayret readily agreed:* PI-ELDM, JAM, CL.

166. *"Mr. Dominique Cayret . . . twenty-five dollars":* LPCCR, Land Sale No. 10041, recorded June 28, 1880.

166. *The Judice Store opened its doors:* Tax Assessment Rolls, Parish of Lafayette, 1881 and 1882.

166. *"ninety-five dollars cash":* LPCCR, Land Sale, recorded February 24, 1881.

166. *"being erected":* ibid.

166. *"a servitude . . . embarking of passengers":* ibid. The section house was torn down in the 1950s and the depot in the 1970s (PI-CL, JLR, HNS).

166. *the stationmaster's residence:* PI-MAD, CL, ELDM, JAM.

166. *vintage Dominique Cayret:* PI-MAD, CL, ELDM, JAM. The stationmaster's home, with its two majestic live oaks in the front yard, is as impressive today as it was over a century ago. The address is 921 Cayret Street, Scott, Louisiana.

167. *giant live oak provided shade:* The oak died in the 1970s.

167. *Julie Nita Cayret:* OCP.

167. *Anaïs Bella Judice:* ibid.; Anders, *Early Families* (Judice Family); Taylor, "Judice," 115.

CHAPTER 19

168. *midlevel, white-collar management position:* Clarke, 411–12.

168. *"He must be . . . of his town":* ibid., 411.

169. *a love interest to develop:* ibid., 411–12.

169. *common industry practice:* ibid., 38–39.

169. *lived in the section house:* PI-EB, HNS, CL.

169. *four-seater outhouse:* PI-EB, HNS, CL; Clarke, 156.

169. *The center of railroad activity:* PI-EB, HNS, CL; LPCCR, 1892 Map of Scott, Notary Records Book #18864.

169. *a large room filled with benches:* PI-EB, HNS, CL.

169. *downsized . . . to a whistle-stop:* J. T. Mulkern was transferred to Jennings Station in 1898 and was replaced by a depot agent (PI-MAD). The depot was torn down in the 1970s (PI-EB, HNS, JLR, CL).

170. *one of the wealthiest . . . men in Lafayette Parish:* LPCCR, Succession of Alcide Judice, # 2620, April 16, 1908; *Lafayette Daily Advertiser,* April 9, 1984.

170. *a magnet for virtually all . . . activity:* PI-EB, HNS, CL. The Judice Store still stands today at its original location at 910 Alfred Street, corner of St. Mary Street, in Scott, Louisiana. At this writing it serves as a flea market. Across St. Mary Street, a "feed and seed" store occupies one of Alcide Judice's original warehouses. For more on passenger train service at Scott Station in the 1890s, see *Southern Pacific Railroad Schedule Book,* 1893.

170. *established a post office:* Adams, 5:10.

170. *fourteen producing farms:* Tax Assessment Rolls, Parish of Lafayette, 1896 and 1897.

170. *Worked by tenants and sharecroppers:* ibid.

171. *fast farm-to-market delivery:* ibid.

171. *His stock portfolio:* LPCCR, Succession of Alcide Judice, #2620, April 16, 1908.

171. *a charter member of its board of directors:* LA, September 8, 1894.

171. *largest shareholders and a founding member:* LG, December 12, 1895.

171. *attend the 1893 Chicago Word's Fair, officially called the Columbian Exposition:* LA, July 15 and August 5, 1893.

171. *not reaching Scott . . . until 1926:* OCP.

172. *a six-thousand-pound searchlight:* Burg, 198–202.

172. *the Ferris wheel:* ibid., 224.

172. *Buffalo Bill's Wild West show:* Blackstone, 26; Burke, 198–200.

172. *the experience of a lifetime: LA,* August 5, 1893.

172. *"the big merchant from Scott Station": LA,* April 6, 1895.

172. *purchased one-fourth of an arpent:* LPCCR, Succession of Martin Begnaud, # 21862, June 6, 1896.

172. *located north of and alongside the railroad track:* LPCCR, Deed of Sale, #12206, October 7, 1882.

172. *The two bachelors: GBC,* 9; LPCCR, Succession of Alexandre Begnaud and Eliza Constantin, #2140, December 17, 1898.

173. *a saloon:* LPCCR, 1892 Map of Scott, Notary Records Book #18864.

173. *Begnaud's Tavern:* ibid.; *LA,* December 7, 1889. Based on the 1892 map of the area of Lafayette Parish that became Scott, Louisiana, the site of Begnaud's Tavern is now occupied by a private residence at 1002 E Street.

173. *different in both appearance and personality:* PI-JB, HLB, RBA.

173. *purchased another parcel of land:* LPCCR, Deed of Sale, #15422, March 17, 1887.

173. *Begnaud's General Store:* Tax Assessment Roll, Parish of Lafayette, 1888.

173. *not as large as the Judice Store:* LPCCR, 1892 Map of Scott, Notary Records Book #18864.

174. *five cotton gins:* The names of the gins were A. C. Prejean's Gin, Alexandre Delhomme's Gin, Prejean's Gin, P. A. Chiasson's Gin, and A. Nero's Gin (*LA,* November 14, 1896).

174. *"Martin Begnaud shipped . . . parish":* ibid., August 23, 1890.

174. *persuading farmers . . . to raise more chickens:* PI-JB, HLB, RBA.

174. *"There are two crops . . . eggs and babies": LA,* April 13, 1889.

174. *"Martin Begnaud has a corner . . . egg center":* ibid., March 29, 1890.

175. *expanded the tavern:* ibid., December 7, 1889.

175. *purchased 150 acres of land:* Tax Assessment Roll, Parish of Lafayette, 1895.

175. *"the enterprising merchant": LA,* August 23, 1890, August 11, 1894. Based on the 1892 map of Scott, the original site of Begnaud's General Store is presently occupied by a private business at 1006 E Street, Scott, Louisiana (LPCCR, 1892 Map of Scott, Notary Records Book #18864). In 1902, Begnaud's General Store was purchased by Luke LeBlanc, a sweet potato and lumber merchant of Scott. By rolling it over huge logs pulled by teams of mules, LeBlanc moved the big store about 200 yards north to his property. He converted the building into a beautiful home that still stands at 1115 St. Mary Street. It is a private residence (PI-CBLM, GM).

175. *Jules Guidry opened . . . third mercantile store: LA,* November 2, 1889.

175. *first "Coffee House":* ibid., December 7, 1889.

175. *opened a sugar mill:* ibid.; PI-CL, EB.

175. *the Hotel St. Paul: LA,* November 2, 1889, December 7 1889.

175. *a dance hall:* ibid., November 2, 1889.

175. *three hundred people attended:* ibid., January 18, 1890.

176. *regularly scheduled dances . . . and benefits:* ibid., November 2, 1889, December 7, 1889, May 10, 1890, August 23, 1890, September 5, 1891, October 16, 1893.

176. *baseball games:* ibid., July 20, 1889, November 2, 1889; *LG,* September 15, 1894; PI-CL, EB.

176. *played on a diamond . . . in a pasture:* Hock, 117.

176. *presented with a keg of beer: LA,* July 20, 1889, October 19, 1895; *LG,* March 6, 1897. Begnaud's Tavern and Peck's Coffee House were razed around World War I and replaced by other homes and businesses. Also, around this same time, the St. Paul Hotel was converted into a private residence, which it remained until the 1960s, when it was torn down. The Scott Pharmacy, 1000 St. Mary Street, corner of E Street, occupies the original site of Peck's Coffee House. On the original site of the hotel, directly across St. Mary Street from the Scott Pharmacy, stand a pool hall and dry cleaners (PI-EB, JLR, JB, CL).

176. *The first school: LA,* April 6, 1889.

176. *privately built and operated:* ibid.; PI-EB, JB, SLP.

177. *built a new Scott School:* Begnaud, *Superintendents* (A. Edgar Martin); *LA,* December 7, 1889, September 22, 1894, September 29, 1894, October 19, 1895; PI-PMPG, GP, MNMP.

177. *provided free transportation: Lafayette Daily Advertiser,* August 9, 1984; Toups, 27; PI-BNCA. A private residence located at 935 Old Spanish Trail and surrounding grounds occupies the site of this first Scott School. So many children attended as a result of Judice's student transportation system that in ten years enrollment exceeded capacity and a new, much larger, school was built on the present site of the Louis Leo Judice Elementary School. The 1895 school was razed (PI-GP, MNMP. PMPG, SLP, ER).

177. *"Educate the Child":* Tombstone of Alcide Judice, Sts. Peter and Paul Church cemetery, Scott, Louisiana.

177. *on the San Francisco and New Orleans line: Southern Pacific Railroad Schedule Book,* 1893, 464.

178. *a new stationmaster arrived:* PI-MAD, ELDM.

178. *"Muldoon": LA,* March 29, 1890, September 15, 1894.

178. *he was a Yankee:* Mulkern-Cayret Papers.

178. *In exchange for citizenship . . . served four years:* ibid.

178. *he entered the cooperage business:* ibid.

178. *J. T. graduated from Baylies:* ibid.

178. *his first independent posting:* ibid.

178. *wiry, strong, and very short: LA,* March 29, 1890, March 14, 1891; PI-MAD.

178. *One of Mulkern's best friends: LA,* July 20, 1889.

178. *"good Confederates":* ibid.

179. *"Blue and grey were once more united":* ibid.

179. *Mulkern wed . . . Cecile Cayret:* Mulkern-Cayret Papers.

179. *"beautiful and impressive": LA,* September 19, 1891.

179. *married in her slippers:* PI-MAD.

179. *"for an extended bridal tour": LA,* September 19, 1891.

179. *"Judging from . . . busy this Fall":* ibid.

179. *the village's first and only mansion:* PI-BNCA.

180. *estimated thousand volumes:* ibid.

180. *French was the only language spoken:* ibid.

180. *regarded with awe and admiration:* The Judice mansion was torn down in the 1960s. The United States Post Office of Scott, Louisiana, a bank, several small businesses, and several private homes occupy the original site (ibid.; PI-JLR, HNS, SLP, CL).

180. *Dominique Cayret died:* OCP; Tombstone of Dominique Cayret, Sts. Peter and Paul Church cemetery, Scott, Louisiana.

180. *Too frightened to live in the country:* LG, July 27, 1895; PI-ELDM, JAM.

180. *buried on his land:* In 1906, Hortense Duhon Cayret and her children would donate several acres just to the west of her husband's grave for the construction of Saints Peter and Paul Catholic Church. In time, the land surrounding the Cayret graveyard would become the cemetery for Sts. Peter and Paul Church parish. Dominique Cayret's two sons-in-law, for whom 1891 was such an eventful year, would later join their father-in-law in the little graveyard: Alcide Judice in 1908 and J. T. Mulkern in 1926 (Baudier, 515; OCP; Cayret-Mulkern Papers; PI-ELDM, JAM; tombstones of Dominique Cayret, Alcide Judice, and J. T. Mulkern, Sts. Peter and Paul Church cemetery).

CHAPTER 20

181. *"the old Democratic warhorse":* LG, December 7, 1895.

181. *He was a permanent fixture:* ibid.; LA, December 10, 1897, August 31, 1889, November 2, 1889; LG, February 9, 1895.

182. *the Alliance held many rallies:* LG, February 9, 1895.

182. *among the founders of . . . Bi-Metallic League:* LA, June 29, 1895.

182. *forced to downplay . . . its position:* Current et al., 476–97, 555–65.

182. *high tariff position was acceptable:* Hair, 88, 246–47.

182. *the controversial Louisiana Lottery:* Wall, 210–17.

182. *Alexandre Delhomme . . . rallied the opposition:* LA, May 3, 1890, September 26, 1891.

182. *The Louisiana Lottery Company:* Hair, 201–202.

183. *the lottery merely switched sides:* Wall, 210–11.

183. *P. G. T. Beauregard and Jubal A. Early:* ibid., 211.

183. *a lock on the legislature:* ibid., 210–12.

183. *"like the French royals . . . forgotten nothing":* Gill, 124

183. *noblesse oblige:* Hair, 21.

183. *Most yeoman farmers . . . in this Democratic camp:* ibid.

184. *referred to the governor as McLottery:* ibid., 136–40.

184. *pro-Nicholls and antilottery rallies:* LA, May 30, 1890, November 22, 1890, July 4, 1891, September 26, 1891.

184. *Delhomme's closest political allies:* LA, December 10, 1887, August 31, 1889.

184. *twenty-five-year life of the lottery:* Hair, 201–202.

184. *The second—and last—chance:* ibid.

184. *Two Republican candidates:* Wall, 222.

185. *a statute prohibiting all lotteries:* ibid.

185. *cease use of the U.S. mail:* ibid.

185. *only within the boundaries of the state:* Hair, 224.

185. *abandoned its recharter fight:* Gill, 142

185. *took two key steps:* Dawson, 191.

185. *Foster made his political peace:* Hair, 258.

185. *John N. Pharr:* ibid., 252, 256–58.

185. *brought his own considerable assets:* Wall, 232.

186. *a rare free-silver Republican:* ibid.

186. *Known as the Populists:* Hair, 252–54.

186. *Wilson-Gorman Act:* ibid., 256.

186. *every sugar planter . . . rallied to the Pharr banner:* ibid.

186. *a reform movement called the Citizens' League:* ibid., 258.

186. *the most significant vote of all:* Wall, 232–33.

186. *known as the Fusion ticket:* ibid.

186. *white supremacy was the pivotal issue:* Ayers, 290–92; Barry, 103, 124.

186. *Night riders, imitators of the Ku Klux Klan:* Hair, 185, 196, 262.

186. *they were called Regulators:* ibid.

186. *At the state level, candidates:* ibid., 262–64.

187. *Locally, there were races for sheriff:* LA, April 25, 1896, April 4, 1896.

187. *the popular "cowboy" sheriff of Lafayette:* LG, December 7, 1895; Perrin, ed., 203; Conrad, ed., *Biography,* 1:114.

187. *Ike and his widowed mother had moved:* Conrad, ed. *Biography,* 1:114.

187. *Raising livestock was Broussard's lifetime avocation:* ibid.

187. *Broussard was a Baptist:* ibid.

187. *his wife was also a Protestant:* ibid.

187. *a regular visitor to the balls:* LA, March 14, 1891, September 5, 1891, September 26, 1891.

188. *"400 white persons were in attendance":* ibid., April 18, 1896.

188. *raided the opera house:* ibid.

188. *Broussard's opponent in 1896. . . . not a political asset:* Fortier, 3:86–87; Perrin, ed., 212; *Mayors of Lafayette,* 7; LA, June 23, 1908; PI-ECCR, FR.

189. *Democrats were on the defensive:* Hair, 258–65.

189. *"hayseed, canejuice . . . wool":* ibid., 257.

189. *"John Nigger Pharr":* ibid., 256.

189. *Twenty-one lynchings:* ibid., 262.

189. *A typical but not isolated example:* ibid., 263.

189. *Foster received 3,093 votes:* ibid.

189. *Statewide, the vote was 116,216:* ibid., 262.

190. *He carried the latter 1,509 to 654:* LA, April 25, 1896.

190. *The precinct, or "box":* ibid.

190. *Ike Broussard was reelected:* ibid.

190. *The Boudreauxs had supported the incumbent:* PI-FSL, CL, JLR.

190. *were both reelected:* LA, April 25, 1896.

VII: THE TRIAL
CHAPTER 21

193. *forty-seven degrees:* WR, February 25, 1897.

193. *"One day," he replied:* TD, February 26, 1897; DP, February 26, 1897.

193. *between one and two thousand people:* Bee, February 26, 1897; TD, February 26, 1897.

193. *The first would-be spectators:* Bee, February 26, 1897; *TD,* February 26, 1897; *DP,* February 26, 1897.

194. *attempted to enter the courtroom with his . . . shotgun:* PI-JB, HLB.

194. *A heated argument took place:* PI-JB, HLB.

194. *the crowd cleared an aisle: TD,* February 26, 1897.

194. *Under armed guard:* ibid.

194. *The smoldering spectator:* ibid.

194. *hundred members of the jury pool . . . assembled:* LPCCR, Seventeenth Judicial District Court Minute Book, 1897, p. 408.

195. *TWELVE MEN, GOOD AND TRUE: DP,* February 26, 1897.

195. *Louisiana Code of Criminal Procedure: Acts Passed by the General Assembly . . . ,* Act 30, 1878, Act 135, 1898; *Louisiana Code of Criminal Procedure,* Articles 799 and 841.

195. *only four jurors had been seated: DP,* February 26, 1897.

195. *it would seek the death penalty:* ibid.; *Bee,* February 26, 1897; *TD,* February 26, 1897.

195. *automatic grounds for dismissal: Acts Passed by the General Assembly . . . ,* Act 30, 1878, Act 135, 1898; *Louisiana Code of Criminal Procedure,* Articles 799 and 841.

195. *Emile Romero was the fourth. . . . Judge Debaillon overruled his father-in- law's motion: DP,* February 26, 1897; *TD,* February 26, 1897.

196. *reserved a bill of exception: DP,* February 26, 1897; *TD,* February 26, 1897; *Bee,* February 27, 1897.

196. *supreme court would then consider: Bee,* February 27, 1897.

196. *defense used one of its peremptory challenges: DP,* February 26, 1897.

196. *Jury selection continued until 7 P.M.:* ibid.; *TD,* February 26, 1897.

197. *Twenty-six . . . had been dismissed:* ibid.

197. *Martin Begnaud's brother-in-law: GBC,* 37.

197. *married to one of Martin's nieces:* ibid., 55.

197. *The jury . . . consisted of:* LPCCR, Seventeenth Judicial District Court Minute Book, 1897, p. 408.

197. *all were farmers:* U.S. Census, 1900, Population Schedule, Lafayette Parish, La.

197. *There were no objections: DP,* February 26, 1897.

197. *Judge Debaillon declared court adjourned:* LPCCR, Seventeenth Judicial District Court Minute Book, 1897, p. 408.

197. *the fire was not severe: DP,* February 27, 1897.

CHAPTER 22

198. *another cool, clear morning:* WP, February 26, 1897.

198. *courtroom doors be opened at nine: DP,* February 27, 1897.

198. *every place a person could stand had been taken:* ibid.

198. *hoping for a little more decorum: TD,* February 27, 1897.

198. *Ernest Blanc appeared "confident" and Alexis "smiled": DP,* February 27, 1897. The official record of the trial is contained in the records of Lafayette Parish Clerk of Court office and consists of one page (LPCCR, Seventeenth Judicial District Court Minute Book, 1897, p. 409).

198. *"I am a practicing physician . . . portion of the breast": TD,* February 27, 1897.

199. *"The wound that . . . a triangular instrument":* ibid.

199. *A bill of exception:* ibid.

199. *"the instrument shown him . . . found on Begnaud":* DP, February 27, 1897.

199. *would have been fatal:* ibid.

199. *"I am a practicing physician . . . Martin Begnaud":* TD, February 27, 1897.

199. *the wounds to the neck . . . were lethal:* ibid.

200. *"Mr. Begnaud in his life . . . a man of courage":* ibid.

200. *"My opinion as to why . . . which checked him":* ibid.

200. *"The only way . . . a revolver was placed at his head":* ibid.

200. *William B. Stansbury:* ibid.

200. *Debaillon declared a recess:* DP, February 27, 1897.

200. *did not want the twelve to hear opposing arguments:* Bee, February, 27, 1897.

201. *"promises, threats and inducements":* DP, February 27, 1897.

201. *it reserved another bill of exception:* ibid.

201. *"Alexis had not struck a blow at Begnaud":* TD, February 27, 1897.

201. *he had to walk only a few feet:* DP, February 27, 1897.

201. *Asked that the jury again be removed:* ibid.

201. *"Eloquently":* DP, February 27, 1897.

201. *he had made only one promise:* TD, February 27, 1897.

202. *extended conversations . . . conducted in French:* DP, February 27, 1897.

202. *Debaillon sustained the defense's objection:* ibid.

202. *their confession had been given freely:* TD, February 27, 1897.

202. *The jurors were brought back:* ibid.

202. *they had identified it as the murder weapon:* DP, February 27, 1897.

202. *The district attorney thanked him:* ibid.

202. *found a key to his brother's store:* ibid.

202. *the state offered the file in evidence:* TD, February 27, 1897.

202. *Begnaud also validated the testimony:* ibid.

202. *He testified that he had been present:* ibid.

203. *The defense called only two witnesses:* DP, February 27, 1897.

203. *"reputation for quiet, industry and good behavior":* ibid.

203. *he would call for closing arguments:* ibid.

203. *"the people demand their punishment":* ibid.

203. *"It was unparalleled . . . history of barbarism":* ibid.

203. *"they were united . . . in death":* ibid.

203. *Defendants had not taken the stand:* ibid.

203. *"Mr. Begnaud" . . . "his magnanimous and noble stand":* ibid.

204. *he almost certainly meant Simeon:* TD, February 26, 1897.

204. *"the twelve men good and true":* DP, February 27, 1897.

204. *"Vengeance is mine . . . laws of the state":* ibid.

204. *Carefully explained . . . "qualified verdict":* TD, February 27, 1897.

204. *"Look at these two young men . . . to hang them":* DP, February 27, 1897.

204. *"motherless, fatherless and friendless":* ibid., February 28, 1897.

204. *"cruel and a relic of barbarism":* ibid., February 27, 1897.

204. *Governor Mouton was the last:* TD, February 27, 1897.

204. *"If you shut your ears . . .":* ibid.

205. *"stand up for Louisiana":* DP, February 27, 1897.

205. *He urged them . . . guilty:* ibid.

205. *Judge Debaillon then charged the jury:* ibid.

205. *"if the jury was satisfied . . . equally guilty":* ibid.

205. *"a confession . . . the highest kind of evidence":* ibid.

205. *out fifteen minutes:* ibid. While the *Daily Picayune* reported that the jury deliberated fifteen minutes, the *Times-Democrat* had the time as twenty-five minutes (*TD*, February 27, 1897).

205. *At 11 o'clock they filed into the crowded courtroom:* DP, February 27, 1897.

205. *"Guilty as charged in the bill of indictment":* ibid.

205. *"Well, I guess it's only a matter of a few days now":* ibid.

205. *Homer Mouton . . . wept:* ibid.

205. *He then declared court adjourned:* ibid.

205. *shook hands with each of their attorneys:* TD, February 27, 1897.

205. *guaranteed another overflow audience:* DP, February 28, 1897.

206. *they would die together:* TD, February 27, 1897.

206. *appealed to the Louisiana Supreme Court:* DP, February 27, 1897. With an air of certainty, the headlines in *L'Abeille de la Nouvelle-Orléans* of February 27, 1897, read, in French, "Lawyers for the Defense Will Appeal to Supreme Court of Louisiana."

206. *a lengthy, in-depth interview:* DP, February 28, 1897.

206. *"splendid health and spirits":* ibid.

206. *"great good humor":* ibid.

206. *"talkative and full of questions":* ibid.

206. *"A strange admission":* ibid.

206. *the deep "fraternal affection":* ibid.

207. *eager to begin . . . an appeal:* ibid.

207. *vetoed the recommendations:* ibid., February 28, 1897.

207. *"Why should we? . . . prolong our troubles":* LA, March 6, 1897.

207. *"rough-looking men":* DP, February 28, 1897.

207. *hang the jury first:* ibid.

207. *"provided for all emergencies":* ibid.

207. *The entire budget . . . $2,300:* Police Jury Minutes, Lafayette Parish, 1897, 58.

207. *appropriated by the parish police jury:* ibid., 56.

207. *billed the police jury on a monthly basis:* ibid., 78.

208. *"The verdict . . . quiet as usual":* DP, February 28, 1897.

208. *decided on the sentencing date:* ibid., March 5, 1897.

208. *all parties were present:* TD, March 5, 1897.

208. *only a few visitors in the courtroom:* LA, March 6, 1897; Opelousas Courier, March 6, 1897.

208. *The Judge asked . . . anything to say:* TD, March 5, 1897.

208. *He then pronounced sentence:* DP, March 5, 1897.

208. *"In this case . . . July 10th, 1884":* LPCCR, Seventeenth Judicial District Court Minute Book, 1897, p. 411.

CHAPTER 23

209. *nine convicted criminals: Bee,* March 11, 1897.

209. *Lynch fever had cooled:* d'Anglade File, CADN.

209. *recent threats of mob rule: Bee,* March 10, 1897.

210. *"within the four walls . . .":* LPCCR, Seventeenth Judicial District Court Minute Book, 1897, p. 411.

210. *had not been a legal hanging: DP,* April 2, 1897.

210. *a small area that would hold the gallows: TD,* April 2, 1897.

210. *the governor could legally set the date:* ibid.

210. *He proceeded carefully: Bee,* March 17, 1897.

210. *set an execution date within two weeks:* ibid., March 19, 1897.

210. *Construction of the enclosure: DP,* March 10, 1897.

210. *be prepared to travel that night:* ibid.

210. *two . . . young men as auxiliary deputies:* ibid., March 11, 1897.

210. *Broussard himself would be in charge: Bee,* March 10, 1897.

211. *Their most welcome visitors: DP,* March 10, 1897.

211. *The most unwelcome visitor:* ibid.

211. *reporters from the local weeklies: LA,* March 13, 20, and 27, 1897; *LG,* March 20, 1897; *Crowley Signal,* March 27, 1897.

211. *brothers continued to lament: Opelousas Courier,* March 6, 1897.

211. *"We burned the last . . . a just one":* ibid.

211. Meurtre de Martin Begnaud: *Vie,* 5-10; *LG,* April 3, 1897.

211. *a record of their travels: Vie,* 5.

211. *presented the piece to their beloved jailer:* ibid., 17.

211. La Vie Humaine: ibid., 11-16.

212. *Completed on March 8:* ibid., 11.

212. *his third literary effort: DP,* March 11, 1897.

212. *They had nothing to lose: Bee,* March 11, 1897.

212. *The fact that their transfer . . . added bonus: DP,* March 11, 1897.

212. *Broussard's weapon of choice:* ibid.

212. *grabbing the sheriff's side arm: Bee,* March 1, 1897.

212. *gave it to his chief deputy to hold: DP,* March 11, 1897.

213. *frank discussion of the escape attempt:* ibid.

213. *"Boy Murderers": TD,* March 31, 1897.

213. *"young demons":* ibid., March 18, 1897.

213. *forged a second file into a dagger:* ibid.

214. *a second file . . . was found: LA,* March 20, 1897; *LG,* March 20, 1897.

214. *"It can be seen . . . Louisiana": TD,* March 18, 1897.

214. *Robert F. Broussard:* Conrad, ed., *Biography,* 1:116; Broussard Papers; Debaillon Papers.

214. *used the money to buy extra food: TD,* April 2, 1897.

214. *Captain Thomas Fulham: DP,* March 19, 1897.

214. *placed in separate cells:* ibid.

214. THE BLANC BROTHERS . . . DEATH: ibid., March 19, 1897.

215. *Ernest resumed his writing: Vie,* 17-23.

215. *"pay his debt . . . forgiveness of God":* ibid., 22.

215. *drawing . . . figures from history:* The March 26, 1897, issue of the *Daily Picayune* contained several of Ernest's drawings; see the illustrations section of this book.

215. *spent most of his time lying in his hammock: DP,* March 19, 1897.

215. *three of the latter arrived:* ibid., March 25, 1897.

215. *Murphy Foster acted immediately: Bee,* March 17, 1897.

215. *Broussard did not receive . . . until the following week:* Death Warrant File, 1897, Louisiana State Archives.

215. *The three arrived unannounced: DP,* March 25, 1897. For more on Romuald Philip LeBlanc see *History of Vermilion Parish, Louisiana.*

215. *Captain Fulham, unprepared: DP,* March 25, 1897.

215. *It was now only 8:30:* ibid.

216. *"Death Warrant":* Death Warrant File, 1897, Louisiana State Archives.

216. *"We are ready anytime now": DP,* March 25, 1897.

216. *"I see the French . . . sentence commuted":* ibid.

216. *Alexis declined, but Ernest lit up:* ibid.

VIII: The Brothers
CHAPTER 24

221. *morning edition . . . contained a bulletin:* Bee. March 19, 1897.

221. *three . . . gentlemen standing before him: DP,* March 21, 1897.

221. *They introduced themselves:* ibid.; d'Anglade File, CADN.

221. *had not received a fair trial: DP,* March 21, 1897.

221. *"He was satisfied in his own mind . . . being sworn in":* ibid.

222. *"see what I can do for you":* ibid.

222. *"not as an official . . . as an individual":* ibid.

222. *placed the brothers under a deathwatch:* ibid.

222. *Marie Gabriel Georges Bosseront d'Anglade:* Actes de Naissance, Archives de Paris; d'Anglade File, CADN; Annuaires Diplomatique et Consulaire, Archives du Ministère des Affaires Etrangères à Paris.

222. *Both . . . became diplomats:* d'Anglade File; Annuaires Diplomatique et Consulaire, Archives du Ministère des Affaires Etrangères à Paris.

222. *his last year in the Crescent City:* ibid.

222. *encompassing . . . the Blanc brothers affair:* ibid.

223. *received a disturbing letter:* Falk to d'Anglade, March 7, 1897, d'Anglade File, CADN.

223. *"There is not an iota of proof . . . these boys are Guilty":* ibid.

223. *Falk's family was prominent:* U.S. Census, 1900, Population Schedule, Lafayette Parish, La.

223. *D'Anglade sent Falk . . . a reply:* d'Anglade to Falk, March 9, 1897, d'Anglade File, CADN.

224. *Consultations with several attorneys:* J. Numa Augustin and Emile J. Meral, leading members of the New Orleans Bar, were d'Anglade's closet legal advisers in these matters (*DP,* March

30, 1900, November 11, 1925; *Biographical and Historical Memoirs of Louisiana*, 2:248; d'Anglade File, CADN).

224. *The consul general made his personal appeal:* d'Anglade to Foster, March 25, 1897, d'Anglade File, CADN.

224. *"I am aware . . . in behalf of my countrymen":* ibid.

225. *"I have the honor . . . Murphy J. Foster, Governor of Louisiana":* Foster to d'Anglade, March 27, 1897, d'Anglade File, CADN.

226. *Janssens would approach . . . Thomas G. Rapier:* d'Anglade File, CADN.

226. *Rapier was a devout Catholic:* ibid.; Conrad, ed., *Biography*, 2:672–73.

226. *"Your Grace, I have this . . . worse consequences":* Rapier to Janssens, March 20, 1897, d'Anglade File, CADN.

227. *reinstated as the state capital in 1879:* Gould and Powell, 11.

227. *attorney general was still located in New Orleans:* d'Anglade File, CADN.

227. *Cunningham, from Natchitoches:* Fortier, 3:112–13.

227. *a recommendation from the presiding judge:* d'Anglade File, CADN.

227. *He did not discourage d'Anglade's efforts:* ibid.; *TD*, March 23, 1897.

227. *no meeting of the Board of Pardons:* d'Anglade File, CADN.

227. *an emergency meeting:* ibid.

227. *A final draft was agreed upon:* ibid.

227. *each year witnessed a decline:* Jackson, 14–15; Vella, 262–72.

228. *it would cease daily publication:* Schneider, 2.

228. *fourteen active in 1897:* *Bee*, December 1, 1897.

228. *essentially social clubs:* ibid.

228. *"both strangers . . . Penitentiary for Life":* d'Anglade File, CADN.

228. *contained only seven hundred signatures:* ibid.

228. *"I do not consider . . . most heartily":* d'Anglade to Foster, March 26, 1897, ibid.

228. *there would be no reprieve:* Foster to d'Anglade, March 27, 1897, ibid.

229. *"I have received your favor . . . in person":* Foster to d'Anglade, March 29, 1897, ibid.

229. *"no one in the parish would sign such a petition":* Forge to d'Anglade, March 25, 1897, ibid.

229. *Cunningham was candid:* d'Anglade File, CADN.

229. *some friendly advice:* ibid.

229. *approach Debaillon:* Mouton to d'Anglade, March 29, 1897, ibid.

229. *"Having been one . . . 7 P.M.":* ibid.

230. *Mouton agreed to intercede:* ibid.

230. *a forceful case for clemency:* ibid.

230. *"I refuse to recommend . . . in Blanc Brother":* Debaillon to Cunningham, March 31, 1897, ibid.

230. *"As the judge declines . . . to be useless":* ibid.

230. *anger and bitterness:* *Crowley Signal*, April 3, 1897.

230. *defeated there by Julian Mouton:* *LA*, April 25, 1896.

230. *an 864-vote majority:* ibid., May 2, 1896.

230. *he carried Lafayette Parish:* *LG*, April 21, 1900.

CHAPTER 25

231. *telegraphed his Orleans counterpart:* DP, April 1, 1897; Bee, April 1, 1897,

231. *Broussard . . . arrived a little before eight:* DP, April 1, 1897; TD, April 1, 1897.

231. *escorted into the prison bullpen:* TD, April 1, 1897.

231. *The press corps following closely:* ibid.

231. *crowds gathered to watch:* ibid.

232. *added shackles to the prisoners' legs:* ibid.

232. *RIDE TO THEIR DEATH:* ibid.

232. *"I will protect you with my life":* DP, April 1, 1897.

232. *"It is my duty . . . his own duty":* TD, April 1, 1897.

232. *Sheriff Broussard's decision:* LG, March 27, 1897.

232. *"When we get up there . . . quick as you can":* TD, April 1, 1897.

232. *He had ridden over from Abbeville:* ibid.

232. *About three hundred people were gathered:* ibid.

233. *riveted one shackle to Ernest's left ankle:* ibid.

233. *Broussard removed the brothers' wrist irons:* DP, April 1, 1897.

233. *Father Ashley Henry Arthur Albert Knapp:* Knapp Records, Dominican Order Archives, Montreal, Canada; Cormier, 98, 335; *Directory of the English Dominican Province . . . ;* Gumbley, 176.

233. *"received . . . on 22 October, 1887":* Gumbley, 176.

233. *Father Julien Ravier-Boulard:* In the following year, Father Ravier-Boulard was named by Archbishop Janssens as assistant pastor at St. John the Evangelist Church in Lafayette *(Hoffmann's Catholic Directory 1898,* 80).

233. *the missionary would administer . . . the sacrament:* TD, April 1, 1897; DP, April 1, 1897.

234. *his conception of the mechanics of the gallows:* DP, April 1, 1987.

234. *"The doors are worked . . . traps open":* DP, March 31, 1897.

234. *built several years earlier:* ibid., April 1, 1897.

234. *escaped while awaiting execution:* ibid.

234. *"everybody laughed":* ibid.

234. *"intention to give the boys . . . a broken neck":* TD, April 2, 1897.

234. *two black hoods:* ibid., April 1, 1897.

235. *two pine coffins . . . a single unmarked grave:* TD, April 2, 1897; U.S. Census, 1900, Population Schedule, Lafayette Parish, La.

235. *invoice totaling $38:* Police Jury Minutes, Lafayette Parish, 1897.

235. *The ropes . . . greased and stretched:* TD, April 3, 1897.

235. *Jean Begnaud . . . would handle the night shift:* ibid., April 2, 1897.

235. *awarded that honor to his brother-in-law:* PI-JLR, JB.

235. *his best bottle of French white:* TD, April 2, 1897.

235. *the brothers were fast asleep:* DP, April 1, 1897.

235. *Father Knapp . . . administered Mass:* ibid., April 2, 1897.

236. *"steak, potatoes . . . and bread":* ibid.

236. *slices of cake:* ibid.

236. *exact time of the execution:* TD, April 2, 1897.

236. *"Well, will you . . . let us hang":* ibid.

236. *Trains arrived . . . from all directions:* DP, April 2, 1897.

236. *much grumbling and dissatisfaction:* TD, April 2, 1897.

236. *the fence . . . would not survive the morrow:* LG, April 3, 1897; DP, April 2, 1897; TD, April 2, 1897.

236. *agreed to permit viewing:* TD, April 2, 1897.

236. *amused by their notoriety:* DP, April 2, 1897.

237. *they continued to speak to each other:* ibid.

CHAPTER 26

238. *the Blanc's personal jailer:* LPCCR, Seventeenth Judicial District Court Minute Book, 1897, p. 386.

238. *fifty-three years old:* Mouton, 29.

239. *completed several brief compositions: Vie,* 15–16.

239. Meurtre de Martin Begnaud: ibid., 5–10.

239. La Vie Humaine: ibid., 11–16.

239. *four short pieces written between March 9 and March 20:* ibid., 17–23.

239. *A salient omission:* In all the newspaper coverage of the Blanc brothers, only one observer, a correspondent for the *Daily Picayune,* asked them for the Christian name of their father. He found it strange that neither Alexis nor Ernest could remember (*DP,* February 28, 1897). Although they spoke and wrote affectionately of their mother on many occasions, the Blancs never mentioned her given name.

239. *born in Paris:* TD, January 7, 1897.

239. *St. Germain-des-Prés:* DP, April, 1897.

239. *Their father was a clerk/accountant:* ibid.

239. *The Third Republic came into being:* Weber, *My France,* 10.

240. *an era of creativity rarely seen:* Brogan, xxi–xxii; Tuchman, *Tower,* 198–200.

240. *the most important of these reforms:* Elwitt, 203–207; Weber, *Peasants,* Chapter 18.

240. *"lay, obligatory, free schools":* Elwitt, 198–99.

240. *"feared more good than . . . general literacy":* Brogan, 154.

240. *mandatory teaching of physical fitness:* Weber, *Fin de Siècle,* 25; and Weber, *My France,* 207–10, 225.

240. *France went bicycle-crazy:* Weber, *My France,* 213–14; Weber, *Fin de Siècle,* Chapter 10.

241. *Champs de Mars:* Brogan, 282; Shattuck, 18, 51.

241. L'Ouest Sauvage de Buffalo Bill: Blackstone, 2.

241. *"on the edge of . . . the Arc de Triomphe":* Burke, 188.

241. *"Vive Annie Oakley! Vive Annie Oakley!":* ibid., 190.

241. *"In Paris . . . was sold on the grounds":* Blackstone, 133.

242. *offered Buffalo Bill one hundred thousand francs:* Burke, 190.

242. *American Indians came and went:* Russell, 351.

242. *referred to Alexandre Dumas:* TD, January 5, 1897.

242. *Aimard's novels that had stimulated his interest: Vie,* 12.

242. *"All this reading . . . like a magnet attracts iron":* ibid.

243. *"Considering our position . . . kept us anymore":* ibid., 5.

243. *the teenagers arrived in New York:* ibid.

243. *Each purchased a rifle:* ibid., 13.

243. *They lost everything:* ibid.

243. *living in an abandoned cabin:* ibid., 13–14.

243. *both injured in the performance of their new duties:* ibid., 14.

244. *a hospital for the indigent:* ibid.

244. *a local farmer offered them a job:* ibid.

244. *"New Orleans where our language was spoken":* ibid.

244. *"finding nothing to do there":* ibid., 15.

244. *jumped off the train at Scott Station:* ibid.

244. *The month was April, 1894:* ibid.; DP, April 3, 1897; TD, April 3, 1897.

CHAPTER 27

245. *the population . . . was 888:* U.S. Census, 1880, Population Schedule, Lafayette Parish, La.

245. *the population . . . had quadrupled:* ibid., 1900.

245. *Between four and five thousand people:* LG, April 3, 1897; TD, April 3, 1897; DP, April 3, 1897; *Weekly Iberian* (New Iberia), April 3, 1897.

245. *Men and boys predominated:* DP, April 3, 1897.

245. *It was a beautiful, clear spring day:* WR, April 3, 1897; DP, April 3, 1897.

245. *Every road . . . was jammed:* DP, April 2 and 3, 1897; TD, April 2 and 3, 1897; *Weekly Iberian* (New Iberia), April 3, 1897; *Abbeville Meridional,* April 10, 1897.

245. *offering excursion rates:* DP, April 3, 1897.

245. *The "Doodle Bug":* PI-SLP, EB.

245. *it made no stops that morning:* PI-SLP, EB.

245. *Scott Station was deserted:* LG, April 3, 1897; DP, April 3, 1897.

245. *Carencro looked like a ghost town:* ibid.

245. *been filled to capacity:* ibid.

246. *The saloons . . . open all night:* LG, April 3, 1897.

246. *people had staked out claims:* DP, April 2 and 3, 1897; TD, April 3, 1897.

246. *his neck would not be the first one broken:* TD, April 3, 1897.

246. *the only known photograph:* LA, November 13, 1955.

246. *families came with picnic baskets:* DP, April 3, 1897; *St. Landry Clarion,* April 10, 1897.

246. *vendors were omnipresent:* DP, April 3, 1897.

246. *disappointment with the high fence:* TD, April 2, 1897; LG, April 3, 1897.

246. *he would kill any man who tried:* DP, April 3, 1897.

246. *coffee and wine:* ibid.

246. *Father Knapp. . . . until the end:* Bee, April 3, 1897; DP, April 3, 1897.

246. *Alexis had not lost his sense of humor:* Bee, April 3, 1897; DP, April 3, 1897.

246. *The sum total of their earthly possessions:* TD, April 3, 1897;

247. *One was to go . . . to Mouton:* ibid.

247. *a last news conference:* DP, April 3, 1897.

247. *"coolness" and "resignation":* TD, April 3, 1897.

247. *Broussard climbed the scaffold:* TD, April 3, 1897; DP, April 3, 1897.

247. *drop was increased to seven and a half feet:* ibid.

247. *the fifteen men the sheriff had invited:* ibid.

247. *one . . . must be a physician:* ibid.; PI-JB, HLB, RBA.

247. *Three close friends:* PI-JB, HLB, RBA; *LG,* April 3, 1897.

247. *Martin's two surviving brothers:* LG, April 3, 1897; *GBC,* 9.

247. *The list was rounded out:* TD, April 3, 1897.

247. *nine carefully chosen volunteers:* DP, April 3, 1897.

248. *The same protocol was followed:* ibid.

248. *two large basins of warm water:* LG, April 3, 1897; DP, April 3, 1897.

248. *they had not attached the collars:* DP, April 3, 1897.

248. *the collar would only interfere:* ibid.

248. *the handcuffs were returned:* ibid.

248. *Father Knapp arrived:* ibid.; *LG,* April 3, 1897; Knapp Records.

248. *The condemned men were left alone:* DP, April 3, 1897.

248. *read Governor Foster's death warrant:* ibid.

248. *"led by Father Knapp . . . of the Dominican order":* ibid.

248. *"Adieu Ernest, Adieu Alexis":* ibid.; *St. Landry Clarion,* April 10, 1897.

248. *The only woman allowed:* PI-AJB, CBP.

248. *"I'm sorry":* PI-AJB, CBP.

248. *exchanged looks with Benton:* PI-AJB, CBP.

248. *mounted the steps to . . . scaffold:* DP, April 3, 1897.

248. *a sea of humanity:* ibid.

249. *two open coffins:* ibid.

249. *The faces of the brothers were pale:* ibid.

249. *"in a reverent manner":* TD, April 3, 1897.

249. *Ernest would speak on behalf of both:* DP, April 3, 1897.

249. *"Friends—We will . . . au revoir":* ibid.

249. *Ernest Blanc then stepped back:* ibid.

250. *"Good-bye":* ibid.

250. *"You have been . . . are grateful":* ibid.

250. *"Good-bye, boys":* ibid.

250. *"With celerity the sheriff slipped . . . their heads":* ibid.

250. *Broussard jerked the handle:* ibid.; *LG,* April 3, 1897.

250. *the fence collapsed:* LG, April 3, 1897; TD, April 3, 1897.

250. *hung for twelve minutes:* DP, April 3, 1897.

250. *which occurred first for Ernest:* ibid.

250. *pronounced the two dead:* ibid.

250. *Dr. Girard confirm his findings:* ibid.

250. *laid the bodies in the coffins:* ibid.; *LG,* April 3, 1897.

250. *twelve volunteer pallbearers:* DP, April 3, 1897.

250. *"died from a dislocation of the vertebra":* ibid.

250. *The coffins remained opened:* LG, April 3, 1897.

250. *cut the ropes into pieces:* PI-FSL, JLR

250. *remaining segments . . . thrown into the crowd:* PI-FSL, JLR; DP, April 3, 1897.

250. *out to the waiting wagon:* DP, April 3, 1897.

250. *they dropped one of the coffins:* PI-FSL, JLR.

251. *a brief burial service:* DP, April 3, 1897.

251. *driven around. . . to the cemetery:* ibid.

251. "pendu aujourd'hui": Burial Record Book, IV, 366, entry 18. St. John the Evangelist Church, Lafayette, La.

CHAPTER 28

252. *an English translation of* Meurtre de Martin Begnaud: LG, April 3, 1897.

252. *the rights to all the remaining prison compositions:* ibid.

252. *the booklet quickly sold out:* ibid.; LA, April 3, 1897; St. *Martinville Weekly Messenger*, April 10, 1897; PI-JLR, FSL.

252. *mega-articles:* DP, April 3, 1897; TD, April 3, 1897; *Bee*, April 3, 1897.

253. *a major accomplishment:* DP, April 3, 1897; TD, April 3, 1897; Hair, 187–90.

253. *lynch law would have prevailed:* DP, April 3, 1897; TD, April 3, 1897.

253. *Ernest Forge received a letter:* DP, May 8, 1897; LA, May 8, 1897; LG, May 8, 1897.

253. *"New York, May 2, 1897 . . . ":* DP, May 8, 1897; LA, May 8, 1897; LG, May 8, 1897.

254. *Front page headlines:* DP, May 8, 1897; LA, May 8, 1897; LG, May 8, 1897.

254. *Father Forge responded promptly:* DP, May 8, 1897.

254. *an appointment to meet the priest:* ibid.

254. *Theophile Wucher:* "Fathers of Mercy," *The Catholic Encyclopedia*, 5:794–95; Fathers of Mercy Letters, Archives of the University of Notre Dame; *New York Times*, May 4, 1933.

254. *"a warm and personal friend . . . mother of the boys":* DP, May 8, 1897.

254. *"Their family refuses . . . console her in some way":* ibid.

255. *"their alleged trip to France":* ibid.

255. *"did not remember . . . his church there":* ibid.

255. *"Father Wucher answered . . . unnecessary publicity":* ibid.

EPILOGUE

256. *careful examination of the birth records:* Actes de Naissance, 1875–1880, Archives de Paris.

256. *The search was then expanded:* ibid., 1873–1882.

256. *an illegitimate child:* ibid., November 17, 1877, Blanc #2750.

256. *no record of an Alexis Blanc:* ibid., 1873–1882.

257. *equally disappointing results:* Tables Décennales de Naissance autour de Paris dans l'Ancien Département de la Seine, 1873–1882, Archives Départementales.

257. *Likewise, baptismal records:* Les Registres de l'Archevêché: Baptêmes, St. Germain-des-Prés, 1876–1879, Archives de Paris.

257. *they said she died:* Vie, 1.

257. *no listing for a . . . Mlle Blanc:* Actes de Décès, 1893, Archives de Paris; Bureau des Cimetières, 1893, and Bureau des Mairies, 1893, Mairie de Paris

257. *seven . . . when his father died:* TD, January 7, 1897.

257. *said he died in 1889:* DP, February 28, 1897.

257. *a thorough search . . . produced no leads:* Actes de Décès, 1883, 1884,1889, Archives de Paris.

257. *lists for the sixth arrondissement:* Les Cadastres, Serié D1P4; Listes Electorales, 1879–1893, Archives de Paris.

257. *a search of succession (will) records:* Les Registres de Déclarations de Succession, 1882–1894, Archives de Paris.

258. *not really brothers at all:* PI-MPBR.

258. *filled with useful information:* d'Anglade File; Annuaires Diplomatique et Consulaire, 1859–1987; Correspondance Politique et Commerciale, 1897–1918; Correspondance Politique Etats-Unis, vols. 174 et 175; Etat Numerique de la Correspondance Consulaire et Commercial de 1793 a 1901; Dossiers Individuels, Tome I, A-J.

258. *"as an individual . . . French government":* DP, March 21, 1897.

258. *the mysterious letter:* DP, May 8, 1897; LA, May 8, 1897; LG, May 8, 1897.

258. *arrived in the United States on August 24:* Vie,1.

259. *first- and second-class . . . allowed to disembark:* Jonas, 17,125; Pitkin, 22–23; and Shapiro, 119–22.

259. *listed in the SS* Noorland's *manifest:* Passenger Lists of Vessels Arriving at the Port of New York, August 23, 1893, National Archives.

259. *the difference in first names:* PI-JM.

259. *not Emile, but Albert:* Actes de Naissance, November 17, 1877, Blanc #2750, Archives de Paris.

259. *no record of the SS* Noorland: Ship Records, Departures and Arrivals, 1893, Public Records Office, London.

260. *returned to Europe in May 1896:* Vie, 6.

260. *those records were also examined:* Ship Records, Departures and Arrivals, 1896, Public Records Office, London.

260. *any record of their arrival at New York:* United States Immigration and Naturalization Service, Passenger Lists of Vessels Arriving at the Port of New York, July 1, 1896, to January 1, 1897, National Archives.

260. *no evidence that they entered . . . New Orleans:* United States Immigration and Naturalization Service, Passenger Lists of Vessels Arriving at the Port of New Orleans, July 1, 1896–January 1, 1897, National Archives.

260. *"their* alleged *trip to France":* DP, May 8, 1897; LA, May 8, 1897; LG, May 8, 1897.

260. *All these efforts proved fruitless:* Libraries, archives, and court offices in the following cities and towns were contacted: Atlanta; Chicago; El Paso; Helena, Mont.; Indianapolis; Kansas City; Los Angeles; Louisville; New York; Norfolk, Va.; Ogden, Utah; Omaha; Portland; San Francisco; Sacramento; St. Louis; and St. Paul.

260. *burial records . . . give no precise indication:* burial research, St. John the Evangelist Church, Lafayette, La.

261. *she heard elderly visitors:* PI-MA.

261. *examined the site and reached several conclusions:* PI-MM.

262. *"GPR is a non-intrusive . . . subsurface change":* Zenero and Seng, "Geophysical."

262. *"four distinct high . . . of headstones":* ibid.

262. *"The configuration . . . of the remains":* ibid.

263. *two prerequisites must be met:* Louisiana Revised Statute, Title 8, Section 659, LSU Law Library, Baton Rouge.

263. *authorized the disinterment:* Fifteenth Judicial District Court, Docket No. 95- 0035 3-B, 1995, Lafayette Parish.

263. *A letter addressed to the pastor:* Author to the Rev. Msgr. Glen John Provost, March 1, 1995, copy in possession of the author.

263. *enthralled by famous murders:* For more on how notorious murders and murder trials have

captured the imaginations of Americans, see Halttunen, *Murder Most Foul*, and Cohen, *The Murder of Helen Jewett*.

264. *He was elected district attorney:* Fortier, 3:86–87; *Mayors of Lafayette*, 7; *LG*, April 21, 1900; *LA*, November 10, 1904, February 4, 1908.

264. *the most popular watering hole: Jean Begnaud et al.* v. *R. Dugas*, Eighteenth Judicial District Court, October 13, 1906, No. 34291, LPCCR; PI-JB, HLB, RBA.

264. *Jean Begnaud's eldest grandchild: GBC*, 105; PI-ECCR.

264. *Ike Broussard was reelected:* Perrin, ed., 203; Conrad, ed., *Biography*, 1:114; *LA*, January 20, 1904, August 24, 1914, September 26, 1921.

264. *a brief moment of fame:*, *LG*, April 24, 1897.

265. *there were always takers:* PI-AJB.

265. *bitten by a rabid dog: GBC*, 9, 33; PI-JB, HLB, RBA.

265. *"leprosy of the nineteenth century":* Vella, 256.

265. *the family listened . . . until she died: GBC*, 33; Hebert, *Southwest*, 14:33.

265. *the prettiest of the ten:* PI-JB, HLB, RBA.

266. *their last surviving grandchild . . . died:* Brian Gabriel Comeaux to author, October 23, 1995; *GBC*, 35.

266. *Laurence was the younger: GBC*, 9, 35; PI-AJB.

266. *Laurence Arceneaux never married:* Brian Gabriel Comeaux to author, October 23, 1995.

266. *"brutally beaten . . . and vase":* ibid.

266. *Kevin Touchet . . . "no contest":* Fifteenth Judicial District Court, Docket #40408, 1988, Acadia Parish.

266. *in jail for over five years:* Brian Gabriel Comeaux to author, February 26, 1998.

266. *eligible for parole in 2001:* Louisiana Revised Statutes, 15:574.4 and 15:571.4, LSU Law Library, Baton Rouge.

266. *Thomas entered a plea of "no contest":* Brian Gabriel Comeaux to author, February 26, 1998. The case numbers for the actions cited above are, for Kevin Touchet, 60718, and for Shane Michael Thomas, 61424, Fifteenth Judicial District Court, 1991, LPCCR.

267. *"Lucheni . . . piece of firewood":* Tuchman, *Tower*, 101.

Author's Note

By 1896, the year Martin Begnaud was murdered, it was clear that the future of Scott Station was not as a railroad center. The Southern Pacific Railroad Company was consolidating its operations all along the line, and it was inefficient to maintain a full range of services at Scott Station when the company's much larger divisional headquarters was only five miles away at Lafayette. J. T. Mulkern was the last stationmaster of Scott Station. When he was transferred to Jennings Station in 1898, Mulkern was replaced by a depot agent, and the Southern Pacific did not renew its lease on the home built by Dominique Cayret for the stationmasters. It became the permanent residence of Hortense Cayret and her unmarried children. As a result of the railroad's withdrawal, over time more and more people—even its own residents—began referring to the village as simply "Scott." On November 20, 1907, the state of Louisiana officially incorporated "The Village of Scott." The proclamation was signed by Governor Newton C. Blanchard. The U.S. Census of 1910, the first following its incorporation, gave the population as 150. It would take fifty-one years for this figure to reach 1,000, the number needed under Louisiana law for an incorporated municipality to be called a town. "The Town of Scott" was created on July 7, 1964, the result of a proclamation signed by Governor John J. McKeithen. The jump from town to city, which required a population of 5,000, took much less time, only twenty-six years. Governor Charles E. Roemer III affixed his signature to the appropriate proclamation on March 7, 1990, and the settlement founded by Dominique Cayret, Alcide Judice, and the Louisiana Western Railroad became "The City of Scott" (PI-ELDM, JAM, MAD; U.S. Census, 1910, Population Schedule, Lafayette Parish, La.; Louisiana Secretary of State's Office).

BIBLIOGRAPHY

Primary Sources

Manuscripts

Archdiocese of New Orleans Archives, New Orleans

Diary of the Archdiocese, 1888–1897.
Hoffmann's Catholic Directory, 1898.
Ordo List of Clergy, 1896–1897.

Archives des Dominicains, l' Ordre des Dominicains au Canada, Montreal
Knapp, Albert M. Records.

Bibliothèque Nationale, Paris
French Anarchist Movement Files.

Dixie Plantation, Franklin, La.
Foster, Murphy J., and Family. Papers. In possession of Foster family.

Dominican Archives, Philip Memorial Library, Providence College, Providence, R.I.
Catalogue of Letters, 1905

Dominican College Library, Washington, D.C.
Knapp, Albert M. Obituary.

Edith Garland Dupré Library, Jefferson Caffery Louisiana Room, University of
Southwestern Louisiana, Lafayette

Broussard, Robert F. Papers.
Burke, Walter J. Papers, 1835–1941.
Caffery, John M. Papers, 1817–1960.
Debaillon-Mouton Law Firm. Records.
Debaillon, Paul. Papers, 1852–1957.
Givens–Hopkins Families. Papers, 1847–1948.
Griffin, Harry Lewis. Collection, 1905–1964.
Griffin, Lucile Mouton. Collection, 1798–1967.
Pierrotti, Auguste. Papers, 1864–1922.
Rees, Henry, and Family. Papers, 1826–1901, 1974.
Theriot, Marie del Norte. Papers, 1852–1973.
Voorhies, Felix. Papers, 1869–1919.
Voorhies Family. Papers, 1847–1948.

Hill Memorial Library, Louisiana State University, Baton Rouge

Cary, Sylvester L. Scrapbook, 1864–1930.
Comptes-Rendus de l'Athénée Louisianais, 1897–1899.
Garland, Henry Lastraps. Papers.

Historic New Orleans Collection, New Orleans

Municipal Records of New Orleans.
Private Collections.

Howard-Tilton Library, Manuscript Division, Tulane University, New Orleans

Calder, Gertrude. Papers, 1868–1913.
Société de Secours Mutuels des Enfants de la France. Minute Books, 1892–1902.

Lafayette (La.) Catholic Diocese Archives

St. Bernard Church (Breaux Bridge, La.) Parish Brochure.

New Orleans Public Library, Louisiana Division, New Orleans

L' Union Française. Minute Book, 1895–1902.

St. John the Evangelist Roman Catholic Church, Lafayette, La.

Begnaud, Martin. Death Certificate, April 23, 1896.

Blanc, Ernest and Alexis. Death Certificates, April 2, 1897.
Burial Record Book, 1896, 1897.
Funeral Record Book, 1896, 1897.

St. Vincent de Paul Catholic Church, New York, N.Y.
Archival Records.

San Antonio, Tex.
Mulkern-Cayret Family. Papers. In possession of Margery A. Dreeben.

Scott, La.
Cayret, Octavie, and Family. Papers. In possession of Elia Louise D. Mouton.

Slidell, La.
Benton, Hampton. Papers. In possession of Cynthia Benton Prevost.

Texas and Pacific Railroad Archives, Dallas, Tex.
Malone, R. A. "Problems of Railroad Engineering in South Louisiana, 1850–1860."
    1964; in possession of author.

University of Notre Dame Archives, Hesburgh Library, Notre Dame, Ind.
Father of Mercy Letters.
Forge, Father Ernest. Letters, 1866, 1882.

NATIONAL, STATE, AND LOCAL DOCUMENTS (U.S.)

Acts Passed by the General Assembly of the State of Louisiana. New Orleans: Office
    of the Democrat, 1877, 1878, 1879, 1896. Louisiana State University Law Library,
    Baton Rouge.
Annual Report of the Secretary of State, State of Louisiana. New Orleans: Office of the
    Democrat, 1878. Louisiana State Library, Baton Rouge.
Attorney General's Docket Books, 1889–1916. Secretary of State, Louisiana State
    Archives, Baton Rouge.
Criminal Court Judgment Docket Book, 3 July 1888–February 1909. Marion County
    Courthouse, Indianapolis, Ind.
Criminal Court Order Book, Box 28, April 1893–June 1894. Marion County Court-
    house, Indianapolis, Ind.
Death Warrant File, 1897. Secretary of State, Louisiana State Archives, Baton Rouge.

1892 Map of Scott, Notary Records Book #18864. Lafayette Parish Courthouse, Clerk of Court Records, Lafayette, La.

Lafayette Parish, Louisiana, 1823–1892: Computer Indexed Marriage Records. Hammond, La.: Nicholas Russell Murray, 1981.

Louisiana Code of Criminal Procedure. St. Paul: West, 1991.

Miscellaneous Letters of the Department of State, M-179 Reels 959–963; February–April, 1897. National Archives, Washington, D.C.

1905 Map of Scott, Notary Records Book #31477. Lafayette Parish Courthouse, Clerk of Court Records, Lafayette, La.

Notary Records. St. Martin Parish Clerk of Court Records, St. Martinville, La.

Notary Records Books, 1823–1918. Lafayette Parish Courthouse, Clerk of Court Records, Lafayette, La.

Official Journal of the Proceedings of the Senate of the State of Louisiana at the Regular Session. New Orleans: Democrat Publishing, 1877–1879. Louisiana State Library, Baton Rouge.

Police Jury Minutes, Lafayette Parish, 1896–1908. Hill Memorial Library, Louisiana State University, Baton Rouge.

Register of Partitions, 1897, 1898, 1906. Lafayette Parish Courthouse, Clerk of Court Records, Lafayette, La.

School Board Minute Book. Vol. 1, 1906–1909. Lafayette Parish School Board Office, Lafayette, La.

17th Judicial District Court Indictment Book, 1897. Lafayette Parish Courthouse, Clerk of Court Records, Lafayette, La.

17th Judicial District Court Minute Book, 1892–1898. Lafayette Parish Courthouse, Clerk of Court Records, Lafayette, La.

Tax Assessment Rolls, Parish of Lafayette, 1880–1897. Secretary of State, Louisiana State Archives, Baton Rouge.

Transcriptions of Parish Records of Louisiana. No. 28, Lafayette Parish Series 1, Police Jury Minutes, Vol. 5, 1896–1904. New Orleans: Works Progress Administration, 1941.

United States Census, Agricultural Schedules, 1860–1900.

United States Census, Population Schedules, 1810–1910.

United States Department of Agriculture. Weather Bureau Monthly Observations at New Orleans. Vols. 18, 19, January 1896–December 1897. Hill Memorial Library, Louisiana State University, Baton Rouge.

United States Immigration and Naturalization Service. Passenger Lists of Vessels Arriving at the Port of New York, 1820–1897. Lists for June 15, 1896–January 1, 1897. National Archives, Washington, D.C.

United States Immigration and Naturalization Service. Passenger Lists of Vessels Arriving at the Port of New Orleans, 1820–1897. Lists for July 1, 1896–January 1, 1897. National Archives, Washington, D.C.

NATIONAL AND LOCAL DOCUMENTS (ENGLAND AND FRANCE)

Actes de Décès, 1882–1893. Archives de Paris.

Actes de Mariage, 1873–1882. Archives de Paris.

Actes de Naissance, 1873–1882. Archives de Paris.

Annuaire Diplomatique et Consulaire, 1859–1987. Archives du Ministère des Affaires Etrangères à Paris.

Bureau des Cimetières. Mairie de Paris.

Bureau des Mairies. Mairie de Paris.

Les Cadastres. Série D1P4. Archives de Paris.

Correspondance Politique et Commerciale, 1897–1918. Archives du Ministère des Affaires Etrangères à Paris.

Correspondance Politique Etats-Unis. Vols. 174, 175. Archives du Ministère des Affaires Etrangères à Paris.

d'Anglade, Marie Gabriel Georges Bosseront. Dossier. Le Centre des Archives Diplomatiques de Nantes, Nantes, France.

Dossiers Individuels. Tome I, A–J. Archives du Ministère des Affaires Etrangères à Paris.

Etat Numérique de la Correspondance Consulaire et Commercial de 1793 à 1901. Archives du Ministère des Affaires Etrangères à Paris.

Fathers of Mercy Dossier. Archives Nationales, Paris.

Listes Alphabétiques par Arrondissement et par Type d'Acte. Archives de Paris.

Listes Electorales, 1879–1893. Archives de Paris.

Les Registres de l'Archevêché: Baptêmes, St. Germain-des-Prés., 1876–1879. Archives de Paris.

Les Registres de Déclamations de Succession, 1882–1894. Archives de Paris.

Les Registres de Recensement Militaire, 1877–1910. Archives de Paris.

Ship Records. Departures and Arrivals, Southampton and Plymouth. Lists of August 1893, and May–August 1896. Public Records Office, London, United Kingdom.

Tables de Décès, 1882–1892. Archives Départementale (Seine-St.-Denis), Bobigny, France.

Tables Décennales, 1873–1882, 1883–1983. Archives de Paris.

Tables Décennales de Naissances autour de Paris dans l'Ancien Département de la Seine, 1873–1882. Bobigny, Creteil, Nanterre, Versailles. Archives Départementale (Seine-St.-Denis), Bobigny, France.

Tables de Mariage, 1872–1881. Archives Départementale (Seine-St.-Denis), Bobigny, France.

Tables de Naissance, 1875–1879. Archives Départementale (Seine-St.-Denis), Bobigny, France.

NEWSPAPERS

Abbeville Meridional, 1896–1897
Alexandria Democrat, 1876
*Baton Rouge Advocate,*1998
Baton Rouge Weekly Advocate, 1896–1897
Crowley Signal, 1897
Houston Post, 1896–1897
Indianapolis Sentinel, 1893
Lafayette Advertiser, 1878–1900
Lafayette Daily Advertiser, 1960–1996
Lafayette Gazette, 1893–1897
(New Iberia) *Weekly Iberian,* 1897
New Orleans Christian Advocate, 1897
(New Orleans) *L'Abeille de la Nouvelle-Orléans,* 1896–1897
New Orleans Daily Picayune, 1896–1897
New Orleans Daily States, 1896–97
(New Orleans) *Tägliche Deutsche Zeitung,* 1897
New Orleans Times-Democrat, 1896–1897
(New York) *Courrier des Etats-Unis,* 1897
New York Times, 1896–1897, 1933
Opelousas Courier, 1896–1897
(Opelousas) *St. Landry Clarion,* 1897
Paris Evénement, 1897
(Paris) *Petit Parisien,* 1897
Paris Temps, 1897
Paris XIXe Siècle, 1897
St. Louis Republic, 1893–1894, 1896
St. Martinville Weekly Messenger, 1897
London Guardian Weekly, 1998

INTERVIEWS

Abramson, Bella Nickerson Chappuis (BNCA): the great-granddaughter of Dominique Cayret and Hortense Duhon, the granddaughter of Alcide Judice and Anaïs Cayret, and the daughter of Anaïs Bella Bella Judice. March 14, 1994.

Arceneaux, Regina Begnaud (RBA): the great-granddaughter of Alexandre Begnaud and Lise Constantin, and the granddaughter of Jean Begnaud and Emma Constantin. November 30, 1993

Attwood, Mary (MA): curator of the cemetery of the Cathedral of St. John the Evangelist, Lafayette, La. November 15, 1994.

Bacot, J. Parrot (JPB): director of the Louisiana State University Art Museum. November 2, 1994

Begnaud, Henry Lionel Sr. (HLB): the great-grandson of Alexandre Begnaud and Lise Constantin, and the grandson of Jean Begnaud and Emma Constantin. August 23, 1994.

Begnaud, John (JB): the great-grandson of Alexandre Begnaud and Lise Constantin, and the grandson of Jean Begnaud and Emma Constantin. November 29, 1993.

Begnaud, Paul Heywood (PHB): the great-great-grandson of Alexandre Begnaud and Lise Constantin, and the great-grandson of Jean Begnaud and Emma Constantin. September 17, 1994.

Benton, Antoine Joseph (AJB): the son of Hampton Benton Jr. and Odéide Gilbert. October 21, 1995.

Boudreaux, Emick (EB): the great-grandson of Colonel A. D. Boudreaux, the grandson of Olivier Boudreaux and Philomène Begnaud, and the son of André Boudreaux. November 15, 1994.

Broussard, Rita Begnaud (RBB): the great-granddaughter of Alexandre Begnaud and Lise Constantin, and the granddaughter of Jean Begnaud and Emma Constantin. March 2, 1994.

Deville, Laura Belle Domingue (LBDD): the granddaughter of Hampton Benton Jr. and Odéide Gilbert. August 22, 1996.

Dreeben, Margery Albach (MAD): the great-granddaughter of Dominique Cayret and Hortense Duhon, and the granddaughter of J. T. Mulkern and Cecile Cayret. January 4, 1995.

Guidry, Pearl Marie Provost (PMPG): the great-great-granddaughter of Alexandre Begnaud and Lise Constantin, the great-granddaughter of Jean Begnaud and Emma Constantin, and the great-granddaughter of Louis G. Breaux. February 4, 1995.

Hamm, Bob (BH): veteran Lafayette, Louisiana, journalist and broadcaster. His two retrospective feature articles written for the *Lafayette Daily Advertiser*—one in 1955 and one in 1984—kept alive the memory of the momentous events of 1896 and 1897. April 15, 1995.

Jammes, Father Jean Baptiste Marie Camille (JBMCJ): pastor of St. Martin de Tours Catholic Church, St. Martinville, Louisiana. July 20, 1994.

LeBlanc, Constance (CL): born on November 16, 1900, she is the oldest living resident of Scott, Louisiana, at this writing. February 25, 1994.

LeBlanc, Francis Sonny (FSL): the great-grandson of Colonel A. D. Boudreaux, and the grandson of Olivier Boudreaux and Philomène Begnaud. August 22, 1994.

Manhein, Mary (MM): director of LSU Faces Laboratory, Department of Geography and Anthropology, Louisiana State University, Baton Rouge. March 14, 1995.

Martinez, Clara Belle LeBlanc (CBLM): the great-granddaughter of Colonel A. D. Boudreaux, and the granddaughter of Luke LeBlanc. August 25, 1994.

Maurin, Jean (JM): professor of history, University of Paris VIII. February 18, 1995.

Mouton, Elia Louise Doucet (ELDM): the great-granddaughter of Dominique Cayret and Hortense Duhon, and the granddaughter of Desire Doucet and Louise Cayret. December 3, 1994.

Mouton, Georgia (GM): the current owner of the home that was originally Begnaud's General Store. January 17, 1995.

Mouton, Jules Allen (JAM): the great-grandson of Alexandre Begnaud and Lise Constantin, and the grandson of Alexandre Martin and Azema Begnaud. December 3, 1994.

Prevost, Cynthia Benton (CBP): the granddaughter of Hampton Benton Jr. and Odéide Gilbert. October 21, 1995.

Provost, Gabriel (GP): the grandson of Louis G. Breaux. August 24, 1994.

Provost, Marie Noelie Martin (MNMP): the great-granddaughter of Alexandre Begnaud and Lise Constantin, and the granddaughter of Alexandre Martin and Azema Begnaud. August 24, 1994.

Provost, Stephen Lock (SLP): the grandson of Louis G. Breaux. August 26, 1994.

Raggio, Emily (ER): the great-granddaughter of Colonel A. D. Boudreaux, and the granddaughter of Olivier Boudreaux and Philomène Begnaud. August 25, 1995.

Raggio, James Lewis (JLR): the great-great-grandson of Colonel A. D. Boudreaux, and the great-grandson of Olivier Boudreaux and Philomène Begnaud. February 25, 1994.

Resweber, Ellen Cecile Campbell (ECCR): the great-great-granddaughter of Alexandre Begnaud and Lise Constantin, the great-granddaughter of Jean Begnaud and Emma Constantin, the granddaughter of William Campbell and Ellen Eastin, and the daughter of Milton Campbell. August 22, 1994.

Resweber, Francis (FR): a biblical scholar and an authority on the life of William Campbell. August 22, 1994.

Richard, Marie Pauline Boudreaux (MPBR): the great-granddaughter of Colonel A. D. Boudreaux, the granddaughter of Olivier Boudreaux and Philomène Begnaud, and the daughter of André Boudreaux. March 1, 1994.

Sonnier, Hector Numa (HNS): born on September 19, 1905, a lifelong resident Scott, Louisiana, an authority on its history, and the husband of the late Philomene Nola Martin, the daughter of Alexandre Martin and Azema Begnaud. September 20, 1994.

Sonnier, Marie Madeleine Martin (MMMS): her grandfather, Louis Martin of Carencro, was a neighbor and acquaintance of Hampton Benton Jr. June 21, 1994.

Secondary Sources
Books, Articles, and Dissertations

Adams, Donna Burge, comp. *Post Office Records, 1832–1900*. 6 vols. Baton Rouge: self-published, n.d.

Aimard, Gustave. *Les Bandits de l'Arizona*. Paris: E. Ardant, 1882.

———. *Les Bois Brûlés*. Paris: E. Dentu, 1875.

———. *La Loi du Lynch*. Paris: Amyot, 1859.

———. *Les Outlaws de Missouri*. Paris: Amyot, 1868.

———. *Les Trappeurs de l'Arkansas*. Paris: Amyot, 1858.

Allain, Mathé. "Records of Belle-Ile-en-Mer." *Attakapas Gazette* 16 (1981): 103–10; 17 (1982): 76–83; 18 (1983): 73–80.

Allen, Michael. *Western Rivermen, 1763–1861: Ohio and Mississippi Boatmen and the Myth of the Alligator Horse.* Baton Rouge: Louisiana State University Press, 1990.

Ambrose, Stephen E. *Undaunted Courage: Meriwether Lewis, Thomas Jefferson, and the Opening of the American West.* New York: Simon and Schuster, 1996.

Anders, Quintilla Morgan. *Early Non-Denominational Private Schools in Vermilionville (Lafayette) Louisiana, 1867–1905.* Lafayette: n.p., 1968.

————. *Some Early Families of Lafayette, Louisiana.* Lafayette: Sans Souci Book Store, 1970.

Anding, A. A., "Land of Evangeline and Old Spanish Trail." *Louisiana Highway Magazine* 14 (March, 1928): 9–15.

Andriot, John L., ed. *Population Abstract of the United States.* McLean, Va.: Andriot Associates, 1980.

Arsenault, Bona, *Histoire des Acadiens.* Ottawa: Editions Lemeac, 1978.

————. *History of the Acadians.* Quebec: Le Conseil de la Vie Française en Amérique, 1966.

Arceneaux, Maureen. "The Railroad Comes to Acadiana: One Man's Plaintive Response." *Attakapas Gazette* 24 (1989): 169–73.

Arceneaux, Ruth. "The Charles Homer Mouton House." *Attakapas Gazette* 6 (1970): 145–47.

Arceneaux, William. *Acadian General: Alfred Mouton and the Civil War.* Lafayette: Center for Louisiana Studies, University of Southwestern Louisiana, 1981.

Auge, Claude, ed. *Nouveau Larousse Illustré.* 7 vols. Paris: Larousse, 1898–1901.

Ayers, Edward. *The Promise of the New South.* New York: Oxford University Press, 1992.

Baker, Vaughan. "Patterns of Acadian Slave Ownership in Lafayette Parish." *Attakapas Gazette* 10 (September 1974): 144–48.

Balesi, Charles J. *The Time of the French in the Heart of North America, 1673–1818.* Chicago: Alliance Française, 1992.

Bancroft, George. *History of the United States of America, from the Discovery of the Continent.* 6 vols. New York: D. Appleton, 1888.

Barde, Alexandre. *The Vigilante Committees of the Attakapas.* Lafayette: Acadiana, 1981.

Barry, John. *Rising Tide: The Great Mississippi Flood of 1927 and How It Changed America.* New York: Simon and Schuster, 1997.

Baudier, Roger. *The Catholic Church in Louisiana.* 1939; reprint, New Orleans: Louisiana Library Association, Public Library Section, 1972.

Baughman, James P. *Charles Morgan and the Development of Southern Transportation.* Nashville: Vanderbilt University Press, 1968.

Beard, Charles A., and Mary R. Beard. *A Basic History of the United States.* New York: Doubleday, 1952.

Beaumarchais, J. P., et al., eds. *Dictionnaire des Littératures de la Langue Française.* Paris: Bordas, 1984.

Beckwith, Hiram. *The Illinois and Indiana Indians*. Chicago 1884.

Begnaud, Lurnice. "The Begnaud Family: Four Generations in Louisiana." *Attakapas Gazette* 16 (1981): 3–12, 87–96, 131–40, 182–92.

———. *Superintendents of Education of Lafayette Parish*. Lafayette: Lafayette Founders Committee, 1995.

Biographical and Historical Memoirs of Louisiana. 3 vols. 1892; reprint, Baton Rouge: Claitor's, 1975.

Bird, Will R. *Done at Grand Pré*. Toronto: Ryerson, 1955.

Black, Henry Campbell, ed. *Black's Law Dictionary*. St. Paul: West, 1979.

Blackstone, Sarah J. *Buckskins, Bullets, and Business: A History of Buffalo Bill's Wild West*. New York: Greenwood, 1986.

Blanc, Ernest, and Alexis Blanc, *La Vie, le Crime, et les Confessions d'Ernest et Alexis Blanc; ou, L'Histoire d'un Crime Horrible, Ecrits et Signés par Eux-Mêmes*. Lafayette, Imprimerie de la Gazette, 1897.

Blanchard, J. Henri. *The Acadians of Prince Edward Island, 1720–1964*. Charlottetown, P.E.I.: self-published, 1964.

Booth, Andrew B., ed. *Records of Louisiana Confederate Soldiers and Louisiana Confederate Commands*. 3 vols. New Orleans: Commissioner, Louisiana Military Records, 1920.

Bradshaw, Jim. "History of Acadiana: Acadia Parish." Supplement to the *Lafayette Daily Advertiser*, August 26, 1997.

———. "History of Acadiana: Lafayette Parish." Supplement to the *Lafayette Daily Advertiser*, February 24, 1998.

———. "History of Acadiana: St. Martin Parish." Supplement to the *Lafayette Daily Advertiser*, July 29, 1997.

———. "History of Acadiana: Vermilion Parish." Supplement to the *Lafayette Daily Advertiser*, June 24, 1997.

———. "Remembering Our Acadian Heritage." Supplement to the *Lafayette Daily Advertiser*, September 29, 1994.

Brasseaux, Carl A. *Acadian to Cajun: Transformation of a People, 1803–1877*. Jackson: University Press of Mississippi, 1992.

———. *A Comparative View of French Louisiana, 1699 and 1762*. Lafayette: Center for Louisiana Studies, University of Southwestern Louisiana, 1981.

———. *In Search of Evangeline: Birth and Evolution of the Evangeline Myth*. Thibodaux, La.: Blue Heron, 1988.

———. *The "Foreign French": Nineteenth-Century French Immigration into Louisiana*. 3 vols. Lafayette: Center for Louisiana Studies, University of Southwestern Louisiana, 1990.

———. *The Founding of New Acadia: The Beginning of Acadian Life in Louisiana, 1765–1803*. Baton Rouge: Louisiana State University Press, 1987.

———. *Lafayette: Where Yesterday Meets Tomorrow*. Chatsworth, Ca.: Windsor Publications, 1990.

————. "Phantom Letters: Acadian Correspondence, 1766–1784." *Acadiensis* 23 (Spring 1994): 124–32.

————, ed. *Quest for the Promised Land: Official Correspondence Relating to the First Acadian Migration to Louisiana, 1764–1769.* Translated by Carl A. Brasseaux, Emilio Garcia, and Jacqueline K. Voorhies. Annotated by Carl A. Brasseaux and Jacqueline K. Voorhies. Lafayette: Center for Louisiana Studies, University of Southwestern Louisi-ana, 1989.

————. *"Scattered to the Wind": Dispersal and Wanderings of the Acadians, 1755–1809.* Lafayette: Center for Louisiana Studies, University of Southwestern Louisiana, 1991.

Braud, Gerard Marc. *De Nantes à la Louisiane: L'Histoire de l'Acadie, l'Odyssée d'un Peuple Exilé.* Nantes, France: Ouest Editions, 1994.

Brebner, John Bartlet. *New England's Outpost.* New York: Columbia University Press, 1927.

Brentano, Frantz Funck. *The Old Regime in France.* Translated by Herbert Wilson. London: Edward Arnold, 1929.

Brogan, D. W. *The Development of Modern France, 1870–1939.* Vol. 1. New York: Harper and Row, 1966.

Bumsted, J. M. *Land, Settlement, and Politics on Eighteenth-Century Prince Edward Island.* Kingston: McGill-Queen's University, 1987.

Burg, David F. *Chicago's White City of 1893.* Lexington: University of Kentucky Press, 1976.

Burke, John. *Buffalo Bill: The Noblest Whiteskin.* New York: G. P. Putnam's Sons, 1973.

Burns, Francis P. "Lafayette Visits New Orleans." *Louisiana Historical Quarterly* 29, no. 2 (April 1946): 296–340.

Campbell, G. G. *The History of Nova Scotia.* Toronto: Ryerson, 1948.

Carleton, Mark T. *Politics and Punishment.* Baton Rouge: Louisiana State University Press, 1971.

Carter, J. C. "A Century of Progress in Louisiana, 1852–1952." *Southern Pacific Bulletin* 39 (October 1952): 1–55.

The Catholic Encyclopedia. Vol. S. New York: Encyclopedia Press, 1913.

Caughey, John Walton. *Bernardo de Gálvez in Louisiana, 1776–1783.* Berkeley: University of California Press, 1934.

Chandler, Richard E. "A Shipping Contract: Spain Brings Acadians to Louisiana." *Louisiana Review* 8 (1979): 23–81.

Clark, Andrew Hill. *Acadia: The Geography of Early Nova Scotia to 1760.* Madison: University of Wisconsin Press, 1968.

Clarke, Thomas Curtis, et al. *The American Railway.* 1888; reprint, New York: Arno, 1976.

Cleveland, Frederick, and Fred Wilbur Powell. *Railroad Promotion and Capitalization in the United States.* New York: Longmans, Green, 1909.

Cobban, Alfred. *A History of Modern France.* 3 vols. London: Alden, 1962.

Cohen, Patricia Cline. *The Murder of Helen Jewett: The Life and Death of a Prostitute in Nineteenth-Century New York.* New York: Alfred A. Knopf, 1998.

Conrad, Glenn R., *The Attakapas Domesday Book: Land Records of the Attakapas District*. 3 vols. Lafayette, Center for Louisiana Studies, University of Southwestern Louisiana, 1990–.

———., ed. *A Dictionary of Louisiana Biography*. 2 vols. New Orleans: Louisiana Historical Association, 1988.

———. "The Public Land Sales of Southwest Louisiana, 1821–1856." *Attakapas Gazette* 18 (1983): 58; 19 (1984): 66–69.

———. *White Gold*. Lafayette: Center for Louisiana Studies, University of Southwestern Louisiana, 1995.

Cormier, Hyacinthi. *Catalogus Ominium Conventuum et Domorum Provinciarum et Congregationum*. Rome: Richard Garroni, 1910.

Crouse, Nellis. M. *Lemoyne d'Iberville: Soldier of New France*. Ithaca, N.Y.: Cornell University Press, 1954.

Current, Richard N., T. Harry Williams, and Frank Freidel. *American History: A Survey*. New York: Alfred A. Knopf, 1966.

Davis, Edwin Adams. *Louisiana: A Narrative History*. Baton Rouge: Claitor's, 1961.

Dawson, Joseph G. III. *The Governors of Louisiana*. Baton Rouge: Louisiana State University Press, 1990.

D'Entremont, Clarence-Joseph. *Le Canada-Français: Documents sur l'Acadie*. Fredericton, New Brunswick: University of Moncton, 1976.

De Ville, Winston. *Acadian Church Records, 1679–1757*. Ville Platte, La.: Provincial, 1993.

———. *The Acadian Coast in 1779: Settlers of Cabanocey and La Fourche in the Spanish Province of Louisiana During the American Revolution*. Ville Platte, La.: Provincial, 1993.

———. *The Acadian Families: 1686*. Ville Platte, La.: Provincial, 1986.

———. *Attakapas Post: The Census of 1771*. Ville Platte, La.: Provincial, 1986.

Dictionnaire des Auteurs. Paris: Bouquins, 1980

Dictionnaire des Oeuvres. Paris: Bouquins, 1990.

Directory of the English Dominican Province of the Order of Peachers. Rome: Vatican, 1991.

Doiron, Allen, and Fidele Theriault. *La Famille Doiron*. Fredericton, New Brunswick: self-published, 1994.

Dormon, James H. *The People Called Cajuns: An Introduction to an Ethnohistory*. Lafayette: Center for Louisiana Studies, University of Southwestern Louisiana, 1983.

Dumas, Alexandre, fils. *La Dame aux Camélias*. New York: Oxford University Press, 1986.

Eccles, William J. *France in America*. New York: Harper and Row, 1972.

Edmonds, David C. *Yankee Autumn in Acadiana*. Lafayette: Acadiana, 1979.

Elwitt, Sanford. *The Making of the Third Republic: Class and Politics in France, 1868–1884*. Baton Rouge: Louisiana State University Press, 1975.

Estaville, Lawrence E. "Changeless Cajuns: Nineteenth-Century Reality or Myth?" *Louisiana History* 28 (Spring 1987): 117–40.

———. "Were the Nineteenth-Century Cajuns Geographically Isolated?" *Geoscience and Man*, 25 (1988): 85–95.

Foner, Eric. *Reconstruction: America's Unfinished Revolution, 1863–1877*. New York: Harper and Row, 1988.

Fontenot, Mary Alice, and Paul B. Freeland. *Acadia Parish, Louisiana*. 2 vols. Lafayette: Center for Louisiana Studies, University of Southwestern Louisiana,1979.

Fortier, Alcée. *Louisiana: Comprising Sketches of Parishes, Towns, Events, Institutions, and Persons, Arranged in Cyclopedic Form*. 3 vols. New Orleans: Century Historical Association, 1914.

Fredrickson, George. *The Arrogance of Race: Historical Perspectives on Slavery, Racism, and Social Inequality*. Middletown: Wesleyan University Press, 1988.

The Freemason's Companion: A Ritual. Cincinnati: John D. Caldwell, 1874.

The French in New England, Acadia, and Quebec. Proceedings of a Conference Sponsored by the New England–Atlantic Provinces–Quebec Center at the University of Maine at Orono, 1972.

Gaxotte, Pierre. *Louis XV and His Times*. Translated from the French by J. Lewis May. Philadelphia: J. B. Lippincott, 1934.

Gill, James. *Lords of Misrule: Mardi Gras and the Politics of Race in New Orleans*. Jackson: University Press of Mississippi, 1997.

Giraud, Marcel. *A History of French Louisiana*. 5 vols. projected. Baton Rouge: Louisiana State University Press, 1974–.

Glad, Paul W. *McKinley, Bryan, and the People*. New York: J. B. Lippincott, 1964.

Goetzmann, William H. *Exploration and Empire*. New York: Alfred A. Knopf, 1966.

Goins, Charles Robert, and John Michael Caldwell. *The Historical Atlas of Louisiana*. Norman: University of Oklahoma Press, 1995.

Gooch, G. P. *Louis XV: The Monarchy in Decline*. London: Longmans, Green, 1956.

Gould, Philip, and Lawrence N. Powell. *Louisiana's Capitols: The Power and the Beauty*. Lafayette: Galerie, 1995.

Greene, Jack P. *Settlements to Society, 1607–1763*. New York: W. W. Norton, 1975.

Griffin, Harry Lewis. *The Attakapas Country: A History of Lafayette Parish, Louisiana*. Gretna, La.: Pelican, 1974.

Griffiths, Naomi E. S. *The Acadians: Creation of a People*. Toronto: McGraw-Hill Ryerson, 1973.

———. "Acadians in Exile: The Experience of the Acadians in British Seaports." *Acadiensis* 3 (1973).

———. *The Contexts of Acadian History, 1686–1784*. Montreal: McGill–Queen's University Press, 1988.

Grossman, Joel B., and Richard S. Wells. *Constitutional Law and Judicial Policy Making*. New York: John Wiley and Sons, 1980.

Guaranty Bank and Trust. *Lafayette: Its Past, People, and Progress*. Baton Rouge: Moran, 1980.

Gumbley, Walter. *Obituary Notices of the English Dominicans from 1555–1952*. London: Blackfriars, 1955.

Haggerty, Richard H. *Dominican Republic and Haiti Country Studies*. Washington, D.C.: U.S. Department of State, 1989.

Hair, William Ivy. *Bourbonism and Agrarian Protest: Louisiana Politics, 1877–1900*. Baton Rouge: Louisiana State University Press, 1969.

Halttunen, Karen. *Murder Most Foul: The Killer and the American Gothic Imagination.* Cambridge: Harvard University Press, 1998.

Hebert, Donald. *Acadians in Exile.* Cecilia, La.: Hebert Publications, 1980.

——. *A Guide to Church Records in Louisiana, 1720–1975.* Eunice, La.: Hebert Publications, 1975.

——. *Southwest Louisiana Records: Church and Civil Records of Settlers.* 39 vols. Rayne, La.: Hebert Publications, 1974.

Herbin, John Frederic. *A History of Grand-Pré.* 4th ed. Bowie, Md.: Heritage Books Reprint, 1991.

Hero, Alfred Olivier. *Louisiana and Quebec: Bilateral Relations and Comparative Sociopolitical Evolution, 1673–1993.* Lanham, Md.: University Press of America, 1995.

Hock, Nancy Tulloch. "Recreational Pursuits of Lafayette Parish Residents, 1890–1899." *Attakapas Gazette* 12 (1977): 114–24.

Hoffsommer, Don L. *The Southern Pacific, 1901–1985.* College Station: Texas A&M, 1986.

Holmes, Jack. *The 1779 "Marcha de Gálvez": Louisiana's Giant Step Forward in the American Revolution.* Baton Rouge: Baton Rouge Bicentennial Corporation. 1974.

Holy Bible: King James Version. Camden, N.J.: Thomas Nelson, 1972.

The Holy Bible. Translated from the Latin Vulgate. New York: C. Wildermann, 1911.

Hume, Matin A. S. *Spain: Its Greatness and Decay (1479–1788).* 3d ed. London: Cambridge University Press, 1925.

Images de Lafayette: A Pictorial History from the Historic Photo Collection of O. C. "Dan" Guilliot. Lafayette: n.p., 1992.

Index to the William McKinley Papers. Washington, D.C.: Government Printing Office, 1963.

Jackson, Joy. *New Orleans in the Gilded Age: Politics and Urban Progress, 1880–1896.* Baton Rouge: Louisiana State University Press, 1969.

James, C. L. R. *The Black Jacobins: Toussaint L'Ouverture and the San Domingo Revolution.* New York: Random House Vintage Books, 1963.

Jehn, Janet. *Acadian Exiles in the Colonies.* Covington, Ky.: self-published, 1972.

Jennings, Francis. *Empire of Fortune: Crowns, Colonies, and Tribes in the Seven Years War in America.* New York: W. W. Norton, 1988.

——. *The Invasion of America: Indians, Colonialism, and the Cant of Conquest.* Chapel Hill: University of North Carolina Press, 1975.

Jonas, Susan, et al., eds. *Ellis Island: Echoes from a Nation's Past.* New York: Aperture Foundation, 1989.

Jones, Stanley. *The Presidential Election of 1896.* Madison: University of Wisconsin Press, 1964.

Kamen, Henry A. F. *Spain, 1469–1714: A Society of Conflict.* New York: Longmans, Green, 1983.

Karl, Thomas R., et al. *Statewide Average Climatic History: Louisiana, 1891–1982.* Asheville, N.C.: National Climatic Data Center, 1983.

Kasteel, Anne-Marie. *Francis Janssens: A Dutch American Prelate.* Lafayette: Center for Louisiana Studies, University of Southwestern Louisiana, 1992.

Kellogg, Louise Phelps. *Early Narrative of the Northwest, 1634–1699.* New York: Scribner's, 1917.

Kennedy, J. H. *Jesuit and Savage in New France.* New Haven: Yale University Press, 1950.

Kenneson, Claude. "Lafayette Parish Place Names." *Attakapas Gazette* 10 (1975): 206–209.

Kirby, Robert L. *Kirby Smith's Confederacy: The Trans-Mississippi South.* New York: Columbia University Press, 1972.

Koenig, Virginia. *Meurtre de Martin Begnaud par Ernest Blanc.* Lafayette: n.p., 1974.

LeBlanc, Dudley J. *The Acadian Miracle.* Lafayette: Evangeline, 1966.

Lemee, Patricia Ruth. "Tios and Tantes: Familial and Political Relationships of Natchitoches and the Spanish Colonial Frontier." *Southwestern Historical Quarterly* 101 (January 1998): 341–58.

Longfellow, Henry Wadsworth. *Evangeline: A Tale of Acadie.* 1847; reprint, Toronto: W. Briggs, 1908.

Loveland, Anne C. *Emblem of Liberty: Lafayette's Image in the American Mind.* Baton Rouge: Louisiana State University Press, 1971.

McKernan, Maureen. *The Amazing Crime and Trial of Leopold and Loeb.* 1924; reprint Birmingham, Ala.: Notable Trials Library, 1989.

MacLean, Harrison John. *The Fate of the Griffon.* Chicago: Swallow, 1974.

McLure, Mary Lilla. *Louisiana Leaders, 1830–1860.* Shreveport: Journal Printing Company, 1935.

McNaught, Kenneth. *The History of Canada.* New York: Praeger, 1970.

McPherson, James M. *Battle Cry of Freedom.* New York: Oxford University Press, 1988.

Mamalakis, Mario. *If They Could Talk! Acadiana's Buildings and Their Biographies.* Lafayette: Lafayette Centennial Commission, 1983.

Mann, Robert. *The Walls of Jericho: Lyndon Johnson, Hubert Humphrey, Richard Russell, and the Struggle for Civil Rights.* New York: Harcourt Brace, 1996.

Mayors of Lafayette, 1884–1976. Lafayette: Lafayette Founders Committee, 1975.

Meinig, D.W. *The Shaping of America: A Geographical Perspective on 500 Years of History.* Vol. 1. New Haven: Yale University Press, 1986.

Millet, Donald J. "The Economic Development of Southwest Louisiana, 1865–1900." Ph.D. diss., Louisiana State University, 1964.

———. "Southwest Louisiana Enters the Railroad Age: 1880–1900." *Louisiana History* 24 (Spring 1983): 165–83.

Mowat, R. B. *The Diplomacy of Napoleon.* London: Edward Arnold, 1924.

The New Oxford Atlas. Prepared by the Cartographic Department of the Oxford University. London: Oxford University Press, 1975.

Nouveau Larousse Illustré. Paris: Larousse, 1971.

Oates, Stephen B. *The Fires of Jubilee.* New York: Harper and Row, 1975.

Odom, Edwin Dale. "Louisiana Railroads, 1830–1880: A Study of State and Local Aid." Ph.D. diss., Tulane University, 1961.

Olcott, Edward R. *The Louisiana Magistrate and Parish Officers' Guide.* 3d. ed. New Orleans: James A. Gresham, 1883.

Palmer, R. R., and Joel Colton. *A History of the Modern World.* New York: Alfred A. Knopf, 1984.

Parkman, Francis. *Pioneers of France in the New World.* 1897; reprint, Williamstown, Mass.: Corner House, 1970.

Perrin, William Henry, ed. *Southwest Louisiana Biographical and Historical.* 1891; reprint, Baton Rouge: Claitor's, 1971.

Pickering, Danby, ed. *The Statutes at Large.* Vol. 24. Cambridge: Printer to the University, 1769.

Pitkin, Thomas M. *Keepers of the Gate: A History of Ellis Island.* New York: New York University Press, 1975.

Potter, David M. *The Impending Crisis.* New York: Harper Torchbooks, 1976.

Pourciau, Betty. *St. Martin Parish History.* Baton Rouge: self-published, 1985.

Prescott, William H. *The Conquest of Mexico and the Conquest of Peru.* New York: Random House, n.d.

Rawhyk, George A., *Nova Scotia's Massachusetts: A Study of Massachusetts–Nova Scotia Relations, 1630 to 1784.* Montreal: McGill–Queen's University Press, 1973.

Rees, Grover. *A Narrative History of Breaux Bridge, Once Called "La Pointe."* St. Martinville, La.: Attakapas Historical Association, 1976.

Reeves, Miriam G. *The Governors of Louisiana.* New Orleans: Pelican, 1962.

Richard, Carl J. *The Louisiana Purchase.* Life Series, No. 7. Lafayette: Center for Louisiana Studies, University of Southwestern Louisiana, 1995.

Rieder, Milton P. Jr., and Norma Gaudet Rieder. *The Acadians in France, 1762–1776.* 3 vols. Metairie, La.: self-published, 1967.

———. *The Crew and Passenger Registration Lists of the Seven Acadian Expeditions of 1785.* Metairie, La.: self-published, 1965.

Robichaux, Albert J. *The Acadian Exiles in Chatellerault, 1773–1785.* Cecilia, La.: Hebert Publications, 1983.

———. *The Acadian Exiles in Nantes, 1775–1785.* Harvey, La.: self-published, 1978.

———. *The Acadian Exiles in St.-Malo, 1758–1785.* 3 vols. Eunice, La.: Hebert Publications, 1981.

Romero, Sidney James. "The Political Career of Murphy James Foster, Governor of Louisiana, 1892–1900." *Louisiana Historical Quarterly* 28 (October 1945): 1129–1243.

Roustang, François. *An Autobiography of Martyrdom: Spiritual Writings of the Jesuits in New France.* Translated by Sister M. Renelle, S.S.N.D. St. Louis: B. Herder Book Co., 1964.

Royster, Charles. *The Destructive War: William Tecumseh Sherman, Stonewall Jackson, and the Americans.* New York: Alfred A. Knopf, 1991.

Russell, Don. *The Lives and Legends of Buffalo Bill.* Norman: University of Oklahoma Press, 1960.

Ryan, Mary C. *The Louisiana Purchase: Milestone Documents in the National Archives.* Washington, D.C.: National Archives and Records Administration, 1987.

Sanders, Mary Elizabeth. "List of Owners and Slaveholders of the Attakapas." *Attakapas Gazette* 11 (1976): 84–91.

Sauer, Carl O. *Seventeenth-Century North America.* Berkeley: Turtle Island, 1980.

Sayers, Isabelle S. *Annie Oakley and Buffalo Bill's Wild West Show.* New York: Dover Publications, 1981.

Schneider, Linda. *Louisiana Newspaper Project.* Baton Rouge: LSU Libraries, 1992.

Segura, Pearl Mary. "Amand Broussard *dit* Beausoleil." *Attakapas Gazette* 18 (1983): 147–53.

Sellers, Alvin V. *The Loeb-Leopold Case.* Brunswick, Ga.: Classic, 1926.

Senior, Donald, ed. *The Catholic Study Bible.* New York: Oxford University Press, 1990.

Shanabruch, Charles. "The Louisiana Immigration Movement, 1891–1907: An Analysis of Efforts, Attitudes, and Opportunities." *Louisiana History* 18 (Spring 1977): 203–26.

Shapiro, Mary J. *The Story of the Statue of Liberty and Ellis Island.* New York: Vintage Books, 1986.

Shattuck, Roger. *The Banquet Years: The Origins of the Avant-Garde in France, 1885 to World War I.* Salem, N.H.: Ayer, 1969.

Smith, Virginia Rogers, and Judith Dinkle Smith. *Searching for Your Ancestors on Microfilm.* Baton Rouge: State Library of Louisiana, 1992.

Social Research Class. *Scott—Where the West Begins: A Sociological Survey of Community Life.* Lafayette: University of Southwestern Louisiana, 1951.

Stubbs, William C. *A Handbook of Louisiana.* New Orleans: New Orleans Picayune, 1895.

Taylor, Gertrude. "Fortune and Misfortune: The Sorrel Family in Louisiana, 1763–1900." *Attakapas Gazette* 21 (1986): 179–91.

———. "Judice, A. Genealogy." *Attakapas Gazette* 20 (1985): 98–116.

———. "Land Settlement in T9S, R4E." *Attakapas Gazette* 18 (1983): 120–21.

———. "St. Martinville to Sorrell." *Land Grants along the Teche.* Lafayette: Center for Louisiana Studies, University of Southwestern Louisiana, 1979–1980.

———. "A Village Called *Pont des Breaux.*" *Attakapas Gazette* 19 (1984): 99–106.

Taylor, Joe Gray. *Louisiana: A History.* New York: W. W. Norton, 1976.

———. *Louisiana Reconstructed, 1863–1877.* Baton Rouge, Louisiana State University Press, 1974.

Terrell, John Upton. *LaSalle: The Life and Times of an Explorer.* New York: Weybridge and Talley, 1968.

Thompson, J. M., *Napoleon Bonaparte: His Rise and Fall.* Oxford: Basil Blackwell, 1952.

Thwaites, Reuben Gold, ed. *The Jesuit Relations and Allied Documents, 1610–1791.* 73 vols. Cleveland: Burrows Brothers, 1896.

Toups, Kathleen, ed. *Scott: A History of the Church Parish and the Town.* N.p.: n.p., 1960.

"Tour of Inspection Made by the Sieur de la Roque." *Report Concerning Canadian Archives for 1905.* 3 vols. Ottawa: Canadian Printing Office, 1905. Vol. 2, Note A: 1–172.

Tuchman, Barbara W. "Mankind's Better Moments." In *Practicing History.* New York: Ballantine Books, 1982, pp. 227–43.

———. *Practicing History.* New York: Ballantine Books, 1982.

———. *The Proud Tower: A Portrait of the World before the War, 1890–1914.* New York: Macmillan, 1966.

Vella, Christina. *Intimate Enemies.* Baton Rouge, Louisiana State University Press, 1997.

Vermilion Historical Society. *History of Vermilion Parish, Louisiana.* Dallas: n.p., 1983.

Voorhies, Jacqueline K. "Kabahonosse." *Attakapas Gazette* 6 (1971): 150–51.

———. *Some Late-Eighteenth-Century Louisianians: Census Records of the Colony, 1758–1796.* Lafayette: Center for Louisiana Studies, University of Southwestern Louisiana, 1973.

Wall, Bennett H. *Louisiana: A History.* 3d ed., Wheeling, Ill.: Harlan Davidson, 1997.

Warburton, A. B. *A History of Prince Edward Island.* St. John, New Brunswick: Barnes, 1923.

Weber, David J. *The Spanish Frontier in North America.* New Haven: Yale University Press, 1992.

Weber, Eugene. *France Fin de Siècle.* Cambridge: Harvard University Press, 1986.

———. *My France: Politics, Culture, Myth.* Cambridge: Harvard University Press, 1991.

———. *Peasants into Frenchmen: The Modernization of Rural France, 1870–1914.* Stanford: Stanford University Press, 1976.

Wilder, Mitchell. *The Wild West; or, A History of the Wild West Shows.* Fort Worth, Tex.: Amon Carter Museum of Western Art, 1970.

Williams, T. Harry. *History of American Wars from 1745 to 1918.* New York: Alfred A. Knopf, 1981.

———. *P. G. T. Beauregard: Napoleon in Gray.* Baton Rouge: Louisiana State University Press, 1955.

Willie, Leroy E. *Galvez and Other Louisiana Patriots.* Baton Rouge: Sons of the American Revolution, 1995.

Winters, John D. *The Civil War in Louisiana.* Baton Rouge, Louisiana State University Press, 1963.

Winzerling, Oscar William. *Acadian Odyssey.* Baton Rouge: Louisiana State University Press, 1955.

Woodward, C. Vann. *Origins of the New South.* Baton Rouge: Louisiana State University Press, 1951.

Wrong, George M. *The Rise and Fall of New France.* 2 vols., New York: Macmillan, 1928.

OTHER PRINTED MATERIAL

Lafayette Parish Historical Sites Inventory. Section II—Structures. Lafayette: Lafayette Council of Governments, 1977.

Louisiana Trails Advisory Council. Report to the Governor. Baton Rouge: n.p., 1975.

Martin, Philip. *Généalogie de la Famille d'Alexandre Begnaud et Lise Constantin.* Lafayette: n.p., 1902.

"Morgan Whitney's Louisiana." Program of Whitney Photography Exhibit, Louisiana State Museum and Whitney National Bank, 1997–1998.

Mouton, Franklin III. *The Moutons: A Genealogy.* N.p.: self-published, 1978.

Proceedings of the New Orleans, Algiers, Attakapas, and Opelousas Railroad Convention. New Orleans. 1851. Microfilm # 1054, Louisiana State University Library.

Sanders, Mary Elizabeth. *Records of the Attakapas District, Louisiana.* 3 Vols. n.p.: typescript, 1974.

Southern Pacific Railroad Schedule Book. San Francisco: n.p., 1893.

Thom, Evelyn Martindale. *Lafayette Honors Baton Rouge with a Visit on the Fiftieth Anniversary of American Independence.* Baton Rouge: Baton Rouge Bicentennial Commission, 1975.

United States Newspaper Program. National Union List, 1985.

The World's Columbian Exposition. Chicago: J. W. Ziegler, 1893.

Zenero, Roberta, and David Seng. "Geophysical Evaluation of a Burial Site: Lafayette, Louisiana." November 20, 1995.

ACKNOWLEDGMENTS

As memory serves, I was about ten years old when my mother, Regina Begnaud Arceneaux (1919–1994), first introduced me to the story of the murder of Martin Begnaud. Mother was known to all as NaNa, and this book is dedicated to her memory. She was named for an aunt who, in turn, was named for her aunt; the latter is the Regina Begnaud whose tragic denouement is recounted in the epilogue of this volume. My mother and her family, the Begnauds of Scott, Louisiana, refused to allow the account of the murder of their kinsman to fade from memory. I am indebted to this family—my family—for the gift of this very personal historical memoir.

In 1995 the good people for whom I work, the board of directors of the Louisiana Association of Independent Colleges and Universities, generously granted me a sabbatical leave that enabled me to complete much of the research for this book. Then and now, they are: Samuel Dubois Cook and Michael Lomax of Dillard University, Eamon Kelly and Scott Cowen of Tulane University, Father Jim Carter and Father Bernard Knoth of Loyola University, Ken Schwab of Centenary College, Bob Lynn and Rory Lee of Louisiana College, Father Tom Chambers of Our Lady of Holy Cross College, Norman Francis of Xavier University, and Jim Firnberg and Mike Smith of Our Lady of the Lake College. They have been unflagging in their encouragement and support.

A very special thanks to my two part-time research assistants, Henry O. Robertson Jr. and Kay S. Martin, who worked tirelessly in tracking every possible document, book, fact, etc. that I needed, if it existed. Unfortunately, many did not. These two professionals gave freely of their advice and guidance from the very beginning of this project to its completion. In addition, Henry (and my wife) were the first persons to read the first (of many) drafts of the manuscript. Our lively debates served as the intellectual stimulus that I needed on so many occasions when I felt overwhelmed by the stacks and boxes of documents, books, and articles and entertained grave doubts that the resulting manuscript would ever be published. Henry was a graduate student in the history department at Louisiana State University when I first engaged his services on this project. I took so long to complete the book that Henry had time to complete his Ph.D., do some part-time teaching, be invited to and participate in numerous job interviews, and—finally—accept a tenure-track faculty position at a college. Dr. Robertson has the potential to become one of the great historians of the twenty-first century.

I would still be working on the manuscript or would have quit long ago but for Christine Amond Sonnier, my assistant, who taught me how to use a personal computer and compatible software. Patiently, Chris instructed me on the incredible advantages of composing on the computer screen as opposed to pen and paper. I thank her for her sedulity, and I want to take this occasion to apologize to her family for the many desperate late-night and weekend phone calls to her home when I just knew that I had lost an entire chapter, only to have Chris work her magic and make it reappear. My colleagues Betty Young and Mary Ann Coleman were both helpful and understanding.

I want to thank my father, Teddy Arceneaux, for sharing with me, over the course of a lifetime, his in-depth historical knowledge of his (and my) hometown, Scott, Louisiana. A complete grasp of the full story of the origins of Scott Station would not have been possible without his counsel. Many thanks to all the people who allowed themselves to be interviewed for this book. Son LeBlanc, Bella Abramson, Elia Louise Mouton, J. Allen Mouton, and the late A. J. Benton were extraordinarily helpful and made major contributions.

We all stand on the shoulders of giants. This is especially true for historians. I would like to mention five whose pioneering work on Acadian history is profound and upon whose research and wisdom I have heavily relied: Carl A. Brasseaux, John Bartlet Brebner, Glenn R. Conrad, Naomi E. S. Griffiths, and Oscar W. Winzerling. Stephen White is the director of the Centre for Acadian Studies at the University of Moncton, New Brunswick, Canada. Anyone interested in doing research in Acadian genealogy should first pay a visit to him and to the Centre's incredible holdings. It was Professor White who steered me through the intricate web of my distant ancestry and the movements of the Doiron and Bernard families before, after, and during *le Grand Dérangement*. I also wish to thank Winbourne Magruder Drake, Edwin Adams Davis, Burl Noggle, John Preston Moore, and Jane Lucas deGrummond. I am grateful to the administrators and editors of the LSU Press for their professionalism and their dedication to excellence. I particularly enjoyed working with Gerry Anders.

Words cannot express my appreciation for all the many contributions made by my wife, Patsy, to the completion of this book. A real trouper, she served as editor, adviser, photographer, and artist. Cheerleader and gentle critic, Patsy was always at my side. Finally, I wish to thank my agent/attorney/son, Scott B. Arceneaux, for his expert legal advice, and my other children, Ted, Angelle, and Leah, for their interest and encouragement.

Of course, all errors—while inadvertent—are my responsibility.

INDEX